Books by

LOUISE HALL THARP

Champlain: Northwest Voyager

Company of Adventurers
The Story of the Hudson's Bay Company

The Peabody Sisters of Salem

Until Victory
Horace Mann and Mary Peabody

Three Saints and a Sinner
Julia Ward Howe
Louisa, Annie and Sam Ward

Three Saints and a Sinner

Three Saints
and a Sinner

—

JULIA WARD HOWE,
LOUISA, ANNIE AND SAM WARD

by

LOUISE HALL THARP

WITH ILLUSTRATIONS

Little, Brown and Company · *Boston* · *Toronto*

The author wishes to thank Appleton-Century-Crofts, Inc., for permission to quote from SAMUEL GRIDLEY HOWE and STEPPING WESTWARD by Laura E. Richards (Copyright 1935 by Laura E. Richards and Copyright 1931 by Laura E. Richards); Coward-McCann, Inc., for THE HORSE AND BUGGY AGE IN NEW ENGLAND by Edwin Valentine Mitchell (Copyright, Coward-McCann, Inc., 1937); Dodd, Mead and Company for A DIPLOMATIST'S WIFE IN MANY LANDS by Mrs. Hugh Fraser (1910); E. P. Dutton & Company, Inc., for THE FIFTY BEST HISTORIC AMERICAN HOUSES by Ralph E. Carpenter, Jr.; Harper & Brothers for MEMORIES GRAVE AND GAY by Florence Howe Hall; Houghton Mifflin Company for JULIA WARD HOWE, 1819-1910 by Laura E. Richards and Maud Howe Elliott; The Macmillan Company for UNCLE SAM WARD AND HIS CIRCLE by Maud Howe Elliott (Copyright The Macmillan Company, 1938); Stanford University Press and Carvel Collins for SAM WARD IN THE GOLD RUSH edited by Carvel Collins (Copyright 1949 by the Board of Trustees of Leland Stanford Junior University); University of Minnesota Press for THE MYSTERY OF A PUBLIC MAN by Frank Maloy Anderson.

To my father
Newton Marshall Hall

Held we fall to rise, are baffled to fight better,
Sleep to wake.

— BROWNING

Contents

All illustrations appear between pages 22 and 23

Three Saints and a Sinner

CHAPTER ONE
This Was New York

"HEAVEN save the ladies, how they dress!" Charles Dickens, seated in an upper window at the Carleton House, looked down upon "the best part of Broadway" and made this observation for the record. He was visiting New York City, and the year was 1842.[1]

"The beautiful metropolis of America" was "not so clean as Boston," Mr. Dickens observed. His hotel was at the corner of Frankfort and William Streets and his view of Broadway included the tip of City Hall Park. He deplored the droves of marauding pigs that patrolled the gutters, acting as unpaid although official garbage collectors. And the New York traffic was also disconcerting. "No stint of omnibuses here!" exclaimed Dickens. "Half a dozen have gone by in as many minutes. Plenty of hackney cabs and coaches too; gigs, phaetons, large-wheeled tilburies and private carriages — rather a clumsy make, and not very different from the public vehicles but built for the heavy roads beyond the city."

Casting an appreciative eye at the ladies, "What various parasols! what rainbow silks and satins!" Dickens remarked. If the Ward family carriage had come by at that moment, he might have added a paragraph to *American Notes*. Built for heavy roads it certainly was, but it was canary-yellow in color, with sky-blue cushions. And the three enchanting Ward sisters had been known to dress alike — in yellow bonnets and sky-blue pelisses to match the carriage!

"The three Graces of Bond Street," their friends called these Ward sisters — the eldest of whom Charles Dickens was soon to meet. They were Julia, Louisa and Annie — young, unmarried and each an heiress. Even if the girls had been unattractive, Bond Street would have been a Mecca for fortune hunters, now that their father, Samuel Ward, the banker, had died. Their uncle John Ward, and their brother Sam, would have no enviable task helping the Ward heiresses to choose husbands from among their many suitors. Uncle John and brother Sam were further hampered by the fact that the girls had minds of their own.

Julia, the eldest, was so brilliant that it was not her fault if she often seized the center of the family stage. She was a little thing, just a quarter of an inch over five feet tall — all flash and fire. She had red hair, the lovely cream complexion that was more admired than almost any other form of beauty — and blue eyes that laughed when she seemed most serious. She spoke and read French, Italian and German; wrote poetry and sang arias from the operas. "Diva Julia," they called her when she sang, and she was indeed the leading lady in her own and everybody else's drama.[2]

Personally, Julia Ward disliked the perfect oval of her face, calling it merely "round." Her white shoulders, well-developed bosom and tiny waist were assets which she used well. But her red hair — called unfashionable — she chose to like, in defiance of fashion's decree. When she met a man who collected "Rossos" — red-haired friends, sure to prove congenial — she agreed that here was a good idea. Perhaps Julia Ward was not actually what could be called a beautiful young girl; but, like a fine actress, she gave the impression of beauty whenever she chose. One thing Julia Ward could not do. She could not pass unnoticed.

Louisa, second of the Ward sisters, would soon be known as "the beautiful Miss Ward." And this time, the description was strictly true. Louisa was as dark as Julia was fair. She parted her thick, dark hair above her serene brow, looped long locks over her ears — a style as hideous as it was fashionable, except that to Louisa it was most becoming. Her high-bridged nose gave character to a face that might otherwise have been merely pretty, while Louisa's lovely dark eyes deluded many a young man into thinking she would melt into his arms. It was true that she was gentle, getting herself engaged to more than one man at a time, rather than breaking hearts by saying no. And it was true that her Uncle John promptly disengaged her. But the proud tilt of her head, the firm chin line, should have given warning. Louisa Ward would show strength of purpose when faced with adversity.

With two such sisters, how could Anne Eliza Ward be anything but "little Annie"? The youngest of seven children, Annie's birth had been the cause of her mother's death. She was shy and self-effacing, as though possibly some overzealous relative had told her how, at first, her father had rejected her. Yet surely she knew her father had loved her dearly. She was a sort of elfin child, with big dark eyes, pointed chin and wistful smile. At Newport, during her childhood's summer days, it was little Annie who knew where the wild flowers grew and where the birds had hidden their nests. It would take all of an artist's skill to paint little Annie's subtle smile — the flowers braided in her hair.

In 1842, when Charles Dickens visited New York, Annie and Louisa were just out of school and always close companions. Their sister Julia shone before their dazzled eyes like the bright star that she really was. Who but Julia Ward could have stolen a scene at a dinner given for that greatest of dramatic personalities — Boz himself? When this astounding event happened, Annie and Louisa were impressed, of course — but not surprised.

Julia might not have been at the Dickens dinner at all, however, if it had not been for her brother Sam. That Sam and Julia should work together with spectacular results was already a well-known phenomenon in the Ward family. Sam was the eldest of the banker's children. Upon his father's death, Sam had inherited not only a good-sized fortune but his father's place as head of the firm of Prime, Ward and King. He was trying hard to fill his father's shoes. But Nature had fashioned Sam in a different mold. He had outstanding talents when it came to spending money, rather than earning or conserving it. A worse banker than Sam could hardly be imagined — nor a better friend maker.

Sam Ward would have liked to be tall and handsome. He was not. He was short and slightly bandy-legged. When he was a child, his mother had begged him to wear a nightcap lest the family trait of baldness overtake him. He must have let the warning go unheeded for his bald head was the delight of cartoonists when his fame, as King of the Lobby, Forty-niner, follower of the turf and Wall Street plunger, brought him several fortunes, briefly enjoyed. Sam would have liked to be a good banker. In his own way he was a genius, nonetheless.

Applying his unique ability not to banking but to friendship, Sam Ward "did more than any one man to make Charles Dickens's stay in New York memorable." Sam said so himself.

He also achieved the impossible for his sister Julia. Four days after the Boz Ball, that "tallest compliment ever paid a little man," [3] Sam got an invitation for Julia to go to the Dickens dinner at the City Hotel. This was a much more exclusive affair than the ball — with only two hundred and thirty people attending; Washington Irving being master of ceremonies. And it was for men only.

No one could have been more pleased than Sam to execute such a *coup d'état* — unless it were Julia, bidden to accompany Mrs. Charles Dickens and "a group of ladies" to the City Hotel. There, in an anteroom at the end of the banquet hall, the novelist's wife was to be installed where she would be neither heard nor seen. Equally in purdah for the occasion were Mrs. Brevoort, New York's leading society matron, Miss Catharine Sedgwick, American novelist, and other noted ladies.

It was a man's world and Mrs. Dickens's unseen ladies-in-waiting knew it. They were grateful when they were allowed to have the door of their anteroom ajar. By craning their necks, they could see Washington Irving, handsome and elegant but obviously nervous. They saw him slip the memorized manuscript of his remarks under his dinner plate and someone whispered to Miss Julia Ward, "He'll break down — he always does." [4] Julia could only agree, for she knew Irving well. He had been one of only two guests outside the immediate family at her brother Sam's wedding. But Julia regarded Mr. Irving as old — for he was the friend of John Jacob Astor, grandfather of Sam Ward's young bride.

It is to be hoped that Miss Julia Ward and the other ladies had already dined. But if not, they were privileged to peek through the door and watch the gentlemen eat. They could even see the guest of honor, Mr. Charles Dickens, with his "rings and things and bright array." And when the long meal with its multitude of courses was over at last, the fortunate ladies could hear applause and see Mr. Dickens being led to the platform.

But just before the speech began, the unprecedented happened. To put it in the words of Philip Hone, former mayor of New York, famous diarist and neighbor of the Ward family, somehow the ladies "got possession of the stage behind the president." Mr. Hone would not have believed it if he had not seen it and his choice of words conveyed his horror. Miss Julia Ward, recalling the scene long later, said that "someone brought a whispered invitation."

Could that someone have been her brother Sam? Julia Ward did not say, but it would have been like him. [5] His eyes (sometimes so like his sister's) must have gleamed with mischief — and with pride also, for

Julia surely looked enchanting — whether she wore the pale-blue satin looped with lace; whether she wore camellias or white roses "à la victime" in her hair! Stepping politely aside and walking demurely behind the formidable Mrs. Brevoort, Miss Julia Ward nevertheless drew men's admiring glances — all two hundred and thirty of them.

"Heaven save the ladies, how they dress," Charles Dickens might have said again if he had looked behind him. Or he might have said something less charitable, for he cared little for sharing the limelight, even for a moment.

But Julia Ward, if she blushed at all, blushed with pleasure at the sensation she and her fellow partners in crime were making. In years to come, all she would get at first was just "a whispered invitation" — but she would step right up to the platform, wherever she might be. She would gladly share the platform with other women. But if called upon to step to the center of the stage, she would never hesitate.

At last a day would come when the honors would all be for her — for Julia Ward Howe. She would be equal to any occasion, her quick wit sparking out in repartee during debate — never a line forgotten when she read her poems. The applause of both men and women would be hers one day, and many an ovation. But there were long years between, and tears as well as joys to come. Meanwhile, with blue eyes flashing in appreciation of the scene, Miss Julia Ward listened and learned.

CHAPTER TWO

Three Graces of Bond Street

"WHEN Broadway ended at Union Place and the Astor House was new, when water was peddled in barrels at a cent a gallon . . . Bond Street was one of the best known streets in the city and none stood higher as a place of residence." So said *Valentine's Manual*, referring to the golden days of nineteenth-century New York. Leading into Broadway just below Washington Square, Bond Street was country property when Samuel Ward the banker bought newly laid-out lots for himself and his family. Bond Street might as well have been called Ward Street for, at one time or another, as many as twelve houses were occupied by members of that remarkable family. No wonder Julia, Louisa and Annie sometimes complained that they never saw anyone except their relatives. No wonder visitors from Boston were a welcome diversion.

Colonel Samuel Ward, patriarch of the family, lived at Number 7 Bond Street [1] with his bachelor sons, Richard, John and William. His son Henry lived at Number 18, and after the old Colonel died, John and Richard made Number 8 a family meeting place.

The Ward sisters had other neighbors, of course, in spite of their half-humorous, half-serious complaints. At Number 12 lived James Gore King,[2] their father's partner at Prime, Ward and King. He was the son of Rufus King, minister to Great Britain, president of the New York and Erie Railroad. His brother Charles was editor of the *New York American*, and it was Charles King who published Julia Ward's first literary efforts — much to her joy and to the displeasure of some of her Bond Street relatives. "The Royal Family," the Ward sisters affectionately called the Kings. There were four daughters and three sons of a suitable age to become playmates of the younger Wards.

Then there was Albert Gallatin,[3] at Number 5 Bond Street. He had been Secretary of the Treasury under Jefferson, had reduced the national debt and had been thrown out of office for his pains. Gallatin was the first president of the council of the University of the City of New York, and Samuel Ward the banker was first secretary. But Albert Gallatin must have seemed old to the Ward sisters, for he was a contemporary of their grandfather, Colonel Ward.

On Bond Street lived judges, bank directors, merchants and clergymen. The neighborhood was restricted to the extent that purchasers from Samuel Ward the banker promised to build no "slaughter house, smith shop, forge or furnace . . . or any manufactory of glue or gunpowder . . . or any brewing distillery." [4] In view of the fires that devastated downtown New York, Bond Street residents promised to build in brick or stone.

The finest house on Bond Street was The Corner, built by Samuel Ward the banker, in the spring of 1831. He had held the land since 1826, having bought (with his older brother Richard) part of a farm once owned by de Peysters, Kips and others, then by a Jones family, for whom "Great Jones Street," a block north of Bond, was named. Samuel Ward paid $11,000 for 130 feet on Bond Street and 57½ feet on Broadway; and only six years later, when he decided to buy land north to Great Jones Street, the additional 140 feet of Broadway frontage cost $40,000. But Samuel Ward bought when values had just begun to rise, and by selling small plots (one to Philip Hone) on Broadway and Great Jones Street, his profits more than covered the cost of building his mansion.

"Mr. Ward, you are moving out of town," his friends told the banker in 1829 when the family left Bowling Green for their first Bond Street home, at Number 16. This was true, for beyond Bond Street lay open fields, with "a wilderness of rocks, bushes and thistles with here and there a farm house." Twenty years later an afternoon's drive to see the Croton Reservoir, at what is now 42nd Street, would still be a country excursion. The Ward children saw from their nursery windows at 16 Bond Street "the gradual building-up of the street." A fascinating scene it must have been, as huge horse-drawn drays brought brick and marble; as carved marble mantelpieces came packed in straw from the "yard" of Frazee and Launitz.

Julia was the only one of the Ward sisters who really remembered any other home but Bond Street. Yet Bowling Green had been the

Ward children's first playground, little pink ices at tables in Castle Garden their treat for good behavior. Julia and her brother Sam were born on nearby Marketfield Street; Louisa and Annie, at Number 5 Bowling Green. Even after she had lived in Boston fifty years, "I am a New York woman," Julia Ward Howe would often say. She was apt to be annoyed when people seemed unduly surprised.

The Wards had New England roots, nonetheless. Their first American ancestor, John Ward, "sometime cavalry officer in Cromwell's army," had settled in Newport, Rhode Island, soon after the Restoration in 1660. The first American John Ward quite rightly judged that a new land would be more healthy for him and his family after Charles the Second came to the throne. In 1724, his son Richard, having prospered, married a great-granddaughter of Roger Williams and bought himself a splendid house in the center of Newport.[5] The house was not new. Richard might have remembered seeing the cellar dug, the massive beams set and the pilastered chimney rising like a fortress. This was a many-chambered house suitable for a man who fathered fourteen children. Though not the newest house in Newport, this "Wanton-Lyman-Hazard House" survived to become the oldest.

Richard Ward became Royal Governor of Rhode Island. His son Samuel became Revolutionary Governor and one of the framers of the Constitution. But the Ward sisters were rarely told stories of this illustrious ancestor. They were merely given to understand that they had a great deal to live up to and that there would be no excuse for them, if they were lazy or incompetent. All the Wards knew about their great-grandfather's public life. Three times chosen Governor of Rhode Island, he was also a member of the First Continental Congress. It is sometimes said that the leaders of the American Revolution were a mob of have-nots, motivated primarily by greed and the desire to seize land and wealth from Tory neighbors. Proof to the contrary lies in the quality of the members of the Continental Congress, of whom Governor Samuel Ward was an outstanding example. His wealth before the Revolution was estimated at "between fifty and sixty thousand pounds." Much of this, however, was in credit extended to farmers; and after the Revolution debts proved uncollectable. This he foresaw. The large farm was profitable only when properly manned and supervised but when his son Samuel joined Washington's forces the Governor was proud and happy — experiencing only that inner anxiety which every loving parent has to face.

Governor Ward became a leader in the American Revolution, with regret nonetheless. "The Idea of taking up Arms against the parent State is shocking to Us who still feel the strongest Attachment to our Sovereign," he said, "and warmest affection for our Brethren in Britain, and may God in his infinite Mercy grant that We may never be driven to that fatal Extremety but if We must either become Slaves or fly to Arms, I shall not (and hope no American will) hesitate one Moment which to chose, for all the Horrors of Civil War and even Death itself . . . is infinitely preferable to Slavery." [6] This letter was written in December, 1774. By May 26, 1775, Governor Samuel was writing from Philadelphia to his son Samuel who had just become a Captain in the Rhode Island Army of Observation — at the age of eighteen.

Said Governor Ward: " . . . That Love of Liberty and your Country, which you sucked in almost with your Mother's Milk, I flatter myself will excite you to the most noble Exertions, and support you under the most arduous Labours. . . . but remember my dear Son, that besides Bravery — Prudence, Wisdom and Economy are necessary; when your Country calls for your Life, risk it freely — but never wantonly expose yourself or your men. Let Sobriety, Temperance and Virtue direct your whole Conduct . . . be extremely careful of your Men, see as much as possible in Person that they have good Provisions, — compel them to be clean, to dress their provisions well and suffer as little Debauchery and Drunkeness to take footing amongst them as possible. . . ." And at the end of his letter, Governor Ward gave his son a text of scripture to be his guide:

"Remember my Son that unless the Lord keep the City, in vain do the Watchmen watch."[7]

A month later, Governor Ward wrote to Captain Samuel, and his opening sentence goes to the heart of every parent who has been in the same situation: "This is the first Time that I ever wrote to a Person whom I did not know whether to consider as one of this World or of the next." But Governor Ward devoutly hoped that "Heaven had spared" his son — and he was right, though news was slow in coming. Young Captain Ward had joined Arnold's expedition to Quebec and on November 27, 1775, had reached the St. Lawrence River.

"Good God! how various are the scenes I have passed through since I left You the 29th of last May," wrote Captain Samuel, adressing his whole family. "But the wise Men say that life is a Journey. . . . As a summary of the whole, We have gone up one of the most rapid rivers in the world, where the water is so shoal that, Moderately speaking, We have waded 100 miles. . . .

"We were thirty days in a wilderness that none but savages ever attempted to pass," Captain Ward went on. "We marched 100 miles upon short three days Provisions, Waded over three rapid Rivers, marched through snow and Ice bare foot, passed over the St. Lawrence where it was Full of Enemies Frigates, and are now twenty-four Miles from the City to recruit our worn-out Natures."

One of the rivers was the Chaudière and another the Dead River, which a storm with hurricane winds turned into a river of the dead. Provisions were ruined, boats made of green lumber leaked even in good weather and broke up in the storms. Many of the sick were sent back and many men deserted, but Captain Ward lent some of his own courage to his company. Now he was sure that, under General Montgomery, "We shall have the glory of taking Quebec."

The delays, the quarrels between Arnold and other top-echelon officers are now a part of history. When the plan of attack was at last decided upon, Captain Samuel Ward and his men "occupied about the center of Arnold's line," being "ordered to attack the lower town by way of the barriers on the St. Charles River." So wrote a family historian much later, but the action was more like an Indian raid with everything depending on snowfall and darkness and with only thirty men detailed to this dangerous assignment.[8]

Captain Ward and his men plunged through the storm, dragging a small cannon mounted on a sled. Something black loomed ahead. It was the barrier. "After an hour's heavy fighting," they captured this outpost — but time seemed to stand still and no one knew exactly when the sixty defenders surrendered. Now the snowfall, without which the attack could not have begun, turned to rain, which made it impossible for Captain Ward and his men to keep their powder dry. Hammers clicked but there was no answering roar and flash, while the defenders beyond the St. Charles barrier, safe under cover in the houses of the lower town, fired from windows upon the Americans exposed in the street.

Following in the wake of their little cannon, Captain Ward and his men pushed on to a second barricade. General Arnold was led to the rear, gravely wounded. And from the battlements above came the ominous roar of heavy artillery. The attack was no longer a surprise. Captain Ward fought on, taking possession of a stone house where he and a small handful held out for three hours, awaiting promised reinforcements. But nothing was heard from General Montgomery and his main body of attackers. General Montgomery was dead.

Abandoned by necessity and seemingly forgotten, Captain Ward and his remnant of command were taken prisoner near Hope Gate. The name of the place must have seemed ironic to a young officer who had just lost his first engagement. It was while Captain Ward was a prisoner of war that his father died.

Governor Ward knew that he was in grave danger in Philadelphia. Crowded living conditions and the massing of ships at the wharves, as other American ports were British-occupied, brought epidemics which raged unchecked. In 1770, Governor Ward's "Dear better Half" had been laid to rest in the cemetery plot on the Westerly farm — his "Beloved wife Anna in the 43rd year of her age." He had only the children now, to whom he was unusually devoted. He wrote them a long letter of guidance — in case he never came home.

"Strive to promote each other's happiness," said Governor Ward. "Bear with one another's Imperfections, be of one Mind and have one Interest in Everything, as much as may be."

Out of a family of eleven, there were not many left on the Westerly farm to read this letter. Charles, the eldest, had joined the Navy. Samuel was in Quebec; and of the three remaining boys, the oldest was only sixteen but doing a man's work. Governor Ward foresaw difficulties ahead:

"The Estate I have left may, if industriously managed, be sufficient to preserve You all from Want. But without Industry and Frugality You must all come to Distress. Exert Yourselves therefore in your separate Callings . . . but do not make too much Haste to be Rich lest you fall into divers Temptations . . . " (This letter should have been placed before Sam Ward, fourth of the name, in his earliest years. But even so, it is doubtful if anything could have made Sam Ward other than he was — an artist in good fellowship, and in great haste to be rich.)

In Philadelphia, a document was in process of preparation. Governor Samuel Ward took an active part in the writing of this document — it was the Declaration of Independence. But on March 26, 1776, Governor Ward died of smallpox. He died before the Declaration of Independence was signed, but his name should, by rights, have been on it.

Not until after his father's death was Captain Samuel Ward paroled and sent to British-held New York by sea. At the end of 1776 he was exchanged. Now he was at liberty to begin his military career all over again and General Washington, far from holding the young man's defeat against him, made him a major. Major Samuel Ward was with Washington at Valley Forge.

In the spring of 1778, Major Ward went home to Rhode Island just long enough to marry Phebe Greene, daughter of William Greene, soon to be Rhode Island's governor. Then the major returned to defend Fort Mercer at Red Bank, New Jersey — and to evacuate the fort successfully when it became untenable. Major Ward had learned to be the kind of officer Washington most needed — when successful retreat meant ultimate victory.

With his brother-in-law, Christopher Greene, Samuel Ward went back to Rhode Island in 1778 to recruit a Negro regiment. Rhode Island had enacted "the first legislation concerning slavery in America," ordering "the freeing of slaves after 10 years' service." This was in 1652. There were now many free Negro Rhode Islanders and freely they joined the "First Rhode Island Regiment." Their first assignment must have suited them perfectly, for they were to liberate Newport from British occupation. But a storm dispersed the French Fleet, which was to have played a major part in the action, and the land attack was called off. Once more, Samuel Ward — now a colonel — acquitted himself well in retreat. But this must have been his bitterest disappointment.

With the defeat of Cornwallis in 1781, Colonel Samuel Ward became a retired army officer on half pay. The words bring up the picture of an old man, pottering about in his flower garden. But Colonel Ward was only twenty-five years old.

Shipping as supercargo, Colonel Ward voyaged to China and later to England and France. He was in Paris during the French Revolution but took refuge in the country to avoid the "terrible sight" of the executions. Buying judiciously and selling at home to advantage, many supercargoes made money on the "ventures" the captains allowed them to stow on board the vessels. Colonel Ward's brothers and sisters, living in reduced circumstances since the Revolution, were inclined to blame him because he did not immediately make a fortune in silks and tea. "Bear with one another's imperfections," their father had told them, but this they were inclined to forget. It was not Colonel Ward's fault that he had little capital to invest in merchandise. In his journals, he set down information that would be worth more to his sons than any inherited fortune he might have left them.

The United States, so recently become a nation, was now engaged in a struggle for the right to trade with other nations on equal terms. Colonel Ward during his voyages saw how the British were intrenched, with resident agents in all foreign ports who had money to buy when prices were low, storehouses to hold goods off the market and docks for loading British ships when the time was right to ship and sell. The Colonel saw that what his own country needed was a merchants' banking system.

In mapping out a new career, Colonel Ward — still in his early thirties — might have turned to Newport as a base of operations. But Newport was a dead city, her trade in rum and molasses gone and her trade as a fashionable summer resort still far in the future. Providence, having supplanted Newport as the capital of Rhode Island, might have attracted Colonel Ward. Indeed, he sailed from there on his first voyages. But two Ward brothers had already chosen Providence and Colonel Samuel intended to abide by his father's wishes and bear with the imperfections of a large and strong-minded family. They could all "be of one mind and have one interest in everything" much more easily when separated by considerable distance. Boston had sprung into the lead as the merchant city, but Colonel Samuel Ward made a young man's choice. While a prisoner in New York, he had noticed that it had "a harbor of vast importance." To succeed in New York, a man "must have Boston connections," it was said — and Colonel Ward thought he could manage that. In 1791, he chose New York.

A port "of vast importance" New York might some day be, but as the sailing packet from Rhode Island approached her destination, the Ward family saw nothing but a sprawling country town. Here and there, a church spire raised a heavenward finger of warning just as in Providence or Newport; wooden houses clustered near the wharves, as in Boston. But at the wharves lay so many vessels that newcomers always spoke of the "forest of masts" — and beyond the waterfront, stair-stepped gables in brick proclaimed the city's Dutch origin and gave the town a faint foreign accent and a flavor all its own.

Only the previous year, New York had been the young nation's capital, and Federal Hall, all of three stories high, dominated the skyline. Nearby, a white-columned mansion built for President Washing-

ton now housed Governor Clinton. Very shortly the state government
would also desert New York and the city would take over the neoclassic buildings abandoned by two governments. There must have
been those who predicted that New York would now dwindle away,
with ghost mansions falling into decay along empty streets. Colonel
Ward, mindful of the port with its forest of masts, bought city
property here and there, as much of it as he could afford.

At first there was not much cash to spare, however. Colonel Samuel
Ward and his wife Phebe had ten children. Death had taken its toll,
two sons lying buried in Rhode Island. Three sons and a daughter
were to be native-born New Yorkers. And to call off the names of the
sons of Colonel Ward was like reciting the names of the kings of
England. They were Henry, Richard, John and William. Aged five,
when his family made New York their home, was Colonel Ward's
namesake — Samuel Ward.

Manhattan was still an island of hills and valleys, swampland and
meadowland — all through Samuel Ward's boyhood. Streams, some
swift, some sluggish, seeking the Hudson or the East River, would
have rewarded boyhood fishing excursions — if the Ward boys had
leisure hours. Just off Broadway near the present City Hall lay Fresh
Water Pond. It was big enough and deep enough to serve John
Fitch for his experiments with the first steamboat, and the Ward boys
could have seen the wooden hulk, with its iron walking-beam, lying
abandoned on the shore. Pearl Street, beginning just below the pond
and following the East River watershed, curved like the river that it
once was — moving south, then wandering east and turning south
again. The Wards' first home was on Pearl Street. But it was still
called Queen Street by old settlers, for colonial names died hard. In
1806, the Wards moved from 284 Queen Street to Number 8 Fletcher
Street — a byway leading from Pearl to the East River.

A few blocks north of Fletcher Street was Crane's Wharf, where
Colonel Ward set himself up in business. Before long it was Colonel
Samuel "and brothers" doing business at Crane's Wharf — importing
fine Madeira wine; exporting cordage.

Just beyond the wharf, large houses with gardens lined the shores
of the East River, giving way within a few miles to scattered farms.
The ferry to Brooklyn left from a slip, one block below the Ward's
home on Fletcher Street. The "horse ferry," they called it, because a
horse walking a treadmill supplied the motive power. For the Ward
boys a country excursion to Brooklyn was a rare treat.

During the next forty years, "a New Yorker with no very extended acquaintance could tell the names of all the principal merchants and where they lived. Pearl Street and its immediate vicinity was the favorite location," [9] and young Samuel Ward, as he scampered along the street to school, knew everyone and was known by everyone he met. Business associations begun on Pearl Street lasted for three Ward generations.

There was, for example, Mr. Comfort Sands. He lived four blocks north of Fletcher Street at the corner of Pearl and Cherry, in a fine house set in spacious grounds. This house would remain a landmark until it was demolished to make way for one of the piers of Brooklyn Bridge. Mr. Sands was himself a landmark; and in all probability, the Wards were already acquainted with him, for he had been a supplier for Washington's Army. Colonel Ward knew him now in any case, for he was the owner of rapidly expanding ropewalks, making cordage on the shores of the East River, in Brooklyn. Mr. Comfort Sands "believed in Brooklyn."

In 1802, a new name appeared in the New York directory. It was Nathaniel Prime, stock and commission broker, 42 Wall Street. Most New York merchants still had their offices in their own homes on Pearl Street or nearby, but in 1792 the Tontine Coffee House was built on the corner of Wall Street and Water Street and members of the New York Stock Exchange met at this convenient and convivial spot. So Mr. Prime's choice of both a home and an office on Wall Street, though a departure, was nevertheless strategic. In 1810, he moved his home to 10 Broadway, keeping 42 Wall as a place devoted entirely to business. This too was a novel idea — Nathaniel Prime came from Boston.

"Old Nat Prime," they called the Bostonian, soon to become a dyed-in-the-wool New Yorker. For many years, his heavy, squat figure was a familiar sight along Wall Street. According to gossip, he had been "in early life, a coachman to the rich William Gray, an eminent merchant in Boston," but Nathaniel Prime became "the third-richest man in New York."

The first-ranking merchant would of course be John Jacob Astor. His shop, where he first sold his flutes, was on Pearl Street. Like Samuel Ward, Astor's brother Heinrich, who ran a butcher's shop, had also served in the Revolution — but in a far different capacity from the Colonel. From his native village of Wald Dorf, Heinrich Astor had been brought to New York with the Hessians as part of the sutler's train. His brother John Jacob, with his stock-in-trade of flutes, followed. The older generation of Wards and Astors got on reasonably well but it was said that there was little love lost between John Jacob Astor and Nathaniel Prime. Brother Heinrich could be induced to lend money for nothing; but old man Prime wanted plenty of interest when he lent that peddler John Jacob some money to buy furs.

"Old Man Prime was a fearfully long-headed man," related Walter Barrett, at one time his clerk and later the author of much gossiping reminiscence. Prime, according to Barrett, "could see through a millstone quicker than any man in Wall Street," but he was also "frequently sold. On one occasion, a Hartford jockey named Adam Hitchcock sold him a leopard-spotted horse for fifteen hundred dollars. It was all right until the black-and-white-spotted horse got caught out in the rain." If this story were true, then Nathaniel Prime was a better stockbroker than horse trader and — for a former coachman — curiously blind. His humble beginnings were forgotten, not only when he became rich, but because he married Cornelia Sands, daughter of Comfort Sands, whose family had long been landed proprietors at "Cow's Neck," Long Island. The name of their holdings was later changed to Sands Point — not so much in their honor as in deference to the dignity of subsequent Long Island residents who took over after the cows departed.

In 1802, Nathaniel Prime, the newcomer from Boston, needed a clerk in his office at 42 Wall Street. He hired Samuel Ward, Jr., who was then sixteen.[10]

Colonel Ward had graduated in one of the earliest classes from Rhode Island College — later Brown University. But his father, the Governor of Rhode Island, had expressed the hope that the boy would "learn arithmitick and merchants accounts" while in college, and it might be logical to deduce that, while Colonel Ward's French and Latin were both excellent, his "arithmitick" remained faulty. The Colonel allowed Samuel's brother Richard to "read law" but Samuel himself, according to his own account, "went only to the common school." He also knew French and Latin — which perhaps his father taught him, for it was not taught in New York public schools at that time, but only in church-supported or private schools. In any case, mathematics spoke the language young Samuel best understood and there was no place where figures could be better studied — save in a countinghouse.

Samuel Ward brought enthusiasm to his work as he climbed his high stool each morning. If this had not been so, he could never have become Samuel Ward the banker, head of the great house of Prime, Ward and King. That he regretted his lack of educational opportunity is evidenced by the money and hard work he put into the establishing of the University of the City of New York — so that other boys should have the chance he missed. He was also one of Columbia's trustees and to Columbia went all his sons.

All this was in the future. Samuel Ward the banker was now sixteen, and as he walked along the partly filled-in and graded Battery Park at noon, he might easily have seen the girl he was to marry. In 1802, Julia Rush Cutler also lived in New York and "walked by the Battery and the waterside every day." She and two companions were dressed in "Spencers just alike" so that they looked like three sisters.

But Samuel Ward, aged sixteen, would hardly have noticed the gay little girl, even though she had sparkling brown eyes, dark curls and a mischievous smile. Julia Rush Cutler was at this time only six years old.

CHAPTER THREE
Cinderella Story

AT the corner of Bowling Green and Broadway stood a stately Colonial mansion.[1] It had been built for the Collector of Customs in King George's time, and Sir Henry Clinton lived in it during the British occupation of New York. It was the home of the Spanish Ambassador when New York was the Federal capital. A fanlighted doorway was flanked by arched windows and surmounted by a triple window having a fanlight. "A quadrille could be danced" in the fifty-foot drawing room, but while Samuel Ward was growing up, the house was a fashionable girls' school — and later a fashionable boarding-house.

The school was kept by Mrs. Isabella Graham, and Julia Rush Cutler was Mrs. Graham's pupil in 1802. The two other girls who walked with Julia "by the water side" in Battery Park were Mrs. Graham's granddaughters, Jessy and Bella Bethune. "Jessy and Bella and I agree very well, but I want to go home," [2] the six-year-old Julia confessed to her mother, in a letter written for her by Mrs. Graham and addressed to Jamaica Plain, Massachusetts. Julia sent messages to her brother, Benjamin Clarke Cutler, and her two sisters, Eliza and Louisa. They all seemed very far away. "Grandmother keeps school every day," Julia wrote — calling Mrs. Graham by the name her little friends used, and unaware that Mrs. Graham's other activities made her continued school-keeping a remarkable achievement.

At a time when poverty and misfortune were all too often regarded as a punishment for evildoing and no concern of the godly, Mrs. Graham was a pioneer humanitarian. She organized the "Society for the Relief of Poor Widows and Small Children" — having been herself a poor widow in straitened circumstances before her school proved a success. It was Isabella Graham who started what was said to be the first free orphanage. And with grown-up pupils to help her, Mrs. Graham also established the "Magdalen Society" to help "fallen women."

Julia Rush Cutler spent all her most impressionable years with Mrs. Graham. But she had parents of her own, nonetheless. "High Sheriff of Norfolk County," her father was called, and he was a descendant of early New England settlers, if not himself much of a Puritan. He died in 1810 and Eliza, Julia's older sister, was taken out of school to bring up the younger children, their mother being "prostrated with grief."

The Ward sisters knew their Grandmother Cutler [3] very well. She was an entertaining, if sometimes exasperating, old lady with flashing eyes, ready wit and highly developed histrionic talents. She "dipped snuff" and she ate with her fingers whenever they proved more efficient than a fork. She was a lady, nonetheless — her manners having been acceptable in her day and she seeing no reason to change them. She had been the belle of Washington's ball; her uncle had been General Francis Marion, the "Swamp Fox," and she was brought up on one of the fabulous Allston rice plantations of South Carolina. These were facts she never let anyone forget.

The Marions were a Huguenot family of pure French descent and the large measure of wit and social charm attributed to the French seemed to have descended directly through Grandmother Cutler to the Ward children, Julia and Sam in particular.

Grandmother Cutler, whose maiden name was Mitchell, had Allston half sisters. She was married at sixteen to a Dr. Hyrne of Georgetown and she was twenty when she was widowed for the first time. She remembered the many servants, the grand-scale entertaining on the plantation and the luxury of Georgetown life; and when, in 1791, she married Benjamin Clarke Cutler, he was described as "a genial, handsome man much given to hospitality." When he died in 1810, he left his wife very little beyond the rambling old house in Jamaica Plain, five children — and the expectation of a legacy from his rich uncle.

Mrs. Sarah Cutler lived on what she called "a pittance," her economies giving way to fits of extravagance, as she remembered various legacies she hoped to receive from her own and her husband's family. None of these ever came up to expectation. Not even Samuel Ward the banker could help her realize much hard cash from a South Carolina inheritance paid in produce. And the rich uncle left all his money to the Widow Cutler's son, who became a very pious Episcopal clergyman in Brooklyn.

The Widow Cutler's first duty, as she saw it, was to marry off her daughters as soon as possible. What could a penniless gentlewoman do, except marry money? Mrs. Cutler may have had her doubts about Eliza, her oldest daughter. The poor girl's teeth had been horribly neglected and she had "hair moles" on her face. Worse still, perhaps, was Eliza's wit, which had a razor edge. Men shied away from Eliza but gathered around her mother, regardless of her age, to laugh over the old lady's audacious but good-humored sallies. Perhaps some man would want a perfect housekeeper with the heart of gold which Eliza never really concealed despite the lash of her tongue.

Charming little Julia presented no problem. She was pretty, she was gay — and Mrs. Graham had educated her beautifully. In 1812, Mrs. Cutler accordingly arrived in New York and placed her daughters Eliza and Julia in a highly respectable boardinghouse. She stayed a short time with the girls, meeting fellow boarders. There were two brothers, Henry and Samuel Ward, both of them said to be "spoken for." That "satisfied the proprieties," Mrs. Cutler said. She departed, leaving the girls.

Actually, neither of the Ward young men was engaged. "I wish to return to you by the end of this month, as report is busy and my affairs are in everyone's mouth," wrote fifteen-year-old Julia Rush Cutler to her mother. It was the eighth of February, 1812. Samuel Ward had fallen in love with her.

A letter from Samuel Ward, the young banker, was on its way to Mrs. Cutler. Julia warned her mother, "I hope in your answer to S, you have merely given your consent, as I do not wish you to appear anxious for this connection." "It would take volumes to tell you half his goodness," Julia confided to her mother, but to Samuel Ward himself she said only that she "esteemed him highly."

With wisdom far beyond her fifteen years, Julia Cutler insisted that Samuel Ward come to her own home to court her. There were starlit walks around Jamaica Pond for Julia and her Samuel — with the ever-faithful Eliza along as chaperone. There were horseback rides to a high hill for a glimpse of Boston Harbor, blue in the distance. Julia at last confessed that her "esteem" had turned to love.

How could Julia Cutler resist Samuel Ward? He was over six feet tall and the artist who painted him in his youth showed to advantage

Samuel Ward the Banke[r]

From the collection of Sam[uel]
Prescott Hall. Reproduced throu[gh]
the courtesy of Mrs. Eleanor H[owe]
Saunders, granddaughter of J[ulia]
Ward Howe.

Photograph by Reni

Julia Rush Cutler Ward

[T]he wife of Samuel Ward the
[b]anker, by an unknown artist.
[A]ttributed to Charles C. Ingham.
[T]his portrait is the property of
[M]r. Ernest Mailliard of San Rafael,
California.

The Corner, about 1835

A water-color drawing by A. S. Hosier; J. Clarence Davies Collection, Museum of the City of New York. The white columns to the left are on Broadway and are part of Mr. Ward's private picture gallery. The Wards had a small telescope in the cupola.

Samuel Gridley Howe

From a photograph which was later the model for a portrait by John Elliott. (Supplied through the kindness of Frances Minturn Howard.)

Henry Wadsworth Longfellow

Painted by C. G. Thompson in 1840. The original painting is at the Longfellow house (Craigie House), Brattle Street, Cambridge, Massachusetts.

Photograph by Fogg Museum of Art

Charles Sumner

From a drawing by Franquinet. The original picture is at the Longfellow house, Brattle Street, Cambridge, Massachusetts.

Photograph by Frick Art Reference Library

John Ward

The guardian of the Ward sisters, by S. B. Waugh. The original picture is the property of Mrs. John Ward Mailliard, Jr., of San Francisco.

Sam Ward

Painted in Europe by C. Vogel ("von Vogelstein"); owner, William
S. Mailliard, Representative for California, Washington, D.C. The
dog was added later by an unknown artist, at Sam's request.

Sam Ward and His Bride Emily, Daughter of Mr. and Mrs. William
B. Astor. Painted by Anne Hall.

Thomas Crawford

From a portrait belonging to Frances Minturn Howard

Anne Eliza Ward (Annie) in Greek Costume

This painting by an unknown artist is the property of Mrs. Marion-Leigh Moore, granddaughter of Annie Ward Mailliard, San Rafael, California.

Prince Joseph Bonaparte and Adolph Mailliard

The standing figure is Prince Joseph; seated is his cousin, Adolph;
painted by C. Morelli. The original painting is the property of Mrs.
John Ward Mailliard, Jr., of San Francisco.

Young Sam Ward

From a drawing by Franquinet. A New Year's gift from Sam to Longfellow, 1840–1841. The original picture is at the Longfellow house, Cambridge, Massachusetts.

Sam Ward in a Famous Caricature

By "Spy" from *Vanity Fair*

Sam Ward, King of the Lobby

Samuel Ward, Esq.

Painted in Rome, 1884, by John Elliott

Louisa Ward Crawford

By her sculptor husband, Thomas Crawford — and possibly in her wedding dress. This bust, now at the Museum of the City of New York, is the property of Mr. Lawrence Terry and is reproduced by his kind permission.

Louisa Ward Terry

by her second husband, Luther Terry. The portrait, in the home of Mr. Lawrence Terry, Concord, Massachusetts, is reproduced by his kind permission.

photograph by Keith Martin, Concord, Mass.

Julia Ward Howe

Painted from a photograph, by her son-in-law John Elliott, and
completed after his death by William Cotten, Newport artist. The
original is at the National Museum, gift to the Smithsonian Institute
by the late Maud Howe Elliott.

Julia Ward Howe "at Sunset"

In her favorite chair, gift of her brother Sam. Courtesy of Frances
Minturn Howard.

the clear-cut Roman nose, the cleft chin, the wide mouth — serious but not severe. Under Julia's spell, the young banker turned poet and wrote her verses, trying to put into words just what had charmed him. Julia Cutler, not quite sixteen, was like a rose that had "just begun to bloom," he said.

Samuel Ward, at the age of twenty-six, was already a partner of Nathaniel Prime. He was the catch of the town and it was a tribute to the Widow Cutler's strategy that she convinced him he must plead with her to consent to an early wedding.

Colonel Ward, young Samuel's father, was always spoken of as "a gentleman of the old school," with "elegant deportment and mild manner." He was still the army officer, however, and he required obedience from his sons. It was two months after Samuel had written to Mrs. Cutler asking for her daughter's hand before he dared write his father a letter, which started out as a request for permission to marry. "The sage counsels of wisdom and experience do not always tally with the impatience of youth," Samuel began very cautiously. But he ended by making clear his intention. "Be assured, dear father, that I have bestowed my heart on a being in every way worthy . . I am content to wed without your approbation." And Colonel Ward, veteran of so many strategic retreats, knew when to give in gracefully.

The wedding date was set for October, 1812; and Samuel Ward bought a house for himself and his bride. "A little box," he called it, but pride could not be concealed as he described "its situation which is very pleasant and perfectly healthy." The address was One Marketfield Street.

Beginning at Broad Street, which had been a canal in Dutch times, Marketfield Street ran west, skirting the southern side of Bowling Green. There were gateposts at the entrance and the street itself was as old as New Amsterdam, taking its name from the Markvelt of Dutch days. Samuel Ward's new house was probably very old, a "little house which consists of two stories, very small but convenient and suitable for young beginners."

It was somewhat disconcerting to learn that Mrs. Cutler was sending an old family servant into her daughter's new home.. "I intended at first to have but two domestics in our establishment on account of the smallness of our little cage," her future son-in-law remarked. "And I wished dear Julia to acquire with as little trouble as possible, that knowledge of housekeeping which is indispensable." The old servant came, just the same.

The wedding took place on October 9, 1812, in Trinity Church, Boston, with Henry Ward as his brother's "groomsman." Someone said that the Widow Cutler "looked ready to tread the boards in her ancient finery" but actually that was no insult. The departed fashions of her youth suited her and if she made a stage production out of everything she did, she always put on a good show. At the party at Jamaica Plain afterward, Eliza danced in stocking feet, paying the forfeit for being the elder sister but unwed. And Henry "danced in a kettle."

Over hills and down the steep and narrow roads, by stagecoach and then in a hired carriage, went the bride and groom. *And* the bride's sister Eliza. The War of 1812 made the usual travel route, by sailing packet along Long Island Sound, unsafe — hence this long and rugged journey. Very shortly the inland roads would become impassable because of snow. The bride's sister Eliza would have to make a long visit. And to the bride herself, duty had been made clear. She was to find Eliza a husband.

The Primes were the first to entertain the bride and groom. For the occasion, young Samuel Ward the banker hired Huggins, the fashionable hairdresser, to come to One Marketfield Street to dress his wife's hair "very fancifully" — and also her sister Eliza's. Her husband bought Julia a new camel's-hair shawl so large that she "could scarcely wag under it," she said, and her dress, made by the best dressmaker in town, was a sensation at Mrs. Prime's. "At her ball the other night, would you believe it, I was dressed lower in the back than anyone present," she gloated. "I do not think the back of my gown was more than a half a finger long."

Looking about her at the Primes, young Mrs. Ward remembered the house very well. It was One Broadway — formerly Mrs. Graham's exclusive school for young ladies, where Julia Cutler had been a pupil but by no means a wealthy one.[4] In the days when the dwelling became a boardinghouse, Miss Julia Cutler could hardly have afforded to take a small room at the back. And now the sixteen-year-old Mrs. Julia Cutler Ward was guest of honor at the newly restored Colonial mansion recently acquired by Nathaniel Prime, her husband's partner. Julia must have looked and felt like a princess in her white satin ball gown. This was a Cinderella story.

Young Banker Ward's resolutions concerning economy had been broken now and then, it would seem. "Our house is so small, it is to be furnished in handsome style," Julia explained to her mother. Curtains were "made of delicate white dimity with draperies of salmon color" and there were "cornices of a new pattern, green and gold." Her husband went shopping with her, choosing from cabinetmakers' designs furniture to be made to order and buying enough glassware to last a lifetime, as his wife laughingly told him. But all was billed to her husband and one thing troubled Julia. She had no money of her own and her mother was always writing of financial difficulties.

"I enclose you ten dollars," Julia Cutler Ward wrote her mother. "If I can, I will make up the same sum again." This was pocket money which her husband gave her for small purchases, and she dared not ask for more. The whole Ward family was watching her for just such a move. There was, however, her "lottery ticket." Public lotteries had been held in New York since earliest times and for all sorts of purposes from street paving to fund raising for Columbia College. "By the next opportunity, I will endeavor, if my lottery ticket draws, to relieve you of your embarrassment," Julia wrote. She was never a selfish Cinderella princess.

Heavy snows fell in January, 1813. The young Wards, happy and gay, "staid till a very late hour" at one party, then "Rose with sick headaches and pale faces to prepare for another revel." The fresh air cleared their heads as they joined "a party formed to go in sleighs by fine moonlight about three miles out of town to Colonel Harrison's where we had dancing to our heart's content." (Three miles from Marketfield Street would have brought the sleighing party about as far uptown as 42nd Street.)

The sleighing was perfect that year, "one load of young fashionables snowballing another" as they tore along. Miss Livingston "lost her hat and curls." But young Mrs. Ward's curls were natural, and all her own. Her adoring husband, the young banker, described his wife as "one of the most fascinating, bewitching little Sylphs that ever captivated the soul of man!"

And Julia, with a wicked twinkle, said that "Mr. W. has taken infinite pains (with his usual goodness) to correct my faults, to convince me of the absurdity of my ideas on some subjects, to form my mind, to correct my judgment and taste and above all, my temper." As a matter of fact, she had thrown a glass of champagne at him. But she had promised never to do it again.

The young Wards were carefree and happy until April, when their world changed overnight. Young Mrs. Ward told what happened — as soon as she was able. "It is now three weeks since I was attacked by a disorder common to this climate, called inflammation of the lungs. . . . Dr. Post has attended me constantly twice a day. I have been bled and blistered both on my breast and side, and am now, by the Mercy of Heaven, almost restored."

Tuberculosis was so tragically prevalent that Mrs. Ward's sister Eliza only echoed public opinion when she described a frail appearance as a mark of beauty. "Julia, since her illness, has grown wondrous handsome," Eliza Cutler said. "Her complexion is clearer than ever, her figure extremely slim and genteel, and the expression of her countenance is peculiarly interesting."

Dr. Post, New York's leading physician, having failed to kill his patient by bleeding her, now prophesied that young Mrs. Ward would go into a decline.

It was Colonel Ward who probably saved her life. He had taken his family to live on a large farm he had bought at Jamaica, Long Island, and he insisted that this daughter-in-law, whom he now loved dearly, should spend the summer with him — away from darkened rooms, poultices and blood letting. "My own father could not have been kinder to me," Julia said. Obediently, she drank milk and ate the wonderful cheese her sister-in-law Anne Ward could make. There were parties all over the countryside and she went to some of them, riding pillion behind her husband down the leafy lanes and then home early to bed. There would be no gadding about in New York during the coming winter. On January 28, 1814, a son was born to Julia Cutler Ward — and named for his father.

Poor little Sam! He was named for his father the banker, for his grandfather the Colonel, and for his great-grandfather the Governor of Rhode Island. He was not supposed to rest on their reputations. He was expected to surpass all three. And of course, in a way, he did. No other Ward was ever a lobbyist or a Forty-niner. No other Ward ever flew so high or fell so far only to soar again. Moreover, Sam Ward succeeded in being himself at all times and in spite of his ancestors.

Grandmother Cutler had hurried to New York when she heard that the first grandchild was imminent. But she enjoyed the drama of the situation so much — she required the smelling salts or a sip of brandy so often — that there was hardly time to look after the young mother. Subsequently, the Wards were careful to keep her at home and in ignorance of such events.

By May, when her baby was only five months old, young Mrs. Ward again developed "a violent oppression at her lungs"; and this would be the springtime pattern of her short life. This time, she was frightened and remembered the stern teachings of Dr. John M. Mason who used to come to Mrs. Graham's school to teach the little girls their catechism every Wednesday. Mrs. Ward, now only eighteen, "pictured to" herself "the deathbed of a sinner" and "feared that nothing could save" her. They had to give her laudanum to still her weeping. As soon as she was able, she sent for Mrs. Isabella Graham, whom she still called her "dear grandmamma."

Mrs. Graham came at once and "explained the Bible." Perhaps young Mrs. Ward had cared too much for balls and loved too well the beautiful clothes her husband gave her. But it was no sin "to romp and frolic with little Sammy," to be naturally gay, to go to parties now and then and to give them, making her husband proud of her and her home a happy one.

Mrs. Graham brought "joy and peace in believing" and she also had constructive suggestions for a young girl who had feared death and who now wanted to get the most out of life. Seamen, dockers, riggers — all had been thrown out of work in the Port of New York because of the War of 1812. Their families, living nearby but in dark cellars and crowded shacks, were starving. Young Mrs. Ward now learned of these neighbors of hers for the first time, for although they lived so close to her, they were far removed from her happy world. She was not well enough to visit them the way Mrs. Graham did, but she shared food and clothing. She presented their case to friends.

"The new Society is going pretty well," Mrs. Ward was soon able to write. "We are begging donations from all. I gave twenty dollars and have got two donations promised." This was the "Society for the Promotion of Industry among the Poor." It was an effort to educate women so that they could earn money in their homes while caring for their small children, and stress was laid upon sewing, of course — but the problem was far from simple. It would someday occupy the mind and heart of a second Julia Ward.

The year 1814 was full of anxiety for New Yorkers. In October, "We are still uncertain whether or not we shall be visited by the British," Mrs. Ward wrote. New York homes, vacated for the summer, were being opened now but "several ladies are waiting to ascertain whether we are to be honored with a visit . . . before they will put up their curtains." If New York were to be an occupied city for the second time, all windows were to be bare it seemed. But Mrs. Ward's curtains were bravely in place. "After all, if the British do come, we could not be in better hands to be well taken care of than with Mr. Ward," she said. "He is a man of so much judgment and coolness that he always decides for the best!" Surely no husband ever received a better compliment!

"New York money passes at so great a discount that it would be folly to buy Boston goods," Mrs. Ward went on. "As to silver, we never see a sixpence, but use little bills something like Continental money. Boston money passes at a great premium, for more than specie."

With "judgment and coolness" doubtless, Samuel Ward the banker had some time ago possessed himself of Boston dollars. At last in March, 1815, came the news that "Mr. Madison's War" was over. "I think it was a fortnight after the news arrived that they had the illuminations," Mrs. Ward said. She thought the "transparencies very pretty, especially the one showing the Temple of Janus locked up and the key hung up." The Primes celebrated with a party "for two or three hundred people" and Mrs. Ward was well enough to go. The old house, which had now seen one more historic episode, "was beautifully fixed with artificial flowers behind all the lights"; and although Julia Cutler Ward did not say so, she too was beautiful, her dark eyes seeming larger than ever, her pure white skin almost translucent, excitement bringing brilliant color to her cheeks.

In 1815, Julia had a miscarriage — "but fortunately attended without pain or danger," her husband said. In January, 1816, a second child was born to the Wards, a little girl this time, named Julia for her mother. "The first little Julia" they would always call her, for in the spring of 1819 they lost her. In 1818, a second son was born and was named Henry in honor of his father's brother. Two sons were a source of pride and satisfaction, but the "first little Julia" was "so very engaging" in "her blue frock and trousers, white ruffles and little red shoes." Her two Cutler aunts, Eliza and Louisa, vied with each other to serve her. She was such a sunny child — so healthy and so happy!

It was whooping cough that proved fatal. Samuel Ward wrote the sad letter to the baby's grandmother, dating it April 23, 1819. "It is my painful duty to announce to you the decease of our precious little Julia. The violence of her complaint baffled medical skill — it has pleased Heaven to take her from us, and we yesterday with aching hearts committed her mortal remains to the Narrow House."

Samuel Ward's heart ached especially for his young wife, who was expecting another child. "I pray you, write her cheerfully," he begged.

On May 27, 1819, another little girl was born. They named her Julia for her mother — and for the little sister so recently dead. Julia Ward would always remember that there had been a "first little Julia," forever relegating to second place the Julia who was so very much alive. It would take years of experience to teach her that she had been doubly dear to her parents and loved for herself as well as for the sake of another. She would never be described as "engaging." She was much more of a little personality than that, but she engaged attention by fair means or foul. With her white skin and gray-blue eyes, she looked like a little angel. But her hair was red.

This was a tempestuous child. Stupid nursemaids doubtless told her about "the first little Julia," so gentle and so sweet. This second Julia was not sweet. She would be naughty when she felt like it and "at the sight of the rod" she "screamed herself half to death"; but her mother understood her, having been high-tempered herself, she said. Little Julia was generous and affectionate — her storms giving way quickly to sunny smiles. She was never for a moment a sulky child, and patience and gentleness would do wonders for her temper. The Wards would have their gentle daughter, and their daughter with the "uncommonly sweet temper." But they would never have a more interesting or gifted child than the second Julia. Soon she would not have to be called the second Julia, but just Julia Ward — in her own right.

In 1820 a third son, Francis Marion Ward, named for the Revolutionary hero on his mother's side, joined the family and now Sam, Henry, Julia and Francis Marion filled the tiny nursery in that box of a house on Marketfield Street. Moreover, Colonel Ward was a constant winter visitor, having sold the Fletcher Street house and moved his family permanently to Long Island. There were also almost always visiting aunts, a Miss Cutler or a Miss Ward, come to help with the children — or to look for a husband as the case might be. Samuel Ward the banker needed a larger house, and fortunately he could afford one.

The firm of Prime and Ward had become Prime, Ward and Sands in 1816 — Joseph Sands, son of Comfort Sands, having joined them. Once the War of 1812 was over, the cordage business which Comfort Sands had established was booming again as sailing ships were refitted. Hand in hand went the banking business, and with great satisfaction Samuel Ward bought Number 5 Bowling Green — across the park from Nathaniel Prime's great mansion.

Bowling Green was just north of Marketfield Street. In Colonial days, three men, John Chambers, Peter Bayard and Peter Jay, had leased the plot for eleven years — price one peppercorn; and at their own expense they had built a bowling green where they and their friends played this historic British game. Once the fort protecting New York town had stood behind the Green, but it was gone now and upon a ledge beyond the battery a new fort had been built to repel the latest threat of invasion. With the ending of the War of 1812, it was already obsolete, and now, connected with Battery Park by a bridge, it had become Castle Garden. Within its circular walls was an auditorium large enough for the celebration honoring Lafayette on his return to the United States in 1824 — large enough to hold six thousand people when Jenny Lind sang there in 1850. The Bowling Green, with its neat iron fence, was just a step from Battery Park and Castle Garden. The Green was said to be "frequented by the *Jeunesse dorée* of the period" — because their parents lived around the park. Everyone walked in Battery Park, nodding and speaking to everyone else. And in summer everyone, including Mrs. Ward and her sisters, had tickets to the "Marine Baths," great arklike houseboats moored near the Battery where they went to enjoy salt-water bathing "roofed over and closed in on all sides."

The Wards' new house had much larger parlors, and this time the cornices were "dead gold and bright with cornucopias of fruit." New furniture and new carpets were ordered and, as a special surprise for Louisa Cutler, a new "Piano forte." It was Louisa's turn to come to the Wards' now — Eliza having failed so far to catch a husband. The new house would be ready just in time for the Wards to give a party for Louisa.

Louisa had "a most choice collection of beaux" at her party, Mrs. Ward said. About "seventy people came. Mrs. Astor was there, Mrs. King and nearly all the fashionables. Everyone appeared to enjoy themselves . . . almost all stayed till one and some till two." They had music from "a violin and tambourine and danced on the carpet."

Louisa Cutler proved no matrimonial problem. She had a "Murillo-like beauty" and her brother-in-law had educated her beautifully during many previous visits, hiring "Professors" to come to the house. She had an "uncommonly sweet disposition" and by October, Matthew Hall McAllister, a former Princeton law student visiting friends in New York, had seen her and came back again and again to implore her to marry him. His Savannah family was by no means pleased with a bride without dowry; and Samuel Ward, who loved his sister-in-law, thought she could do much better. But Matthew Hall McAllister defied his father and persuaded Louisa that he could not live without her.

So Louisa decided to marry Matthew Hall McAllister. For the second time, Eliza Cutler danced in stocking feet at a wedding and then set out on a wedding journey not her own — this time to Savannah with Louisa McAllister. Samuel Ward gave Louisa a handsome trousseau from Philadelphia and bought Eliza some new clothes too, so that she would "look smart enough for Louisa's new family."

On February 25, 1823, a third daughter and sixth child was born to the Wards. She was named Louisa, in honor of the recently married Louisa Cutler McAllister. Never was there a more obliging child. She actually looked like her beautiful aunt and she was equally sweet-tempered.

Very properly, Louisa McAllister named one of her sons Samuel Ward. But in this case, there was no resemblance. In fact no greater contrast can be imagined than that between namesake and uncle. Ward McAllister, as he called himself, became famous as the arbiter of fashion in New York. Because Mrs. William B. Astor's drawing rooms would hold four hundred people, Ward McAllister listed for her the proper people to invite. His list was the original "Four Hundred." Fortunately, Samuel Ward the banker, that most democratic of men, never lived to see his nephew and namesake achieve this kind of fame! [5]

At the time of her little Louisa's birth, Mrs. Ward received from her husband a gift so lavish that she was ashamed to tell about it. "This morning was out making calls in my new voiture and horses," she wrote, "which is so much admired as to really embarrass me. Mr. W. presented me with a most superb pair of blood bays with black manes and tails, and I think them without exception the handsomest pair I have ever seen."

It was his mother's carriage that Sam Ward remembered, rather than her bay horses. He said that "it was her first and only carriage" and that "it was of a pale lemon color, which may still be seen among the equipages of Berkeley Square, London. It was built in Philadelphia, on C springs, and cost a thousand dollars." When Sam Ward saw carriages like his mother's, the year was 1883. Therefore the carriage chosen by the banker for his wife remained in fashion for sixty years. Sam remembered other things about the day when he first saw his mother's carriage and pair.

"The day was one of unmitigated felicity," he said, looking back.

"It was about the 3rd of May. The books of Prime, Ward and King had been balanced on the 1st and my father stood credited with a hundred thousand dollars."

The firm was not yet Prime, Ward and King, however. From 1816 to 1825, it was Prime, Ward and Sands. Then it was Prime, Ward, Sands and King until 1831. But Sam remembered best the firm name which his father made famous.

James Gore King came into the firm after turning down a offer from John Jacob Astor to manage the American Fur Company, and he was a valuable acquisition — as the other partners were soon to realize. Educated in Europe while his father Rufus King was ambassador to Great Britain, James Gore King had returned to the United States with the boyhood reputation of being "a prodigy of learning." He graduated from Harvard and studied law under Tapping Reeve at Litchfield, Connecticut, but interrupted his career to become Adjutant General during the War of 1812. Next, he took a turn at banking in New York, but in 1818 established the banking house of King and Gracie in London. King's European banking connections, especially with Baring Brothers, were of great value to his new firm. Baring Brothers became the European representative of Prime, Ward, Sands and King.[6]

Young Mrs. Ward knew all the personalities connected with her husband's business, whether she knew anything of banking or not. Her husband's associates and their numerous families all came to her "caudle parties" — remarkable affairs at which hot whiskey punch was served in cups and cakes were passed around as though at a tea. "Everything was in great style," at her latest "Caudle Party," Mrs. Ward said with satisfaction. Each guest "got red as a rooster" from "the steam from the caudle" and some of the ladies "got their bonnet strings untied and fanned themselves." It was a mischievous Mrs. Julia Ward who mimicked the strong German accent of one of her guests, "Vel, Mrs. Vard, that layst cup vas too much!" And it was a well-pleased young hostess who set down the fact that her "Caudle Party," though a great success, "became very fatiguing by the third day."

Little Julia remembered being allowed downstairs for a glimpse of parties in the Bowling Green house. There were crystal chandeliers full of brightly lighted candles and people danced on the carpet while Uncle Henry played the piano. The fine English "piano-forte" was never silent for long when members of the musical Ward family were about. Julia could hardly remember the time when she and Sammy could not dance and sing and pick out a tune.

It almost went without saying that every well-educated young lady could play the piano; but, surrounded by so many musical people, young Mrs. Ward rarely played. She had a different gift all her own. Although it was not entirely a secret, it was not to be mentioned outside the family. She wrote poetry!

"I send you a couple of my effusions which I beg none but the family may see, as Mr. Ward is so very fearful lest I should be discovered as the author," she warned her mother in a letter. "The printed one I wrote the day of the Marquis's arrival after a most fatiguing dinner party." The "Marquis" was Lafayette and the year 1824, and Mrs. Ward's poem, "The Arrival," was not only printed in New York papers but "copied in all the papers in Boston, Philadelphia and Baltimore." She "now had before" her a Charleston paper carrying her poem. This was an "unexpected compliment," she said.

Her secret was not well kept. "Dr. Francis, in his blundering kindness, ran about town telling everyone here," Mrs. Ward reported a little later. Dr. Francis had supplanted Dr. Post as the Ward family physician ever since the death of the "first little Julia." It was not that they blamed Dr. Post, but Dr. Francis was such a cheerful, encouraging person and such a good friend.

"I need this encouragement truly," confessed Julia Cutler Ward. "I have not had a soul to read my effusions to. Mr. W. is so indifferent that I now spare myself the mortification of attempting to arrest his attention. He is always in a hurry, or he had rather put it off, or jumps up in the middle recollecting something he must do — and finish another time."

Mrs. Ward's success as a published though anonymous poet continued, and so did her husband's lack of proper appreciation. "Even the piece of 150 lines, which appeared in the last number of the *Atlantic*, he never heard of, until he saw it in print, and then held it in his hand all the way out of town, (for I was by his side) and read the newspapers instead." The *Atlantic Magazine* first appeared in 1823 and it was in 1824 that the Wards went "all the way out of town" together — by carriage to Bloomingdale. Although Mrs. Ward had every reason to be proud of having her poetry published it is possible to feel a little sympathy with Samuel Ward the banker — confronted with 150 lines of verse after a busy day at 42 Wall Street.

When Julia Cutler Ward was included in *Griswold's Female American Poets* her husband was properly proud of her.

CHAPTER FOUR
The Young New Yorkers

IN the spring of 1818, just before his brother Henry was born, Sammy had gone to visit his grandfather on Long Island. This was a temporary arrangement which grew into a permanent one when Sammy, who had been pale, became as "strong as an Apache." In July, 1818, his father wrote that "Sambo goes to school every day." And his mother said that "Sammy walks a mile and a half to school and takes his dinner." [1] It was Cornelius Eigenbrodt's Academy, that was considered within walking distance of Colonel Ward's farm in Jamaica; and Sam Ward was only four and a half years old. His mother had already taught him to read, and by the time he was six he was deep in Caesar's Gallic Wars.

Sam was kept rather short of pocket money, his mother writing him that he must make his "quarter of a dollar" last a month. So as an extracurricular activity, Sam made an investment somewhat prophetic of his future career. There was an older boy named Bilbo who worked on the farm and whom Sam admired greatly. Bilbo said he was going to be a pirate someday, and when he showed Sam "a certain hole in the ground" Sam agreed to put a penny a week in it — being assured that by the end of the year "the fifty pence would be turned to gold by incantations known only to" Bilbo. [2]

But Bilbo was shipped off aboard a man-of-war when it was discovered that he was trying to get Master Sam to run away with him. Sam, going at once to look for his gold, found nothing but pebbles in the hole. It was a lesson he never forgot. On the other hand — as he ruefully admitted in later life — it was a lesson he never really learned either.

Sammy spent his school vacations at home in New York and, when he went back to Grandfather Ward and Aunt Anne, he carried affectionate messages from his mother concerning his welfare. Colonel Ward's unmarried daughter Anne had become a bit severe with the passing years, reading sermons being her only form of recreation. But Sam's mother wrote that it might "improve Sammy's manners" to let him "go to a ball."

In 1824, when Sammy was ten years old, he entered Round Hill School in Northampton, Massachusetts. This famous school for boys was run by George Bancroft and Joseph Green Cogswell. The term had begun when Sammy arrived, escorted by his uncle, Matthew Hall McAllister, who happened to be going that way. They arrived in Northampton in the evening after a long day's journey by coach and Uncle McAllister offered Sam a beefsteak dinner and a night at the inn before going to the school. But Sam, intensely eager for this new experience, declined. They went straight to the school. arriving after the boys had eaten and had gone to bed. After much pounding on the door, a sleepy Mr. Bancroft let them in, and Sam found that his advent was of no particular importance except to himself. This was a blow, but worse followed. He was given "three slices of bread without butter, a glass of water, and sent to bed." Here was another lesson which Sam not only learned but profited by this time. Never again would he refuse the offer of a good dinner.

Being well grounded in Latin, Sam began the study of Greek. At the end of August, Sam wrote his mother: "I assure you that although I am perfectly satisfied with my situation, yet I now begin to feel not exactly homesick but as if I wanted to get home very much. And I really do."

Sam had missed a summer vacation which his sister Julia, although only five years old, would always remember. Their father had rented "a fine country seat in Bloomingdale, six miles from town." Julia remembered that her mother gave her lessons out of doors in the garden and that the French teacher came out from New York in the Bloomingdale stage. There was a rose arbor and Julia remembered that her mother arranged flowers "with great taste." To have flowers in the house — this would always remind Julia of happy times. Her brother Henry, now six, was her constant companion but Francis Marion, being only four, was relegated to the society of his sister Louisa in the nursery. Since Louisa was only a little over a year old, "Manny" tried to tag along after those two superior beings, Henry and Julia — and he was "extremely jealous," Julia remembered. He also had "a painful impediment in his speech," but perhaps that came a little later when the Ward family nursery was suddenly a sorrowful place for reasons beyond the comprehension of a four-year-old.

The Bloomingdale summer was over all too soon, and the family returned to Bowling Green. Sammy came home in September for that longed-for vacation and doubtless there were festivities in his honor. But there would be no three-day Caudle Parties for the grownups this year. There came a time, early in the winter of 1824, when all must be quiet in the Bowling Green house. Henry and Julia, who had been allowed to play downstairs, were herded into their third-floor nursery with Manny and Louisa and told to be quiet even there. Aunt Anne Ward came from Jamaica. She called and went away again. Dr. Post came, and Dr. Francis. The children were used to this sort of thing because their mother was so often ill, and they were not too surprised when their father came to them on the morning of November 2 and told them that they had a new baby sister. He was smiling joyfully. "And she can open her eyes," he said. Her name was Anne Eliza — Anne for Aunt Anne Ward and Eliza for Aunt Eliza Cutler.

Aunt Anne told what happened between November 2 and the night of the eighth. "Our darling Julia had not slept well and was under the influence of paregoric." But after the baby was born, Mrs. Ward "recovered perfectly" and next morning after breakfast, "she sent for us all in. And she looked so well you could hardly believe she had been confined. The dear little babe was lying on her pillow — and a happier group than we were, you cannot imagine."

Aunt Anne went shopping and engaged a "mantua maker." Mrs. Ward planned for the "pelisse" to be cut and sewed in her bedroom, so that she could enjoy watching the process — for she dearly loved the making of clothes. But that night the young mother was "taken with a fever." At eleven the following morning, both Dr. Post and Dr. Francis had arrived but there was nothing they could do.

Mrs. Samuel Ward, now only twenty-eight, had lived with tuberculosis for eleven years. If she had not conquered it, she had fought it to a standstill and she did not intend to die now and leave six children motherless. "Pray that my cough may be removed," she begged. But although the cough troubled her whenever she was in a weakened condition — it was the fever that mounted.

Samuel Ward had summoned the two best doctors in New York. Dr. Francis was already becoming famous for his work in obstetrics. But twenty years would have to pass before Dr. Oliver Wendell Holmes would make his famous study of puerperal fever, cause of so many deaths among mothers in childbed. It would take a still longer time and much more research to show that puerperal or childbed fever was a form of blood poisoning, preventable under antiseptic conditions and at long last curable with new drugs.

Julia Ward, five and a half years old, was awakened in the night on the eleventh of November. "Your mother is dead," they told her and she was taken to her mother's room to kiss a terrifyingly cold cheek.

It seemed to Aunt Anne that "only dear little Sam is old enough to feel his loss," and she piously set about rectifying this state of affairs. At bedtime, "when the children came to say their prayers," she told them that "they could not now ask a blessing on their dear mother. At this, they all cried and it seemed as if their little hearts would break," Aunt Anne wrote, with the air of a good woman who knows when her duty is well done.

The children's father was taken ill with "fever and ague." Several weeks went by; Samuel Ward recovered slowly; and there were those who said that he refused to see his newborn child until Colonel Ward went up to the nursery for the little Anne Eliza and laid her in her father's arms. She was then his favorite, people said, perhaps telling this story to the little girl, whose heart must have been filled with misgiving. Of course her father loved her — Annie knew that. But somehow she had been the cause of her mother's death, a very dreadful thing to think about while not in the least understanding how it could be true.

Samuel Ward sold the house on Bowling Green with all its furnishings. Every room recalled a painful memory of a young wife who had died in her twenty-eighth year and who, in the course of a few short years of married life, had brought her husband more happiness than many men ever experience. Suddenly bereft not only of his mother but of all familiar surroundings, perhaps it was now that little Francis Marion's speech difficulty began. Julia saw closed parlors and furniture shrouded with dust sheets in the Bowling Green house; the parties she remembered seemed like some happy dream. Beyond that, all the Ward childrens' memories were of Bond Street.

At Number 16, the first Bond Street house, the children occupied "that gloomy third-floor nursery" where the three little girls, each with a large family of dolls, played "Mrs. Miles, Mrs. Jones and Mrs. Brown." It was a bright spot in their lives when their father's coachman, "old black Johnstone," lifted them into "the great yellow carriage with the blue linings."

The Ward children learned to ride their ponies in their father's paddock on the corner of Bond Street and Broadway but soon the family coachman had only girls to teach. The three Ward boys all went off to Round Hill school — Henry when he was eight and Francis Marion when he attained the same advanced age. They found Sam, an "old boy" — waiting to welcome and rule them.

According to Sam's letters home, he was a most exemplary boy. He later remembered matters unfit for parental consumption. "Old Bancroft" (who was twenty-seven) was Sam's Greek instructor. Sam's "fair progress" developed into rapid progress, and he was soon launched upon the Greek drama.[3] "Old Bancroft used to make me translate it (*Phèdre*) alone in the P.M. school," Sam said. "Then he would cock over his chair agin the wall and go to sleep and I would read extracts from *Peregrine Pickle* and *Count Fathom* until the boys' laughter woke him up — when I would complain that they were laughing at me.

"I can see the whole scene as I write, even to the falling off of his gold spectacles from his nose as he woke *en sursaut*, and in his efforts to catch them, the dear old sheepskin 'Graeca Major' would fly the other way. What a monstrous old humbug he was then, and what a wonderful young one he is now!"

When Sam Ward made these disrespectful comments, George Bancroft had reached seventy. His many-volumed *History of the United States* was complete at last, but his political career, begun when he became Collector of the Port of Boston, still continued. As Collector, and at Elizabeth Peabody's insistence, he had given Nathaniel Hawthorne that very minor post of weigher and gauger. But unlike Hawthorne, Bancroft loved politics and he had gone onward and upward (helped out also by two wealthy marriages) until he had become Minister to Great Britain and was now — at the age of seventy and when Sam Ward recalled him — Minister to Berlin. "Humbug" or not — it was all in the point of view.

In any case, George Bancroft was a good judge of character when Sam Ward was a boy. Sam was "impatient of slow progress and accurate labor," said his headmaster — and this was true of Sam all his life.

"In mathematics," Sam did not "excel, nor will he," Bancroft said further. "He can get through a course with respectability and great advantage to his mind, but his talents incline him to other pursuits." This was true also, but Bancroft had observed another trait of Sam's — too great a desire to please. Sam would often hesitate to answer a question when "doubtful what bearing his answer may have on the opinion entertained of him." This desire to please, and above all to please his father, led Sam to apply his excellent mind to mathematics. He therefore "excelled" in spite of Bancroft; but it is a temptation to speculate as to what he might have done with his life if he could have developed his real talents in "pursuits" other than banking.

Sam Ward, as his father's oldest son, was predestined for banking, so George Bancroft's system — to discover a boy's bent and then unbend it — was just the thing. Nothing was to be said in Sam's favor because he was the youngest boy in his Spanish class and by far the best student. His French, which he wrote and spoke "with accuracy," was to be looked upon as a pastime; and the set of drawings, over which Sam had labored and which he had just proudly sent to his father as a gift, were not to be praised.

Sam, who was so affectionate and so homesick that he drew hearts at the bottom of his letter and wrote "For Father, the largest part of my heart," waited in vain for a word of appreciation about his drawings. He grew still more homesick, and wrote his father a long carefully worked-out argument in favor of going back to Long Island to become his grandfather's "mainstay in old age." It was all in vain. He must stay at Round Hill and study mathematics. He must set an example to his brother Henry who would soon arrive.

When eight-year-old Henry finally arrived, however, Sam was obliged to write an indignant letter. Henry "never minds me without a great deal of trouble on my part," Sammy complained. It seemed that Henry had climbed to the roof of a shed at school. "I asked him to come down," Sammy related — which is probably not how it sounded to Henry. "He answered, 'I won't' and I had a great deal of trouble getting him down, but I having succeeded, he fell into a passion." The diplomacy for which Sam Ward was to become famous had not quite developed, but he made progress. A few days later, Sammy wrote, "Henry is now becoming a very good boy by degrees, I having remonstrated with him a great deal."

In June, 1829, it was Francis Marion's turn to put in an appearance at Round Hill School. "I like the school better than I expected," Francis Marion said. "We play eight hours and study six hours, the way is we get up at five." He had been led to believe that there would be no play at all.

The Bancroft system of discovering aptitudes in order to suppress them operated in Henry's and Marion's case as it did with Sam. At eight, Henry had "mind enough, at his tender age" to "learn the first principles of Algebra and to reason with Mathematical accuracy." Henry had at once "begun Greek" but so far, it "had not sobered him." So for Henry it was Greek, since he "unites the greatest playfulness with the most uncommon talents," Mr. Bancroft said, and was "as quick to drollery as to understanding." Whether or not Francis Marion's "painful impediment in speech" had left him was not stated, but "Manny," being mathematically inclined, would study law.

With an older brother's superiority, but with real affection, Sam wrote asking after the little sisters left at home. "How do the children come along with their dancing? Ask Julia if she can go chapé to the right and chapé forward? Can she do the anti-chat?" There was no doubt but what Julia and her sisters could do all the steps, for a dancing teacher came to the house to give them lessons. But they had a dull time of it, on the whole, compared to their brothers. It was Julia who envied her brothers the most.

A succession of nursery governesses came and went, teaching the girls to write a delicate, strongly slanted hand and to spell in the British manner. Louisa and Annie wrote ladylike letters and so did Julia when she put her mind on it. Usually, however, Julia had so much to say that her words, the letters half formed, scrambled across the page as though pursued by thoughts too fast for them. Her handwriting resembled her brother Sam's; he, try as he might, never wrote a tidy letter in his life but wrote many that made good reading.

The girls were pleased when they were allowed to go to Miss Catherine Roberts's Day School for Young Ladies on Wabash Street. But the experience proved a disappointment. All that was expected of them was that they memorize page after page of Paley's *Moral Philosophy*. Miss Angelina Gilbert's school on Bleecker Street, not far from Bond, was a little better. Julia gathered from her brothers that chemistry would be an exciting study, and at her insistence Miss Gilbert let her have a chemistry book, but when Julia was told that there would be no experiments allowed she lost interest.

Samuel Ward paid two hundred dollars a term to educate Julia, Louisa and Annie, aged twelve, eight and seven respectively. When the girls reached the age of sixteen Miss Gilbert would consider their education complete, whether they had learned anything or not. Louisa and Annie were inclined to accept this state of things and to take life as they found it. But Julia had been looking into her brothers' books and she knew that there was an exciting world which was forbidden to her as much as though the angel with the flaming sword had personally driven her from the tree of knowledge. It was not fair and she was not going to stand for it.

The first really pleasurable excitement on Bond Street, as far as the Ward sisters were concerned, was a wedding which took place in 1829.

"Is Dr. Francis married yet?" Governor Clinton had asked young Henry Ward.

"No, but he is trying to be," Henry had replied.

On November 16, 1829, Dr. John Wakefield Francis succeeded. He married Miss Eliza Cutler, who had been taking care of the Ward children, her nephews and nieces, ever since their mother died. And so at last the Widow Cutler had married off all three of her daughters — or her daughter Julia had, for before her death young Mrs. Ward had seen Eliza's chances greatly improve, thanks to her care. A dentist had been found capable of repairing Eliza's ruined teeth. Dr. Post had removed the "hair moles" which poor Eliza had never dreamed she could get rid of — and Eliza was "handsome," in her late sister's own words. Eliza "dressed like a lady" and looked "very handsome in the street with her head full of feathers and appeared to enjoy herself." It is to be hoped that young Mrs. Ward, before she died, detected a look of admiration on the part of Dr. Francis for the much improved Eliza Cutler. Eliza had been the unpaid but faithful nurse to all the Ward family whenever they fell ill. She and Dr. Francis knew each other very well long before young Henry observed that the doctor was "trying to get married."

Samuel Ward the banker gave his sister-in-law a white cashmere shawl and a pair of pearl earrings as a wedding present. It was "a small token of affection compared to all she has done for me," he said in the note that accompanied the gift. And he lent the bride and groom the Ward family carriage for their wedding journey. The children, all dressed in their best and allowed to join the festivities, never forgot the sight as old Johnstone drove up to the door. He had braided white ribbons into the horses's manes and tails.

The bride and groom made their home with the Wards — for how could Eliza leave her sister's children? The only difference was that now they called her "Auntie Francis." But if Dr. Francis had not been more or less of a fixture in the Ward household such an uncle would have made a great deal of difference. He was an exuberant little man, fond of the society of actors and writers and unfailingly generous when these became his patients but could not pay. One such was Edgar Allan Poe, who repaid his debts in a description of the little doctor.

"His person and manner were richly peculiar," Poe wrote. Dr. Francis was "short . . . with limbs of great strength, the whole frame indicating prodigious vitality . . ." [4]

The doctor's conversation was "a sort of Roman punch, made up of tragedy, comedy and the broadest of all possible farce." He was "very earnest, intense, emphatic; thumping the table with his fists; shocking the nerves of the ladies. His forte after all was humor, the richest conceivable — a compound of Swift, Rabelais and the clown in the pantomime."

According to Poe, Dr. Francis had an odd way with women. He "pats every lady on the head, and (if she is pretty and petite) designates her by some such title as 'my pocket edition of the *Lives of the Saints!*'" At least in later life, Eliza Cutler Francis was anything but petite for she weighed over two hundred pounds. But her life was sufficiently saintly — she was just an encyclopedia rather than a pocket edition.

Auntie Francis was happily married although she had her trials. It was said that one day at dinner the doctor noticed that her face was flushed. He instantly led her off to his office on the lower floor and, over her indignant protests, bled her copiously. Then he allowed her to go back and finish her dinner. [5]

There was something to be said on the other side. Dr. Francis was one of the few men who could have laughed at all of Eliza's barbed remarks. When told that a Bond Street neighbor "keeps horses, servants" and so on, she retorted, "Oh yes, I know. He keeps everything but the Ten Commandments!" The man soon heard the story, and Dr. Francis might have lost a wealthy patient. But Dr. Francis was not worried about his clientèle. His practice was said to have amounted to "$15,000 annually," which was a large sum for his day. The amount of free medical help he gave was something that few people knew about.

Auntie Francis and her husband did everything they could for the Ward children. Their presence meant much to this naturally lively family while Mr. Ward, who had plunged deep into business to forget his grief, seemed to have lost the knack of being gay. Dr.

Francis brought friends from the theater into the Ward parlors and such remarkable amateurs as Dominick Lynch, wealthy wine merchant, who proved that all the musical talent was not on the stage.

Little Julia used to hide beneath the grand piano to listen to Mr. Lynch and to weep in ecstasy as he sang "Lord Ullin's Daughter" and other Irish ballads — which he said George Moore had written just for him. Mr. Lynch brought the first Italian opera to New York and Julia Ward, aged seven, was allowed to see *La Cenerentola*, with María García who was only sixteen, in the title role of Cinderella. Sammy remembered seeing *The Barber of Seville* at this same time, and when his own tenor voice developed he sang many of the songs he had heard sung by Mr. Lynch — although his own special style was German. Julia later learned to sing by the "García method."

But Boston was not the only city to give the theater a hard time during the first half of the nineteenth century. New York was nearly as hostile. María García sang at a concert in the Bowery Theater in 1827, and that was all right because the concert was for the benefit of the Greeks. But the next year a French dancer appeared in ballet costume and "most of the audience blushingly retired." [6] Prince Achille Murat, who was there, said, "The ladies screamed out for very shame." Although the dancer wore "Turkish trousers" at subsequent performances, the Bowery theater shortly burned down and there were plenty of people who said that it was a judgment upon the wicked stage. With pious Aunt Anne Ward on one hand, and the Reverend Benjamin Clarke Cutler on the other side of the family to influence him, it was ten years before Samuel Ward let his daughters go to the theater again.

Fortunately for the girls, their brother Sam came home from Round Hill School to live on Bond Street and to go to Columbia in 1829. He was fifteen and he would have been proud to read what George Bancroft finally said of him. "It is very seldom that we are able to say so much good and so little ill of anyone as I can truthfully say of Sam," Bancroft had written Mr. Ward. But of course Sam must not be told. "Praise injures him. It makes him first confident, and then of course careless." Sam's "manner" was improved, but was still "not quite correct." He was still "impetuous."

As a result of all the secrecy about his fine mind, Sam had a shock in store. He found the entrance examinations at Columbia "mere play" and he never exerted himself again in college. Columbia was a "kind of Sleepy Hollow in the heart of old New York," he said in retrospect. Every morning he walked downtown from Bond Street past City Hall to Park Place where brick buildings with high chimneys looked down upon a grassy square. The courses Sam took seriously were his introduction to society, both polite and otherwise. At Round Hill, the boys were always hungry and the sin for which Sam was most often punished was slipping off to the village of Northampton to buy pies. Now, in New York, Sam had both freedom and pocket money. Entering "Delmonico's café" for the first time, Sam looked about him "with awe." To be sure, it was expensive and Sam's allowance was still modest, but where else could you get such a "quail and beefsteak" dinner with "chocolate cream and ice mixed" for dessert? Sam developed a passion for oysters and soon became a connoisseur of oyster cellars. There was "Decker's" and there was "Downer's," those "gaudy cellars" ⁷ with thick red carpets spread over long corridors belowstairs, with gas chandeliers (an innovation) and paintings of half-clad women on the walls. "Clerks betting with sharpers" were to be seen there, and "dashing young men, their pockets filled with money." If a "gentleman and a lady" dined alone behind the crimson curtains in one of the gilded wooden booths, it was assumed (at least by the tract-writers) that they were "playing for higher stakes, perhaps a husband's honor or a wife's immortal soul." Sam Ward could satisfy his longing for oysters at much less expensive places where the bill of fare was better. His pockets were not yet "filled with money" although he wished they were, and by careful application to this new course of study he soon learned where to find the best food and where to see the sights — all the way from "Fred's," that "famous old billiard parlor on the southeast corner of Reade Street and Broadway," to Delmonico's on the "west side of William Street."

If Sam entered Delmonico's "with awe," he had something else to say of Columbia. "The duties of the students were light, of the professors still lighter, of the President, lightest of all." Only Professor Anthon excited Sam's respect — "he accomplished more work than any man I have ever known," said Sam. And he was himself a man of tremendous energy — occasionally misapplied.

Sam Ward graduated from Columbia in 1831 at the age of seventeen, after gracing those particular academic halls for only two years. He had entered with advanced credit in almost everything. The career of banking now opened before him with its probationary period on the high stool of a clerk in his father's office at 42 Wall Street. To Sam the prospect was anything but alluring and he begged to go to Boston to study higher mathematics under the great navigator, Nathaniel Bowditch.

It would seem that Sam had a series of personal interviews with Dr. Bowditch, then engaged in his monumental work in astronomy. Sam rushed back to his room after each interview and wrote down the words of the mathematician. His romantic imagination was fired by astronomy, and he soared joyously into infinity — but nothing could have been further from banking, with its constant call upon judgment and common sense. Sam wrote his father about the balls he had *not* attended.

Sam was delighted when he was appointed to the examining board at West Point "in the summer of 1832." "In those days it was a kind of frolic," he said, and he might just as well have called it a farce. "The gentlemen" of the board were "entertained at Cozzen's Hotel" where the cellar was "overflowing with wine when Uncle Sam paid the bill." Sam's "education at the old farm" — his grandfather's in Jamaica — had "made him a tolerable 'taster' and the hardy life" he had led had given him "a tolerable constitution — two elements likely to compose a good drinker. When therefore this convivial board discovered that I had an aptitude for Euclid as well as for Madeira, they appointed me honorary chief examiner," Sam said.

Now the farce began — as Sam Ward told it:

"I speedily became popular with the cadets; many of whom I helped through the mire of confusing equations, or assisted with a suggestion as to how to complete their geometric figures on the blackboard.

"When the most satisfactory examination for many years had been completed, and I had helped to draw up the Visitors' Report to the Secretary of War, the Board celebrated with a dinner at the Superintendent's, Colonel Sylvanus Thayer. To prepare myself, I swam the Hudson, from Cold Springs to West Point, and was the only guest at the dinner who was not afterwards taken to the hotel in an ambulance!"

Sam returned to New York, still unready to become a clerk in Wall Street. He said he was "surprised" and "flattered" one day when his father came home to Bond Street to dinner — which was at three in the afternoon — and said that Professor Charles E. Davis and Captain Ross from West Point had called at the request of Colonel Thayer to offer "the post of Assistant Mathematical Professor" to young Sam. Flattered though he was, Sam had to think fast, for his father was willing to let him postpone banking in favor of West Point. He needed to know "military engineering," Sam said. Perhaps his father should first send him to Europe "to study in France and Germany" and meanwhile he would like to "go to Newport and ponder among its rocks and surf, the problems" of his "future career."

At eighteen, Sam Ward's gift of diplomacy was developing.

CHAPTER FIVE

"Julietta"

"IT was the fashion then at Newport to lease for the summer a farmer's house on the Island and not live in town" — so said the incurably social-minded Ward McAllister, who, as a small boy, was included in the Ward family gatherings every summer. Up from Savannah by packet came the McAllisters — the Ward childrens' Aunt Louisa and their various first cousins. From Brooklyn came the Reverend Benjamin Clarke Cutler, their uncle, bringing with him their Grandmother Cutler, as spry and witty as ever. Auntie Francis came, escorting the Ward children and bringing her own — one of them named Samuel Ward Francis, of course.

"Well do I remember, with my uncle Samuel Ward and Dr. Francis of New York, building bonfires on Paradise Rocks on the Fourth of July and flying kites from Purgatory," wrote Samuel Ward McAllister, recalling Newport in the days before it became the famous summer resort. In 1831, Samuel Ward paid to "Geo. Bailey of Newport, $238.50 for myself and children." And in 1834, Mr. Ward "hired a house belonging to the Widow of Commodore Perry" and "paid for two boarders in each room of the house." These Newport summers Mr. Ward himself shared only for a few weeks at a time. Like many other devoted fathers, he stayed in New York where, at his office in Wall Street, he labored daily in his family's behalf.

In March, 1831, Samuel Ward began to build "The Corner." [1] This was the fine mansion of his dreams which his neighbor, Philip Hone the diarist, would refer to as "a noble house." Eventually, it would contain every good thing that money could buy — including a picture gallery, one of the first in New York. Contemporary canvases would outnumber old masters, for Samuel Ward believed in helping young American artists. The "picture room," as he called it, was finished in

1836 — when Mr. Ward said he hoped it would "repay the labors of the road," for architects and builders alike had been baffled by this difficult assignment.

The Ward children were in Newport in July, 1832, when their father wrote them that "the new house is coming along finely . . . the upper rooms are done." Water had been "found at 37 feet 3 inches and an iron pump installed." No need to send a servant to the public pump at the corner of the street as in Marketfield Street days — when the water brought home with so much trouble was brackish to the taste because of tidewater seepage. No need to patronize the water-barrel man who came through Bond Street.

A center hallway was flanked by two great drawing rooms facing Bond Street. Behind them, and looking out on the Bond Street garden, was the dining room; and on the Broadway side was a room called "Mr. Ward's study." The picture gallery ran along Broadway and a lower story partly below ground housed the kitchens and an office for Dr. Francis.

Marble mantels were carved to order at the shop of Frazee and Launitz, a new firm. They had a gifted young apprentice, now eighteen, who far surpassed the other marble carvers, and he was given this important order. Dark, handsome and as powerfully built as a stone-cutter needs must be, Thomas Crawford might have been seen in the Ward half-finished parlors, supervising the setting of his caryatides — marble maidens who carried marble lintel and mantelshelf upon their uncomplaining heads. Soon Thomas Crawford would be off to Rome and a career as a sculptor, all unmindful of a pretty little girl named Louisa Ward who would grow up admiring his work. Louisa was now nine years old. She would be twenty when they met.

In the summer of 1832, the Ward children had been hurried to Newport earlier than usual. Asiatic cholera had broken out in New York. In mid-July and over a three-day period their neighbor Philip Hone mentioned 411 new cases and 234 deaths from cholera. Newport proclaimed a quarantine and "no one could come ashore from the steamboats." Henry Ward, who had stayed behind with his father and was giving good satisfaction as a clerk at 42 Wall Street, was trapped now although he had planned to take a vacation very shortly. Samuel Ward the banker would not have left his business if he could — and Grandfather Ward had already refused to retreat from the unseen enemy.

Broadway, always so crowded, was soon almost deserted. Mr. Ward, riding on horseback to work as was his custom, saw no one in the street and only a few faces peered at him from behind closed windows. Dr. Francis, in his gig, was almost the only passerby on Bond Street. The Ward childrens' uncle, the Reverend Benjamin Clarke Cutler, remained in Brooklyn to bury his parishioners and this too was courage, for cholera was supposed to be "in the air."

On August 16, it fell to Henry Ward, now fourteen, to write to his brothers and sisters in Newport. The weather had been "intolerably hot," he said. At half past eleven the evening before, Miller, Colonel Ward's man, rang the doorbell. Colonel Ward was stricken with cholera.

Mercifully, young Henry was not allowed to go with his father. Death from cholera was horrible. Colonel Ward's four sons were summoned: Samuel, Richard, John and William. All except William lived on Bond Street and all reached his bedside in time. They had one comfort: death from cholera was swift. Colonel Ward, a debonair old gentleman of seventy-six, had now lost his last engagement. It did not seem possible that he could be dead.

Late in the autumn the embargo was lifted and Samuel Ward the banker arrived in Newport, exhausted from living in a plague-ridden city and burdened with grief over the death of Colonel Ward. He was shocked to see his son Sam come in from duck hunting, as cheerful and happy as a boy could be. It was not that Sam Ward was heartless, however. He was particularly vulnerable to grief. It was just that his was a spirit that could not grieve overlong. Letters from his grandfather, written in graceful Old World style, he kept always. He remembered his thrill of excitement when he saw his grandfather's commission, signed by General Washington. And they were always keeping "fête days" at Jamaica, pledging each other's health and standing to toast General Washington in old Madeira taken from a British ship in privateering days. Sam owed his easy, elegant manner to his grandfather the Colonel — and part of his charm.

Sam — who was soon in his father's good graces again — postponed his decision on the West Point offer, and obtained permission for that European tour he wanted. Of course Sam knew better than to call it a tour — he was to study at the University in Paris and in Germany, whither American students were flocking in increasing numbers. Sam's father took him back to New York to call on friends and collect letters of introduction to European bankers and mathematicians. Albert

Gallatin gave him a letter — but Sam collected a few on his own from Dr. Francis's more exciting artist and actor friends. Letters acquired for him by his father from clergymen and missionaries remained among Sam Ward's papers — unpresented.

Sam Ward arrived in Paris, wide-eyed and comparatively innocent. All his life, he had been kept very short of pocket money with the idea of teaching him prudence; he was now given an unlimited letter of credit!

His first Paris contact was Jules Janin, French dramatic critic and novelist. Sam dearly loved the theater, and he had never had more than a taste of it, just enough to whet his appetite. Now Sam discovered what money could buy in the way of exquisite little dinners at elegant restaurants, with Monsieur Janin as guest of honor, ladies from the stage for decoration — and other young men as guests who were also on tour at the expense of wealthy parents. Sam lingered in Paris much longer than he was supposed to, and it is doubtful if he matriculated at any university other than that of experience.

With Jules Janin, Sam was taken to meet the great Rachel in her dressing room after a performance of *Phèdre*. She had acted her important scenes under such emotional stress that her Greek robes were wet with sweat, Sam observed — and as he sat talking to one of the finest actresses France had ever known, he remembered reading *Phèdre* (and *not* reading it) at Round Hill School. That was not so long ago, but he had come a long way. Taken to hear Paganini practice in his rooms, Sam was astonished to learn that the great violinist spent hours playing the guitar to keep his fingers supple. Sam also played the guitar very well, and he felt a kinship with the concert artist. He was learning to talk with people on their own chosen ground; questioning, admiring — with great charm. They said it was Sam Ward whom Janin had in mind when he wrote *The American in Paris* and it was true that Sam behaved very much like the wealthy young man in the novel. But people would always be linking Sam Ward to characters in fiction. He delighted in the society of writers, and his was the bold, bright, larger-than-life personality that any writer would like to capture on paper.

Sam finally tore himself away from Paris and by devious routes, and in his private carriage, arrived at the University of Tübingen, Württemberg, Germany. The university, founded in the fifteenth century, was everything Sam had hoped. There were old buildings, old houses, a castle in the town, and students who behaved like a chorus in light opera — or so it seemed to Sam. He promptly learned the German *Lieder* for which he was to become famous in many a parlor back home. Sam went to school at least long enough to meet a very earnest and very poor German student by the name of Charles F. Mersch. They studied together, and, at Sam's expense of course, they traveled together — becoming well acquainted with various innkeepers' daughters. Eventually, Sam wrote a thesis in German and received a most ornate piece of parchment — his degree from Tübingen.

All during his European tour, Sam kept a diary which it was said he let his sister Julia read when he got home. One volume at least belonged to her years later, and it began in 1834 when Sam "arrived in Paris for the third time." This was not like Sam's first wide-eyed arrival, for now he knew all the ropes. He "took tickets for tomorrow night, *Don Juan* at the opera" and "who the Devil should" he "behold in a pastry cook's shop but Miss Florentine — along with Eliza and Papita." [2] "Florentine" was not necessarily the lady's name but it was sometimes the name of all ladies in her line of business.

Sam rose late next day, breakfasted at one P.M. and went to smoke his cigar in the "*passage de l'opéra*." He was not too surprised to "meet for the 2nd time, Florentine." He had been lonely the night before, he said, back in the same old hotel and even the same room he had occupied before — but without his former companion. So now he "went home with" Florentine and "found there," along with other girls — another man. "I am then informed that, since my departure, he has been the *Amant*," Sam sadly wrote in his diary. "Alphonsine always remains," he was told — but he did not care for Alphonsine.

Sam was informed that the following day would be Florentine's "fête day" and that "she has suddenly become fond of money . . . and a gentleman coming in, I am dispatched." Not too cast-down, Sam was "well pleased" with the opera, *Don Juan*, but afterwards at the door he met his rival "who runs for a hack while I wait for F. I put them in a *fiacre* together and go home to my solitary bed," he said.

The following afternoon Sam went to the rue Coquenard — "where I find F to give her 50 francs in petite monnae." Florentine was "rendered excessively kind by my present and on my taking leave, promised to come and have breakfast with me on Monday the 11th." But if Florentine thought she was Sam's only friend, she should have read the next sentence in his diary. "Turning down rue Cadet, met Pauline, who has recovered her health at the expense of her utterance — then met Marie who is glad to see me."

Sam Ward was beginning to think in terms of a literary career. First, he planned to write a comprehensive history of mathematics, to please his father. For this, the plodding but accurate Mersch was to come to the United States to act as Sam's secretary. Meanwhile, now was the time to gather material for the poems and novels which would be Sam's real life work. He observed and recorded accordingly: While at Florentine's "see the manner of providing mistresses for country friends exemplified in the case of a neat and modest young girl whom F is packing up and off — to her old keeper, the Commandant Dupont at Valenciennes." Sam actually wrote part of a novel in French, explaining later to his exasperated father that this language now came more naturally to him than English. If Sam could have kept the forthright simplicity of his diaries when he wrote for publication, he might have realized a cherished ambition. In any case, he enjoyed collecting his material.

But Sam had not quite forgotten Bond Street. A few days later he met an American sea captain "who informs me, that much is said in N.Y. last winter of the gay life I was leading in Paris — my father always silent." So Sam sent his father his thesis in German and his Tübingen degree and promised to come home soon. Meanwhile he needed more money because he had just bought, from the widow of Adrien Marie Legendre, the mathematician's entire library. Sam said that this was a chance of a lifetime and that the books would sell for twice what he paid for them. For once, he was not exaggerating. Legendre had been Professor of Mathematics at the École Militaire; and in the United States, at that time, there was no mathematical library to compare with the one Sam Ward was bringing home. If he were to teach at West Point, he needed "the best books," Sam said, and he certainly had them. Blissfully unaware that a major financial panic was building up in America, Sam was hurt and surprised to receive a sharp note from his father telling him to stop spending money and to come home at once.

Sam came "directly home" by way of Heidelberg, Stuttgart, and London. It was in Heidelberg that he met the best friend he ever had; the only man who never exploited him for the sake of his money or cheated him because of his kind heart and unsuspecting spirit. Sam had gone to an evening party in honor of Mrs. William Cullen Bryant and her daughter, who was later the wife of Parke Godwin, editor of the *New York Evening Post*. This was during the winter of 1835 when Bryant imagined, for a brief period, that he could retire and devote himself to poetry, living upon his one-third interest in the *Evening Post*. But Sam told the story himself of his meeting, at the Bryants' party, with Henry Wadsworth Longfellow.

"I accepted, little dreaming that I should there meet and make a friend in whom I never failed to find the most tender and loving sympathy." [3] Sam's cousin, George Washington Greene, already knew Longfellow and "had so frequently praised him" that Sam could hardly wait to meet the professor from Portland, Maine. Usually, such a meeting proves disappointing; "with me, it was a case of love at first sight," Sam said. He loved the "ruddy face, eloquent eyes and abundant locks." The two young men left the party together and Longfellow "walked home with" Sam to the "Balischer Hof, where we talked till dawn." The next time they met, both young men would be back in the United States; and then, and upon many subsequent meetings, Sam would greet Longfellow with an exuberant kiss on each cheek — Continental fashion. Cambridge would be astonished. Sam would produce from the side pockets of his loud-patterned greatcoat bottles of Rhine wine; and at Craigie House on Brattle Street the two friends would drink many a toast in the tall green glasses which Longfellow had brought back from Germany and always used on these convivial occasions.

But meanwhile, Sam Ward proceeded on his roundabout journey home and while traveling through Stuttgart he saw the "Royal Review of the Household Troops." Jerome Bonaparte, who had married the king's sister, galloped up and down in the uniform of "a Württemberg warrior," Sam said. "It was my first sight of a live Bonaparte. Later, I met in London and America his charming brother Joseph, ex-king of Spain." Sam also met Louis Mailliard, a son of His ex-Majesty's by a lady other than his wife. Louis Mailliard was King Joseph's private secretary, the father and son relationship being no secret and considered no disgrace. Monsieur Louis Mailliard had been very properly married to Marguerite Redet, the daughter of one of Napoleon's equerries, and their son Adolph was also in London. Sam Ward did not know, or had forgotten, that his mother had once met the ex-king of Spain and had been entertained at dinner at King Joseph's fabulous palace in Bordentown, New Jersey. The next time Sam met Adolph Mailliard, it would be in New York and in Bordentown. But not even the imaginative Sam could have foretold at this time that Adolph would become a candidate for membership in the Ward family!

By means of various artful excuses, Sam managed to stay in Europe for four years. But on Friday evening, September 20, 1836, Sam Ward reached New York, took an omnibus and rode up Broadway alone. There on the corner of Broadway and Bond Street stood his own house, which he had never before seen completed. Sam ran up the marble steps and pulled the knob of the doorbell. A servant came in answer to the distant tinkle.

"Is Mr. Ward at home?" Sam asked.

"No."

"Where is he?"

"At Newport."

"With the family?"

"Yes, with the family. Mr. Ward has bought a magnificent country house there, and he will not be back until next week. But Dr. Francis is here, as well as Mr. Henry Ward."

"Is there a room vacant?"

"What do you mean, sir! Do you take this for a tavern?" [4]

Sam was having his fun, which lost nothing in the telling. Of course by this time his brother and the doctor had found out who was at the door. There were "transports of joy, shrieks and vivas." They "laughed and talked till dawn."

Sam "showed himself about town a bit" — not only himself but his Paris clothes. Then he went down to Newport. Although it is highly improbable that the Wards' servant would have told a supposed stranger that "Mr. Ward had bought a magnificent country home," it was true that the banker had a big white clapboard house with rooms enough to accommodate the large family of children, aunts and cousins. It stood on the corner of Bellevue Avenue and Old Beach Road, next door to what is now the Redwood Library. With that irrepressible humor that was part of his charm, Sam remarked that at church on Sunday the clergyman read the parable of the "Prodigal Son." It did not take Sam long to reinstate himself in his family's good graces, however. He described his reception in Newport: "Three angels embrace me, strangle me, call me 'Brother!'" [5]

"Never were three girls more thoroughly different in character than my sisters," Sam said, getting acquainted with them all over again. In 1836, Julia was seventeen, Louisa thirteen and Annie only twelve.

Annie was "affectionate and highly sensitive," her brother thought. Louisa was "proud yet warm-hearted" — and Julia? "Jule, poor Jule," was "the victim of a thousand false inquietudes and sensibilities. Smiling before you," she "wept in secret," and Sam was told that recently she had locked herself in her room "for five days in succession, writing some sort of essay!"

Francis Marion looked askance at his sister Julia's literary efforts, as did the rest of the family. "Much does she seem revolving over some plan for literary distinction, but this, I hope, she will lay aside when she grows older and wiser," he said.[6] Now that brother Sam had come home, Julia had an ally at last. He saw no reason why Julia should not be a writer if she wanted to, and when she confided her secret — that she was writing an essay on Goethe — he thought it was a fine idea.

Joseph Green Cogswell, Sam's former tutor at Round Hill, was pretty much at the root of the whole matter, having fired Julia's imagination with his talk of Goethe, whom he had known personally in Germany. George Bancroft had withdrawn from Round Hill School in 1831, Mr. Cogswell buying him out, with the help of a loan from Samuel Ward, and trying to run the school alone. Cogswell had failed, another school position proved impossible and he had now taken shelter under the Wards' hospitable roof as tutor to the Ward daughters. Here at last was the opportunity the girls had longed for and they promptly chose subjects their brothers had studied and which were denied them in polite little day schools for young ladies. Louisa began Algebra with "Coggie" and astonished him with her progress, Annie's capacity to read and understand an immense number of books was equally gratifying — and Julia plunged into German, making rapid progress. Mr. Samuel Ward's kindest acts seemed to bring him trouble, however. Now that he had befriended Cogswell, he found a copy of Goethe's *Faust* in Julia's possession. Had she read this dreadful book? Julia had indeed. Fortunately, it was some time before Julia's essay on "the minor poems of Goethe and Schiller" appeared in the *New York Review*.

Samuel Ward the banker had his difficulties with his daughters, surely. Julia, being the oldest, was the first to become romantically involved. Her father had expected it, but when it came he felt entirely unprepared. He forgot that her mother had been only fifteen when he himself proposed marriage, and he now sternly broke up Julia's first affair. So Julia confided in her father's friend, Major David Bates Douglass. Having been a Professor of Mathematics and Engineering at West Point, Major Douglass liked and understood young people. He was often at the Wards' house, where he and Mr. Ward discussed the plans he had drawn for New York University's romantic Gothic buildings on Washington Square — which Mr. Ward's donations would help to build. After serious work was over, Major Douglass had been known to linger and take part in charades with Julia Ward, her sisters — and his own daughter Sarah. It was not surprising that Julia sometimes thought Sarah's father understood her better than did her own.

In August, 1834, the fifteen-year-old Julia wrote to Major Douglass. She was in Newport, which she had always loved, but now she felt that all was forever changed. "Since I have been here, I have not enjoyed one moment of happiness," Julia wrote. It was because of "Dear T——." There was cholera in New York as usual, and Julia was anxious. "When you see —— tell him to be careful for my sake." Julia signed herself "Juliet," but in her postcript her sense of humor bubbled up in spite of her romantic grief. "Lord Capulet, alias Samuel Ward, sends his regards."

Evidently Major Douglass knew who T—— was, but Julia was disappointed when he did not answer her letter. In September, she wrote again. "We have done everything that could enliven the solitude of the country, we acted some charming 'tableaux vivants' which I will explain to Sarah on my return. . . . I could think I have been happy but for the remembrance of ——, whose image, sleeping or waking, continually pursues me. How hopeless is my passion, returned as I am assured it is, with all the ardor of youth; why must we both be unhappy from the difference of our station? But my resolution is taken, whatever it may cost me. Cease to love him, I cannot — but I shall never behold him again. I shall see him once more, but tell him that I have done wrong in exciting in him a feeling which can never be gratified, that we are separated by obstacles which nothing can remove, and that we must part forever! May he be happy . . . for me nothing remains but submission. The tears blind my eyes as I write."

"Your little Julietta" she signed herself, but once more the spark of humor was not entirely drowned in tears. After quoting "Oh that I were a glove upon that hand . . . " Julia Ward added, "Father says he does not see why any man should wish to be a 'mitten' on a girl's 'paw'!"

"Julietta" said that she had no skill in letter writing, but she managed to describe the feelings of a teen-age girl very well. "My mind seems to me to be a perfect chaos of different elements confusedly blended together. . . . I feel as if I were endeavoring to untangle a skein of silk. . . . I know I have talents . . . energies . . . feelings and affections . . . how to regulate these I know not, perhaps time, experience or friendship may teach me." [7]

During the following summer, a sea captain by the name of Russell E. Glover, and a man probably nearer Julia's father's age than her own, asked her to stroll with him in the Newport garden. As soon as they were alone, he solemnly took out his calling card, wrote something on it — turned on his heel and left her. Almost unable to believe her eyes, Julia read, *Russel E. Glover's heart is yours.*

Again Mr. Samuel Ward had to break the news that his daughter Julia's hand could not be promised. But Julia was not interested in Captain Glover so this time the role was not that of Lord Capulet, for which Mr. Ward could be thankful. Of course, further trouble was just around the corner. Captain Glover had sailed to Greece, found a Greek boy, the son of a petty chieftain, who was the captive and slave of the Turks. Captain Glover bought the Greek boy, brought him to the United States in 1828 and had him sent to school. In 1834 the boy was at New York University, sent there by a group of missionary-minded people whose contributions, nevertheless, left him hungry and much in need of clothes. The good-hearted Captain Glover probably never realized that Miss Julia Ward was much more interested in the Greek boy than in himself.

The boy's name was Christodolous Leonidas Miltiades Evangeles [8] but fortunately he was always called "Christy." Although he did not know exactly how old he was, he thought he was nineteen in 1835. He was so unusually handsome that his portrait was painted by Edward D. E. Green, by Robert Weir and by Jane Stuart, daughter of Gilbert Stuart. "The Greek Boy" the paintings were usually entitled, but they were exhibited in various places under various names. Samuel Ward bought Weir's picture for his private gallery, and the Greek Boy himself became a sort of public idol, symbolizing America's feeling for the Greeks under Turkish oppression. Ladies old enough to know better wrote poetry dedicated to Christy, and by the time he was sixteen he "lectured" on Greece to sympathetic audiences. In spite of all this, Christy behaved himself very well, and in his delightfully frank diary he told his experiences.

In 1835, Christy "accepted Mr. Samuel Ward's proposition, which is to carry me through Columbia and Seminary in Greenwich and then send me to my dear Country Greece." Christy planned to be a clergyman, but at times he saw himself as a statesman or a general leading victorious Greek armies against the Turks.

"I here represent Greece and I visit in the highest circles of society," Christy wrote in his diary. "And also, from what they tell me, I am the only person (or young man) with whom Mr. Ward ever permitted his Daughter to go walking out or be alone with in any manner whatsoever."

Christy took "Miss Julia Ward" to St. Thomas's Church to see "the farewell to the first two Protestant Episcopal missionaries to China." He sat with "Miss Julia Ward" at a "glee party for the benefit of the blind," and she gave him "Dr. Howe's book on the Greek Revolution to read."

This was a very proper friendship until Christy went to Newport with the Ward family and Julia, discovering that Christy kept a diary, prevailed upon him to let her read it. Much that Christy commented upon, Julia took for granted. "Broadway, throughout the year is in some place or other stopt up or tearing down." She knew that. There was "a genteel side of Broadway," where it was proper to walk, and Julia Ward had grown up knowing which side of Broadway to walk on.

Christy had a few things to say about prevailing fashions. He did not like "proud fellows with a pair of whiskers like a pair of shoe-brushes, courting rich, ugly girls with mouths big enough to swaller [sic] an alligator." He did not approve of girls "dressed like wasps, in places almost cut in two, then a little below . . . stuffed out with goodness knows what, to be big."

A few personalities came in for comment. Commodore Vanderbilt, for example, "is a tall rich fellow, lives in East Broadway . . . I saw some very pretty girls at his house — for which I like him better." When Christy met Miss Catharine Sedgwick, he commented: "Miss Sedgwick, the great American Authoress, appeared very moody. She looks as though she had just come from a sacrifice to Pan. I was quite pleased with her."

What really impressed Julia Ward, however, was Christy's interest in girls her own age. He had fancied himself in love with one after another of her schoolmates and she herself came at the end of the list. Here was a challenge. But first Julia wrote a poem for Christy on a blank page of his diary. She called him a "coquette," which was quite true. With more truth than poetry she proceeded:

He falls deeply in love with each girl that he sees
And then goes and whispers his thoughts to the trees.
There's Sukey and Polly and Graham, I trow
And poor Julia Ward with her hands white as snow —
And pretty Miss Randolph and lovely Miss Post
(I think if he gets her, she'll soon rule the roast) . . .

It was a long and teasing poem, and poor Christy was offended. Then the next thing he knew he was enslaved. He forgot Julia Post, Maria Graham and Polly Ann Gibson. Christy taught Julia a song in Greek and he took her to "First Beach" where they sat on the rocks and he "comforted her about her soul." The Ward boys teased him unmercifully, but surely there was never such a girl as Julia! "My sweet Euphrosene" he called her.

"I love this young and most intelligent lady," said Christy in his diary when he returned to New York in October. He began to consider how to "muster up courage" to ask Samuel Ward for his daughter's hand.

But in his efforts to keep his romance a secret until the proper time, Christy ran afoul of one of Julia's ever-present aunts. Under close questioning, he assured Aunt Louisa McAllister, who was visiting her brother in Brooklyn, that he planned to marry a Greek girl after he returned to his own country. Christy had been living at the Bond Street house, but now he was sent to live with Reverend Benjamin Clarke Cutler. And Aunt Louisa's report of the conversation so exasperated Julia that, as Christy put it, "Julia treats me differently. She says I have deceived her."

This time, Samuel Ward's intervention was not needed. The romance was over. But it is to be hoped that Major Douglass, in the privacy of Mr. Ward's study, had not laughed at "Lord Capulet." Christy promptly fell in love with Sarah Douglass, and now it was the Major's turn to play Capulet.[9]

After a few blighted schoolgirl romances, Miss Julia Ward decided that a literary career would be the thing. Perhaps she hoped that her father would approve. But this, in Mr. Ward's opinion, was the worst caprice of all, and he decreed that she should stay in New York with him during the summer, while the rest of the family were in Newport. At a loss to know how to bring up a motherless daughter, it was now that Mr. Ward gave Julia her mother's letters to read, and she wept in secret for the mother she needed so much. The series of letters must have made one thing seem clear to Julia: that a happy marriage was most desirable but that eventually the birth of a child proved fatal. This was the sort of fear that could not be told, however, and Julia tried hard to please her father. She concealed her tears and wrote amusing letters to her sisters in Newport.

"By a strange and inexplicable caprice, Papa took it into his head today that I must make some pies," Julia wrote — knowing full well that it was all part of the campaign to make her more domestic and less literary. She described the "miseries of pie-making, of kneading up and rolling out the paste, of stewing, sweetening and worse still tasting the gooseberries, of daubing one's self with butter, lard and flour — hands, face and clothes; of tearing the paste to pieces in trying to transfer it from board to dish! In two hours" she "made three pies." "My only consolation is, that though I made them, father will have to eat them," she said.

Brother Sam's return had brightened the horizon for all three Ward sisters, however. Already his friends were coming to see them and Julia added a postscript to her letter. "Professor Longfellow paid us a visit on Sunday and will dine with us today. Longfellow must be a strong-fellow to masticate the paste I have prepared for him."

Alas for Mr. Ward's plans — Longfellow brought to Julia a new intellectual pursuit. He discussed *Beowulf* with her, and she promptly got herself an Anglo-Saxon grammar and started to read *Beowulf* — which was not her father's idea of how she should spend her time.

Louisa, who could also be humorous when she chose, wrote to ask if "Jolie Julie" had "misbehaved." If so, she suggested a punishment. "I shall shut you up in your room with nothing but bread and water, and what is worse yet, you shall have nothing to read but your Anglo-Saxon grammar and *Beowulf* and if that does not give you a distaste for all sorts of *wolves* (not excepting those *Long Fellows*) I do not know what will."

Julia was at last allowed to go to Newport and Louisa came to New York to take her place and learn the domestic arts. This was by no means as difficult for Louisa as for Julia, but she looked forward to letters from Newport with news of how the rest of the family fared. Julia wrote that she still had not "misbehaved" but that she had been on an excursion with Longfellow. "We passed yesterday at Fall River, an ugly, dusty little place, we visited factories and saw the famous skeleton in armor, which was found there some years since." Julia suggested to "Longo" that he write a poem about this mysterious warrior.[10] Knowing about her secret ambition and the little notebook of poems, to which Julia added from time to time, Longfellow hesitated to accept the idea. But Julia assured him that skeletons were not her style.

A little over a year went by and Longfellow's "Skeleton in Armor" was done — a long poem in manuscript, which he said was too long for him to copy off and enclose in the letter he was writing Sam Ward. But Sam replied in great excitement:

"I mentioned to Clark . . . that you had composed a delightful poem. He told me that the next *Knickerbocker* is to have an original poem from Halleck, Bryant, etc. etc., in short is to be a crack number. He says he expects one from you, subject unknown. My description of 'The Skeleton in Armor' excited all his cupidity and I advised him to offer you $25. there for."

This was the first time that Sam Ward acted as Longfellow's literary agent, but it was by no means the last. Both young men felt that twenty-five dollars was a substantial amount; but the time would come when Sam would obtain a really high price in New York for one of Longfellow's poems.

CHAPTER SIX

The Astor Wedding

FOR some time after Sam Ward returned home, purchases which he had made in Europe continued to arrive at the Port of New York. Mr. Pescatori, a banker, left at the office of Prime, Ward and King a package confided to his care by the artist, von Vogelstein. It contained the portrait of a young man, seated at the foot of a tree, a light whip in his hand.[1] "It *purports* to be you," Samuel Ward the banker told his son Sam, without enthusiasm. Yet it was a charming painting in clear, translucent color, showing a young man with hair elegantly curled, a delicate mustache outlining full, sweet lips, and a silky Van Dyke beard concealing not too strong a chin. Sam was delighted with a portrait which made him look so much like a poet or a novelist. But he had been told to report daily at his father's office, and he could only conclude, from his father's tone of voice, that velvet coats and frilled shirts were not to be worn on Wall Street and that the novel he had begun must be finished at night or not at all.

Sam said that he "determined to excel all" his "father's clerks" and that he put in nine or ten hours a day at the office.

But Julia remembered that Sam's first day's performance at the office had been so faulty, that her father, on reviewing it, exclaimed, "You will play the very devil with the checkbook, sir, if you use it this way." How could a young man, now twenty-two and with a German degree in mathematics, fail in so simple a task?

Sam entered his father's employ at a crucial time for Prime, Ward and King. The panic of 1837 had begun, and Sam must have seen the hungry mobs in the streets.[2] Wholesale grocers in Washington Street were raided and four or five hundred barrels of flour and wheat were broken open, their contents thrown in the gutter. This was in protest against high prices, but the flour destroyed could not be replaced because Western farmers had turned to land speculation. For five years, previously, "the rage for speculating in lands" had "led to great over-trading. Men had run in debt far beyond their means of paying . . . Immense amounts of specie had been transferred to the West to pay for public lands, for the government" refused "any other kind of payment."

With New York specie drained away, merchants and bankers turned to Great Britain for loans, but "the Bank of England had extended itself beyond all precedent in granting credit for business ventures in the United States. Finding its gold reserve reduced, the Bank of England refused to discount the commercial paper of eight English banks having large commitments in the United States." Baring Brothers, correspondent of Prime, Ward and King, was one of these.

Young Sam Ward, Jr., the fledgling banker, understood only vaguely why his father was so anxious and hard to please. He knew that his father called countless meetings of fellow bankers, from which he emerged depressed in spirit as never before. On May 8, 1837, the Dry Dock Bank of New York failed. On May 10, all the New York banks suspended specie payment, and Samuel Ward considered this an act of bad faith and a breach of honor. He had fought against it, but he had been outvoted. When Sam said that worse things could happen than suspension of specie payment, Mr. Ward could not agree. Yet, from a banker's viewpoint, worse followed when several states repudiated their debts, and New York showed signs of doing the same.

To Mr. Ward, it was like seeing his country defeated by an enemy to have banks failing and states dishonoring obligations. James Gore King hastened to London while Samuel Ward pleaded with leaders in New York State to delay. And then, at the last moment, the Bank of England lent Baring Brothers five million dollars in gold to be distributed among the New York banks; the consignment being to Prime, Ward and King. Prime, Ward and King negotiated a loan for the State of New York, which was promptly repaid. Specie payments were resumed by the end of May, and the crisis was over. Sudden as the panic seemed, it had been years in the building and no one knew the strain under which Mr. Ward had been suffering.

But if Sam failed to appreciate his father's anxiety, he recognized drama when he saw it. A dray piled with kegs had come rumbling over the cobblestones from the waterfront and had pulled up at 42 Wall Street. Men began to carry kegs marked "P. W. & K." up the stairs. It was the gold from England! Sam rushed home to tell the girls and also his father who was ill at the time.

Sam's father began to have hopes of him — if only he would marry and settle down. But Sam, at twenty-four, said he would not marry till he was thirty. It was the sort of statement on the part of an attractive bachelor that invited retraction. Sam's letter to Longfellow, written a few months later, described his state of mind concerning Emily Astor, daughter of William B. Astor and John Jacob Astor's grandchild.

"You ask me whether the romances have fled." But Sam was still more determined to be a poet and a novelist. "They have not left me — yet no longer haunt me in shadowy outlines of heavenly forms. The visions of youth and hope and loveliness have become one glorious and thrilling reality. Out of the perfumed incense I have so long burned to my unknown divinity, the Goddess herself has appeared." Emily Astor, "little Emily, pale and sweet," was the "goddess." She was only sixteen in 1837 when she and Sam Ward became engaged.

Now at last Julia and Louisa Ward were allowed to visit houses other than those of relatives on Bond Street. There were musical evenings at Emily's grandfather's house on Broadway. "My little songbirds," John Jacob Astor called Julia and Emily, beating time to their music and joining in the chorus. Sam delighted the old man with his German *Lieder* and this was a surprise — a young man who could sing in German the songs John Jacob Astor thought everyone had forgotten.

Parties at Emily's house on Lafayette Place were more formidable, but Julia and Louisa Ward enjoyed them just the same. Emily's mother, the former Margaret Armstrong, had been educated in France; her father claimed descent from Scottish nobility, and her grandmother had been the wealthy Alida Livingston. William B. Astor was called many things but "sociable" or "genial" were not among them. It was his wife who filled the brick mansion with guests representing the highest level of society.[3] "Her notions of propriety in dress were very strict," Julia Ward discovered. "Jewels were not worn in the daytime. Glaring colors and striking contrasts were to be avoided." But Julia was thrilled by her first glimpse of the world of fashion. Her father gave her "a beautiful diamond ring." Her hair was dressed for these formal occasions "in intricate braids worn low at the back." It was "pomaded" to make it darker, for light red-gold was still unfashionable. But she had no jewel for her hair and Julia Ward was much cast-down. She was to be "first bridesmaid" at Emily's wedding. Emily's grandfather had given the bride a "diamond star," and how would the first bridesmaid look without so much as a gold chain and ornament hanging upon her forehead, Oriental style? She begged her father for a "ferronière" and he gave her "a very pretty string of pearls, having a pearl pansy and drop in the center."

Sam Ward and Emily Astor were to be married at the bride's home on January 25, 1838. Considering the constant entertaining that went on, it seems strange that only two guests outside the immediate families were invited. They were Washington Irving and Fitz-Greene Halleck. Irving had recently completed *Astoria* from John Jacob Astor's papers and notes, and from a firsthand survey of the Northwest. Irving genuinely admired John Jacob Astor, and presented him as one of the builders of the nation — which he was. Since Astor's fortune had been made out of the misfortunes of others in many instances, this favorable light pleased the old man, who had begun to think in terms of another world where there would be no barter. Fitz-Greene Halleck had been Astor's secretary for years, forsaking what his friends believed would have been a brilliant literary career. Perhaps, in selling his services, Halleck forfeited great fame; but he was no servant: he was a friend.

Julia Ward was in her seventh heaven over the wedding festivities and her sister Louisa no less so, if less articulate about it. Annie was not included in the bridal party, which may explain in part her paleness and "languor." Annie was fourteen, the same age as Alida Astor, the bride's sister, who was of course a bridesmaid. But there was nothing to do about it except that Annie might have profited by a white moiré silk dress like her sisters' instead of having to swallow the medicine Dr. Francis gave her.

Henry Ward was in Europe, since it was at last his turn to make the grand tour. Julia therefore wrote him about the wedding. "We were sorry that you could not be at dear Sam's wedding," she said. She and her father had wanted the wedding postponed till Henry's return, but Sam would have been a poor sort of bridegroom to consent to that. Instead, the wedding was "hastened because of the precarious state of Mr. Astor Senior's health and his anxiety to see his favorite grandchild married." The old man would last another ten years but Emily was indeed his favorite and the $20,000 promised her "upon her marriage or upon attaining 21 years" was hers now — but most certainly in trust and not to be turned over to her husband. This is not to say that, as yet, the Astors disapproved of Sam Ward. They admired his father, his family was distinguished and they were pleased with the match.

"Weddings are generally anything but gay," Julia wrote. "This was the most cheerful that I ever saw. . . . The bridal train consisted of myself and Mr. Jones, Louisa and Robert Walsh, Miss Alida Astor and Marion." In all probability, "Mr. Jones" was Frederick Jones, who had been at Columbia with the Ward boys.[4] He afterward married Lucretia Stevens Rhinelander, and was the father of Edith Wharton — the whole family being friends of the Wards. Robert Walsh was also a Columbia classmate who visited the Ward sisters in Newport. And "Marion" was of course Francis Marion Ward, now a senior at Columbia.

Julia, as first bridesmaid, "pulled off the glove with great dexterity," she said. "Sam and Emily went through the service with calmness and self-possession. They were married by Mr. Eastburn who read the service beautifully."

This was an evening wedding, and "at ten o'clock the doors of another room were thrown open and we all seated ourselves at a table which resembled the entertainments in the Arabian Nights. The supper was magnificent," but Julia "could not say that we did it justice, for we were all too gay to eat; the Doctor told some of his best stories and when the clock struck twelve we could scarcely believe it." The "Doctor" referred to must have been Dr. Francis, considered as a member of the family and not an outside guest like Halleck and Irving.

There was probably no wedding trip. The bride and groom stayed "at the bride's house until the first day of February," when they "received their friends." This receiving of friends took the form of "a grand ball," at which "Sam, Emily and I are going to sing some trios," Julia said. And when the ball was over, she was still gasping over the "floor of the ballroom" where a "floral design had been traced in colored chalks." And she still felt sadly abused because just as "the evening was at its height," her father "gravely admonished" her that "it was time to go home."

From the Astors', Sam and his bride went to live at The Corner until their own house at Number 32 Bond Street should be ready for them. The house was the gift of Samuel Ward the banker to his son, who in turn presented it to his wife — much to the satisfaction of the Astors, who knew a good piece of real estate when they saw one. The house was still standing exactly one hundred years later when Sam's niece, Maud Howe Elliott, saw and described it: "a handsome brick building with keystone arch, fanlight and marble steps and iron railing."[5] A staircase circled from lower hall upward four flights, the lightly soaring spiral outlined by the mahogany handrail's smooth curve. Ceilings "showed the touch of a master modeler's hand" but the master was not Thomas Crawford this time — for he had reached Rome, the land of his heart's desiring.

As the wife of the eldest son, little seventeen-year-old Emily Astor could now be the official chaperone for the motherless Ward sisters. Not that their father let them go out very much — but there were parties around the corner on Lafayette Place, and best of all were the parties in their brother's new home as soon as it was finished. Sam worked hard at banking, at least in his own estimation — but he was also serving a brilliant apprenticeship as the future famous host.

CHAPTER SEVEN
End of an Era

THE Ward sisters were no longer schoolgirls. Even little Annie was fifteen, and tinkled the piano adequately, if not brilliantly like her sister Julia. She had no further need of dancing masters now that her older brothers were at home to teach her all the newest figures. Louisa had put away her algebra textbooks and only Julia had formed a life-long habit of study, although as yet she hardly realized it. Their tutor, Mr. Cogswell, left them, accepting the opportunity to escort William B. Astor's son, John Jacob, 3rd, to Europe.

Sam Ward had suggested to Mr. Astor that Longfellow be chosen as traveling companion for the young man, and Professor Longfellow was much disappointed not to receive the assignment. Longfellow was tired and temporarily discouraged with his teaching duties at Harvard. Moreover, Miss Frances Appleton had refused again and again to marry him, and he was determined to forget her if he could. A long European journey would be just the thing.

Curiously enough, Cogswell departed for Europe with regret. He was leaving a lady whom he addressed as "dearest, fairest, brightest, purest, best and best beloved." [1] This long letter, which he wrote in diary form, remained among the papers of the Ward family with the notation attached to it in another hand to the effect that Cogswell's "Goddess" was Julia Ward. Poor "Coggie's" passion was unrequited, however, and there were those who said he transferred his affections to Louisa. Again "Coggie" was doomed to disappointment, and upon the retirement of Fitz-Greene Halleck he became secretary to John Jacob Astor. He persuaded Astor to purchase earthly immortality by endowing the Astor Library — since the old man was still anxious about a possibly bleak eternity. It became Cogswell's delightful duty to purchase all the best available books in Europe and America and no one was better fitted for the task. He had been early a widower, never re-married but continued to be the Ward sisters' good friend, often escorting them to Boston and return via the Long Island Sound steamers. As a book collector Coggie spent a much more peaceful life than he might have had as Julia's or Louisa's husband.

Prosperity followed troublous times in the banking world and Samuel Ward should have been able to take life a little more easily now that his children were growing up. He was often ill, suffering from rheumatism, which, though painful, he did not consider dangerous. When his children urged him to take a vacation he refused, the habit of work and of worry having become too firmly entrenched. Instead of spending the summer of 1839 in Newport, he remained at his desk in New York, going only briefly to Rokeby, summer home of the Astors on the Hudson. Sam and Emily had a little daughter, born in 1838 and named Margaret Astor Ward; and Samuel Ward went to see "Miss Margaret," although he might have hesitated to admit how much he loved the child. He was anxious about Emily's saddle horse — he thought it was "too tall for her" and promised to find her a better one.

By the end of August, when Samuel Ward the banker finally arrived in Newport, he could not rest. Sam had taken his place at 42 Wall Street and perhaps his father could not forget the affair of the unbalancing checkbook. Certainly Mr. Ward had not forgotten the panic of 1837, and he wrote anxiously about a "specie pool" he feared might be forming. But "they cannot hurt New York if true to herself," he said. Although the country was "in a sound condition" he foresaw that there would be "small profits this year" for Prime, Ward and King — and Sam was to watch his personal expenses and be careful in furnishing his house.

In November, all the Wards were back in New York. Samuel Ward had been ill with rheumatism in Newport and he now had an extremely severe attack of what Dr. Francis called "rheumatic gout." Dr. Francis suggested a trip abroad and the children agreed that "it would be far pleasanter" for their father "than a winter of confinement to his room — with Wall Street so near." It was understood that Julia would go with her father, and she began to save her allowance to spend in Paris. On November 24, Francis Marion wrote cheerfully of the proposed journey. Three days later, at noon on November 27, 1839, Samuel Ward the banker was dead.

Philip Hone expressed the grief and concern of the outside world. "There are few citizens of New York whose death would have caused such a void in the circles of active business and social intercourse as Mr. Ward's; the moving spirit of a great financial concern. He was a rich man and made good use of his money; and such men are not easily spared at this time." Christy Evangeles had long since discovered that "Mr. Ward . . . distributed no less than $15,000. to the poor every year" and this did not include boys like Christy who were given an education and young artists like Thomas Cole, to whom a large commission from Samuel Ward had marked the beginning of a successful career.

But the outside world never realized what a shock Mr. Ward's death was to his children. They had depended on him far too much and they were pitifully unprepared to live without him. The girls, now heiresses, knew nothing about the handling of their own money. Sam was the least ready of all to take over the heavy responsibility of a great banking firm — and he realized this as he wrote to Longfellow, expressing the impact of his loss.

"I have received a terrible and stunning blow — I am as one ship-wrecked, who finding himself suddenly cast upon the waters, struggles for self-preservation and the safety of those who cling to him. . . .

"Or I am as a child of some old warrior of feudal days to whom devolves the two-handed sword of his sire who perished in the battle-field. . . . God help me!" [2]

Uncle John Ward moved from his own house at Number 7 Bond Street to live with his nieces — for the faithful Auntie Francis had by this time a small family of children and she wanted a home of her own. Of course she moved only a short distance along Bond Street and if the girls were ill she would come post haste. It was said that she cured more of her husband's patients with her nursing than he did with his medicines.

Uncle John was a broker, and his reputation was for honesty above all things. Tall, heavy-set and wearing a perennial "brown scratch wig," he looked every inch the President of the New York Stock Exchange — as in fact he was from 1831 to 1833. A bachelor, he was sure he knew just how to bring up young girls. He agreed with his late brother that the girls should be much more domestic, and with this in mind he brought home lengths of silk and told them to begin making their own clothes.

This was startling, but Julia, Louisa and Annie were a match for him. They would need a dressmaker to give them lessons, they said. To this, Uncle John agreed — but Annie was in the end the only one who could really be said to have made a dress herself. Uncle John was encouraged, however, until he came across a favorable notice of Julia's essay on Goethe. He could not help a feeling of pride and he brought it home to show to her. "This is my little girl who knows about books and writes an article and has it printed," he said — "but I wish she knew more about housekeeping." Eventually, Julia herself admitted that "this was a sentiment which in after years I had occasion to echo with fervor." [3]

Uncle John Ward differed from his brother Samuel in various ways. Samuel Ward had given up smoking in order to set his sons a good example while they were growing up. Uncle John was never seen without a good cigar. During his last years, Samuel Ward the banker had progressed from a temperate use of wine to total abstinence, locking up his fine wine cellar. Said Philip Hone at the time of Samuel Ward's death: "He became all of a sudden a total abstinence man, at a time of life when the experiment was dangerous, and drank nothing but water, when in my judgment a moderate use of the good wines which he had in his cellar would have been congenial to health." Uncle John had the wine cellar unlocked again when he took up his residence at The Corner. He agreed entirely with Philip Hone — in fact he was a member of the "Hone Club," a small but convivial group of men dedicated to the art of good dining.

In all fairness, however, it must be admitted that Uncle John suffered greatly from gout. It did not improve his disposition to sit in a chair with a throbbing and swollen foot propped upon an ottoman in front of him while in the next room assorted young men sang love songs to his nieces. This bringing-up of girls was proving harder than he thought — and all the young men who gathered around them seemed trifling and untrustworthy.

Louisa, at seventeen, was already "the beautiful Miss Ward," and to Uncle John's horror he discovered that for the last four months she had considered herself engaged to a young man from the South — a Newport visitor. Inquiries were made about the suitor and the letters received from a man who signed himself "W. Stevens of St. Croix" were devastating. "If I had a sister, I would sooner see her married to a leper than into a family whose unkindness to the fair sex seems to exist as a disease of the blood." Now Uncle John got his initiation in the role of Capulet as he sternly told Louisa that she must give up her young man. Louisa shed tears but recovered quickly. Then came the matter of a ring. This time, she had managed to keep the affair quiet, and it was her brother Francis Marion who was her confidant and who told her she had done right to return this ring to the hapless young man who had given it to her. The keeping of this secret was doubtless beneficial to Uncle John's blood pressure, but he grew suspicious all the same. Louisa was so very beautiful!

It was decided to sell the Newport house and Francis Marion, in Cambridge studying law, spoke for all the Ward children when he said, "It made me very sad to think that the happy days at Newport could never return, for it is a spot to which we are all attached by all the earliest associations of our childhood and nowhere on earth will the ocean ever appear so beautiful to us, the sky so blue, or fields so lovely." Marion hoped that someday he might "have a small cottage near Newport in one of its sequestered glades." [4]

Sam also loved Newport, especially the duck hunting. But he now spent his summers with his wife's family at Rokeby. It was conveniently near New York and Sam was seriously trying to become a banker. He wrote to Longfellow, describing his perplexed state of mind, knowing well that Longfellow would understand. "My hands are full of threads and sometimes I pull right, and at times wrong and once in a while they break. . . . I am eliminating a few of the impossible quantities from the equation of life and when I have accomplished some one or two thousand projects, may be able to resolve it. Some men contrive to freeze their dreams and lo! the enchanted castles in the air are present with every ornament and device — others neglect the crystalizing moment and suffer [their dreams] to evaporate and become air-castles indeed."

Sam saw himself clearly yet was powerless to do anything about his faults. "We continue the firm," he said. "My father's place will be mine as soon as I can fill it. . . . To say that I fear giddiness were to confess myself vain of the height I may have been raised to by circumstances — but for some time, *blickauf* must be my motto — I do not feel secure upon the hillside."

Henry Ward had returned from Europe and had gone back to his desk at Prime, Ward and King, content apparently never to aspire to his father's place because he happened to be the second son. Yet he had gone willingly to work for his father, had done so well that his salary was increased and he had pleased his father mightily by being more interested in his work than in how much he made in wages. This was the boy so full of "drollery" in school, but he was now a steadying influence for Sam. Henry was engaged to a banker's daughter, Mary Ward of Boston — of an entirely different Ward family. Her father was Thomas Wren Ward, representative of Baring Brothers, and Mary had a brother, Samuel Gray Ward. The resemblance both in name and certain tastes to Sam Ward of New York was striking. Mary's brother Sam had banking thrust upon him by birth but preferred the arts. However, Samuel Gray Ward of Boston was so very proper a young man that he was called "the *good* Sam Ward," to distinguish him from the gay Sam Ward of New York, who, it seemed, was to be his brother-in-law.

The shadow of death still hovered over the New York Ward family, however. In October, 1840, Henry Ward, at the age of twenty-two, was stricken with typhoid. He died in his sister Julia's arms. Sam, Henry and Julia — this had been the nursery triumvirate. Julia's sense of security had been shaken by the sudden loss of her father, and Henry was her second great loss — drawing her closer to Sam in love but not in confidence. The date of Henry's birth never came around without his sister Julia's remembering it, and on the day of his death she relived the tragic scene all the years of her life.[5]

Sam, in his letter to Longfellow, told of his own grief at the loss of Henry. "To lose a dear brother is like dying oneself and surviving it. How shall we ever be gay more? The song and dance will need his stirring voice and nimble step . . . a glad boy of twenty-two."

But death was not through with them. Four months later, on February 16, 1841, Sam Ward again wrote to Longfellow — joyfully at first, announcing the birth of a son. Emily was "extremely well and making me quite happy, doubly so indeed that my dear Wife should have got through her trouble so bravely," Sam said. Two days later, Sam wrote again. Emily Astor Ward was dead.[6]

"I thank God that my little babe is doing well," Sam said, but this third letter to Longfellow, dated February 21, he left unfinished until morning and in the morning the picture had changed. "My little boy exhibits . . . symptoms of languor and drowsiness which disturb me. It is so sweet a babe and endeared by such a tie to my innermost heart." Sam Ward's first little son lived only a few hours more.

With this new and unexpected blow, everybody seemed to forget a little girl, Margaret Astor Ward, just two years old when her mother died. Everyone except Louisa Ward, who took to her heart her little niece. If Sam had to be away, it was Louisa who went to his house every morning to have breakfast with Maddie. Louisa began to teach Maddie to read, and wrote her notes reminding her to be good because people would not love a spoiled child. Julia marveled at Louisa's patience. "I am not good with children," Julia confessed. "For their own sakes, I should almost be willing not to have any."

After the death of Henry, The Corner was no longer the same happy place. Francis Marion was going to New Orleans to represent Prime, Ward and King's Southern interests — no one was left except the three girls and the Uncle John. And now Sam's home was also a bereaved and lonely one. The sensible thing to do was for Sam's sisters to come and keep house for him — with Uncle John still the kind but bewildered guardian to the heiresses. Accordingly, in 1842, the Ward heirs sold The Corner to Joseph Sampson, auctioneer, for sixty thousand dollars.

Now the Ward sisters came to understand the meaning of the words "breaking up a home." First, the great picture gallery must be cleared. The family portraits — Governor Richard Ward painted in a glorious red coat by Smibert; Governor Richard in later life by Copley — five generations of family portraits all the way to little Annie in Greek costume — must stay in the family. But the pictures acquired for the gallery were more of a problem. Enormous paintings bought for Mr. Ward in Spain were allocated to each daughter as part of her patrimony under the assumption that each girl would someday have a home of her own large enough to accommodate a "Magdalen" or "The Dying Hercules." Huge canvases by Thomas Cole — "Childhood," "Youth," "Manhood" and "Old Age" — had been uncompleted at the time of Mr. Ward's death, and they were sold. The "Greek Boy" by Robert Walter Weir was sold; but "St. Nicholas" by Weir was kept to bring joy to future generations of small children. Lesser decisions had to be made, day after day. Whether to sell the red porcelain dinner set and keep the blue; where to store mahogany parlor furniture, what to do with marble-topped tables and Wedgwood mantel ornaments — three young girls had no idea.[7] They worked so hard every day and they were so tired every night that at last they began to think they never wanted to see anything connected with the past again. This was the end of an era.

The Ward sisters lived with their brother Sam from 1842 until 1844, when their uncle's house at 8 Bond Street was ready to receive them. Favorite pictures went first to Sam's — where some remained — then to Uncle John's. Family papers found their way from one Ward attic to another, their last resting-place eventually forgotten. And the marble bust of Samuel Ward the banker stood on its pedestal in Sam's house looking down on a new era of which he could not approve. Julia put a flower in the folds of the Roman toga and kissed the cold lips — her father in marble. She loved him and he seemed hopelessly remote.

There was an air of determined cheerfulness about the Ward brothers and sisters as they tried to put their lives together again. Julia continued a close friendship with Mary Ward, the girl who was to have been her sister-in-law, and wrote her long letters, signing herself "Jules." [8]

"I wanted to see something of society, it seemed hardly fair that I should never give myself the opportunity of judging or being judged by it," Julia explained as she told of her winter at Sam's house. "Our party comes on Friday night. . . . We have given 200 invitations which comprise the cream of New York Society. Of course one third of these will decline. The carpet is taken up, the floor planed in one room, the other is covered with a linen cloth — the music will be beautiful, and the whole — if you could come." And Julia offered her friend Mary the escort of John Louis O'Sullivan, a most attractive young man from Bond Street. "John O'S. will bring you, he is now in Boston, or James Lawrence who has promised to come."

Julia thanked Mary for the gift of a wreath of artificial flowers, something no girl could be without, evidently. "It is more becoming than anything I have," Julia said, "I wear it 'en courronne' around my head, a little low in front, with the two roses on the left side. They do not wear wreaths around the braid now, but on top of the head, a little to one side."

Mary did not get to Julia's party and so of course her "Jules" had to write her all about it. "I have no news for you, save that our party went off beautifully — the planed floor was as smooth as glass — the music heavenly — the supper superb. We danced till two, and then sat down with John Astor Dickson and half a dozen others to a private spread which was funny and pleasant. . . . I must describe to you my toilet of last evening, it was so pretty — a dress of pale blue silk with blue lace over it looped up with white camellias, the sleeves very short and trimmed with white flowers." Julia did not wear the "courronne" Mary sent her, however — she had "a guirlande à la victime" on her head, and explained that the victim's garland was "the high classic wreath raised in front, composed of white roses, jasmines and so forth, beautifully put on."

Although Julia Ward was garlanded like a victim, it was not she but her admirers who fell victims to her charm. "I have a sweet and most touching letter from Sam Eliot," Julia confided. Although she had sent him away, the letter . . . "brought him back to me in all his beauty, but he is dying, poor child." He had been a friend of Francis Marion Ward's at Harvard while Marion was studying law there, had visited in New York to fall victim to Julia, and he was now suffering from unrequited affection perhaps, and certainly from boredom in Robert Gould's countinghouse. A trip to Europe helped him to recover his health, while Emily Marshall Otis healed his heart. He remained a lifetime friend of Julia's, however.

Next victim appears to have been Mancer Mark Backus, a Columbia classmate of Henry Ward's. He "declared himself" and had to be refused; nor had he "any encouragement to keep the flame awake," but he nevertheless persisted in his suit. Mary Ward wanted to know where he could "find nourishment for his love, this time?" and she plainly implied that Julia had been a flirt and that "for poor Baco's former feeling" she could "allow and understand." Backus, who had taken the gold medal as the head of his class in Columbia, was studying for the ministry, but he changed his mind as to his calling and in 1844 he found a more responsive lady-love, married and "recovered health and spirits." It was true that men have died and worms have eaten them — but not for love. Yet men languished properly after Julia Ward, while her heart remained intact.

While Julia was making her conquests, Louisa proceeded in her own way to be equally attractive. George Hillard, writing to Longfellow, told of the impression Louisa made in 1842 during a visit to Mary Ward in Boston. "The lovely Lousia is here, but I have seen her only once at Mrs. Ticknor's and was charmed with her sunny smiles, her dazzling teeth, her gentle voice and thoroughbred manner. She appears to have more soul than her more gifted sister." Hillard also observed that the Boston Mary Ward was no longer in mourning for her fiancé, Louisa's brother Henry. She would eventually become Mrs. Charles Dorr of Boston. Right now, it seemed as if she might still be a sister-in-law of the Wards, for her brother John was becoming more and more seriously interested in Miss Louisa Ward.

During the happy days at The Corner, Henry Ward often brought his classmate and especial friend John Louis O'Sullivan to the house.[9]

Born in 1813, O'Sullivan was six years older than Julia and a year older than Sam. He had a fine Irish tenor voice, and spoke French perfectly, having been to a military school in France as a boy. Like Sam Ward, John O'Sullivan's optimism was unbounded and he was as gay a companion as Henry. The two older Ward girls at first considered him one of their beaux, but he was attracted to the quiet little Annie. And she, about seventeen when she first knew him well, considered him the most wonderful of all the wonderful young men who gathered at The Corner. But in one important respect, O'Sullivan differed from all the other Bond Street neighbors. He had no money. He taught school, he tutored in French, mathematics and almost all other subjects while at Columbia, where he graduated in 1831 and received a second degree in 1834. Hanging out his shingle in New York, John Louis attempted to support himself and his widowed mother by means of a career as a lawyer with political ambitions. They also lived upon their hopes, for John Louis's mother had a substantial claim against the Government.

Everything about John Louis O'Sullivan was romantic. Little Annie Ward could not have failed to hear that his great-grandfather was a general in the army of Bonnie Prince Charlie. John Louis's grandfather joined the Irish brigade of the French army — but turned up in America serving under Sir Henry Clinton during the occupation of New York. O'Sullivan's grandfather and Annie's, although on opposite sides, might have met. But at this point history and family tradition took divergent paths, and surely the story Annie heard was that John O'Sullivan's grandfather bore the title of Count Bearhaven — this time the gift of the grateful British. Historians question this tall tale and the validity of the title. John Louis's father was an American citizen, and John Louis was born on a British man-of-war off Gibraltar. His father was a sea captain, later consul for the island of Tenerife, and plague had broken out on Gibraltar; the British commander took the family aboard to escape it.

The bright dreams upon which the O'Sullivans, mother and son, lived resulted from their suit against the United States Government for false seizure of the brig *Dick*. In 1822, John T. O'Sullivan, sailing his own vessel and bound for Cadíz, was seized for piracy. But he was not a pirate. In 1836, Congress paid the widow $19,968.08 in compensation for her late husband's brig. The dream of wealth had become reality and John Louis O'Sullivan put his money right back into a dream. With S. D. Langtree, he established the *United States Magazine*

and Democratic Review, commonly called the *Democratic Review.*
Langtree was to handle the business — O'Sullivan was all inspiration.
The magazine was part literary, part political, and O'Sullivan's ideal,
America's "manifest destiny" to protect her lesser neighbors, was the
political theme. In the literary field, all the best writers contributed,
Nathaniel Hawthorne being convinced by O'Sullivan's magnificent
optimism that in the *Democratic Review* he had at last an outlet and a
livelihood. O'Sullivan published more of Hawthorne's short stories
than any other editor did, and even when twenty dollars was all he
could pay on a considerable indebtedness, Hawthorne and "Count
O'Sullivan," as Hawthorne called him, remained devoted friends. In
1841, John Louis O'Sullivan moved his magazine from Washington to
New York. After an absence of about four years, he resumed his
intimate friendship with the Wards which had really never been
broken off. There was one great difference, however. Little Annie had
grown up.

John Louis O'Sullivan wrote in verse exactly how Annie Ward
looked to him now. But it was typical of O'Sullivan that his lines to
a lady should have political overtones. Annie was on her way to Rhode
Island for a visit — it was now the summer of 1842, and Rhode Island
was in the throes of her struggle to amend her constitution. A state
where limited suffrage dependent upon property ownership still existed was not rightly a part of the United States, O'Sullivan contended.
Annie was visiting a foreign land. And so he wrote for her:

Annie's Passport
I'll not describe each separate feature —
   They'd tempt to dwell on them too long —
Suffice it, she's the gentlest creature
   That ere awakened sigh or song.

As lovely as, at eve's soft hour,
   The first star's gentle smile — and yet
Slight as the lily's stem and flower,
   And modest as the violet.

I've known her since she was a child,
   And loved as long as I have known —
The brightest thing that ever smiled,
   The dearest ever smiled upon. . . .[10]

Annie Ward kept all of the poems John Louis O'Sullivan wrote to
her — and there were quite a few. She also kept her own counsel and

if her sisters liked to think that John Louis O'Sullivan called on all three Ward heiresses impartially, Annie said nothing. The fact remained, however, that living with relatives, however kind, was not the same as having a home. All three sisters were in a mood to marry and Annie might have had hopes.

CHAPTER EIGHT
Stormy Courtship

THE Five of Clubs, they called themselves, and so far, at least, these five young men had no idea how great or nearly great they would all become. There were those, however, who called them "The Mutual Admiration Society" and this was not far from the truth. The five were Longfellow, Sumner, Felton, Hillard and Cleveland. All of them had at one time or another been connected with Harvard and all made their mark, with the possible exception of Henry R. Cleveland, "a cheerful, witty instructor" at Harvard whose early death prevented him from fulfilling great promise. For a short time just before Cleveland's death there were Six of Clubs — Dr. Samuel Gridley Howe being added in 1843. Most of them visited Sam Ward in New York from time to time and as soon as Professor Felton laid eyes on the Ward heiresses he practically staked a claim on them in behalf of club members as yet unmarried.

In the category of the unmarried came Longfellow, for he had long been a widower.[1] Sumner was a bachelor and a lonely one, or so he said. And Dr. Howe, although the veteran of at least two love affairs as well as of the Greek campaigns against the Turks, was unmarried and willing to change his state. Part of Professor Felton's work as matchmaker was already done. Dr. Howe and Julia Ward had met.

During the summer of 1841 — the first summer after the death of Henry Ward — Julia went to Dorchester to visit Mary Ward, the girl who was to have been her sister-in-law. They saw only their intimate friends but "Longo and Sumner were very agreeable." [2] One fateful afternoon, Sumner suggested a ride out to South Boston for a call on Dr. Samuel Gridley Howe at Perkins Institute for the Blind. Sumner hired a horse and a smart red-wheeled carriage. Julia put a flower in the professor's hat without his knowledge — then out along the country roads they drove. The Perkins Institute was located in the former Mt. Washington Hotel, a huge affair of many piazzas, one above the other, standing alone in open fields with an old farmhouse dating from Revolutionary days almost its only neighbor. The former summer resort was just under the crest of Dorchester Heights with blue water on two sides and a far-reaching view of Dorchester Bay and Boston Harbor.

Dr. Howe was not at home so the visitors sat down to wait. For the first time, Julia Ward saw blind children "flitting about" — running up and down the long flight of steps from the door of the building to the road, their finger tips just touching the hand rail. Some of the children, born not only blind but sadly deformed, were so shocking to Julia that she shuddered in spite of herself and turned away. Sympathetic and tenderhearted, it seemed more than she could bear. Yet when she looked again at the blind children she saw that they themselves were smiling and happy.

Julia, Longfellow and Sumner were shown into one of the schoolrooms and Laura Bridgman was brought in by her teacher to meet the visitors — a little girl of thirteen wearing a green ribbon bound around her sightless eyes. Dr. Howe's famous pupil, the first blind and deaf child taught to "Communicate," was not at all shy and enjoyed "seeing" people with her quick fingers — lightly touching faces, hair and dress. She turned to her teacher and asked in sign language if Miss Ward were pretty. Her teacher laughed and said "yes," placing her fingers in Laura's palm to make the signs which the child must feel since she could not see them.

Charles Sumner was looking out the window as a splendid horseman came galloping across the open fields. "Here comes Howe on his black horse," he said. And Julia Ward remembered that she went to the window and saw "a noble rider on a noble steed." [3]

When Samuel Gridley Howe came striding into the room, Julia saw a man just under six feet tall but seeming taller by reason of the proud carriage of his head. "A beautiful youth," the Greeks had called him, and his profile followed so closely the Greek ideal that he must have seemed like one of their heroes returned in their hour of need. Tremendous energy and vitality made him seem younger than he was, and probably Julia did not stop to figure out at this time the difference in their ages; but she had been only nine years old when Dr. Howe wrote his *Historical Sketch of the Greek Revolution.* She was fifteen when she found the book in her father's library and gave it to the Greek boy Christy to read. Miss Julia Ward was now twenty-two and Dr. Samuel Gridley Howe was forty. Except for Christy, Julia might never have given more than a passing thought to the struggle for Greek Independence. But as it was, she looked with curiosity at the author who had been eyewitness to exciting episodes. She could see why his friends called Dr. Howe by the name to which his Greek decoration entitled him. He looked every inch the "Chevalier."

Laura Bridgman's questioning fingers had found a gold locket which Julia was wearing and she asked in sign language what it might be. As Laura's teacher interpreted, Julia impulsively took off the locket to give to the child to keep. But Dr. Howe forbade the gift. Laura Bridgman was a celebrated case, often interviewed by doctors, foreign visitors and educators. It would never do to allow her to accept gifts, Dr. Howe explained. The Chevalier must have seemed to Julia like her father, the severe Mr. Ward, as he sternly reproved her. Meekly she told him that he was right indeed, and apologized for her thoughtlessness. She noted with satisfaction, however, that he gave her a second much more intertested glance. It might be fun for Miss Ward if she could make the Doctor respond to her charms in a slightly less fatherly fashion.

A greater contrast can hardly be imagined than that between Dr. Howe and Julia Ward. When she stood she came scarcely to his shoulder.[4] She was as blond in coloring as he was dark. With virility an outstanding characteristic of the Doctor's, Julia Ward was as intensely feminine in appearance as a girl could be. She was born in May and he in November.

When she entered the carriage for the return drive to Dorchester, Miss Ward unfurled a lace parasol to protect her cream complexion. And Dr. Howe, who was proud of his ability to meet sun or snow without flinching, mounted his "demon steed" and rode alongside as escort part of the way. He twitted his friends Sumner and Longfellow on the quality of their livery-stable horse, and Miss Julia Ward noted with secret amusement that he was showing off his own superb horsemanship. She assumed that she would see him again before long, but it appears that she did not.

During the following winter, Julia visited Boston. She made no mention of Dr. Howe and she seemed to have forgotten all about him. Unlike the wealthy young men whom Julia knew best, the Doctor had no time for social calls and parties. Moreover, Julia was enjoying the great sensation of that winter of 1841–1842 in Boston. Charles Dickens had arrived and she had met him.

"Last night I went to a party at Mrs. Shaw's, given to *Boz and me*," Julia wrote to her sisters back home. "At least I was invited before he came here, so I think I will give him only an equal share of the honor. I danced a good deal with some very agreeable partners, and I talked as usual with Sumner, Hillard, Longo etc. I was quite pleased when Boz recognized Fanny Appleton and myself, and gave us a smile and a bow en passant. He could do no more, being almost torn to pieces by the crowds which throng his footsteps. I like to look at him, he has a bright and most speaking countenance, and his face is all wrinkled with lines, not of care but of laughter. His manners are very free and cordial, and he seems to be as capital a fellow as one would suppose from his writings."

Charles Dickens's visit set off a series of parties like a chain reaction — and Longfellow, who went to a good many of them, observed that "Julia" was "enjoying herself much in Boston and making friends and admirers. Felton is in love with her and in speaking of her uses the superlative degree only," Longfellow humorously remarked. He thought "Park Street was never more brilliant than now." This letter was to Julia's brother Sam — "Dickens breakfasts with me Friday. Will you come?" Longfellow urged. "Let me know beforehand for every place at table is precious — but I shall count upon you."

In spite of the social whirl, Miss Julia Ward contrived to do some serious business while in Boston. She had a remarkable faculty for combining business with pleasure. Some of her poetry appeared in John Louis O'Sullivan's *Democratic Review* and Julia had brought along a collection of verses in the hope that Ticknor and Fields would publish a volume. Longfellow wrote that "W. T. was much delighted with Julia's poems" but if this were true then Ticknor's decision not to publish the volume was the more puzzling to Julia. "W.T. . . . agrees with me . . . in regard to publishing," Longfellow said and he too had decided against the project. But everyone underestimated the determination of Miss Julia Ward.

The Ward sisters and their brother Sam were all together on Bond Street in April, 1842, when Longfellow made them a visit. The professor was on his way to Germany, to "take the waters," for he was "out of health and spirits" and had decided to make one last effort to forget the hard-hearted Fanny Appleton who still refused to marry him. He stayed with the Wards until his ship should sail. "I have passed three days very pleasantly here," he wrote, although he admitted that he was impatient to begin his voyage. "The Wards are well; and little Annie smiles meek and childlike as when you saw her." This letter was addressed to Charles Sumner, so presumably it was Sumner who had so described Annie at some previous time. "Julia thinks you might have called a second time to see them. I think likewise, for she is certainly a remarkable person and worth half a dozen calls at least. Louisa you will see in Boston on Friday next. Sam is as multifarious as usual; in the morning reads Livy an hour before breakfast with Mersch; then hurries down to his business; rides on horseback *before* dinner and sings Italian duets *after*.

"I have been this evening to a play called 'Boz.' It is a caricature on Dickens' reception here. Dickens is very well represented by Horncastle. The best joke in the piece is the invitation from members of an Engine Company to see a fire and the accompanying request to know whether he will have a single house burnt, or a whole block. He is also invited to see a steamer burst her boiler on the North River!

" . . . But one of my candles is sinking in its socket. It is nearly one o'clock and I am the only person up, in the house. . . .

"Once more, Benedicite! When this reaches you I shall be rocking on the broad sea. . . .

"*P.S.* At this very moment two voices not the most melodious are singing under the window, 'Thou, thou reignest in this bosom.' A serenade to — which of the three? If to Julia, they will not gain by the transaction. They sing too horribly out of tune.

"They have now got to 'Oft in the Stilly Night' and it is quite tolerable. I expect Sam or Uncle John to interfere: if they do not, I shall."

Longfellow left for Europe before Charles Dickens completed his Western tour of the United States. But whenever any member of the Five of Clubs left Boston or Cambridge the other four wrote long letters retailing all the news. No boarding-school girls were ever more faithful correspondents. Accordingly, then, Hillard announced the presence of "the lovely Louisa" in Boston and Felton wrote of his trip to New York to join in the last farewells to Dickens. He had "a glorious visit" — Howe went with him.

A farewell breakfast was given for Charles Dickens by James Gore King at his country place on the heights of Weehawken, New Jersey. "The house and grounds, the view, the library and the conservatories were all most beautiful," Philip Hone wrote admiringly. He noticed Miss Julia Ward at the party. With her was a stranger — a Dr. Howe of Boston.

"Mounds of superb strawberries were consumed," and then all too soon the men were "driven down to Jersey City where, by previous arrangement, a steamboat was sent to take them aboard." Then all went joyfully "down to Sandy Hook" enjoying a "cold collation, to which and to an infinite number of bottles of Champagne wine, utmost justice was done."

Julia understood that she would not see Dr. Howe again. He and Felton were to take the steamer for Boston as soon as these final fare-wells to Dickens were over. Carriages, which had been patiently waiting in the Kings' driveway, drove one by one to the door to pick up the ladies and take them down the steep road to the Hudson. Horses' hoofs made a hollow tattoo on ferry planking. So often, it seemed, the men went on with their gay adventures while the women went home. Not that Julia had much time to be lonely, however. There was to be a party at 32 Bond Street that evening and she was going to sing. Lorenzo da Ponte had been her singing teacher — the man who wrote the libretti for Mozart's *Marriage of Figaro* and *Don Giovanni*, and Julia knew very well that she sang better than most professional opera singers. She had every right to be called the "Diva Julia."

"A select company of friends assisted at the performance of some divine music and the demolition of a pyramid of strawberries," said Sam, describing his own party. In the midst of it, in walked Felton and Dr. Howe. They had missed the Boston boat.

Julia may have wondered why the evening party seemed suddenly so gay. After the music, she proposed children's games and Dr. Howe laughed with glee to see his plump professorial friend fall over an ottoman and lie kicking his heels on the carpet. They were playing "blindman's buff." When it came to be Dr. Howe's turn to be blind-folded, it was Miss Julia Ward who allowed herself to be caught in his powerful embrace. He flung off the blindfold and looked deep into her eyes and she returned the look, then lowered her lids — for this too was a game she well knew how to play. But the embrace tightened and she felt compelled to look up into gray eyes that seemed to turn blue-gray with lightning in them and it was not a mere boy from Bond Street who held her playfully. The swift color mounted into Julia's cheeks. The Doctor let her go.

"Tell me, Doctor, did you ever kill a man? Doctor — *do* tell me,"

Julia begged. Felton, overhearing, roared with laughter and called Howe "the Turkicide." Julia Ward could hardly fail to observe that Dr. Howe disliked being laughed at more than most people did.

A bread-and-butter letter to Julia was in order, and Howe and Felton wrote one together on a large piece of blue paper which they referred to as Sumner's "bankrupt paper." A neatly ruled oblong occupied the center of the page, and Dr. Howe's remarks filled this with Felton's delightful nonsense running all around it like a frame. It must have taken Julia hours to read this letter and when she finished it she must have been fairly puzzled by it.

Felton pretended to be making a report to the trustees of Perkins Institute in Howe's style. "You will remember that early in June last, I visited New York for the purpose of transacting some business with the Bible Society in that City. . . . During my visit, I was ever on the watch, as is my custom, for fit objects to which our Institution might extend its benevolences. Many eyes I looked at, of many colors, of every shade and hue; some so deep I could not fathom them; some so bright, that my own were almost blinded by their dazzling glances. Once in Bond Street, I saw such eyes and lost all perception of the passage of time. In fact I could not see the hands of my watch, and but for the timely interposition of a friend, I might not have seen them to this day and the Institution, perhaps, would have lost my labors forever. Soon after, and nearly in the same place, I saw a blind boy, who but for his chubby cheeks and blond complexion, I would have taken for a little Indian. He had a curiously wrought bow in his hand and a quiver full of arrows on his shoulder. He stopped me as suddenly as if he knew the Superintendent of the Blind Institution was passing by. For my life, I could not help taking him with me, home. He was admitted to our Institution. Full soon, I found him mischievous, troublesome. . . . I bethought me to arm myself with the shield, helmet and spear which I fought the barbarians with in the Grecian wars. . . . He twanged his bow, the arrow pierced my Grecian shield and inflicted a deeper wound than ever I received in the battlefield from . . . Turkish scimitar."

And Professor Felton, still pretending to be Dr. Howe, summed up the sad case of Cupid's wound. "The case, gentlemen, seems to differ from any we have ever met before, and to require peculiar treatment. I think it will be necessary for me to visit New York once more and lay the subject before the Bible Society. Perhaps they will make an additional appropriation for printing the Apocrypha." [5]

Dr. Howe began his own letter in a light vein also — but he could not sustain it.

He ended lecturing — even scolding — Julia.

"Very happy, fair lady, was the 'gentle Doctor' when he saw the kindly notice vouchsafed to him in your letter to the learned Feltonius; happy although he knew too well that with you 'gentle' and 'simple' are synonymous — happy as when he has been gazing on a star, forgetting . . . simple soul that he is, that for him it only lightened, never warmed, and as he has ofttimes gazed on a such a star and tried to fathom its bright depths, so has he looked down, down into thy lustrous eyes until he lost his senses trying to measure their depth and color. Are thine eyes blue, sweet lady? . . .

" 'Did you ever kill a man — Doctor — *do* tell me!' And I tell thee, méchante, laugh less at others now and you will look back more complacently upon the past when your golden locks are turned to silver . . .

"And so you doubt whether I can take an interest in those who have all their senses! Alas! but I can, and in those even who, having already more senses themselves than fall to the lot of ordinary mortals, are continually taking their senses away from other people . . . " Dr. Howe said that he wished that Julia Ward knew Horace Mann, and he launched out on a long lecture concerning phrenology. It would appear that he was not quite satisfied with the shape of Miss Ward's head, much as he had praised her eyes! He was worried about her "propensities" and he meant that she laughed at people. "And so you think you are 'half spoiled' do you? . . . But you are not spoiled, you only exercise some qualities of your nature to the detriment, not only of others but of yourself. On this subject (if you will only hold still long enough) I will give you a word of friendly counsel. . . ." Dr. Howe did so, not in one word but many. Julia had not been so lectured since she lost her father and she was half angry, half convinced that Dr. Howe was right.

It was abundantly plain that Dr. Samuel Gridley Howe could not bear to be teased or laughed at, but on the other hand he had a sense of humor even though it was limited, and a splendid sense of the ridiculous where others were concerned. "I have gotten . . . Hobbyhorsical," he admitted, on the subject of phrenology. "If I were near you," he said, "I should expect an instant explosion not direct and en face but torpedo-like as is your wont, springing a mine under innocent feet just when we thought we were on firm ground."

Was this in any sense a love letter? Julia Ward was sure it was not, until she reached the last words. "I will not allow anyone but you to be amused at my expense; but you, you may laugh at me, scold at me, do anything, so you forget not that I am truly your 'Gentle Doctor.'"

Professor Felton wrote to Longfellow giving his own version of his and Dr. Howe's visit to New York. "Sam Ward and the sisters three were at home and a more delicious family than they make, I have never seen. They were all in excellent health and spirits, kind and hospitable as any human beings could be. . . . We dined with them on Sunday — spent Sunday evening with them — Monday dined with Dickens. . . .

"By Jove, Longfellow," Felton said, "you are the most insensible block in existence not to fall in love with one of these incomparable sisters. Julia is the most remarkable person I ever knew. Every time I see her, some new power or attraction strikes me; and I am astounded that all unmarried men are not piled up at her feet. If the three destinies could bring matters into such a train as to divide that band of graces between you and Charles and Howe, I should exclaim, 'Nunc dimittis, domine.' Pray think of it."

The "Charles" mentioned as a husband for one of the Ward sisters was Charles Sumner, now a Boston lawyer, with his abolitionist fame as yet unmade. Unless the painter of his portrait flattered him, he was attractive to look at, with hollow cheeks, beautiful but too feminine a mouth, and with a poetic forelock of wavy hair upon his forehead. But which of the sisters had his friend Felton chosen for him? At the time this letter was written, Annie Ward was seventeen, Louisa, eighteen — and Charles Sumner was thirty-one. Julia might have been more suitable in age, for she had just turned twenty-three. But Felton, a plump little man looking the part of an overaged Cupid, felt that Julia's fate was settled.

"We enjoyed this visit beyond anything this mortal life often turns up," Felton said and concluded with a prophecy. "Howe says he has never experienced anything like it except two or three expeditions against the Turks. Between you and me, he was shot through the heart by the Judicious and perpetrated more soliloquies, apostrophies and ecstatic exclamations than I have heard these many years." The Judicious was one of Julia Ward's many nicknames and in Felton's opinion, therefore, only two of the "Three Graces" of Bond Street remained for him to parcel out among his friends. Julia's and Dr. Howe's fate was sealed.

Of course Julia Ward herself had yet to be consulted. She had many suitors. Some hearts she had broken, as gently as she could; some rash young men she had led along, because they rode too high and deserved a fall. At present, Julia's heart was very much her own.

Three months later, or in September, 1842, George Hillard, writing to Longfellow, mentioned matters which were as interesting as they were private and none of his business.

"Howe has gone to New Hampshire and Vermont on one of his flying excursions. I don't know whether he and the 'Diva Julia' are converging or not. He is much captivated but whether she has had the sweet spell thrown over her or is only indulging her love of mischief and giving her victim a little line before she finally lands him high and dry on the sands of rejection to sigh and gasp his life out, I cannot say."

From the moment when she saw him galloping across the fields on his black horse, "the sweet spell" had been thrown over Julia and she was in love with Samuel Gridley Howe. She confessed this long later. But meanwhile there was her pride which matched his — with this difference, that hers could melt. There was her fiery temper and her really magnificent sense of humor. It was a stormy courtship and in February, 1843, Julia was certain that it was all over. She was in Boston visiting Mary and she wrote her brother Sam giving some advice for Louisa which she herself could never follow — wise as it was.

"Howe left early this morning for Hartford without having seen me, and goes to New York before returning here. The object of his visit is not to be mistaken, I find it quite a matter of pleasantry among his friends and his making this trip at this time proclaims quite publicly who it is he goes to see. Longfellow has, I find, been to Mary to request her good offices. I think that the Doctor has acted with a want of delicacy and also of discretion in this matter. I do not think the position he has to offer is one suited to Weevie, who does depend very much on the atmosphere in which she lives. South Boston will not be Bond Street. . . .

"You know Lou's impulsive nature and that, in these things, she is not so discreet as in other things. It is not long since another image was in her heart and before that she was deeply interested in one no way worthy of her . . . She must consider that any step taken in this direction is irrevocable — to accept the Chevalier and then turn him adrift would be impossible. . . ."

So Julia thought that Dr. Samuel Gridley Howe had gone to New York to propose to her sister Louisa. The gossips had been hard at work this time. The members of the Five of Clubs can not be exonerated, but the finger of suspicion points at Julia's dear friend Mary Ward — and Longfellow. But Longfellow had only recently returned to the United States and by his own account he himself had been most favorably impressed by Louisa, so it seems unlikely (as well as out of character) that he should be matchmaking. Writing to Henry Cleveland on January 4, 1843, Longfellow told of his homecoming:

". . . And now let me go back a few days. My arrival in New York was not precisely as you pictured it to yourself, instead of standing like Park Street Church and Steeple on the wharf, Sumner and Felton were cosily dining with Howe and Willis at the Globe. It was after dark when the Great Western reached the slip. I went up alone to the Astor House; — thence to Sam Ward's. . . ."

Short, stout Professor Felton and tall, thin Charles Sumner ("Park Street Church and Steeple") were at the Wards' by this time. "Joyful was the meeting." Longfellow's friends had "been on board the vessel" but had somehow missed him. He proceeded to describe Louisa Ward.

". . . The lovely Louisa made an impression on my heart like that made by Fanix in Calderón's *Principe Constante*, when she lay down in the bed of flowers ('Sobra un cartre de Carmin . . . un foso de esmaralida') — and emerald is the hue of hope! Alas, we ended the night in an *oyster cellar!* Precisely as you imagined."

With all her mind and heart taken up by Dr. Howe, perhaps Julia did not notice how much impressed Longfellow had been by her sister Louisa. But according to portraits of both girls, Fanny Appleton and Louisa Ward strongly resembled each other. Emerald was "the hue of hope"; but when Longfellow saw again his much-loved Fanny, he could no longer "look upon her face without emotion" and say, "It is ended." And it was Fanny who at last gave him reason to hope. Scarcely a month had gone by and the gossips would have to talk fast, but perhaps Julia Ward had heard that Longfellow was at last going to marry Miss Appleton. If he then recommended Louisa Ward to Dr. Howe and asked Mary's "good offices" — it was still an unlikely story, but a young woman as much in love as Julia might believe it!

"South Boston would not be Bond Street" — Julia Ward never wrote a truer word, and for a few days she was sure she could take her own advice — if she ever needed it. Then Dr. Howe came back from New York and Julia wrote a letter to her brother Sam. She had given away her heart and, as she told of it, she wrote a love poem in prose.

"The Chevalier says truly — I am the captive of his bow and spear. His true devotion has won me from the world and from myself. The past is already fading from my sight; already I begin to live with him in the future, which shall be as calmly bright as love can make it. I am perfectly happy to sacrifice to one so noble and so earnest, the day-dreams of my youth. He will make life more beautiful to me than any dream. His affection for me, he says and I believe, had not wavered, has not been transferred to another. . . ."

CHAPTER NINE

Crowded Honeymoon

JULIA WARD would be twenty-four years old on May 27, 1843. Nothing on earth could have prevented her marriage to Dr. Samuel Gridley Howe if she chose to have him for her husband, but she knew what Ward family tradition required. "Our engagement awaits only your sanction to be acknowledged," she wrote to her brother Sam — "yours and the approval of my dear sisters and uncle. Give me, dearest brother, your fraternal blessing and let me tell you that, although I have chosen for myself an older and more experienced guide than yourself, I do not expect to find anywhere a kinder friend than you have been to me. . . ." [1]

It was considerably harder for Dr. Howe to write Sam Ward a proper letter. "Since Julia regards you 'in loco parentis,' " he began — and that was about as well as he could do. He stated with a certain amount of pride that his income was three thousand dollars a year and that he could afford to marry. It is not exactly unusual for a man in love to have little use for a future brother-in-law and Sumner's opinion of Sam Ward was more charitable than Dr. Howe's. "I disagree with Sam Ward on almost every human topic," Sumner said, "but when I have talked with him five minutes, I forget everything save that he is the most delightful company in the world." Dr. Howe would not even allow that Sam had this much charm.

Comments from the Ward family were not favorable. "A mere pittance" Sam called Dr. Howe's income. And Francis Marion, at home for a short time, congratulated himself on returning to New Orleans. " . . . just in time to escape being scratched by that confounded bit of New England granite." He knew that his sister Julia was really in love, however, and her temper he knew of old. "For Heaven's sake don't show Julia this" he said at the end of his letter. Perhaps a delay might cause Julia to change her mind and the Ward family favored a long engagement if any, but their hopes were disappointed by Julia's next letter from Boston.

"The Chevalier is very presumptuous" — he "says he will not lose sight of me for one day, that I must stay here until he returns with me to New York. The Chevalier is very impertinent, speaks of two or three months when I speak of two or three years and seems determined to have things his own way — but dear Bunny, the Chevalier's way will be a very charming way and is, henceforth, to be mine."

With or without Ward consent, news of Julia's engagement was circulated in February and letters about it were exchanged among the Five of Clubs like valentines. "I should be very selfish," Dr. Howe told Longfellow, "could I garner the joy I feel in my own heart and not impart a portion of it to my friends — especially to you who have felt such an interest in my *affaire de cœur*. I need say but one word, — 'Julia loves me' — and you know all the rest."

Like most people with but one word to say, Howe used many more in praise of Julia, to which Longfellow replied, "My dearest Chevalier, from the deepest dungeons of my heart, all imprisoned sympathies and affections of my nature cry aloud to you, saying 'All hail!'" Among all of Howe's friends, Longfellow was "the oldest friend of your fair young bride," he said.

One by one, the notes of congratulation came in from the Five of Clubs. More interesting, but a little less like valentines, were the letters they exchanged among themselves. These were very serious young men and quite possibly Miss Julia Ward had poked fun at every one of them at one time or another. "Felton will write about Howe's engagement to a fine, young, buxom damsel of four and twenty, who is full of talent — indeed carrying almost too many guns for any man who does not want to be firing salutes all the time," Longfellow said.

And Hillard wrote, "The piece of news which interests us most is Dr. Howe's engagement to Julia Ward — the Diva, as she is generally called among the club. Howe is very happy — his whole heaven being painted with purple streaks of love and hope. I hardly know the lady myself well enough to judge how wisely and well he has chosen, but her intimate friends all value and admire her much, and that she has had the good sense to choose a true and good man, and give up all hope of a brilliant establishment (which in all probability she might command) is in itself an excellent trait in her nature." Hillard had his doubts, however. "I have not been altogether pleased with what I have seen of her, though there is certainly much to admire and doubtless to love." Hillard had had doubts about his own marriage, as Elizabeth Peabody discovered without too much difficulty. He was Sumner's law partner (and Hawthorne's lawyer), but much preferred a literary career. When he published his *Six Months in Italy*, that "glorified and even glorious guidebook," he would dedicate it to Louisa.

Julia finally returned to Bond Street, her future husband coming with her as he had promised to do. It was March 29, 1843, when Dr. Samuel Gridley Howe wrote to Sumner— calling him "Don Carlos," surely a name of Julia's devising — "Here I am, in the very central Power of Paradise and surrounded by three Divinities, who, angels as they are, play the very devil with one's heart. I am so very happy that I am really frightened: what does it mean? Is it not some illusion? I never saw anything like it before: no one ever did — as for all the happiness they tell you about in novels, it is all humbug: the authors were never here in this library: they never knew the Graces, so how should they conceive what happiness is? I shall be back in your miserable old Boston on Friday morning, I am afraid; and shall have to stay an everlasting three days. . . ."

Julia's sisters complained bitterly. She had returned to them in body only, while in spirit she floated far above the clouds. The wedding date was set for April 23 and Uncle John, who had recently acquired Number 8 Bond Street, would have his parlor furnished just in time. But Julia, who had always loved to plan parties, could not be brought down to earth long enough to make out lists of guests or choose a caterer. She could not be made to shop for her wedding dress, but would only say she wanted something simple — white and lovely. Louisa and Annie were in despair.

Together, the younger girls chose white muslin, fine as a cobweb, and had it made up for Julia with lace inserts at each flounce.[2] A lace stole went over her shoulders and her wedding veil was of finest embroidered net. Julia's little white satin shoes were square-toed like a ballerina's.

Longfellow, Felton and Sumner went with Dr. Howe to New York to help him claim his bride. It was typical of Longfellow to remember Henry Cleveland, who must be lonely as well as ill and to write an account of the wedding to Mrs. Cleveland, for his benefit. The Bostonians set out on April 18. "We were to have taken the *Mohegan*, but

she blew up a day too soon, as you doubtless saw by the papers," Longfellow said.

The *Narragansett* was the boat which the bridegroom and his party
boarded and Longfellow talked with the steward about the accident
to the sister ship. No one had been killed but, in the general alarm, one
young man had jumped overboard followed by some hunting dogs he
had with him — and they all had to be fished out of Long Island Sound.

"Then it was not a *bad* burst?" queried Longfellow.

"Oh, no," replied the steward. "It was a very good burst and
seemed to give general satisfaction."

The party had arrived safely in New York and Longfellow was
seated in his room at Sam Ward's house, writing of his adventures. But
Charles Sumner was elsewhere, probably at Number 8 Bond Street,
closeted with the bridegroom and Uncle John Ward. Uncle John had
placed before Dr. Samuel Gridley Howe a paper called an "ante-nuptial
agreement" concerning his niece Julia Ward's private fortune. Charles
Sumner, the best man, on reading it, announced that it was a most
iniquitous document and that the bridegroom was under no circumstances to sign it.

Dr. Howe said that he did not know that Julia Ward was wealthy
and that he would have preferred "a penniless bride." This, Uncle John
very definitely did not believe.

Thomas Wren Ward of Boston had furnished Mr. John Ward of
New York with information concerning the future husband of the
eldest of the Ward heiresses. On the moral side, he must have given
Dr. Howe a handsome recommendation. In point of heredity, the
Howe family was as old and as completely English in origin as the
Wards.

Abraham Howe, Freeman, died in Roxbury Massachusetts in 1676
and on Dr. Howe's mother's side, Richard Gridley came to Boston in
1630 aboard the *Griffin*, was Captain of "Ye Ancient and Honorable
Artillery Company" after 1658 and "one of the richest men in town."
Like the Wards, the Howes and the Gridleys had been Patriots during
the Revolution with one member of the Gridley family at the Boston
Tea Party and another who was designer of the Bunker Hill fortifica-
tions. Abraham Howe, in 1645, signed a covenant to assist in establishing
what is now the Roxbury Latin School, but subsequent Howes moved
to Boston and Dr. Howe's father owned ropewalks near the present

site of Charles Street which prospered until the War of 1812. At that time, rope was supplied the frigate *Constellation* and never paid for by the Government.[3]

The Howes lived in a stately old house on Pearl Street in Boston, with fine mahogany and family silver attesting to generations of good taste and good fortune. There were six children, of whom Dr. Howe was the youngest son. A brother Edward was lost at sea; a brother Joseph became president of the New England Glassworks. Sisters were notable housekeepers, married and otherwise — models of housewifely perfection, at least in their brother Samuel's eyes.

Although Uncle John Ward could have pointed to more noteworthy public men in the Ward line, he would not have bothered to do so. Even the fact that there had been no banker among the Howes was forgivable, but the ominous note, from Uncle John's point of view, was that Dr. Samuel Gridley Howe seemed perversely proud of it. The doctor was actually proud of his paltry three thousand a year; he scorned wealth and had no intention whatever of improving his lot. All he wanted to do was to improve the lot of blind children, idiot children, prison inmates, the insane — and other unfortunates. And now the doctor wanted to marry an heiress. Uncle John Ward really loved his nieces, and if he ever saw a fortune hunter he thought he saw one now.

It is impossible not to reflect on how much easier everything would have been if Julia's parents had lived. Her father was a philanthropist as well as a banker. He had built a great fortune with some of the joy of a mountain climber in scaling a high peak, but he had never forgotten the responsibilities of his wealth. He must have known of Dr. Howe's work in behalf of the Greeks, and Christy Evangeles was not the only boy to whom Mr. Ward gave an education. He would have sympathized with Dr. Howe's present work, perhaps contributing to the cause. And Julia's mother, recalling early married years when money had not been plentiful, could have helped her daughter become a good housekeeper. Julia's mother even knew how to be a housewife and a poet — with an unpoetical husband.

The "Indenture made this 26th day of April, 1843 between Julia Ward of New York, single Woman . . . and Samuel G. Howe of the City of Boston"[4] had to be drawn up, however, since Julia Ward was without parents and an heiress. The agreement, rewritten at Charles Sumner's insistence, had to be signed; and hard feelings so engendered must be faced and eventually forgotten. But there were tears in store for Julia, and many a time she must have wished that she had been indeed a "penniless bride."

The "ante-nuptial agreement" first listed that part of Julia's fortune which she owned in equal shares with her brothers and sisters. This was downtown New York real estate — houses and land in Pearl Street, one on Beaver Street and lots on Exchange Place and Maiden Lane. Then there was real estate which belonged to Julia alone, her brothers and sisters owning other property of equal value. She owned three lots on the south side of 60th Street; five on the west side of Third Avenue; a large parcel on 58th Street, and Numbers 159 through 168 on the west side of Second Avenue. She had one lot which ran through from 34th to 35th Street on the west side of Eighth Avenue, and there was still more property on Eighth Avenue itself. "The said Julia" was "also possessed of . . . divers sums of money now invested in bonds and mortgages, or in stock and other securities." There was an "undivided residue" of her father's estate still to come to her. All in all, it was a formidable list of assets, and the agreement set up a trust fund for Julia with her brother Sam and her Uncle John as administrators. The Wards had seen many a case of business failure with creditors taking every cent both husband and wife had in the world; they had seen a widowed wife losing two thirds of her own money because her husband died without a will.

Much of Julia's uptown real estate was in undeveloped property which produced no income. It was proposed that she receive three thousand dollars a year — the equal of her husband's income — the rest of her money to be reinvested for her own and her children's benefit. It seems as if all would have gone smoothly but for Dr. Howe's best man. Sumner's contention appears to have been that Julia's income and capital should have been turned over to her husband, to deal with as he pleased; and now, although drugged with love, Dr. Howe's fierce personal pride stirred in its sleep. In the end, they compromised. Ten thousand dollars was to be set aside to be paid to Dr. Howe on demand, for a house and furnishings when the married pair should need such things. And how about this European wedding tour they were planning? Uncle John had demanded. Proudly Dr. Howe asserted that he himself was paying all the costs.

Unhappy over the clash, all parties signed the agreement. Uncle John and the Chevalier discovered a mutual respect for each other, but Sumner remained a target for Uncle John's wrath. Sumner would attract that wrath again. As for Sam Ward, whose duty it would be to pay over Julia's quarterly income — he could hardly tell which member of the wedding party he detested most, the groom or the best man. The whole family felt "scratched by that bit of New England granite" now about to become a member of the family. But Sam's natural good nature prevailed, and he resolved to make the best of it.

In the long pier glass in Uncle John's parlor at Number 8 Bond Street the Three Graces were reflected together as maidens for the last time. And for the first time, perhaps, Julia wore her diamond pin, "one of the diamonds" being her mother's, the rest from the Chevalier "as a wedding gift." The groom himself was resplendent in blue broadcloth coat with brass buttons, white brocaded waistcoat and fawn-colored trousers. Charles Sumner carried for him the "slender gold band" with the words engraved inside it, "Julia Ward, S. G. Howe, April 26, 1843." And then came the word they meant to live by: "Truth." [5]

"Julia looked and behaved admirably well," Longfellow said. "The wedding was a pleasant one — a very pleasant one."

But obviously Longfellow had been afraid that Julia's unquenchable sense of humor might assert itself even at her own wedding. And afterwards it did. "But at supper, her natural roguery broke out," Longfellow said, "and seeing Sumner bend over, and utterly engaged in talking to a lady, she could not help slipping two of their silver spoons into his pocket." Longfellow was shocked although he admitted that it "was an innocent jest, in which we all joined." Only a few knew how well Sumner deserved the punishment of all that laughter at his expense.[6]

On May 1 the newly married pair arrived in Boston to join another wedding couple and leave with them for Europe aboard the Cunard liner *Britannia*. The other bridegroom was the Honorable Horace Mann, and the other bride was the faithful Mary Peabody of Salem. New York visitors who came to wave farewell to the Howes said they had never seen anything quite like the Boston bonnets at the wharf. They could have had Miss Elizabeth Peabody's bonnet in mind, for she was there.

Horace Mann had been a tutor at Brown when Samuel Gridley Howe was an undergraduate there. In recent years, Howe and Mann had become fellow crusaders for improved public education. Mr. Mann passed his forty-ninth birthday aboard ship and although Mary Peabody was ten years younger, she seemed an elderly bride to the twenty-four-year-old Julia. "Mr. and Mrs. Mann are very loving," Julia said, catching the bridal couple in an embrace. "She wears a monstrous sun-bonnet — he lies down in his overcoat."

The Manns were to travel in Europe with the Howes — or so the two husbands of the two brides had decided. And in strictest Ward tradition, Julia had brought a sister along on her wedding trip! "Little Annie" had been so "pale and drooping" that Uncle John had decreed a European journey for her with the newly married Howes as chaperones. Later, sister Louisa and assorted Ward cousins would join them. It was to be a crowded honeymoon.

Perhaps only Louisa, who was very close to Annie, suspected a possible cause of Annie's drooping spirits. And even Louisa had never seen all the poems of John Louis O'Sullivan's which Annie kept hidden away. There was one written on Annie's eighteenth birthday which might have marked the end of Annie's hopes — flattering though the verses were. O'Sullivan pretended that "fifty years have passed away" and he wrote twelve stanzas of pretended recollection.

> The hair which underneath the snowy fold
>   Of that sweet cap, now spreads its whitest snow,
> How beautiful, when eighteen summers old,
>   It lay upon how beautiful a brow!
> If you would like to see what it was then,
>   I still can show a treasured specimen. . . .
>
> I've been a little famous since that day,
>   For some good done, and God knows how much evil
> Turned some things topsy-turvy, and they say
>   In politics have played the very ——.
> A desperate radical in legislation
>   And twice President of this great nation. . . . [7]

This was all very well and a charming birthday salutation, but O'Sullivan went on to speak of Annie, fifty years hence, as a "stately old granny" and to refer to "my Ada's grandchildren." And Annie's name was not Ada.

In 1846, John Louis O'Sullivan was married, but not to Annie and not to Ada. His wife's name was Sarah Rodgers; whether her life was happy or not, it was at least eventful. O'Sullivan was Minister to Portugal when he persuaded his friend Nathaniel Hawthorne to invest in a gold mine which brought them little if any gold. He had a faculty for

CHAPTER TEN
Sam's Medora

THE Wards were a closely knit, devoted family. They also paid a great deal of attention to each other's affairs, causing explosions of family temper and mutual recriminations which outsiders could never understand. Of course if an outsider had said half the things they said to each other they would have turned upon the wretch with one accord. Julia, while on her honeymoon, heard things about brother Sam and spoke her mind concerning his conduct.[1] "I am given to understand that he is making a donkey of himself by sending Medora Grymes bouquets which she gives away, boxes, and a riding whip which he himself deserves to feel. Whatever may happen hereafter — her present engagement should make her sacred — he has no right to approach her in any way until her engagement is broken off."

For some time now, Sam Ward had banished his grief for his young wife Emily Astor. He was once more the popular beau, exchanging quips with all the belles at all the balls. Some of his repartee he relayed to the patient Longfellow.

"If you will not dance with me tonight, will you dance with me next winter?" he had said "to a young Belle who is always engaged."

" 'With pleasure, unless Miller's prophecy is fulfilled in April,' " the girl replied.

" 'In that case, we will waltz in Heaven,' " replied the gallant Sam, " 'and let me add that such a prospect will make a very pious man of me, until April.' "

The world did not come to an end on April 3, 1843, although William Miller and his followers were ready in their white robes. From the state of mind of members of the Ward family and others, it might as well have — when Sam got himself engaged to Medora Grymes that fatal year!

'Oh he is such a wonner.' I do not like that pretty women should pay him so many compliments — it will turn his little head. He is almost well and so handsome!"

Julia wrote a long letter in diary form which she posted at intervals to her sister Louisa. Staccato sketches of new acquaintances were deft and to the point. "Annie and I went alone to a rout at Mrs. Sidney Smith's and were announced as 'Mrs. 'Ow and Miss Vord,' — did not know a soul, Annie frightened, I bored — got hold of some good people, made friends, drank execrable tea, finished the evening with Sir Sidney himself and came off victorious — that is to say, alive. Sir Sidney like old Mrs. Prime, three chins, and such a corporation!

"Landsdowne is a devilish good fellow, Ho, ho! he wears a blue belt across his diaphragm and a silver star on his left breast and makes himself at home in his own house — he is about 60 with Marchioness to match, side-dishes I presume but did not inquire. . . ."

Julia's diary letter contained references to Howe's prankish humor, which she had just begun to experience. Her husband "came to bed with his hat on in the dark the other night, and once before with his hair mittens, which frightened me." Louisa, who could not remain unmarried much longer, might just as well learn what to expect from a strictly masculine idea of fun.

Sam's Medora

THE Wards were a closely knit, devoted family. They also paid a great deal of attention to each other's affairs, causing explosions of family temper and mutual recriminations which outsiders could never understand. Of course if an outsider had said half the things they said to each other they would have turned upon the wretch with one accord. Julia, while on her honeymoon, heard things about brother Sam and spoke her mind concerning his conduct.[1] "I am given to understand that he is making a donkey of himself by sending Medora Grymes bouquets which she gives away, boxes, and a riding whip which he himself deserves to feel. Whatever may happen hereafter — her present engagement should make her sacred — he has no right to approach her in any way until her engagement is broken off."

For some time now, Sam Ward had banished his grief for his young wife Emily Astor. He was once more the popular beau, exchanging quips with all the belles at all the balls. Some of his repartee he relayed to the patient Longfellow.

"If you will not dance with me tonight, will you dance with me next winter?" he had said "to a young Belle who is always engaged."

" 'With pleasure, unless Miller's prophecy is fulfilled in April,' " the girl replied.

" 'In that case, we will waltz in Heaven,' " replied the gallant Sam, " 'and let me add that such a prospect will make a very pious man of me, until April.' "

The world did not come to an end on April 3, 1843, although William Miller and his followers were ready in their white robes. From the state of mind of members of the Ward family and others, it might as well have — when Sam got himself engaged to Medora Grymes that fatal year!

catching the bridal couple in an embrace. "She wears a monstrous sunbonnet — he lies down in his overcoat."

The Manns were to travel in Europe with the Howes — or so the two husbands of the two brides had decided. And in strictest Ward tradition, Julia had brought a sister along on her wedding trip! "Little Annie" had been so "pale and drooping" that Uncle John had decreed a European journey for her with the newly married Howes as chaperones. Later, sister Louisa and assorted Ward cousins would join them. It was to be a crowded honeymoon.

Perhaps only Louisa, who was very close to Annie, suspected a possible cause of Annie's drooping spirits. And even Louisa had never seen all the poems of John Louis O'Sullivan's which Annie kept hidden away. There was one written on Annie's eighteenth birthday which might have marked the end of Annie's hopes — flattering though the verses were. O'Sullivan pretended that "fifty years have passed away" and he wrote twelve stanzas of pretended recollection.

> The hair which underneath the snowy fold
>   Of that sweet cap, now spreads its whitest snow,
> How beautiful, when eighteen summers old,
>   It lay upon how beautiful a brow!
> If you would like to see what it was then,
>   I still can show a treasured specimen. . . .
>
> I've been a little famous since that day,
>   For some good done, and God knows how much evil
> Turned some things topsy-turvy, and they say
>   In politics have played the very ——.
> A desperate radical in legislation
>   And twice President of this great nation. . . . [7]

This was all very well and a charming birthday salutation, but O'Sullivan went on to speak of Annie, fifty years hence, as a "stately old granny" and to refer to "my Ada's grandchildren." And Annie's name was not Ada.

In 1846, John Louis O'Sullivan was married, but not to Annie and not to Ada. His wife's name was Sarah Rodgers; whether her life was happy or not, it was at least eventful. O'Sullivan was Minister to Portugal when he persuaded his friend Nathaniel Hawthorne to invest in a gold mine which brought them little if any gold. He had a faculty for backing a good cause by doubtful means, and in his zeal to save the Cubans from the evils of Spanish rule he consorted with gunrunners, much to the embarrassment of his Government. "Handsome, charming . . . and unlucky, but an optimist to the last," Julian Hawthorne said, and he was right about O'Sullivan.

Annie's heart was not by any means broken although she may have thought it was. She was pale and thin when she embarked upon her sister Julia's honeymoon voyage but her new brother-in-law took a doctor's pleasure in trying to effect a cure. "My sweet little sister-in-law proves very interesting, not only to me but to all who see her, especially W.W. who is our fellow passenger," Dr. Howe said.[8] And the mysterious Mr. "W.W.," after they landed in England, added himself to the party.

The Manns, the Howes, Annie Ward and her admirer proceeded by way of Chester to London. They saw Charles Dickens, who conducted a sight-seeing tour of the seamier side of London for the men of the party only. But he invited the ladies to dinner and so did Forster, biographer of Dickens. It was at the Forsters' that Dickens twitted Mrs. Julia Ward Howe for being a loving bride. "He slid down to the floor and, lying on his back, held up one of his small feet, quivering with pretended emotion. 'Did she call him darling,' he cried."

Banking associates of the Ward family showered the Howes with invitations and long was the list of titles which Julia jotted down in her letters to Louisa. Dr. Howe's reception in the houses of the great was a drama in itself. He attended functions gotten up to honor two daughters of a famous banker — and stole the show. Dickens's *American Notes* had made a sensation, and the women especially had read about the blind and deaf little Laura Bridgman. So here was a character literally right out of Dickens. Curiosity changed to admiration, for Howe was no bent and twisted Cruikshank caricature. This was Tennyson's England as well as the England of Charles Dickens, and Dr. Samuel Gridley Howe had the eyes of a knight of the Holy Grail. He had injured his knee on shipboard but even his slight limp and his pallor from recent confinement indoors made him the more attractive. Although he had left Byron's helmet at home, the story of his Greek career, even his face and figure, denoted shining armor.

"We are too young to be noticed," Julia wrote of herself and Annie, with pretended jealousy and just a grain of truth. "We are very demure and have learned humility. Chev receives a great deal of attention. Ladies press forward to look at him, roll up their eyes, exclaiming,

There were no stars of television, stage and screen; no girls chosen to be Miss 1843 of state or nation. But there were "beauties." Sam's Medora was a beauty. She was painted by popular artists, whether they had ever seen her or not, she was daguerrotyped and eventually photographed. Sleepy-eyed, with small mouth and plump cheeks, she would register no emotion whatever as she gazed from the pages of Mrs. Caroline Kirkland's *Book of Home Beauties.* It did not do justice to Medora to call her a *home* beauty, however. She was a ballroom beauty, though not invited to every New York ball.

Sam's Medora was the daughter of John Randolph Grymes of New Orleans. Her parents were now divorced — and in their day divorce was never mentioned except behind closed doors. It was no fault of their daughter's, but there were houses, Mrs. William B. Astor's for example, where Medora was not received.

Actually, her name was not Medora. It was "Marie Angeline, who signs herself Medora" on deeds to property she later acquired.[2] But she was every bit as beautiful as people said. Long after the sentimentalized portraits had faded, a niece described her as she appeared to the discerning eyes of a child.[3] "Her coloring was like that of a June rose." It was summertime, and her little niece saw Medora "standing before a Louis Quinze dressing table, looking at herself in the glass as she arranged her dark hair in wide braids low over her ears. There was a plate of ripe strawberries on the dressing table and a mixture of sweet, unfamiliar perfumes in the air." Medora was wearing "an embroidered white muslin peignoir that had an under-robe of pink silk just the color of her cheeks. The sun came into the big luxurious bedroom through green Venetian blinds and one long shaft lay on the moss green carpet." Medora smiled at her little niece and "held out the plate of strawberries." Getting out her guitar, she "sang the songs that had sung her into" Sam Ward's heart — "Oh bring to me my Arab Steed!" and "My earrings, my earrings, I've dropped them in the well."

Who could blame Sam Ward for loving his Medora! Many people did blame him, however, and when Medora announced her engagement to a Frenchman by the name of Delauney, Sam was still more severely censured for refusing to give her up. Longfellow assumed that Sam's romance was over. "From my heart of hearts, I sympathize with you, my dear Sam," Longfellow wrote, "yet when I think out of what a labyrinth you have escaped, I am not sure that this is not one of those disappointments which are 'better than success': cutting down through

the white marble to make a goddess, you have struck the *blue vein* —
you have discovered the blemish."

The Howes and Annie Ward were traveling in England when the
news reached them, in June, 1843, of Longfellow's engagement to
"Fanny Appleton, the much-loved and never forgotten Fanny," as he
put it. Sam Ward hastened to Boston to the wedding on June 13.
"Longfellow's wedding was very beautiful, and the bride and groom
models of firm conviction and confiding affection," according to Sam.
"Cogswell and Ned Perkins assisted, I was Master of Ceremonies and
helped demolish the wedding cake. We drank champagne to their
felicity till midnight."

In Fanny Appleton Longfellow, Sam Ward now gained a new confidante for his romantic difficulties. After a few months, Medora
changed her mind about her French lover, Delauney, and agreed to
marry Sam, but Sam's friends had doubts. During one of his flying
visits to Cambridge, Sam gave Mrs. Longfellow one of Medora's "notes
to read." The love letter was in French, "gracefully tender." And Sam,
getting Mrs. Longfellow "in a corner . . . poured forth a volume of his
feelings, past and present." Once Fanny Longfellow had been reluctant to marry but now she was the happiest of brides and she hoped to
see all her friends equally happy. "It seems such a strong attachment
on both sides, that I wish to hope for the best for it, as do Sumner
and Henry," she said. She encouraged Sam — "but everybody here
thinks themselves bound to prophesy as unkindly as possible." Mrs.
Longfellow thought that Medora's mother's "unhappy example,
shunned by all as she is, is anything but a temptation to an evil course,
and is more likely to act as a warning . . . on a young girl. She knows
that Vice is hideous."

Fanny Longfellow's Boston and Berkshire friends were not such
true Christians as she. "Sarah Sedgwick looked as morally severe as
possible because I praised her [Medora's] grace, as if even God's gifts
to her should not be admired but only considered as possible misfortunes."

There was the chance, of course, now that Medora had changed her
mind, that her former fiancé, being a Frenchman, might call out Sam
Ward. In New Orleans, Francis Marion Ward had recently fought in
a duel for far less cause. In certain quarters, gossips held their breath
in pleasant anticipation of what could only mean tragedy, no matter
what the outcome. But Mr. Delauney was a practical and civilized
Frenchman. He offered to sell to Sam Ward the trousseau which he

had ordered in Paris for Medora and Sam took up the offer, thereby doubtless netting Mr. Delauney a nice profit. The boxes from Paris arrived just in time for the wedding of Miss Medora Grymes to Mr. Samuel Ward, at the bride's mother's estate on Staten Island, September 20, 1843.

"I do not think Sam is very wise," said Fanny Longfellow, "but prefer to hope, now that he is married, that he may make her too happy to go astray."

In Medora's circle there were few if any such good friends as the Longfellows, however. It was said that immediately after Medora's marriage, August Belmont insultingly stationed his finest carriage and pair before her door. Sam let himself be goaded into buying equally fine horses. The new Mrs. Sam Ward's door was now 32 Bond Street and for this reason the Astors were her bitter enemies.

But the effect of Sam Ward's marriage was beneficial to the health of old John Jacob Astor — at least as Henry Brevoort told it to Washington Irving. "Old Mr. Astor still holds out and is better, body and mind, than he was before you left us," said Mr. Brevoort, dating his letter October 18, 1843. "An untoward event has just happened in his family, which has stirred his ire; a thing which always does him good. Master Sam W—— has married Miss Medora Grymes and settled upon her *his* house in Bond Street, which house had been purchased, and previously given or settled upon his first wife, but by our laws became his after her decease. This affair sticks deep in the old man's gizzard. He views it as a sort of impeachment of his accustomed sagacity; a sort of outwitting and over-reaching in the art of bargaining. Previous to the marriage, he sent for the bold Samuel — not to remonstrate with him about the step he was taking, but to warn him that unless his g.g. daughter was not withdrawn from the protection he had provided and placed in the hands of her grandmother, Mrs. W. [Mrs. William B. Astor] means would be adopted to deprive him of the property he had accidentally acquired. To this Master S. bowed in submission."

The house at Number 32 Bond Street had been given to Sam Ward by his father the banker. It had been furnished by Sam himself out of his income while working for his father, and although given to his wife, Emily Astor, it reverted to Sam upon her death — exactly as Henry Brevoort had said. Whatever means the Astors might have adopted would have had a rough time in court, and they probably knew it. But there was no question but what Sam and his Medora could have more fun without little Maddie to look after. Sam loved his little daughter — he was a tender-hearted person. He handed her over to the Astors with regret, but with no misgivings, and all her life Maddie was good to her father — or as good as her grandparents would allow her to be.

There was more to the story, however. Louisa Ward was staying at Rokeby to be with her little niece, now four years old. When the news of her brother's impending marriage reached the Astors, Mr. William B. Astor ordered the carriage. "Miss Louisa Ward is going back to town," he said. Louisa was proud, her brother Sam had once remarked, and he was right. She departed, her beautiful head held high and all her tears unshed till she reached the shelter of Uncle John's house on Bond Street. Never again would she "feel the little necklace of Maddie's arms!" And how she loved the child! It speaks well for both of them that later when Margaret Astor Ward was old enough to choose her own associates she became the friend as well as the devoted niece of Louisa, of Julia Ward Howe and of Annie as well.

The William Astors had "taken this new alliance in great dudgeon," Henry Brevoort observed. They "have resolved never to hold intercourse or to speak to their much over-rated son-in-law. Both parties came into collision a few days since, at a great *fête champêtre* given at Highwood by J. G. King — but there was no recognition and the A's left the field very prematurely to the victorious Sam, who, with his wife, were the lions of the day."

"Another rencontre took place upon the occasion" but this one was "much more amusing and characteristic. Mr. Delauney, who had been jilted by Sam's Medora, approached her with true French nonchalance — took both her hands and congratulated her on the happy event (not of his having been jilted) and clapping his hand upon Sam's shoulder, exclaimed, '*Eh bien, mon ami, comment ça va?*' "

Sam Ward was riding high. He loved the limelight into which his marriage to Medora had thrown him and he was supremely confident that he was about to make a tremendous fortune. His gifts to Medora were lavish. Her sapphires, a necklace, bracelets and earrings. proved worthy of comment by the press and he invited the Longfellows, when they were in New York, to come out to his Staten Island "villa" and try his new saddle horses. Mrs. Longfellow heard favorable comment. A "Mrs. Burke" had said that "the ladies here are greatly pleased with Medora and if Mama will only retire, her success will be certain — that she was often invited without her mother last year and, as Mrs. Ward, will take her own stand." Fanny Longfellow had only slight misgivings. "They will doubtless live very dashingly," she said, and Sam was "not the man, I fear, to elevate her character."

The Longfellows saw Louisa and thought she looked ill. She had been going to a doctor without avail and they could not know that her illness was of the spirit and that there was nothing a doctor could do. Through no fault of her own, she had received a blow to her pride at the hands of the Astors. And some one had fallen in love with her again — John Ward of Boston this time. Louisa was not sure of her own mind, and the engagement was called an "understanding" — which no one understood.

One of the Ward cousins, arriving in London, told Julia all the news and she promptly addressed her brother Sam. "Did Lou or Uncle John refuse John Ward? [4] Beware of governing Lou too much, — dear child, she is too pliant almost. One must not pull her about. Coz told me about it to my great surprise. I did not think he would feel at liberty to propose for her at this time. I hear that Uncle, with his customary generosity, attributes the plot to me. I *could* swear and the doctor does at this most unkind suspicion. . . . I thank God that I am incapable of the worse than indiscretion of making up so doubtful a match — yet if Lou wished it, she should have her way. I hope she acted for herself."

Louisa's Rhode Island cousin, George Washington Greene, was in New York but was soon to return to his post as United States consul in Rome. Like Sam, he had known Longfellow abroad, forming a lifelong friendship. He attempted great things in literature, achieving high-flown language, ancestor worship and a faculty for spending other peoples' money. But he was now only thirty-three with some of his mistakes before him. Longfellow suggested that Louisa go to Rome with her cousin George Washington Greene and join her sister there. The Manns were going home. Julia's cousin was going home. Of course Dr. Howe could have no possible objection to continuing his travels with his wife and two sisters-in-law instead of one.

From Vienna, in October, Dr. Howe wrote a long letter to Sumner, describing just what it was like to travel with a wife and only one sister-in-law and the letter contained advice to Sumner as to the proper way to make a European tour. "Travelling fast through foreign countries is no way to know them," Howe said; he regretted that he had no information to offer on the political situation in France, Belgium, Switzerland, Bavaria and Austria. He explained the reason. [5]

"A bachelor breakfasts in the coffee rooms and learns something from his neighbors, or from the waiter, or even boots; he accosts men in the passageways and in the shops; he profits by the chattering of his valet . . . his barber, his cicerone; everywhere and from everybody he learns something.

"The family man, however, must forgo most if not all these means of getting information; he walks with his wife on one arm and his sister on the other so that he cannot run into passersby purposely, beg their pardon and make that an introduction to an acquaintance; he sits at table flanked on each side by a formidable wall of wadded silk, that cuts him off from any intercourse with his neighbors, nor can he hobnob with any stranger that takes his fancy.

"It is the same everywhere — in the public conveyances, on the steamers, at the Baths, wherever he goes, he is as much cut off from the crowd he wanders among, as if he had a policeman on either arm to keep him silent. On the road it is the same or worse, he is bound up in his carriage, the direction given to the courier and the good man is transported to another city like a bale of goods."

But Dr. Howe realized that he was talking like a bachelor who regrets his lost freedom and he hastened to point out advantages to his newly married state. One could "expect . . . infinite pleasure from the constant presence of a beloved companion who clings closer to you from the strangeness of everything about her; who holds your hand at table so that you cannot eat, who kisses you every moment when you are alone, who even in public promenades will continue to touch her lips to your shoulder, or to transport a kiss on the end of her finger to the back of your hand; a being whose constant presence, like the heat of the sun, makes constant and pleasant day, even in the darkness of storm. A companion who throws around everything you do, the charm of agreeable appreciation for future reminiscence."

Julia read the letter over her husband's shoulder. Was he tired of the long honeymoon and the feminine web she and her sister Annie so delicately spun about him? Some of his remarks, though humorous, were a trifle too true. She added a postscript of her own.

"My dear Sumner, I have been reading the admirable account of Annie and myself . . . and can only advise you not to get married, or if you do, not to take your wife abroad. She will certainly keep people from running against you in the street, she certainly will sit by you at breakfast and at dinner and may even wear wadded silk if the weather be cold. She may compel you to ride in a comfortable carriage instead of being tossed about in a musty, greasy diligence, wherefore, my dear Sumner, do not marry, for great are the miseries of femininity and we all malae bestiae."

They were on their way to Rome when Dr. Howe had news for Sumner in a letter which he marked "confidential." Julia, "with blushes and hesitation," had told her husband that they were going to have a child. "Since then, how much we have rejoiced together; how we have tasted in advance the bliss of parental love; how we have formed plans for its future; how we have felt the force of this new life which rivets us together for aye. And she — oh how much more than I."

By December 11, Bond Street had been bereft of all its Graces and they were all with Dr. Samuel Gridley Howe in his lodgings in Rome. Louisa described her arrival on that day. "We walked up stair after stair until at last, in the fourth story of the Torlonia Palace," she discovered Julia and Annie. "I opened the door and stood curtsying to them for several minutes before they knew me but when at last they did recognize me, what a scream of joy there was! I cried, Annie laughed and Jule stood by in mute astonishment."

The address in Rome was Via San Niccolò da Tolentino, a street which opened into the Piazza Barberini with its famous fountains of the Tritons. All around were ancient palaces, some of them still occupied by Italian nobility, others rented to tourists like the Howes or to artists. The great Thorwaldsen's studio was nearby. And a new personality appeared on the family horizon, whose importance no one as yet recognized. This was Thomas Crawford, the sculptor.

Thomas Crawford was American-born but his father, Aaron Crawford, was born in Ireland and went to Dublin University. Tradition said that the Crawfords were landed gentry who disapproved of their son's marriage, causing him to come to America, but late in life, Jennie Crawford, a maiden sister, "destroyed all family papers." Thomas Crawford was born in New York City on March 22, 1813, and he was now thirty years old. All who saw him spoke of his six-foot stature, "straight and muscular," his "marked and handsome features, thick chestnut hair" and "blazing blue eyes under a broad white forehead." Once seen, Crawford was a man never forgotten.

From his earliest years, Thomas Crawford was independent — he caused his parents great anxiety by running away to join a band of wandering musicians. The walls of his room were covered with his drawings and he knew he had found the right career for himself when he ran away to work for a wood carver. Although his sister Jennie denied it, Crawford's home life was most unhappy. This he confided to Louisa Ward when at last he met her and found her willing to listen to all his thoughts, hopes and dreams.

At the age of nineteen [6] Thomas Crawford went to work for the firm of Frazee and Launitz. Mr. Frazee was a sculptor and had made the portrait bust of Samuel Ward, Louisa's father. When Crawford went to work for him, Frazee was an architect, designer of the New York Customs House, and Launitz was a monument-maker. Already, Crawford owned a collection of plaster casts, bought one by one with hoarded pennies the way most boys collect stamps or arrowheads. His favorite cast was a frieze in relief, "The Triumph of Alexander" by Thorwaldsen. This Danish sculptor was Crawford's hero; and Mr. Launitz, a Russian, had *almost* studied under him — having worked in his uncle's studio in Rome, said uncle being a pupil of Thorwaldsen. Such secondhand inspiration was not going to do for Thomas Crawford. He determined to study under the great Thorwaldsen in person.

Crawford's early work for the wood carver gave him great skill in detail but also harmed him by leading him to emphasize detail at the expense of simplicity. It was good for him to work in stone with Frazee and Launitz, except that a wave of enthusiasm for the ornate was beginning to be felt and, when young Crawford proved capable of forcing into stone designs which would have been permissible only in wood, clients were delighted and orders mounted. Thomas asked for more money. He was refused, so he went back to the wood carver and soon had the satisfaction of being sought out and rehired at a better wage by Frazee and Launitz. After work he attended evening classes at the National Academy of Design.

In 1835, the firm said good-by to their gifted employee. Mr. Launitz gave Crawford two letters of introduction, one to a doctor of medicine in Rome and one to Thorwaldsen. In a boyishly enthusiastic letter home, Crawford told of his adventures. He entered Rome "seventy days" after leaving home and he had been so homesick he "almost regretted the step" he had taken. But on Washington's birthday he had gone to a party at the American consulate, given by George Washington Greene. There he had met Thorwaldsen and walked with the great man that evening, down the Monte Quirinale by the light of a full moon. Thorwaldsen was a tall man with flowing white hair, with "mildness" his "prevailing characteristic together with love for his art . . . and the vivid ambition of his youth which still remains."

Thorwaldsen's early struggles made him "kind to beginners and penniless artists."

Next morning young Crawford presented himself at Thorwaldsen's door by appointment and was greeted warmly by the great man himself, who wore "his study gown and cap which were of silk and velvet and had been presented to him while in Denmark as a memento of affection. He wore them for the givers' sake and not for show" and the silk robe "was splashed with clay." The richness formed a contrast with the simplicity of his apartments: " . . . his bed had no hangings and the brick floor was uncarpeted."

Thorwaldsen was "finishing a noble statue of colossal size for the Protestant Church at Copenhagen." After "turning the statue" for the eager and excited young Crawford "to see in a better light," Thorwaldsen took the young man into another room "in which stood an old-fashioned escritoire and from this he brought out drawing after drawing, unrolled and explained each with unaffected dignity . . . like Ulysses teaching the youthful Telemachus."

Young Crawford was surprised and overjoyed when he was accepted by Thorwaldsen as a pupil. Yet how could the old man have refused so ardent a student? "There is but one other young man besides myself in the studio," Crawford said — "he is a native of Rome. Thorwaldsen visits us once a day, corrects what he sees wrong with our work and after some words of encouragement, leaves us." And now young Crawford's dreams were all of gods and goddesses. He sought out all sorts of translations from the classics, and his imagination seethed with classic compositions as he worked under Thorwaldsen with passionate intensity.

Like most young artists, however gifted, Crawford had much to un-learn as well to learn. "Mass before detail — mass before detail" said Thorwaldsen to a young man who could model a flower down to its last stamen and too often did so. "These few words, 'mass before detail' gave me more insight into my art . . . than all else put together," said Crawford. But the age in which he lived was against him and the craze for detail increased.

Not content with studying under Thorwaldsen by day, Crawford worked at night in the mortuary, dissecting and drawing under Comuccini, an Italian artist noted for neoclassic and religious painting. Crawford made himself a reference library by drawing sheet after sheet of one-half life-size studies of "every bone and muscle and sinew in the human body." On the Via del Orto, he found a studio that would do, although it was not large enough to impress clients — if he ever had any. He invented a lamp to fasten to his head like a miner's lantern so that he could work at night. And in ten weeks he modeled seventeen portrait busts "at a day laborer's wages," since, at the age of twenty-four, a young man's "life savings" are not large and funds were running low.

An original composition was maturing in Crawford's mind. He would need a large block of marble and it must be pure white in accordance with the fashion of his day. There must be no "blue vein" which Longfellow had referred to as the ruin of an artist's work. Crawford's friends told him he was insane to go ahead with his statue of Orpheus before someone had promised to buy it from the plaster model. But Crawford ordered the stone — Serravezza marble from the Carrara district, whose quarries had supplied artists for the past two thousand years. While waiting for the Serravezza (more "modern" than the "old Carrara") Crawford modeled an equestrian statue of Washington — although no one had ordered that either.

Crawford was working on his "Orpheus" when he met Charles Sumner — in Rome for his health. They struck up a strong friendship while Crawford modeled Sumner's subtle, intellectual features, so much admired by his friends. Then Sumner went home and Crawford existed on almost literally a crust a day while he worked on his "Orpheus." But the god with his magic lute failed to charm any dollars from a client.

Thomas Crawford, nevertheless, was in a state of exaltation over his first important work. He tried to put into words for his sister at home what he felt about his "Orpheus," now completed in 1839.

"I am writing in the midst of a terrible thunderstorm," he began. "Incessant flashes dart every moment into the windows of my Studio. My statue of Orpheus is before me, and when I look upon it in the midst of this thick darkness, which is lighted occasionally by a glare of red light, it is difficult to persuade myself that this inanimate creation of mine is not starting from its pedestal and actually rushing into the realms of Pluto." Crawford had shown Orpheus as shielding his eyes with one hand as he gazed into Hades in search of his lost Eurydice — the sleeping Cerberus at his feet. The young god seemed on the verge of plunging forward, and his face in spite of its classic lines was touching in its look of grief and courage. "I have been thinking of the story about Phidias and his wonderful statue of Jove," Crawford said. "You know that upon finishing it, the Sculptor requested some sign from the God, to know if he were pleased with the representation; it seems that the *nod* was given for at that moment the statue was circled with lightning. . . . Were we living in that age, or were ours the religion of the ancient Greeks, I too might interpret the sign in my favor."

But the gods first punished their votary, for Crawford's long privation and strain told upon even his fine physique. And now the second letter of introduction proved important, as Dr. Ruga came daily and free of charge to attend a young sculptor "ill of brain fever." George Washington Greene, American Consul, took Crawford into his own home to care for him.

Crawford's health recovered but his purse did not. There came the inevitable night when he was down to his last "paul." He had not enough to pay for a good dinner, but *Il Trovatore* was playing and he had enough money to get in. After the opera was over he walked for hours through silent, sleeping Rome. This was to be his last night —before he gave up art to eat, becoming a day laborer in good earnest. Next morning he went to a small café near his studio — not for breakfast since he had no money, but to ask for his mail which was delivered there. For weeks there had been no letters for him, but today there was one from Charles Sumner.

Sumner had been circulating a subscription among his Boston friends to buy the Crawford statue of Orpheus and present it to the Boston Athenæum.[7] A sum of twenty-five hundred dollars had been subscribed, of which Mr. Sumner enclosed three hundred as an advance payment. It may be presumed that Thomas Crawford had breakfast at the little café after all.

The purchase of his "Orpheus" was the turning point for Thomas Crawford. "Mr. Tiffany of Baltimore ordered of Thomas Crawford a statuary group, entitled 'Lead us into the Life Eternal'." Jonathan Phillips of Boston, wealthy patron of the arts, wanted an "ideal statue," the subject of Crawford's choosing, and Mr. Tiffany would take a copy when it was done. Crawford's success was not confined to his countrymen. Prince Demidoff, a young Russian nobleman who was spending money sensationally in Rome and Paris, wanted two bas reliefs, "Heracles arrested by Diana in the act of carrying off the golden stag" and "a group of centaurs." These commissions, while in progress of completion, were to be seen at the artist's "new, large studio fitted up in the Piazza Barberini."

Very probably Louisa Ward had seen Crawford's "Orpheus" in

Boston, for she visited there in 1842 when it was the talk of the town. The Boston Athenæum at that time occupied a former Perkins mansion in Pearl Street and when the "Orpheus" arrived it proved too big to go through the door. A little house had to be built for it in the garden. It nearly broke Crawford's heart to learn that his "Orpheus" had been damaged in transit. Both legs at the knee and at the ankle had to be mended by a local sculptor — who did the job very badly, as it later turned out. But all these matters only added interest to the statue. Bostonians visited the "Orpheus" in great numbers and were not disappointed. Somehow, Crawford's "Orpheus" had a quality of immortal youth; and descendants of grim Puritans, with textile-mill money in their pockets, began to wonder how they could get away to Rome for a holiday before they grew too old to enjoy it. Mere mortals began to indulge the hope that one of Crawford's gods in pure white marble, brought home from Rome to adorn a Beacon Hill parlor, might somehow bring with it lost youth and Roman sunshine.

Dr. Howe brought letters of introduction from Charles Sumner to Crawford, who soon became a frequent caller at the Via San Niccolò da Tolentino. Julia and Annie were delighted with the artist, now thirty-two, whom Dr. Howe called "young." But Thomas Crawford was naturally high spirited and Dr. Howe had doubts. He felt that he "had not penetrated through the rather abundant persiflage which, like the bubbles in champagne, keep one from the true taste of the vintage." The truth was that Thomas Crawford had dared to laugh at phrenology!

George Combe, the phrenologist beloved of Horace Mann and Dr. Howe, was now in Rome. Daily, he and Dr. Howe wandered through the museums measuring the marble busts of Roman emperors and, with historic hindsight, concluded much from improper bulges and low brows. Crawford laughed and said that Roman sculptors flattered their clients just as he did — making Roman jaws more formidable just as he himself rendered Boston foreheads more intellectual than life. Crawford even said there was no such thing as the "tyrant type."

Thomas Crawford's joyous presence continued to brighten the Howes' apartment and Dr. Howe's doubts began to fade. "I am more struck every day by the amazing fertility of his fancy," Dr. Howe said. "Perhaps it is because I have not known other artists intimately, but there seems to me a profusion and variety in his artistic conceptions which must be rare indeed. In the merest spirit of play, or rather in no spirit at all but the excitement of ridding his imagination of something that is pecking at it for birth and existence, he throws off sketches which would render a common artist great."

Now came the beautiful Louisa Ward to join her sisters in Rome. Dr. Howe reported that "as for Louisa, she seemed in rather a low state of health" when she reached Rome. Soon he said that she was "already better." The ancient city of Rome seemed to cast a magic spell over Louisa. Thomas Crawford was her first new friend — a laughing, joyous companion, riding the crest of a wave of success. It seemed as if fate itself had taken a hand in behalf of both of them.

CHAPTER ELEVEN

A Tempest on Bond Street

LOUISA Ward came to Rome "under a sort of engagement to John Ward," Dr. Howe said. This was John G. Ward, son of Thomas Wren Ward, Boston banker. "It should not have been talked of publicly as such; at any rate, they are not engaged now nor is there any likelihood of their being while she is abroad." Dr. Howe wanted Charles Sumner to do something about the rumor in Boston. "I authorize you to contradict any report of their engagement whenever you may chance to hear it, although of course you will not seek opportunities of bringing it up."

The trunks, boxes and bandboxes which Louisa had brought with her to Rome contained beautiful clothes which Uncle John had encouraged her to buy; and her cousin George Washington Greene had assured her that the Roman social season would be just beginning, the balls would be dazzling. George Washington Greene had lived abroad since he was sixteen when he came in search of health. A generous allowance, his delicate health (which he managed to protect for a total of seventy-two years) and vague literary aspirations, plus a talent for friendship, provided him with a delightful life. But the family money had been running dry when Greene became American Consul — taking his duties lightly and his social life seriously. He was Crawford's good friend, and visitors to the Consulate were sure to hear of the wonderful American sculptor whose studios they must visit. He could and did introduce Louisa Ward to Italian high society.

The Howes and Wards attended Prince Torlonia's ball, "a fashionable, brilliant, beautiful affair according to some, showing the munificence of the noble host," said Dr. Howe sarcastically.[1] In his opinion it was "vulgar, stupid, tawdry" and the Prince was "a purse-proud Dives." The "Austrian Ambassador's ball" was more of the same. "Greene's introductions are worth little," Dr. Howe concluded — although it was all in the point of view. But even the girls admitted that small private parties were the most fun.

There was the evening when Julia sang more beautifully than anyone. So said her proud husband. "After several English ladies had tried their hands at Italian music and gained the usual marks of applause . . . a few forced tappings of kid gloves, Julia was led to the pianoforte. There was very soon a marked difference in the kind of attention paid to the singer, the low whispering around the piano, the more audible voices in the far corners . . . now ceased entirely and everyone became a listener. She sang beautifully, far better than she usually does — and when she ceased, reaped the reward of hearty and unqualified praise, which you may imagine was to my ears very sweet music itself. 'An American lady! Eh — *possible!* 'Pon honor, most exquisite execution — quite an honor to the country,' etc. etc."

At the Howes' apartment, they had "the merriest times." There was "tea, then music" and they "waxed warm with fun and laughter." An elderly widow danced a Virginia reel and they all "shook wrinkles out of brows where they had been undisturbed for years." It was like a party at Bond Street, Dr. Howe said, and he could speak no higher praise. Yet here was proof that it was not actually Bond Street which spelled good times, but Julia's special gift of communicating joy, of showering a largess of gaiety — which she had brought with her to Rome and would carry everywhere — unless the love and appreciation she needed failed her.

Dr. Howe's dearest wish had been to travel on to Greece and show his wife and his two sisters-in-law the scenes of his early triumphs. He was still a hero in Aegina, where a colony of refugees owed its existence to him. But the Howes had reached Rome by coastwise steamer and Julia had been horribly seasick. Her child was now due in two months and she could not face another coastwise voyage. Dr. Howe thought her foolish and almost went without her, but gave up his trip "out of a sense of duty to her." Perhaps if he could have realized that Julia expected to die in childbirth he might have substituted for "duty" the word "love." Born fearless, Dr. Howe could not understand fears, either secret or avowed. Be it remembered that he thought highly of duty. When his duty was to Julia she had reason to be content.

Dr. Howe grew restless in Rome waiting for his child to be born. Every evening he went horseback riding on the Campagna with Annie and rejoiced in her fine horsemanship and "the bright hue of her

[once] pale cheeks." Annie's restored health "and Julia's happiness compensate me for what otherwise I could not endure," Dr. Howe said — "the comparative loss of my time." Among Julia's own Bond Street contemporaries she had never met a man who minded having nothing to do. Before long, " a year without work is too much for me," Dr. Howe confessed. But he found a solution: "I am now engaged in getting up a school for the Blind here." He met with many difficulties, including a suspicion of his motives, but finally succeeded in having a few blind children of kindergarten age come to his apartment daily. Dr. Howe's glimpses of the excessive poverty that went hand in hand with wealth, and the indifference of the wealthy to the plight of the poor, disgusted him with Rome.

But Rome was a world in itself which contained within it many worlds — a universe in miniature. While Dr. Howe was discovering the world of poverty, Thomas Crawford was leading Louisa Ward into the world of art. Confidingly she followed and together they shared his enchanted Rome of classic sculpture, Renaissance grandeur and modern endeavor. A visit to a museum would be followed by an hour's call at Crawford's studio. When they left the old palace it was to go to the Pincian Gardens where bright new carriages were driven up and down and ladies' parasols looked like a circling rainbow. For propriety's sake, Annie Ward went along, just as her Aunt Eliza Cutler had once done — only now when they sought out the highest hills it was not a glimpse of Boston harbor but a view of St. Peter's dome which they admired. This was a splendid idea — to show Louisa all the famous views of Rome, Thomas Crawford discovered. While she obediently looked into the distance, he could study her perfect profile. What poise she had — what unconscious elegance to the tilt of her head! Or was it the modeling around her eyes that made her so beautiful? Little Annie watched them both and smiled.

But Thomas Crawford must work at night if he dreamed away the daylight hours with Louisa. He had "recently received an order from Perkins for $3000 to execute something chosen by himself." This was probably James Perkins, wealthy Boston art critic, whose son, "Charlie Perkins," was in Rome, a frequent visitor to the Howes' apartment. Charles C. Perkins was studying art and they said that he could have been a good painter if he had not been so well off. In any case, Perkins's money was well spent, from Crawford's point of view. "I always know when he [Crawford] has been at work all night," Dr. Howe said, "for he comes to us with bloodshot eyes and flushed cheeks, while his hands are cool." The Doctor read Crawford a long lecture on the care of his health — which the artist did not heed.

On March 12, 1844, Dr. Howe wrote joyfully to Sumner: Thanks be to God, Julia is safe and I am the happy father of a little girl." Theodore Parker, the great Unitarian preacher and future antislavery crusader, was in Rome and the Howes asked him to christen their child. She was to be named Julia for her mother, and her grandmother, and since little girls were rarely called "junior" — or "third" — and since she was born in Rome, they were calling her Julia Romana. A quizzical gleam came into Dr. Parker's eyes. When the Howes returned home they would in due course have a son, he supposed. Would they then want him christened "Samuel South Boston?"

Samuel Gridley Howe had never been so happy. "Dearest Charlie," he wrote, "would that you were here right now, — your straps unbuttoned, your waistband also, your feet in my red slippers, a glass of Orvieto in your hand, your sweet smile on your lips, — just as you used to sit in my easy chair of a Saturday night. . . . Julia has gone to bed with her dear charge, dearer to her and to me every day. . . . The girls too have retired and I linger for a word with you. If I, unworthy sinner that I am, enjoy this much happiness, how much more would you, whose affections are warmer, whose nature clamors louder for sympathy, whose heart is more tender. Do you know how I feel? . . . As if I had gotten into Paradise and left my best friends outside." But Charles Sumner would see them all soon. They were coming home.

It was springtime in Rome and from the gardens of the Barberini Palace the wistaria sent waves of perfume over the high stone wall into the narrow street. Thomas Crawford and Louisa Ward saw no beauties now in ancient Rome more wonderful than the new beauty in each other. They came hand in hand to Dr. Howe. They were in love. They were going to be married.

This should have been the right moment for the announcement and in many ways it was. Dr. Howe was a most happy father and he had become increasingly well impressed with Thomas Crawford. He knew that Louisa had been engaged at least twice before but this time she had found a real man and never before had anyone seen such a light in her eyes. "I could not help congratulating her heartily," Dr. Howe said. Thomas Crawford wrote to Louisa's Uncle John Ward, not asking for her hand but announcing their intention to marry at once.

But it was not thus, in a foreign land and without the consent of her guardian, that a Ward heiress could be married. Uncle John wrote a fiery letter forbidding the match. Dr. Howe received a blast reminding him that he was supposed to see that Annie and Louisa "formed no lasting attachments" and should have prevented this disaster. In Uncle John's vocabulary, the words "artist" and "impecunious" went together.

The Howes set out on the long journey home by way of Paris and London, taking Annie and Louisa with them. Crawford was not a man to take no for an answer and he followed. In London there were more letters waiting for the Howes. "We had a hurricane last night blown straight across the Atlantic from New York and bowing all our heads while it prostrated poor Louisa," Julia said. "They are very unwise people, those in Bond Street and take the means to favor the very thing they wish to retard. Crawford is in Paris but will be in London in a day or two. He will be in a tempest too, if they give him Uncle John's letter." The Howes, between them, had just barely prevented Louisa from marrying Crawford in Paris. Now they managed to make her promise to wait until she got home and had a good talk with Uncle John. Crawford would sail for the United States at once and it was decreed that he should not sail on the same ship as the Howes. He was going to have it out with Uncle John Ward, he said, and they were all a little afraid of Crawford's hot temper. Yet ardor in a lover is hardly a fault.

Heading her letter Paris and dating it March 30, 1844, Louisa replied to a letter from her Uncle John.[2] "And do you look forward to our return with a great deal of pleasure, dear uncle, and are you happy that I am going to stay the next year and a half with you instead of passing it in Rome? I too am happy sometimes, that I am to be married where I was born and where I hope to die. I will not say anything to you about Crawford. You will know him soon enough, only whether you like him or not, dear uncle, you must in no way endeavor to break off my engagement, for indeed I cannot again be launched upon the wide waters of affection without an object — and such a one I shall not easily find again. But enough of this, for we shall soon talk things out face to face and we shall understand them better.

"And now let me thank you for your kindness in fitting up Number 8 so conveniently, as Sam writes you are doing. Perhaps you will not care to have me with you — I should be very sorry, dear uncle, if such should be the case, for Annie would not stay where I am not wanted.

Yet I can find pleasant homes elsewhere, either with Jule or Sam or I can go to housekeeping. But surely you must love me. You have always loved your dear little Lutie so very much — and I can always *make* you love me as much as I please. I have written you a great deal of nonsense, dear good little uncle, but you, in your letter today, begged me to write."

Thomas Crawford reached the United States ahead of the Howes and Louisa Ward. He paused in Boston, therefore, to see friends and gather in a pocketful of commissions. Friends of both the Wards and Crawford were taking sides like spectators at a tournament. Some of the spectators, Charles Sumner, for example, insisted on entering the lists in favor of his champion, thereby damaging Crawford more than he helped him. The Longfellows were more tactful. They asked Crawford out to Cambridge to dinner and to spend the night. The colonial mansion on Brattle Street, where Longfellow had long been a lodger, had been bought by Fanny Appleton's father and given to the Longfellows as a wedding present. Craigie House had been done over exactly to their taste and in this most beautiful of homes, Fanny sat down to write about her husband's friends and how she made them welcome. It was September 13, 1844.[3]

"Crawford dined and passed the night with us and has just returned to Boston." Mrs. Longfellow had been most curious to see the artist for she had seen his "Orpheus" at the Athenæum. "At first he [Crawford] rather suggests the country school master which Hillard took him for," Mrs. Longfellow admitted. But he "improves like all good things, with time. He appears to have a very energetic character and I should think would mold the yielding Louisa as easily as his clay — but will she stay in any fixed shape and is he not subject to a cruel ordeal in his present position here?" Mrs. Longfellow rather underestimated Thomas Crawford. "I cannot help feeling anxious for him, as he has an ardent and sensitive nature — and he knows his own mind better than she does, I fear."

Crawford left with the Longfellows a copy of "the engraving" of a proposed statue of Washington which he had "modeled in case it should be wanted. It is simple and dignified and the dress is military and yet not a uniform — would satisfy all tastes very well — a cannon and balls are behind his feet — one hand touches his sword and the other holds a scroll, the Declaration of Indepence. It is dedicated to Mr. Sparks." Thomas Crawford had come to the United States to claim a bride but it was like him to bring along proof that he could produce a public monument designed to "satisfy" everyone — and just in case it should be needed. This business acumen should have pleased Uncle John had he known about it — and if he had been in any mood to be pleased.

On the way home from Europe with the Howes and her sister Annie, Louisa had met Arthur Mills, an Englishman, son of Colonel Dudley Mills and a young man "of good family, highest qualities, gentleness and charm." Naturally enough, he had fallen desperately in love with Louisa during the long voyage. He was in every respect the opposite of the tempestuous Crawford and when he made his appearance at Number 8 Bond Street he looked to Uncle John like the answer to prayer.

The fact that Howe and Sumner sponsored Crawford only strengthened Uncle John's championship of Mills. Charles Sumner had written a letter in behalf of Crawford accusing Louisa of being "vacillating" and her brother Francis Marion took up the gauntlet for her. "I cannot tell you how much displeased I am with Mr. Sumner's remarks," he wrote to Dr. Howe. "I cannot think of such interference with any patience. Please let me know as soon as possible whether these learned opinions of Sumner's have been given by request or volunteered by him. Your letter to Sam today [October 14] speaks of 'curses not loud but deep' and I feel sorely tempted to come on and change the snarl of these kind friends to a howl — damn their souls."

Hating quarrels as she did, Louisa had no choice. She went into a decline in the most approved fashion for young ladies in trouble over love affairs. Naïvely, Francis Marion said that Lou was weakened by Dr. Mott's treatments — although her cough had loosened and the doctor was quite confident he could "affect a cure." Good news was that "for the last two weeks, Uncle and Sam and Annie have abstained from the subject of C. entirely."

But the best news of all for Louisa was that by October 23, Thomas Crawford had arrived in New York — not for the first time but this time determined not to be put off any longer. He walked down Bond Street where some of his best work as a stonecutter's apprentice still graced the parlors at The Corner. Number 8 Bond Street could have contained some of his marble maidens, for it was built in 1830, John Ward being the third owner. Thomas Crawford had come a long way since the days when he worked for Launitz and Frazee and the Wards had been their richest clients. Now the apprentice had come to marry the Ward heiress, and he meant to have her.

As soon as Thomas Crawford appeared, Louisa Ward began to have second thoughts about a decline and early death. Her family behaved very well when it came to a showdown. "We are keeping her quiet and calm and amused," Marion said. "C. is a constant visitor. He spent Sunday evening with us — and could not have been more politely entertained were he a crowned head.

"That he is poor, perhaps of humble origin, obliged to remain abroad for some years to come, are not to me objections," Francis Marion said — "provided his positive qualities ensure Lou's happiness and comfort." At least, the whole Ward family were able to concede that Thomas Crawford had "positive qualities." Louisa's cough miraculously vanished, her strength returned and she set her wedding date — November 2, 1844.

Dr. Howe warned his friend Crawford about the "ante-nuptial agreement." It proved to be identical with Julia's, but there was no trouble over it this time. Louisa gave her uncle power of attorney to handle her affairs in this country and Crawford made it clear that he felt competent to support a wife and that her money was her own affair. With the commissions he had already received and those in his pocket, he could afford all the sugar-white marble he needed; his capacity for work was unlimited — his creative imagination was the capital he could depend upon though banks should fail. Even John Ward, broker, was impressed with this kind of artist.

It was an evening wedding at the home of the bride's guardian, Mr. John Ward of Number 8 Bond Street. Never would Bond Street see a happier or more beautiful bride. Louisa wore a crown of flowers, small in circumference and set at the back of her queenly head. Fastened to the back of the little crown was a lace veil, concealing yet revealing her white shoulders.[4]

Julia was at the wedding but Annie was the bride's only attendant. Once more the Reverend Benjamin Clarke Cutler came over from Brooklyn to perform the marriage ceremony for the second of his Ward nieces, and Annie told how "well" Louisa "behaved and how beautifully" she "looked." But Louisa herself said that there was "one thing that Annie could not describe, and that is my real happiness."

Thomas and Louisa Crawford planned to go South on their honeymoon. In Savannah, they would visit the aunt for whom Louisa was named, Mrs. Matthew Hall McAllister, and it was to her cousin, Julian McAllister, now a student at West Point, that Louisa wrote telling of her wedding and her plans. She promised to send him news from home; but the bride and groom went first to Hamilton Grange.[5]

This estate in the country overlooking the Hudson would eventually be cut through by 141st Street. Here Alexander Hamilton had built a mansion and planted a group of thirteen trees to represent the states of the Union. Across the smooth lawn to the river, Hamilton walked on that fatal morning of July 11, 1804, to his rendezvous with death. Sam Ward had just acquired Hamilton Grange and it was in the old mansion that Louisa began her life as the wife of an artist. Every morning, her husband set out for New York to make contacts and solicit work in portraiture.

Thomas Crawford excelled in the art of modeling portraits in clay — later to be put into marble. They were sensitive, poetic, and somehow the individual personality of his sitters managed to survive the coldness of stone. There was nothing funereal in the bust of Charles Sumner, for example — it was lively and intimate. The Sumner bust, modeled in Rome, remained in plaster for several years, but in 1839 Crawford "had it put into marble and sent it to Sumner's mother." While it remained in Crawford's studio, it bore mute but eloquent testimony to what the young sculptor could do and when it arrived in Boston, Sumner brought everyone to see it who could possibly wish to be similarly immortalized. While staying at Hamilton Grange, Crawford acquired New York commissions for a bust of Mathias Bruen, wealthy China merchant whose granddaughter had been one of Louisa's schoolmates. "Miss Schermerhorn" consented to be done in marble; and Philip Hone, whose daughter was Mrs. John J. Schermerhorn, made the following entry in his diary for December 28, 1844:

"I presided this evening at a meeting at the Astor House for a number of gentlemen, the object of which was to raise $10,000 to send Mr. Crawford the sculptor to Kentucky to take a cast of Mr. Clay and to execute a statue in marble of that noble but ill-used patriot."

Thomas Crawford now had traveling expenses for himself and his bride. They could soon start southward on their honeymoon.

While Crawford was at work in New York, Howe and Sumner were busy in his behalf in Boston, circulating a subscription for a Crawford bust of Josiah Quincy, President of Harvard. The Ward brothers, Sam and Francis Marion, were asked to put down their names. Francis Marion answered characteristically: "I am fully aware of the importance of giving Crawford a start and will gladly join you in a subscription for the bust of Quincy. Now I would, as far as I am concerned, gladly give you a handsome sum for any other purpose than the one you name — for I have a most inveterate dislike for old Quin, who once accused me in no very measured terms of riotous and disorderly conduct . . . after a supper party. Not but what he was perfectly right, as to facts, but he took such a view of them . . . that I never intend to forgive him. So you may put down $100 for me under Sam's name, adding of course what he intends to give himself. It may be all wrong, Doctor, but I cannot screw myself any higher."

"Pray let me know when to expect Lou," Julia wrote, from her new home, the "Doctor's Wing" at Perkins Institute. Annie had already arrived and the three sisters were to have a last reunion before Louisa sailed for Europe. There was one old friend in Boston who would find that it took courage to meet Louisa Ward now that she was Mrs. Thomas Crawford. Julia dined with the Thomas Wren Wards and found this out. "John came up to me and talked and asked when Mr. and Mrs. Crawford were to come. Poor fellow, he had overtaxed his strength and was forced to turn instantly away. It touched me to the heart, and looking at his pale face, I felt with some bitterness that Lou had done him a lasting mischief." Julia seemed to have forgotten how rapidly the hearts she herself had broken managed to mend.

By July, Louisa, Annie and Julia were together in South Boston while "Crodie" went daily to Cambridge to model Mr. Quincy and then later to Salem to do, under the direction of a Salem lady, a portrait bust of her deceased husband. There were boat trips and picnics — a "fishing frolic" to Cohasset for the girls and Dr. Howe. And then all of a sudden, the summer was over and it was time for the sisters to separate. "The only sadness in my life," said Louisa, "is parting from Julia and Annie." Those two, with her "dearest Crodie" made up all the world to her.

All the portrait busts in clay had been cast in plaster and then tenderly packed in straw and crated to go to Rome to be put into marble. The many crates attested to the success of Crawford's stay in the United States and it might seem as if the young couple would begin their life in easy circumstances. But although fees were fairly high, payment came in installments, one when the cast was done, another when it went into marble and a third payment upon delivery. Costs must be met all the way, with freight charges among the heaviest, and there was always the risk that a dissatisfied patron might break his contract and refuse to pay installments. The Crawfords were grateful when Uncle John Ward gave Louisa a bank draft for five hundred dollars as a farewell present. Julia predicted that Louisa would spend the money for clothes in Paris, but "Contrary to your predictions, Dudy dear," Louisa wrote, "I have bought only a hat and a shawl and a plain mousseline de laine dress." She was saving her money to furnish a home — and they were expecting a child.

There was one luxury which Thomas Crawford insisted upon. The public diligence from Paris to Châlons took thirty-four hours. Louisa must have a private carriage, and one with springs! From Châlons they would take the boat to Avignon, the diligence from Avignon to Marseilles would have to serve, and then a boat again to Rome. They had with them McDonald, Louisa's maid, a dog named Cato, a bird in a cage — and a mountain of luggage. But they reached Rome safely, early in December, and Louisa was delighted to find that they could have the old quarters in the Via San Niccolò da Tolentino.

"You cannot imagine how comfortable the old rooms are," Louisa said. It was December 4 and she thought that perhaps the next time she wrote it would be "of myself and baby too."

Among the first to greet the young couple was George Washington Greene, Louisa's cousin and Thomas Crawford's friend and benefactor. Taking Crawford aside, Greene explained that he was embarrassed for money and that a loan of a few hundred dollars would be appreciated. What could Crawford do but agree — in fact he was more than happy to help. But soon Greene needed more and still more money.

"I suppose you will hear very exaggerated accounts of Greene's flight to Paris," Louisa wrote on December 17. "He was obliged to make off with himself and his family, Monday night. His debts and creditors have been becoming very burdensome, and as he could not climb on Crawford's shoulders any more, and as Charlie began to resist his frequent demands for cash, he found it safest to run, and has left his library to be sold and pay off old scores as far as the money will go. It is, I assure you, a most disgraceful thing and will injure the American reputation in Rome. . . . We are too thankful he is gone, however, for he has been a constant annoyance to us since the first day we arrived in Rome. He seemed some evil genius in our path, crying gold, more gold, and never once thanking one for assistance rendered." But Louisa was ever gentle and forgiving. "I would not trample on a fallen man," she said. "Let him go in peace." Poor Greene spent most of his time in Paris not so much "trying to get some employment," as Louisa assumed, but in writing pathetic letters until Sumner, Longfellow and Felton raised money to get him home, where he made a new start and began his historical writing. A plaster cast of a bust of George Washington Greene by Thomas Crawford — hollow-cheeked and interesting — came to rest in Longfellow's study at Craigie House.

"We of course shall not get back a penny of all the money C has been lending him [Greene] in years past," Louisa said. But already she was looking forward and not back. "Can nothing be done about the Equestrian statue in Washington?" she wondered. The city of Washington was in the process of being adorned with monuments, and although Crawford had left engravings of his design among his friends, Sumner had yet to become a Senator and Louisa's brother Sam had not begun his reign in Washington as King of the Lobby. Yet influence was needed, as Louisa knew. "I fear me much that Powers or someone else will get the order away from the good Crodie and I must say I think he deserves it," she wrote. "And it would at once make his studio *the* studio in Rome, for no one has had an Equestrian statue to make since Canova and Thorwaldsen and it is here considered a great honor."

Hiram Powers (whose competition Louisa feared), although born in Vermont, grew up in Cincinnati and acquired both fame and skill as a maker of waxworks for Dorfeuille's Western Museum. He was nearly ten years younger than Crawford and before coming to Europe he had "taken likenesses" in Washington, making useful acquaintances as well as good portrait busts. He had a gift for publicity and he was now living in Florence where he headed a rival American art colony not to be underestimated by the American artists in Rome. In his portrait work particularly, Hiram Powers deserved his fame. But Louisa need not have worried, for the "Washington Monument" finally turned out to be an obelisk and all the American sculptor rivals could agree in condemning it.[6]

Crawford would get his "Equestrian" but he would have to wait. There would be triumphs and disappointments as for most young married people, with quiet happiness outweighing all else as they spent evenings, Crawford "with his books of engravings," Louisa with her sewing. "We do not talk much but we are silently happy," Louisa said. And in the daytime, while her husband was at his studio, Louisa passed some hours at the piano with old music books, or she walked as far as the church of Santa Maria degli Angeli with old Cato, the big black dog brought from America for company.

Louisa was "seated at the foot of one of the Egyptian columns" in the old church one day, when "in came the Emperor of Russia and the whole of his suite. The Emperor passed me," she said, "honoring me with a most complimentary stare." But she was anything but pleased. "I would I could have looked the vexation I felt at him," she said. The Emperor had just given a large order, "for the amount of 411,000 dollars," to an Italian sculptor "and he drove right by" Crawford's studio without so much as getting out of his carriage and coming in. "And I, like a dutiful wife, cried very much indeed," Louisa admitted, "not for the money but for the honor. You are proud when people come to see your husband and sad if you think he has been overlooked."

It was not until February, 1846, that Louisa was strong and well enough to write of the birth of her first child. There had been no doctor in attendance, only the *levatrice* or midwife, and Louisa was in labor for fifty-two hours. Small wonder that she had "fallen into a kind of lethargy" and had not been expected to live. But now all that was forgotten and Louisa remembered only "the exquisite joy" of hearing her child's voice. They had named the baby Annie, for Louisa's younger sister. The little girl was delicate, "did not cry yet never seemed to sleep" and in temperament would prove as unlike her aunt Annie Ward as any child could be. But her mother was never lacking in love and patience.

"My life is a truly happy one," Louisa said. "Have I not the kindest, most devoted husband and the most lovely, fair baby . . . ? God gave me a happy heart."

CHAPTER TWELVE
Royal Bordentown

UNCLE JOHN'S double parlors at Number 8 Bond Street had now been the scene of two weddings. Two of the Ward heiresses had been launched upon the sea of matrimony with a suitable amount of champagne and also with preliminary fireworks. Uncle John would surely have liked to breathe a sigh of relief and start planning a dinner for the Hone Club — composed of men only. But there was still "little Annie."

Even Louisa assumed that Annie would enjoy a spinsterish sort of life, as she wrote from Rome that her sister must be sure to accept the two kittens someone had offered and have them brought upstairs to the back parlor of a winter's evening to amuse her "with their antics." Uncle was to go down the street to get "Cousin Annie," his brother's maiden sister-in-law, to come and spend the evening at Number 8. They were to have the teakettle brought upstairs from the basement kitchen along with the tea things because "it is so pleasant to hear a kettle singing on the hearth." Miss Anne Hall, little Annie and Uncle John would gather around the center table after tea and look at books of engravings brought home from Rome. Louisa Crawford, happily married and in her own apartment in Rome, could afford a pang of homesickness as she conjured up the charming scene.

Miss Anne Hall had come to New York when her sister Eliza married Henry Ward, in 1818. Her sister Abby Maria married William Greene Ward in 1830 and Miss Anne, living with first one sister and then the other, had painted miniatures of all the Wards — particularly the children. She was the first woman to become a member of the National Academy of Art, and she deserved the honor — as her many charming miniatures proved. She had a decorative gift, fragile blue morning glories being almost a signature. Her designs for Bible School

certificates, showing angel children, proved popular and she would
certainly enjoy the engravings from Rome and perhaps also the company of Uncle John, remaining Ward bachelor. But Uncle John and
"cousin" Anne Hall could hardly be considered gay companions for
Annie Ward, who was not quite twenty-one.

So far, only a major with a German-sounding name had the temerity
to call on Annie — and risk meeting Uncle John. Julia observed a typical scene when she came to visit soon after Louisa's wedding, and she
put it into dramatic form for Annie's amusement.

Major Tochman, a gentleman who wrote, lectured, and was musical,
was calling and the scene was a room at Number 8 Bond Street. There
were sounds of a piano. "At the last line of the duo, the door opens,
Uncle John enters." Annie and the Major "start back — all three stand
silent for a minute. Uncle John clears his throat. Tochman fidgets.
Annie sighs. . ."

UNCLE: (*holding out his hand without looking at the Major*): How
d'ye do, sir.
MAJOR (*shaking it eagerly*): Very well, very well Mr. Ward, I thank
you. (*Another long pause.*)
UNCLE: Well, Nan, and who has she seen today?
ANNIE: Oh, dear Uncle, I have seen Aunt Henry and Aunt Eliza and
Aunt Maria and Aunt Gertrude.
UNCLE: H'm. Very warm day, sir.
TOCHMAN: Yes, Mr. Ward, very hot, very hot, sir! (*A long pause. John
brings in dinner.*)
TOCHMAN: I stay too long, sir, I must go, sir, good afternoon, Mr.
Ward, good afternoon Miss Annie.
UNCLE (*reluctantly*) Won't you stay to dinner?
ANNIE: Do-o-o-o stay, Major Tochman.
TOCHMAN: I don't know, sir, I am very busy, sir, but since you are so
kind, Mr. Ward. (*They sit down. Tochman eats heartily, looking at
Annie between every mouthful. Annie, confused, picks a little bread
to pieces but does not eat.*) [1]

In June, 1845, Annie visited Julia who was expecting her second
child. The faithful Tochman followed, being an acquaintance of Dr.
Howe's and having negotiated an invitation to visit Perkins Institute
from the unsuspecting doctor.

Dr. Howe's troubles began again although now he must have reflected with satisfaction that there was only one more unmarried Ward
heiress who could be placed in his care. Dating the rough draft June 27,

1845, Dr. Howe set to work, scratching out and rewriting lines of a most difficult letter. "My DEAR MAJOR, Before I knew Miss Annie's sentiments, I told you that I should never interfere to prevent her accepting any man whom she deliberately chose, even though he were a Turk." [2]

Looking at the last word he had written, Dr. Howe paused. Everybody knew how well the Chevalier Samuel Gridley Howe, champion of the Greeks, liked Turks. Perhaps the expression was a little too strong. He struck out "Turk" and started over: "I never offered you any other encouragement." Annie had just come to her brother-in-law's office at Perkins, holding in her hand a letter from Tochman "which she said she did not wish to open or answer." Dr. Howe was firm with her. "She was induced however, to open it out of respect to you," he told the Major. "She then asked me to take it and answer it as I thought proper.

"Having learned from her, that she does not and never did entertain the slightest partiality for you, and that she positively declines any correspondence with you, I must, as her brother, beg you not to pursue this course any further."

Poor Major Tochman! This was not all. Annie did not even know what she had done with the copy of his "lecture" he had lent her, nor with his letters which she wanted to return. They might be locked up in New York with some of her sister Lou's things, she thought. But if she ever found them she would send them back. Dr. Howe told Major Tochman that he "was sorry such an unpleasant termination" came to the Major's visit, but he made it clear that Tochman had better leave.

At the same time, a frequent caller at the Howes' study was suddenly conspicuous by his absence. Meeting Charles Sumner in Boston, Dr. Howe asked him why he came "so seldom." "With great meaning" Sumner replied, " 'Uncle John.' "

Back to Number 8 Bond Street went Annie Ward; back to singing teakettles, purring kittens and all the comforts of spinsterhood with which to await her twenty-second birthday. At 32 Bond Street, her brother Sam was living "very dashingly" as Mrs. Longfellow had predicted; but even there, Annie Ward was "Aunt Annie," for Sam and Medora had a son, born in 1844. His name was Samuel Ward. He would be the fifth Samuel Ward, poor child, but he would have little time either to live up to his name or live it down, for he died at the age of twenty-two. In 1846, Medora had a second son, named this time in honor of his mother's family — John Randolph Ward. Medora, who was so beautiful that according to *Harper's Weekly* she was "considered by New York artists as an incarnation of Aphrodite," was doubtless lovelier still as a young mother. Sam Ward, her proud husband, gave her diamonds and emeralds to be commented upon by the press along with her already famous sapphires.[3]

If life at Number 8 Bond Street was too quiet for Annie Ward, her brother's house at Number 32 went to the opposite extreme and was much too gay. Annie was welcome at all the parties. Medora, if not noted for firmness of character, was nevertheless amiable and willing to please if she could do so without too much trouble. She was willing to go shopping with Annie and help her choose becoming colors. But the contrast between the beautiful Medora and the shy Annie Ward was bound to be painful.

Annie's brother, Francis Marion, now in New Orleans, understood. He wrote hoping his "dear Puss" was "enjoying Society more" and "without feeling too much gratitude to the person with whom" she "might chat or dance." Along with this advice, Francis Marion sent a gift. "When Lucretia Jones was here, I commissioned her to buy for you a beautiful Havana muslin, which I hope has come safely to hand. I have also written to Medora to have it made up for you in the very most becoming manner."

Perhaps the Havana muslin had come to hand and Annie was wearing it when she met a new and most remarkable young man at her brother Sam's house. The young man was tall and slender and accounted by all to be most handsome. His silky reddish beard was clipped short, making his pink and youthful countenance the more guileless — an effect which was doubtless the opposite of what he intended. With him at Sam Ward's was "the Prince" — or Joseph Bonaparte, his friend and inseparable companion. The more princely of the two young men, however, was Adolph Mailliard of the silky chestnut beard.[4]

Adolph and Sam Ward were old acquaintances. They had met abroad when Sam was on his famous European tour and Sam had heard then that Adolph's father was the natural son of Joseph Bonaparte, elder brother of Napoleon. Ex-king Joseph Bonaparte died in 1844, leaving M. Louis Mailliard executor of his estate.[5] In 1846, Adolph Mailliard, as co-executor with his father and with power of attorney, came to the United States and to Prime, Ward and King — now Prime, Ward and Company — to consult Sam in connection with $162,951.51 worth of stocks and bonds held by the late King Joseph in America.

Point Breeze, King Joseph's American palace at Bordentown, New Jersey, now belonged to his grandson, Prince Joseph; but it was also Monsieur Louis Mailliard's home for life, under the will. There were apartments at Adolph's disposal.

Business naturally brought Adolph to 42 Wall Street, New York City, and pleasure led him to the home of the beautiful Medora at 32 Bond Street. This was, nevertheless, a most remarkable young man. Medora spoke "a flashing and trenchant French," which Longfellow had once complimented — but Adolph Mailliard preferred to talk to little Annie Ward. Her pretty French accent had been learned in earliest childhood from exiled French gentlefolk who came to Bond Street to teach her, and she had a still more rare accomplishment. She listened! Medora sang charmingly to the accompaniment of her own guitar and Adolph had a fine singing voice of which he was proud. But again — Miss Annie listened.

Before long, Adolph bent his steps to Number 8 Bond Street to sing to Annie alone. It must have seemed incredible to him that Annie was French only on her mother's side, and that by way of those early Huguenot ancestors in the Carolinas. Annie Ward looked more French than many a French girl. Her hair was very dark and she had succeeded in growing up to a rather large nose which, in childhood, had kept her from being called pretty — interesting though she always was. Her remarkably fine dark eyes had always been her greatest asset. The shyness which the extrovert Ward family deplored in Annie struck Adolph Mailliard as delightful. She had the manners of a French convent-bred young girl frightened yet fascinated by her first glimpse of the great world.

Adolph danced beautifully and knew how to kiss a lady's hand so that the American girls he met — accustomed to a manly handshake — nearly swooned with delight. Annie, even when she was an odd little pixie of a child, had always been graceful, and she danced as though the fairies had taught her — as well as the French dancing master who came to her father's house every week during her childhood. Perhaps, according to her brother Marion's idea, Annie showed too much gratitude when Adolph Mailliard chose to chat or dance with her. In Adolph's eyes, Annie's gratitude was only the proper tribute to his princely attractions. He found her irresistible.

Among Adolph's attractions was the fact that he was just out of prison. What other young man of Annie's acquaintance could say as much? Adolph [6] had been in Tuscany where he had indulged in a little plotting, presumably in behalf of some of those ex-royal blood relatives of his, forever trying to regain a lost throne. Tuscany, now under Austrian rule, was an excellent spot for a Bonaparte to start a revolt, provided the people could be persuaded that the freedom they wanted would come by means of a different dictator. This time, however, the Austrian rulers had been too much on the alert, the young man was thrown into prison and Adolph's father was very angry about the whole thing. He said that the Princess Zenaïde and her husband Prince Lucien must have been to blame; that they had gotten Adolph into jail and should get him out again. The Princess Zenaïde replied with spirit saying that it was the boy's own fault, that her husband could do nothing because her brother-in-law Prince Murat was having trouble with *his* conspiracy to seize the throne of Naples. It was a little different however when it was found that the Princess Zenaïde's son, Prince Joseph, was mixed up in the affair. Purses were slipped into the right hands, doors opened while heads were turned the other way — and Prince Joseph with Adolph Mailliard escaped to America — all in the best Bonaparte tradition.

Poor Uncle John Ward! Now when he heard music in the drawing room the caller was no tongue-tied Major with a German-sounding name. It was a young Frenchman more princely than a prince, with elegant manners and an air of having come to stay. Uncle John's little "Nan," instead of spending her time with elderly aunts, was making hot chocolate (not even honest English tea) for a young man who said no one ever made it half so well before.

It must have come as a surprise to Uncle John to learn that Adolph Mailliard was not born in France. His father and mother had come to America immediately after their marriage and Adolph was born in King Joseph's palace in Bordentown. But he never knew his mother. She died ten days after his birth, and all he had to remind him of her were some prettily painted wild flowers in water color — token of a gently bred young girl in a land where even the flowers were strange to her. When Adolph was two and a half years old, he was sent to France to his mother's parents and when still a small boy to French boarding schools and then to the Collège Henri Quatre. This was the education for a young man of fashion, and Adolph made the most of it.

At eighteen, Adolph was made his father's assistant. It was no fault of Adolph's if he failed to inherit his father's business acumen and if nothing in his education so far had prepared him to handle large sums of money in trust for the Bonapartes. Adolph was a charming companion for young princes, and he had an accurate eye in judging horses.

Of course Uncle John Ward's immediate reaction was a strong disapproval of Annie's choice. Yet in a remarkably short time he "became reconciled to the match" for Adolph had a way with him even when it came to the crusty old President of the Stock Exchange. Annie's brother Francis Marion heard the "Pidge" had "bright dreams" — and had "heard Mailliard well spoken of." Of course Sam favored the match with enthusiasm.

Charles Sumner wrote to Annie from Boston:

"I have just seen a young man with a fascinating smile, and a mild, genial manner, who takes a deep interest in you. I am told that you will receive with indulgence, the felicitations and benedictions which I am prompted to speed to you. I liked him very much, and in the short hour of a breakfast, learned to feel the sweetness, the amiability, the excellence of his character. His countenance is lustrous with beauty.

"As I write this note, at the desk by the window in the back drawing room, the smoke ascends from the red funnel of the steamship which is to bear him across the sea. May he return in good time, to make you happy in his love, as he cannot fail to be in yours."

This was high praise indeed and there was almost a note of relief in it all. Now Uncle John Ward could not say that the bachelor Sumner had designs on Annie.

Unfortunately, Sumner did not say where "across the sea" Adolph was going but it would appear from other letters that he and Prince Joseph Lucien had come from New York to Boston to catch the Cunarder bound for England and that Adolph, at any rate, went to his father on the business affairs of the Bonapartes. Perhaps, in true French fashion, he went also to ask permission to marry.

When Longfellow heard of Annie Ward's engagement, he too sat down to write, dating his letter March 6, 1846.

"I heard but two days ago of your engagement, and take the first moment of leisure to send my heartiest felicitations and my best wishes. I was at Julia's on Saturday. She was expecting the arrival of Monsieur Mailliard and his friend the Prince. The good Doctor was rather eager and restless; and insisted upon driving to town though it was late at night and the roads were bad, to see if the gentlemen had arrived. 'Why are you so anxious about the matter?' I said.

" 'Because they are friends of Annie,' was his answer; and this gave

me a suspicion of the truth though nothing more, for they kept your
secret well.

"Julia, the Doctor and Sumner all speak in the warmest terms of
Monsieur Mailliard. I have not had the satisfaction of seeing him, but
I am sure I should like him."

The following May, Annie went to South Boston to stay with Julia.
Her Adolph was on his way back to her, and again it was Longfellow
who looked on and wrote of Annie. On May 16, 1846, according to
Longfellow's diary, he went from Cambridge to Boston to do a few
errands and then, with his friend Felton, to the confectioner's shop in
Tremont Row. "Then we took ices at Mrs. Mayer's," Longfellow said.
"While seated at our little round table in the corner, Annie Ward and
Fanny Bruen joined us. Annie is looking for her French lover in the
steamer of Monday."

The wedding date was set for June 27 and for the third time the
Reverend Benjamin Clarke Cutler was summoned from Brooklyn to
perform the ceremony for one of his Ward nieces. For the third and
last time the double parlors at Number 8 Bond Street were decked for
a bride. Now, however, the Three Graces of Bond Street were not
together, for Louisa was far away in Rome. Julia faithfully wrote to
Louisa all the details that a sister would long to hear.

Annie's wedding took place in the morning. The bride wore "white
tulle, trimmed with lace which cost $200 or more. . . . Much presents,
splendid dresses," Julia said, calling her own dress "the most splendid
of all" because it was the one Louisa had sent her from Paris. Annie
was "very lovely in her wreath and scarf . . . graceful and poetic.

"Annie behaved beautifully. The company was gay and pleasant —
most of the guests stayed all morning and ate oceans of fruits and ices.
The *buffet* was very handsome in Weller's best style. At three o'clock,"
Annie "slipped off her wedding dress, slipped on a pretty dark silk, ate
a sweetbread and was handed into her carriage to go to the boat. Poor
Uncle cried bitterly as he put her in! Annie also cried but with very
sunshiny tears." Like the traditional third princess in the fairy tale —
little Annie had found her real prince at last. She was on her way to
royal Bordentown!

Curiously enough, no "ante-nuptial agreement" had been drawn for
Annie and no trust fund set up. There were therefore no wedding-eve
recriminations, but if Uncle John had trusted Dr. Samuel Gridley
Howe as much as he trusted Adolph Mailliard what heartaches might

have been avoided! Then Charles Sumner, as lawyer-best-man, could have raised no storm to trouble Julia's peace for years to come. And if he had provided no trust fund for Louisa, how surprised Uncle John would have been to discover that the artist, Thomas Crawford, was most reluctant to handle New York funds and real estate from a Roman studio. Uncle John had been a devoted guardian to his nieces and he had loved them all; Julia with her incurable flame of independence; Louisa with her confidence in his indulgence — and little Annie whom he might secretly have hoped to keep by his hearth forever. Now poor Uncle John made his final error in judgment as he turned over to Annie's husband all her funds as the law allowed.

A little over a month after the wedding, "Adolph Mailliard and his wife Anne Eliza" sold New York real estate, receiving seven thousand dollars, and within four years thereafter Adolph had realized 27,410 dollars in cash by liquidating his wife's holdings.[7] It was all in a good cause, for there was their magnificent Spring Villa in Bordentown to show for it, with its acres of formal gardens, the stables and the horses which made the Mailliard name famous on both sides of the Atlantic. What a delight it was to Adolph that his Annie rode so well! His first gift to her was a fine saddle horse.

Travelers from New York to Bordentown went by water to Perth Amboy, then overland by coach. Bordentown was a busy place for it was the port on the Delaware River for Philadelphia-bound steamboats. Within a few years after Annie's marriage, the Camden and Amboy railroad made Bordentown an important junction and the railroading Van Rensselaer family built a great square house on the bluff overlooking the river. Local ironworks supplied ornamental railings, wrought-iron trellises complete with iron grapes, and fences featuring sheaves of wheat for the handsome homes which were built in Bordentown's iron age of prosperity.

But in 1846, when Annie began to look upon Bordentown as her home, it had a Colonial charm not dependent upon the iron age. Brick houses, built before the Revolution, lined the main street, their doors opening directly upon the sidewalk; their formal gardens at the back hidden by high walls. The addition of wrought-iron balconies such as are usually connected with New Orleans, gave Bordentown a curious air of being both early American and French. Long before Annie Ward Mailliard ever saw it, Bordentown had actually been both French and royal.

Short streets ended suddenly, giving way to farms, and on the highest bluff overlooking Cross Creek, where it joins the Delaware, stood ex-King Joseph Bonaparte's fantastic palace. Point Breeze it was called; the first white wooden palace having been built about 1817 but later destroyed by fire. When Annie came to Bordentown, she saw the second house, a huge brick mansion stuccoed over and painted white, with columned entrances surmounted by balconies and approached by flights of marble steps. The mansion was built on an eighteen-hundred-acre estate, and surrounded by gardens laid out "in the style of the Escorial in Spain." King Joseph, having briefly occupied the Escorial, knew what he wanted. Gardens gave way to deer parks through which twelve miles of carriage roads and bridle paths wound their way — some of them connecting Point Breeze with Lake House, the white painted villa which King Joseph built for his two daughters, the Princess Charlotte and the Princess Zenaïde.

Across the public road from Lake House was a French boarding school for young ladies and this house Adolph bought — adding to it extensively and making it in every way deserving of its name, Spring Villa. The brook which ran through Adolph's formal gardens fed the royal lake across the road on which gondolas floated in summer and where in winter village young people were allowed to come to skate. King Joseph died in 1844, so Annie never saw him, but she was told how he used to come down to the lake to watch the skating and skid oranges and pennies across the ice for the youngsters to scramble for — a truly feudal scene.

Underground passages connected the princesses' villa with their father's palace, and at the foot of the bluff on Cross Creek another underground passage ran inland to the palace. A small ship coming from France could sail up the Delaware, enter Cross Creek and tie up at King Joseph's wharf. Then, sight unseen, a person could enter the tunnel and arrive secretly and safely within King Joseph's royal abode. It was generally believed that Joseph Bonaparte had planned all this for his brother, Napoleon. Joseph himself understood the art of escape and he never came away empty-handed. Goods of all kinds could also be carried, sight unseen, through the long brick-lined tunnels, and townspeople had it that there was buried treasure almost everywhere at Point Breeze.

CHAPTER THIRTEEN

Annie and Adolph

ADOLPH continued to act as his father's agent for the estate of King Joseph's heirs. As there were eight of these princes and princesses, all of them desirous of more money than even their extensive American investments could produce, Adolph's lot was not a happy one. He much preferred to raise race horses. It was a joyful occasion therefore when Adolph's father, Monsieur Louis Mailliard, arrived from France.

Annie gained a new and devoted friend in her father-in-law. Monsieur Mailliard was an old man with a most active life behind him and a longing for tranquillity, a garden and a chance to do a little hunting with dog and gun. Soon he would find a villa just outside of Paris to which to retire on the pension left him by his father, King Joseph. But meanwhile, it was delightful to discover that he had a pretty daughter-in-law who spoke French fluently, understood it perfectly — and had a talent for listening to an old man's tales.

Part of Monsieur Mailliard's purpose in coming to America was to superintend a sale of Joseph Bonaparte's household belongings for the heirs had little use for anything but cash.[1] There had been a sale in 1845, but when a second sale took place in 1847 Annie and Adolph bought furnishings for their own Spring Villa — with Monsieur Mailliard along to help them choose the choicest articles. As they walked through the echoing rooms at Point Breeze, it was not difficult for Monsieur Mailliard to recreate for Annie the days of bygone splendor.

A great hallway ran from front to back, dividing Point Breeze. Four doors, two on a side, led to the main rooms and Monsieur Mailliard remembered every picture on the now partially bare walls, every marble-topped table, every ebony chair. Had he not made the inventory in his clear, precise hand? He regretted that the painting by David, "Napoleon Crossing the Alps," was gone from the billiard room. "Paint me calm upon a fiery steed," Napoleon had said, and David had obeyed. But the painting had gone back to France and Monsieur Mailliard was sorry — he liked paintings of horses. *"La Toilette de Venus"* still ornamented the billiard room; a *"sujet galant,"* Monsieur Mailliard said, and he was amused to observe that it was a little too gallant for Annie. She blushed like a schoolgirl, married woman though she was, and surely Adolph had here a treasure of a wife. Chuckling, Monsieur Mailliard led her across the hall, through the library where Annie had a tendency to linger, and across the small antechamber to the great reception hall.

This was the climax the old gentleman had prepared, and Annie's gasp of amazement was his reward. Six great windows rose from floor to ceiling with pier glasses in gold frames between them. At each end of the room towered a carved marble chimney piece, legacy of Cardinal Fesch to King Joseph Bonaparte. A huge center table topped with black marble gave back somber reflections now that no lighted candles crowded the vast crystal chandelier above. A Gobelin rug with a medallion and portraits of the entire Bonaparte family had been protected from the moths by camphor and lay rolled up at the end of the room. Monsieur Mailliard advised strongly that Annie and Adolph acquire this treasure, and Annie fell in love with the blue merino, yards and yards of which had hung upon the walls of the great reception room. There was enough and to spare to make wall hangings and curtains for Spring Villa. They bought much more — so much in fact that the great Gobelin rug eventually went to Annie's sister Julia Ward Howe, to be hers and her children's delight for many years.

As Monsieur Mailliard, sitting in Annie's handsome drawing room, looked about him at familiar chairs and tables, paintings and bronzes, he could reflect that the past was not forgotten and that the future looked bright. Annie was expecting a child, and a grandchild was what the old gentleman most ardently desired. If he was disappointed, on April 2, 1847 — when the grandchild was a girl — he did not say so. She was named Louisa, for her mother's favorite sister, and this too was acceptable to Monsieur Louis Mailliard — but he was pleased when they gave the name the French form, Louise; and touched when he learned that the little girl's middle name was Marguerite in honor of her French grandmother who had died in a strange land so many years ago. Annie promised that their first son should be named Louis.

Not Louis but Joseph, Monsieur Louis Mailliard protested. Joseph in honor of the royal great-grandfather. When the time came, Annie compromised by calling her son Joseph Louis to please an old man who loved her. Meanwhile there was so much that Annie wanted to know about this strange family she had married into — and no one was more pleased to tell her than her father-in-law.

Everything semed to come right out of one of Annie's favorite romantic novels — including the way in which Bordentown, New Jersey, came to shelter Bonapartes. "The Emperor, unrolling a map of the United States, in the presence of Joseph, placed his finger upon a spot in New Jersey and said. . . . 'If I am ever forced to fly to America, I shall settle somewhere between Philadelphia and New York, where I can receive the earliest intelligence from France by ships arriving at either port.'" But the Bonaparte kingdom in America began to shape only "a few days after Waterloo" and by that time it was too late for the Emperor to profit by his plan. Napoleon had been captured and Joseph Bonaparte was in flight when he stopped for luncheon "in a hotel in the city of Blois." There he met James le Ray de Chaumont, son of a French nobleman who had loaned his personal fortune to the United States during the American Revolution. The debt had been paid in American land and Monsieur de Chaumont had been forced to become in effect a real estate agent in order to collect his patrimony. While the two men sat at luncheon, one of them with vast American acres for sale and the other with a sudden need to leave the country, "a train of heavily loaded wagons stopped under the windows of the hotel." King Joseph said that the wagon train was his and that the goods included "among other things, a great quantity of silver and jewels." [2]

James le Ray de Chaumont unrolled a map. He agreed to take the wagon train which King Joseph said was worth one hundred and twenty thousand dollars and in return he deeded to the former king 26,840 acres which seemed — at least according to the map — to be within easy access of New York and Philadelphia. Changing his name to the Count de Survilliers, from a village on one of his confiscated estates, ex-king Joseph Bonaparte made good his escape to the United States in 1815. But he was shocked at the size of the new country. The domain he had purchased was in northern New York State on the Canadian border, and eventually he took possession of it. Meanwhile, he settled in Philadelphia.

"King" Joseph was well received in Philadelphia, so the story went, until he met Anne Savage, daughter of a Quaker shopkeeper who sold him a pair of suspenders. The king, now the Count de Survilliers, then sold her the idea of becoming his mistress and he set up an establishment for her in the best Continental manner. Probably the ex-king of Naples and of Spain never did understand why Philadelphians were so shocked and indignant. According to his lights, he had treated the girl handsomely. Turning his back upon unappreciative Philadelphia, the Count de Survilliers bought the Bordentown acres and built Point Breeze. For Anne Savage, he built "a charming house called 'Rose Hill,' close by the estate." This was an episode which Monsieur Mailliard probably omitted to tell Annie.

Joseph Bonaparte's retreat from Waterloo was not his first flight and he had long since learned not to leave the field empty-handed. As King of Naples, he had done a good job administering the government and much against his will he obeyed his Imperial brother's command to assume the throne of Spain — for Spain was a trouble spot. It was said that he refused to go to Spain to become King unless the people wanted him. And so (as the story goes) Napoleon ordered money strewn in the streets of Madrid to ensure a large crowd and an enthusiastic welcome. The enthusiasm vanished along with the coins and eventually Joseph, with his unhappy wife, Julie Clary, daughter of a Marseilles silk merchant, left Spain in haste; in anger also — but not without newly acquired possessions.

Annie Ward's father and mother had once dined with King Joseph at Point Breeze and perhaps he showed them the room lined with cabinets where he kept his treasure — Spanish and otherwise.[3] He was fond of displaying to guests strange things they afterwards described — "clusters that looked like jewelled handles of swords, others like portions of crowns rudely broken off; others still like lids of small boxes; many were ornaments entire."[4] Then there was "the crown and ring" which Joseph had intended to wear "when king of Spain; also the crown, robe and jewels in which Napoleon was crowned." When their eyes were "sufficiently dazzled with the display of diamonds and emeralds," King Joseph would touch "another spring, which gave to view another set of drawers" in which he kept "many of Napoleon's valuable papers. . . . Treaties and letters were carefully bound round with ribbons and fastened with jewelled clasps."

It took Annie Mailliard a long time to piece together the story of the jewels, and it was her nephew, F. Marion Crawford, who finally wrote part of it down from various sources including his Aunt Annie's notes. Annie enjoyed most Monsieur Louis Mailliard's own experiences — especially the affair of the iron box. This treasure-hunting tale Annie wrote down for her children as nearly as possible the way their grandfather had told it to her.[5]

"It was a voyage of more than ordinary rigor," Monsieur Mailliard would begin, recalling his journey from America in 1817. The ship on which he sailed was dismasted off the coast of Ireland and "rolled helplessly in the trough of the waves." It was he who "first saw the reef." Crew and passengers gave themselves up for lost, but the ship struck during a falling tide and before it broke up Irish fishermen managed to row out from shore and all the people were saved.

Young Louis Mailliard journeyed on. He had been commissioned to call on Queen Julie, who was in Italy, and invite her to join her husband in Bordentown. But the "Countess," as it was now proper to call her, refused. She was not well, she said. It was her daughter "the vivacious Princess Charlotte" who came to Point Breeze, but not until 1821. And it was in 1823 that the Princess Zenaïde came to Bordentown with her husband, the Prince of Canino.

Ah, but the story of the treasure hunt! An old man remembers so much! Little Annie must understand that when King Joseph fled from Spain he bought himself a castle in Switzerland. He lived at the Castle of Pranguins until the "Hundred Days," when he joined his brother Napoleon in France. But it had seemed a wise idea to leave behind certain especially choice gems. They were put in an iron box and it was Monsieur Louis Mailliard's idea to hide them in the ground in a place in the castle park where he had seen a great number of foxes' dens.

When Monsieur Mailliard returned alone in 1817 and reached the village under the walls of the castle of Pranguins, he "deemed that caution would be necessary." The mayor of the village had been a friend of King Joseph. So after contacting the mayor, Monsieur Mailliard "disguised himself as a half-blind old man, harmlessly mad and seeking an imaginary coal mine in the grounds of the castle." He posed as an Englishman, unable to understand French or German — or to answer questions. The mayor would satisfy village gossips with the story trumped up between them.

And here Monsieur Mailliard would usually pause and sigh, looking at his daughter-in-law, little Annie Ward Mailliard, sitting there with her needlework in her hand, raising her dark eyes and begging him to go on. A young man disguising himself as old — it had seemed such an amusing idea at the time. Now he no longer needed to play the part.

But he remembered everything. He had gone to the place in the woods where the foxholes were. But the ground was covered with snow and nothing looked the same! He found his landmarks, or so he hoped, and marked out a square. For hours he dug — remarkable what strength the supposed old man had, probing the frozen ground with his crowbar, opening up a foxhole with his shovel. But he found no iron box.

The next day was Sunday, and the mayor agreed to come by in his carriage to take him to church — using a road near but not in sight of the foxholes. Then early to work went Louis Mailliard. He marked out another square and dug where foxes had been at work before him. He prodded with his crowbar — one last jab and he had struck something harder even than the frozen soil. Monsieur Mailliard was still struggling to get the iron box out of the ground when it came time for the mayor's carriage. He ran to a nearby knoll (forgetting his role of old man, it would seem) and waved and whistled. The mayor came to help and together they carried the box.

It always amused old Monsieur Mailliard to watch Annie's eagerness as she made him tell exactly what the box contained. Actually, the paper which young Louis Mailliard signed and gave the mayor as a receipt said only "sixteen precious stones, one of them square" and "three other packages." But when Monsieur Mailliard brought the jewels safely to America he listed them in a small paper-bound book along with the ultimate fate of each. This little book remained in Annie and Adolph's possession long after the jewels had left the Mailliards' keeping and their owners had gone the way of all flesh.

The little notebook, in Monsieur Louis Mailliard's careful hand, read in part:

1834: The two big diamonds, the white square and the black, have been sold to M. Aguado in Paris for 210,00 francs.

The great pearl, sold to Mr. Emmanuel for £700.

All entries were in French, the word *gros* being used to describe jewels much larger than merely *grands*. Not all the entries concerned sales of jewels. The "pink diamond" had been "given to Princess Charlotte in London and carried away by her." But Princess Charlotte had paid 100,000 francs for "the diamond necklace coming from Madame." Monsieur Mailliard's last entry was dated 1840 and concerned "the great emerald ring set with diamonds" which had been sold "to Mr. M. Laurière for £890."

Monsieur Mailliard had recorded many gifts to the family: an order of the Legion of Honor set with diamonds for King Joseph's brother

Jerome; family miniatures set with pearls — he could not now recall them all, although his daughter-in-law was always willing to listen. He took out the gold repeater from his pocket and gently touched the spring. A tiny chime told the hour. And the watch had been the gift of King Joseph, now dead. Had he told Annie about the watch? But the hour was late and he must go. It was a matter of pride with him to occupy his own apartments in the partly dismantled Point Breeze. His also to give to his son was the "farm of Grosville . . . containing 250 acres, more or less" according to the will of Joseph Bonaparte.[6]

Although looking forward to retirement, Monsieur Mailliard lingered in Bordentown. He wanted to teach his little granddaughter to speak perfect French, and perhaps he was waiting for his namesake, who was not born until June, 1852 — and was called " 'Poleon" for short. Adolph paid "too much attention to his horses," Monsieur Mailliard complained. But Annie made no complaint of any kind. She was a happy person.

Julia Ward Howe, coming to visit her sister Annie, was astonished by several things. Annie was "handsomer than ever before." And she was no longer even a little "afraid of her men servants"!

CHAPTER FOURTEEN
Sam Ward, Forty-niner

THE CORNER, home of Samuel Ward the banker, still stood on Bond Street and Broadway; a monument to solid industry and conservatism — though occupied by strangers. All of Samuel Ward's children had now left Bond Street with the exception of Sam, the banker's son and heir. Looking about him and noting all the changes, Philip Hone had something to say about his world of 1847 and about bankers as he had known them. In the early days, "proud and aristocratical, they were the only nobility we had. Now we have none."

The new generation, to which Sam Ward belonged, was proud to be sure — but only purse-proud. Walter Barrett, clerk at Prime, Ward and King, summed up Sam: "He drives fast horses." Sam was always under pressure to spend money and where his father saw a sound bank as a symbol of the integrity of a state and of a nation, Sam saw banking merely as a way to get rich. Sam was sure that there were ways of getting rich much faster than his father ever dreamed of — just as there were fast trotters to drive instead of dependable carriage horses.

It did not take Sam long to discover that his personal charm and powers of persuasion had their uses even in banking. There were younger men in the old firm now: Edward Prime had taken his father Nathaniel Prime's place — Deming Duer, son-in-law, and A. Gracie King, son of James Gore King, had come in and Sam was made a partner just before his father's death. Sam found he had a gift for making a speculation seem like a sure thing to his contemporaries and together they talked down the older men, a few lucky turns giving them unbounded confidence. Foreign exchange was the thing to play with. They were sure they knew when to buy or sell gold. It seemed of little consequence to Sam when James Gore King pulled out, taking his sons with him. There were a few high words, with Uncle John and William

Ward, associated stockbrokers, looking on anxiously, yet siding with their nephew.

The argument stayed within the office at 42 Wall Street and when Mr. King started a new firm, nothing was given out publicly except one significant statement: "A diversity of views as to the proper scope and business of the house, led in 1847 to its dissolution." J. G. King, under the firm name of James G. King and Sons, continued doing business in the old style of Sam Ward's father. Prime, Ward and Company added Uncle John Ward and Uncle William Greene Ward to their list of partners. Uncle John was the only pessimistic member of the firm.

Optimism was not all a matter of Sam Ward's imagination. The very air of New York crackled with it. Papers were full of the exploits of General Winfield Scott in Mexico — he was the national hero and reverses had yet to be met, the death toll counted. There was famine in Ireland but, with a wonderful feeling of warmth and generosity, Uncle John Ward and his friends gave up two of their regular Hone Club dinners and donated three hundred and sixty dollars, which the dinners "with fine wines" would have cost, to the fund for loading a ship with grain for Ireland. Irish immigrants arrived in the United States, wave upon wave of them. They had come to build railroads although as yet they knew it not.

In the autumn of 1847, George Templeton Strong, a much younger diarist than Philip Hone and one who had known the Ward boys at Columbia, noted that something was wrong with the bankers, Prime, Ward and Company. Heading his entry *September 7, Tuesday*, Strong wrote: "Prime, Ward and Company in serious trouble — nothing has saved them from a smash but King's personal exertions, which prevented a whole ream of bills from coming back on them. Very creditable to King, especially considering the circumstances under which he went out of the firm, and that he is now leader of a rival banking house. Common report says that Barings did the clean thing and accepted all the bills that were out. But I know of one batch ($15,000) that's come back. In the case of any other house, I should say the diagnosis was very unfavorable, but these people are strong enough to weather a good deal."

This opinion, that in Prime, Ward and Company there was strength, was based on the reputation of a great banker now dead. On Saturday, September 9, a letter had to be written to Dr. Samuel Gridley Howe:

Prime, Ward and Company have found it necessary to suspend payment — this is sad news to communicate to you. I will only add that neither Julia's nor Louisa's property are intermingled with my business.

I must retire from John Ward and Company. William Harryl will go in under the firm of Ward and Company.

WARD

Sam immediately resigned his trusteeship of Julia's inheritance, as did her Uncle John. Samuel Gridley Howe became co-trustee with James K. Mills, a Boston banker who also in due course failed. Dr. Howe had been fighting for control of Julia's money ever since their marriage. He distrusted and despised his brother-in-law, Sam, and now he had the satisfaction of having been right all along. The blow to Ward family pride was something he could not sympathize with, but it must have surprised him to discover how little happiness there was merely in being right.

Now the Doctor would demonstrate the proper way to handle money. He and Mr. Mills sold Julia's New York real estate; Bostonians both of them — they knew that upstart city could never expand as far as 64th Street, for example. Dr. Howe was sure that South Boston with its beautiful harbor views was the coming fashionable residential district and he bought lots all around the Institute on streets as yet to be laid out. His plan was to build and rent dwellings, but he found building costs higher than he expected so the land lay idle, producing nothing but taxes. Land values rose, nevertheless, and Longfellow wrote that Howe was making a good deal of money in South Boston real estate. Of course Julia Ward Howe was not consulted. She was just told where to sign her name.

The news of the failure of their father's firm was followed by a still greater blow to the Ward sisters. Their brother Francis Marion died in New Orleans of yellow fever — September 3, 1847. He was the brother, high-tempered to be sure, who nevertheless patched up his quarrels. "When we meet, Chev and I will smoke pipes, rub noses and be friends," he assured Julia after a particularly acrimonious exchange of letters concerning Louisa's engagement. He was the brother who encouraged little Annie to think well of herself, sending her a muslin in which, he said, she would look "sweet as a rose." He had been in love with a Miss Wadsworth of a famous New York State family, but at the age of twenty-seven he was still unmarried, and in New Orleans he wrote of good business prospects for the family firm. He was in good health and had a fine horse he loved to ride along the riverbank of an evening. News of his death reached his sisters before his last cheerful letters — so full of life. Now there was only one living son of Samuel Ward the banker: Sam Ward the bankrupt.

Julia went to New York to see her Uncle John. "I found Uncle in great agony and depression of mind," she wrote. "Poverty is little to him, but bankruptcy looks hideous and frightful. He has given up everything to his creditors. Prime and Ward is utterly broken up — they will hardly pay thirty cents on the dollar.[1] Sam has nothing left but his house which, being settled on Medora, cannot be touched. He bears up wonderfully, says he can work, will pay off all his debts and be well off someday.

"They are ruined by very extravagant speculations in flour and by holding a large amount of paper of houses which have failed in England. People blame Sam excessively as the author of these speculations." But Julia had talked to her favorite brother, who could always put her under his spell. She thought people were "unjust" and that Sam "was but one of three and Uncle and Prime, who knew him so well, should have looked after him sharply and restrained him."

At this time, Sam Ward was thirty-three years old but he agreed heartily that he should have "been looked after" and "restrained." "He says himself," Julia quoted, " 'I have committed a grievous error, but it was the business of these gentlemen to hold me back. I have done nothing to which they have not assented.' "

Sam had rented his house at 32 Bond Street for twelve hundred dollars a year. "It will be all his income for some time to come," Julia predicted — not as yet aware of Sam's unusual gifts. Medora had departed to her mother's home on Staten Island, where her mother made it clear that Sam Ward would not be welcome. Medora's mother was the one person in the world entirely impervious to Sam's charm and when Medora seemed inclined to continue to see him, she and the children were shipped off to New Orleans. Perhaps Medora never put up much of a fight. She was an excessively beautiful woman whose greatest charm was her acquiescence. But she did not give up Sam completely — she wrote him letters and sent him Longfellow's latest book of poems when it came out.

Under her mother's watchful eye, doubtless Medora took her famous jewels with her. Yet somehow, Sam Ward got together a small stake for a new venture. With creditors hot on his trail, the source of this capital was his own affair, kept strictly secret. Visiting in New York about a month after the crash, Dr. Howe noted the differing attitudes of his in-laws. "Poor Uncle John" was "deeply distressed," for daily he faced creditors such as small merchants who were friends of his, now ruined in his fall. But Sam's fertile brain was already alive with schemes for making a new fortune. Dr. Howe found "poor Sam, fidgetty and trying to be cast down!"

Since Annie had no trust fund set up for her, it is reasonable to suppose that when Prime, Ward and Company failed she lost heavily. But Annie was the one who now offered a shelter to the homeless Sam. She invited him to come to Bordentown to stay "for an indefinite time" and she "really felt proud of" her "good, kind Adolph when he seconded this proposal and added that he only wished it were in his power to help poor Sam in any way."

Sam was to go out daily with dog and gun as he had loved to do as a boy. "I am going to make him help me by reading German with me," Annie said, "and every time the gun is put up, *Wilhelm Meister* shall be brought out . . ." Thus Annie planned to bind up the wounds of the beloved brother whose pride was hurt to be sure, but whose optimism was not dead nor even sleeping.

Carrying his gun among the reedy marshes of Cross Creek, Sam planned his return to prosperity and his future triumphs as a child imagines the day when all who have punished him will hang their heads in shame and beg his pardon. Adolph had a room at Spring Villa where no one entered but himself and invited guests — as his sister-in-law Julia noted with slight rancor. Here, in the evening and at Adolph's invitation, came Sam Ward and his cousins, Henry and Ward McAllister — young men equally in need of a quick fortune. They talked far into the night. What plans were made, dismissed, and made again! What dreams began to assume reality! Gold had been discovered in California.

It was agreed that Mersch, the German student who had been Sam's secretary of late years and who shared Annie's hospitality, should set out for California by way of the Isthmus. But he would not carry with him the picks and shovels, the pans associated with gold digging. He would carry merchandise for which the miners would literally pay an equivalent weight in gold.

In December, 1848, the plans were revised. Mersch set out ahead, going overland; Sam and the McAllister cousins would go by way of the Horn. "Sam paid me a short, sad visit before starting for California," Julia said. She played the piano for him and they sang together the songs he had learned in Heidelberg and had taught her in happier days. Sam cried. "I do not even know now whether he has gone or not," Julia said on December 31, 1848. "It is a sad ending for him."

Sam had not yet left, but on April 6, 1849, he was in the Straits of Magellan and this was no "sad ending" but a glorious beginning of adventure, as he well knew. Although he expressed proper doubts and misgivings in his letter to Annie, Sam could not repress the rising of his spirits. He loved to travel and there never was a better traveler, for no opportunity escaped him. Going ashore at "Rio Janero" he paid his respects to Dom Pedro II, Emperor of Brazil. This audience Sam recalled to the emperor years later when previous acquaintance served his ends. Having made friends with the emperor, Sam sailed on, marveling at the seamanship of the ship's captain in making a landfall "as a rifleman hits a bull's eyes." The Straits Sam found "a singular region," where the perpetual snows, the clouds, "a rainbow variety of hues" delighted him. There was a "sunset surpassing Newport in its most brilliant evenings" and Sam could think of no higher praise. Cape Possession reminded him of Staten Island.[2]

Sam's ship was the side-wheeler *Panama*, making her first voyage to the Pacific. Passengers who had crossed the Isthmus came aboard the *Panama* on the Pacific side. Among these was Jessie Benton Frémont on her way to join her husband, the pioneer explorer and first (provisional) governor of California. He had been attempting to find passes across the Rockies and the Sierras for a railroad when gold was discovered on his California land. General Frémont was a controversial figure but of great importance in San Francisco, and Sam Ward had no trouble at all in being agreeable to his wife — about whose attractions there was no controversy.

The *Panama* arrived in San Francisco on June 4, 1849, burning her planking to keep up steam. And if Sam Ward might be said to have already burned his bridges — he was ready to build new ones.

Sam did not attempt to describe the Golden Gate and San Francisco Bay. They were unlike anything he had ever seen before — even Newport and Staten Island. There were days when the sky was blindingly blue, and the hills, improbably sharp and steep like scenery on a stage, seemed to move in close as though to tempt the uninitiated into a brisk climb that would prove fifty miles in length. The air, more exciting than the vintage wines Sam loved so well, went to his head. Then would come the heat haze and the hills would slip far away. Exposed earth upon their slopes, which had been red, now changed to rose; and once-green live oak blurred to blue like the soft fire and blue lights in an opal. An opalescent light bemused the senses till — almost mercifully — the fog came in. Sam was no artist, although he had friends who were. He was only rarely a poet but tried earnestly to be one, and so the magic site of San Francisco was not lost upon him. The tent and hovel city he saw before him was full of people, hungry for every commodity — and with gold in their pockets.

Almost immediately, Sam Ward became a member of the group that built and managed Long Wharf. Nothing was more needed than a good wharf in a harbor so deep that the longest anchor chain never reached bottom. Sam had every reason to expect success, and he got it. Next he went into partnership with Rodman M. Price to form a mercantile and auction house under the name of Ward and Price. This too prospered mightily, and with fantastic speed.

This is not to say that Sam Ward became a different person — all work and no play. Far from it. There were dances where "the girls spoke only Spanish" and where his cousin Hall McAllister "didn't have much fun" he said — but Sam spoke Spanish fluently. There were faro games where a man could lose every dollar, and poker games at the various so-called clubs where it was possible to come out ahead once in a while. Sam "liked cards but was not a winning player." He liked dealing with people better, and it struck him at once that in that city of tents there should be a ball given "in the best style of New York." Sam was the man to organize a really big affair. Since statuary was a prerequisite of elegance, Sam provided statues. He hired stevedores, "stripped and whitewashed them and had them hold aloft pitch pine torches" to light the great warehouse where the banquet and dance was held.

The story was that Sam also bought a beached ship and converted it into a hotel. The fact that he failed to mention this in letters to his sisters, to whom he wrote in rather pious vein, bears out tradition — that the hotel was not exactly prissy. There were girls of all sorts and Sam was broad-minded in the Parisian sense. His hotel was a big success while it lasted.[3]

Be it understood, however, that Sam was entirely on the side of the law. He arrived in San Francisco on June 4 and by the eleventh he had signed a petition for a mass meeting in Portsmouth Square to elect delegates to form a government for upper California. In July, Sam was among those citizens meeting on the Plaza to organize the "Law and

Order Party" to arrest the "Hounds," a gang of cutthroats who were terrorizing honest citizens. Sam was listed as a member of the First California Guard. Or, as Longfellow had once said, Sam was "as multifarious as ever."

As Sam Ward told the story, he was the one who set up his cousin Hall McAllister as a lawyer. Meeting up with a ship's crew who said they had been swindled by their captain, Sam brought them around to McAllister and, as of that moment, McAllister had a practice.

The Frémonts were settled in their new house just outside of town soon after Sam and his fellow voyager Jessie Frémont arrived. "Mr. Frémont bought a readymade Chinese-built house that fitted together like a puzzle. Pleasant men rode over constantly when the day ended, and in frontier fashion ate with us," Jessie Frémont wrote. She described the "keen, high vitality and the exhilaration of unexpected and great success" which added "their spur to the many charming men who had come out in quest of fortune and found it . . ." And "Sam Ward of epicurean fame, a most agreeable man" came often to see the Frémonts.[4]

Sam Ward's success in California was more exhilarating than most people's because of his recent humiliation in New York. But *he* had expected it. Had he not said he would soon be rich again? As profits from the auction house rolled in, he bought San Francisco real estate — not by any means for cash of course. Why tie up cash when it could be doubled again and again as he bought and sold on credit?

On January 1, 1850, Sam set out for New York, having made a fortune in California in about six months. Even his friend Mersch, the plodding German scholar for whom Sam had once tried in vain to obtain a professorship at Harvard, was listed in a volume called *A Pile*. Sam, by his own account at least, owned forty thousand dollars' worth of San Francisco real estate and "all told, made a quarter of a million dollars." He went home to New York to start a new banking firm: Ward and Price. Perhaps it was these days that people had in mind when they made the comment that "Sam Ward *strutted* — even when sitting down."

Sam sailed on the steamer *Oregon*, which had on board gold bullion which Bayard Taylor (a fellow passenger) described as "the most important which ever left San Francisco." Taylor thought it was worth "about two millions of dollars," and if this was an overestimate Sam Ward would never have been the one to contradict. Sam had gold of his own — nuggets which he would have made into ornaments for his sisters and for Medora.

The story which circulated afterward about Sam's return was probably apocryphal — yet typical enough to be true. He was said to have told an old prospector friend that he went at once to see his Medora. He arrived late at night. All were asleep, so he woke up Medora by flinging gold pieces at her bedroom window. This was without doubt the best way to awaken this most beautiful of women, and Sam and his Medora joined forces again — though briefly.

CHAPTER FIFTEEN

Flood Tide

THE flood tide which had led Sam Ward on to fortune would bring good fortune to his whole family as well — if he could so arrange it. Sam's sisters had stood by him in his days of disgrace and now he urged them to enjoy a holiday in Europe while he made money for them at home, in gold mines and California real estate. Annie and Adolph proceeded to sell most of the rest of the New York real estate left to Annie by her father. Why hang on to land in 34th Street, for example, when they could sell it for fifteen hundred dollars and brother Sam could buy them a California ranch complete with gold mine? Seven other transactions totaled around twenty thousand dollars. Now Annie and Adolph could enjoy a belated but splendid European honeymoon, and Adolph, while abroad, could buy pureblooded Jersey cattle and English fillies with which to improve his already famous Bordentown stock.

The Crawfords, Louisa and her husband and their two little girls, Annie and Jennie, were visiting in the United States during this fortunate year of 1850. Thomas Crawford had been most successful. The little apartment on the Via San Niccolò da Tolentino was a thing of the past, and the Crawfords had taken a ninety-nine-year lease on the Villa Negroni — "a great pile, golden gray with age, its enormous windows set four-square to the world, its topmost terrace open to the winds and commanding a view of the entire city below." [1] It stood on the outskirts of Rome and no one foresaw the day when a railroad station should take its place. Louisa and her sculptor husband lived literally like a prince and princess and Louisa longed to share her palace with her sisters.

Although the lucky year of 1850 had not yet begun, the times were already auspicious for an American sculptor with Roman training. Cities all over the country were emerging from the pioneer stage and there was wealth with which to gratify a newly awakened civic pride. The national capital was being decorated with all sorts of statuary, and provincial cities vied with each other in ordering public monuments to departed heroes. Boston, increasingly the "hub" of the universe and by no means provincial, led the way with Bunker Hill Monument. Horatio Greenough won this commission with his design for an obelisk he was said to have drawn while still in college. The choice of Greenough was fair enough, for he was born in Boston. But Thomas Crawford saw a trend which alarmed him as he attempted to arouse interest in his own design for an equestrian George Washington. "Pagodas, columns, arches, obelisks," had become the rage — Boston having set the style.

Thomas Crawford need not have worried but his annoyance was understandable. He wrote complaining of "conceited committee men who, with a sheet of paper and a pen" now had "the impudence to scratch down three lines and say, 'There's your monument.'" He had not much hope when, in Bordentown, he chanced upon a newspaper article about the competition sponsored by the city of Richmond, Virginia. The contest was almost over and there were those who said afterwards that Crawford worked in great haste. It was true that he worked at top speed because that was the way he always worked. He sent a sketch in just before the contest closed but he had been ready with his idea for the past seven years.

The big news came during the first week in February, 1850. Thomas Crawford had won the Richmond competition and a commission worth fifty-two thousand, nine hundred and seventy-five dollars. Sam happened to be visiting in Bordentown and his own triumphant state of mind only made him rejoice the more over Crawford's good fortune. It was an occasion for the best wines in Adolph's cellar to be brought forth, and amid toasts to success it was decided that Annie and Louisa should both go to Richmond with Thomas Crawford.

To Charles Sumner, his first patron and still his friend, Crawford wrote: "I have doubled the cape at last, thank God, and the rest of life's voyage promises an accompanyment of sunny weather."

The man who presented himself before the Richmond committee in no way resembled "a country schoolmaster" like the Thomas Crawford of six short years ago. His clothes were tailormade and supervised by Louisa's excellent taste. His fine linen handkerchiefs were a small luxury which delighted his sensitive artist's touch, and his children all remembered the aroma of the high quality cigars he smoked. The Viking mustache which adorned his clear-cut features gave him a more modern look than the equally handsome Adolph Mailliard's chin whiskers did. Thomas Crawford's eyes, however, remained his salient feature; their brilliant blue was always commented upon.

There were many details to be settled after winning the Richmond contest. While some papers were signed February 8, the final contract was not signed until June 27, 1850 — for "One equestrian group representing George Washington on Horseback, the portraiture and costume to be similar to that represented by Houdon's Statue of Washington, now in the Capitol of the said City, the group to be enriched with the proper introduction of gold on such parts of the costume as may require it . . ."

Richmond was taking no chances. In 1833, Greenough had produced a marble seated figure of Washington designed for the rotunda of the Capitol. He had attired the Father of his Country in a Roman toga which covered, moreover, less than half of what the well-tailored toga of Roman days would have concealed. Drapery hung from Washington's upraised arm, other covering had he none above his waist. When the statue arrived, it proved too big to go through the door to the Rotunda, which had to be widened. No sooner had the huge piece of marble been placed under the dome than the floor began to shake and the monument was "speedily withdrawn to the outside" [2] — or as speedily as that much marble could be moved. An uproar was already going up. What was George Washington doing, sitting around without any clothes on? Greenough, hurt and unhappy over this Philistine attitude, pointed out that this work, which he considered his greatest, was designed for "interior viewing." It still seemed to the simple-hearted American public that George Washington should not have been shown as though sitting in a Turkish bath.

Thomas Crawford was willing enough to dress General Washington. He further agreed to produce "One full length pedestrian statue of Thomas Jefferson and one of Patrick Henry." Later still, more "pedestrians" were requested, the delighted Richmond Monument committee adding General Andrew Lewis, George Mason, Thomas Nelson and John Marshall, "the portraits of each to be taken from the best likenesses to be obtained and the costumes to be in the dress most commonly worn by each in the performance of his public duty."

Except for the fact that traffic officers had not yet been thought of, even in New York, it seems a pity that a bronze policeman was not commissioned to direct all these pedestrians. But if Thomas Crawford had misgivings, he said nothing. Experience had taught him that the artist is at the mercy of his clients and he signed the contracts. By raising the height of the pedestal and the equestrian statue, he did what he could to restore order and balance, but he must have breathed a sigh of regret for his first fairly simple sketch. There was nothing else he could do except to go about hunting up portraits of deceased patriots and making sketches of them which never seemed to please the descendants.

Thomas Crawford was not to carry away 52,975 dollars in his pocket. For the equestrian, he would eventually receive 30,000 but he would get only 10,000 in advance, for which he must post a bond. Uncle John Ward attended to that for him. When the statue should leave Crawford's studio in Rome, in plaster on its way to be cast in bronze in Munich, the artist would receive 15,000 dollars upon presentation of a certificate signed by an accredited United States agent. Payment for the equestrian when cast in bronze would be 7500 dollars and for a pedestrian 2250. In case of Crawford's death, his models would belong to Richmond and his heirs would be paid for as much work as he had accomplished. There was one bright spot, however. Insurance and freight from Europe to the United States were to be paid by the city of Richmond. The committee assured Crawford that they would have a navy vessel come for General Washington and the rest, as soon as they were cast in bronze.

Thomas Crawford hastened back to Rome to begin work on the Richmond monument. His family and assorted in-laws could follow at their leisure and he would meet them in Paris, but meanwhile his hands longed for clay and his heart was already back in the Villa Negroni gardens. Prince Massimo, owner of the villa, had given Crawford permission to build studios over the ruins of the reservoir of the Baths of Diocletian. Twelve studios were now strung out along one side of formal gardens, built no doubt from stone pre-cut by ancient Romans, as was the villa itself. Here and there an ancient inscription appeared in the walls, honoring some dead emperor, or a fragment of carving, votive to some long forgotten god. Crawford was no archeologist. A really fine fragment of carving he treasured, having it set lovingly where it would catch the right light. But he indulged in no historic reconstruction for he believed in himself and his own era.

Roman marble cutters, gifted with the copying eye and hand but with the light of originality gone out, worked for Thomas Crawford for a few dollars a month, so that in his "twelve grand studios the incessant clang of mallet and chisel" rang from "a hundred busy hands to keep pace with the workings of his mind." Unconsciously, Thomas Crawford applied American methods of mass production to art without realizing that results might fall short of the standards set by Praxiteles. After all, only one temple at Milo stood in need of one Venus in ancient days, while in America hundreds of parlors were incomplete without a piece of statuary by Thomas Crawford. Who was Crawford to deny his countrymen (or women) the right to culture? And now at last Thomas Crawford was to supply the American public with examples of his art which would be theirs to look at free of charge, any time they pleased. With a sense of high exaltation, Thomas Crawford went back to Rome and hired more assistants.

Crawford now experienced the full meaning of that "tide" in the "affairs of men" which leads on to fortune. He offered sketches for competitions to decorate the new national Capitol Building in Washington, D.C., and won commissions with his design for the "north pediment"; for bronze doors for the Senate wing, and for his "Armed Liberty" to cap the dome. Crawford's doors, though later much criticized, had charm. His pediment would not stand the test of time but "Armed Liberty" proved one of his best and genuinely enduring works.

Into "Armed Liberty" Crawford put his whole heart and his philosophy concerning his country and her place in the world of nations. She shall hold "a sheathed sword to show the fight is over for the present," Crawford said, but "her sword is ready for use whenever required." "Armed Liberty" would stand upon a globe with the Americas uppermost to show her "protectorate over this hemisphere" and in Crawford's first design she wore the Phrygian cap to denote freedom for all. Jefferson Davis objected to this on the ground that it was "the badge of the freed slave" — which was exactly what Crawford intended. He was forced to change his design, however, and gave Liberty a helmet with an eagle on it, " a bold arrangement of feathers suggested by the costume of Indian tribes." As Crawford's sculpture "The Dying Indian" showed, he had great sympathy for this disappearing race, and this time no one seemed to mind if he expressed it. Patiently, Crawford remodeled a third time, explaining to his political art critics that in his opinion Freedom should be represented, not by a fainting Victorian female, but by a strong woman "able to bear the brunt of war."

Said Thomas Crawford, "Liberty requires hard fighting and I fear always will, to retain the independence bequeathed to us by the great men of our revolutionary period." The proportions for his statue, he said, were "derived from the cross on St. Peter's" in Rome.[3]

Meanwhile Louisa and the children, Annie and Adolph with off-spring, and at least part of the Howe family prepared to make a Roman pilgrimage. Julia was the one to whom a vacation in Rome meant the most. Among the three Ward sisters, her marriage had proved the most difficult of adjustment, and in 1850, it seemed to her that she and the Chevalier might really have lost the road to happiness. Perhaps if they could go back to Italy and relive some of the sunny hours of their honeymoon, they might find the way to each other's hearts again.

Dr. Samuel Gridley Howe was a reformer, whose mission in life was to change the world in which he lived. Crusader for freedom, leader of the blind — his life was heroic and his world the better for his efforts. But it was unfortunate that the desire to change his fellow human beings should be so deeply ingrained in Dr. Howe that he should marry a young woman to reform her. In Dr. Howe's words, Julia Ward had been "a New York belle — apparently an artificial one — possibly by some thought a beautiful one" when they met. "The true woman . . . had like to have been stifled," he said, and Julia was to become "a wife who lives only for her husband." [4]

Very much in love, Julia had promised to give up everything that had pleased her in the past. But Dr. Howe was absent many long hours while engaged in good works, and it was puzzling to have him resent the creative work in writing and music which Julia resumed to fill her lonely hours. Society, as such, Mrs. Julia Ward Howe relinquished without regret. But friendship was another matter. While living at Perkins or nearby, friends came seldom to see them, and the generous, outgoing heart of a girl who had always lived in a large and loving family grew sick with loneliness. Nevertheless, Julia tried hard to make herself over to suit her reformer husband.

Dr. Howe should have been happy with a wife who obeyed him implicitly — yet Longfellow wrote that "Howe" was in "a nervous, morbid state." He had "no enjoyments in social intercourse, being painfully conscious of the passing of time, as if life itself were slipping from under his feet. At the Asylum, a bell rings every quarter of an hour — a constant *memento mori;* and wherever he goes, he hears this melancholy bell." [5]

Julia had never spent so much as one night in an institution before her marriage — she had never been to a hospital, nor even to a boarding school. She had called at Perkins Institute for the Blind, but had never asked where led the gray marble corridors, raying out from the foyer of the old hotel. Upon marriage, she found that one corridor led to her home — the Doctor's Wing. Two stair steps went down to dining room and kitchen, spiral stairs wound upward to parlors, up again to a pair of bedrooms and higher still until they reached two servants' rooms under the roof. The former Mt. Washington Hotel had once been "modern," but now it was no longer new. Young Mrs. Howe, who was expecting her second child, noticed what would ever after connote the Institute: there was "a smell of water-closets."

One of a young wife's first pleasures is to arrange her own home in her own way. But when Julia Ward Howe arrived in South Boston, she found that her husband's sister, Miss Jeanette Howe, was housekeeper in chief of the Institute, with the Doctor's Wing — where she also lived — her special charge. Julia's trunks and bandboxes and the baby Julia Romana's complicated impedimenta made a shambles of Miss Howe's orderly rooms, and Miss Howe explained that this must not be. It was important to the blind to have "a place for everything and everything in its place." The blind and deaf Laura Bridgman also lived in the Doctor's Wing. Again Julia did her best to give perfect satisfaction — this time to her husband's sister as well as to her husband. But people with such intangibles as poetry and music on their minds find extreme tidiness difficult of achievement.

Young Mrs. Howe had many Boston friends, and she looked forward to entertaining them in her own home. She and her husband decided upon a dinner party once a week, which was a modest program according to Bond Street standards. It was now that Julia wished she had paid more attention to the household arts the way her father and Uncle John had urged her to do. At The Corner, one summoned the housekeeper and planned with her the details of all dinner parties. Obviously, Miss Howe was not the sort of housekeeper one summoned. Miss Howe was not even the sort of sister-in-law who stands behind a young wife and helps her to appear a more accomplished hostess than she really is.

"My husband's eldest sister, who lived with us and who had held the reins of housekeeping until my arrival, was averse to company and usually absented herself on days of dinner parties," Julia Ward Howe wrote long later. "In her absence, I often did not know where to look for various articles requisite and necessary." [6] No one who has ever coped with a strange kitchen could fail to appreciate the scene, with its ultimate tears of frustration. In time, Julia could laugh.

There were servants of course. Immigration was at a high level and there were women willing to work for little more than food and shelter. Moreover, since Mrs. Howe's income was the equal of her husband's, she expected to pay good wages. But Dr. Howe fired the cook in order to save money every time his wife went on a visit, and once at least the servant of his own choosing proved difficult to train. She was a girl from the "Idiot School" in which Dr. Howe was interested, and she could count as far as seven, after which she said "many."

These were minor vicissitudes. Julia managed to laugh more often than she cried and Hillard, who was apt to disapprove of Julia, said "she makes Howe an excellent wife, and shows great character in the quiet ease with which she adapts herself to her new situation." All might have been well but for the question of money. A series of letters to and from Dr. Howe tell the story.

Upon his return from Europe, Dr. Howe found that he had overdrawn his letter of credit with Baring Brothers by about three hundred dollars. He wrote to Sam Ward presenting a draft for an advance on Julia's income for the coming year.

"There is nothing due Julia at this time," Sam replied.

Becoming very angry, Dr. Howe wrote to Charles Sumner to know if the fact that they now had a child altered the "ante-nuptial agreement." It did not.

"My wife had as free and entire control of her property before marriage as I had of mine," Dr. Howe wrote, but this was inaccurate. The Ward heiresses before marriage received an allowance like schoolgirls and had nothing to do with their capital. In order to pay Julia an advance, some of her investments would have had to be liquidated, Sam finally explained — but Dr. Howe's pride had been mortally wounded.

"I have pondered again and again upon a plan of living entirely upon my income and refusing to touch a cent of Julia's," he wrote. "It is true that we should be cramped upon $3000 per an. but I, for my part, had rather live ever so poorly than have the infernal mortification of receiving the dolings-out of rents etc. from such a man as my worthy beau frère."

The Wards discovered that Dr. Howe had "sought a legal opinion" as to their right to keep Julia's money in their own bank. The Wards were "riled" and Dr. Howe used exactly the same expression as letters were exchanged which should never have been written. Dr. Howe put into execution his "plan." He had Julia sign a paper agreeing to turn over to him every cent she should ever receive and Julia was willing, being ever most generous-hearted. He did not tell her what he was going to do with the money, allowing her to assume that it went to pay general expenses. When she asked him for small sums he was "illiberal with her as to money," which surprised her.

Dr. Howe next returned Julia's money to her family but still without telling her what he had done. She found out when she went to visit on Bond Street. On July 5, 1845, Dr. Howe wrote to his wife's uncle, John Ward:

"I have always regretted that Mr. Samuel Ward did not comply with my request to keep secret my resolution about not receiving Julia's income; I never told her about it, nor my best friend, until I found it generally talked about in the family. I should have been the only sufferer, but by letting Julia know about it, she is made to suffer vexation; this however *is not my fault*, though it makes me sad to have anything displease her, it cannot make me change what has become to me like a principle.

"Mr. Samuel Ward's views differ so much from mine as to what is delicacy and self respect; and our correspondence has been so unpleasant that we had better never have any business relations.

"I once signified to him that I would like to have a change in one of the Trustees and to have . . . the right to ask for a settlement without having it considered as a favor. He at first made no objections . . . but he afterwards saw fit to change his mind and to refuse attention to my request. Then came the demur in accepting my draft for so petty a sum as $300 . . . I have now had six months to get cool; I see myself obliged to encroach on my little capital and know it must before many years come to an end; nevertheless if Julia's income were the equal of John Jacob Astor's, and I could have it by submitting to be advised and tutored by Mr. Samuel Ward, I would reject it: I prefer my independence.

"At the beginning of the year, Julia gave me an order to receive all her rents; that order I sent to you Trustees and requested you to do what you deemed proper in the case, as I should not call for the money. Next January and as many Januarys as I am in life, I shall ask her to do the same; and I trust she will ever love me enough to prefer to live with me in poverty than to ask me to submit to what I must deem humiliaion."

Julia Ward Howe had dearly loved her father and perhaps she still felt a longing for a father's protection when first she met Dr. Howe. Certainly Dr. Howe belonged to a previous generation in his attitude. At times, while growing up, Julia had resisted her father's authority, for hers was a passionately independent spirit; but she always found him reasonable though stern. Now she faced a new situation. "Coldness" on Dr. Howe's part met her efforts to reconcile what was no more than a family quarrel. No one could ever accuse the Wards of being cold, whatever else their faults; and to have her husband cold to her was something Julia minded more than all else.

Every January "as long as he was in life" Julia Ward Howe handed over to her husband the entire proceeds of her patrimony — never seeing anything more than the paper she signed. Even with the failure of Prime and Ward when Dr. Howe was made co-trustee with Mills — the paper had to be signed. Obedience was what her husband demanded — obedience as blind as that of his pathetic little charges at the Institute. Julia Ward Howe had promised to "love, honor and obey" and this she did. But nothing on earth could make her *think* the way her husband did on all subjects — although she agreed with him on major matters of social reform — and nothing could quench her spark of humor. For example, referring to arrangements she did not like concerning a visit to Annie, "but Chev's will be done in Bordentown as it is in Boston," she said, the wicked spark of mischief gleaming right through the words.

Julia Ward Howe freely blamed herself and often referred to her "faulty years" when adjustments to married life were painful. If Dr. Howe ever thought that he was in any way to blame, he did not commit it to writing. Yet to be always right is not necessarily to be happy. Dr. Howe was oppressed by the feeling that he was not properly appreciated both in his home and at the Institute, and for a short time he toyed with the idea of going to New York to engage in some sort of business. He had little doubt that he could do better than the Wards. But he could not take orders from anyone, as his wife remarked, and therefore it would be hard for him to find a position he could fill without experience. When the Perkins trustees granted him his leave of absence to go to Europe for his health he was gratified. He had gone to several watering places in the United States — one of them at Northampton, Massachusetts, where the old Round Hill School buildings were now used to accommodate guests. Perhaps the waters in Germany might help Dr. Howe's violent headaches, although they had failed to cure Longfellow's broken heart.

CHAPTER SIXTEEN
Passion Flowers

ON March first, 1850, Dr. Samuel Gridley Howe wrote to his sister-in-law, Annie Mailliard. "Annie-Louisa popped in upon us very unexpectedly, after hardly a tap at the door, the evening before last," he said. "Julia was much surprised but glad to see her; so are we all." The little girl was not to be named "Annie-Louisa," however — she was Laura Elizabeth Howe, named not for her mother's sisters but for a sister of her father's and for Dr. Howe's pupil, Laura Bridgman.

The letter which Annie received a few days later from her sister Julia told a slightly different story. It was the baby's father who was really surprised. "Chev was summoned but refused to remain. 'I shall hear you downstairs before you will want me,' he said and descended to the library to finish a letter to Mr. Mann." Julia sent for him again, however, and after half an hour of severe pain, the child was born. Dr. Howe then returned to his letter to Horace Mann, in which he announced the birth of his fourth child and praised his wife's Spartan behavior — as well he might. Laura Elizabeth was to be a much-traveled young lady, for within "a fortnight" after her mother's letter was written, or when she was about six weeks old, she was on her way to visit her Aunt Annie in Bordentown along with her mother and father, her two sisters, her brother Harry, Miss Fanny Jarvis from the Institute and a nursemaid.

"Pray tell Adolph that I feel really ashamed of quartering myself upon him, with such a troupe of infant phenomena, and that I shall hardly dare to ask for admittance when I knock at the door and he comes to open it," Julia wrote her sister. "But indeed, dear Annie, I can't help it this year. Chev is impatient to get away from the spring winds and we must all go, and we are very grateful that you are willing to receive us for a month." Julia was not really in the least anxious about her reception, for she knew that Adolph Mailliard loved to fill Spring Villa with visiting friends and relatives. Louisa and her children were still in Bordentown. Sam Ward was also a constant visitor, he and Adolph having business together as well as a mutual passion for horses and hunting.

What a chattering of devoted and re-united sisters went on, late in the morning in Annie's dressing room with its hangings of Bonaparte blue merino! At night before the sculptured fireplace, reminiscent of Bond Street, what an orgy of good talk there was with brother Sam to take the lead. Dr. Howe alone was not present — having gone on to Washington. While the family made plans for a trip to Europe to visit the Crawfords, Dr. Howe was not there and failed to catch the Ward enthusiasm. It is doubtful if he could have shared any enthusiasm with Sam Ward, in any case.

While Julia thought of Rome as a place of sunshine and romantic love, the Chevalier remembered instead his days of inaction when all he could find to do with his vast store of philanthropic energy was to start a small kindergarten for the blind. The last place the Chevalier wanted to see again was the scene of his overlong honeymoon. But when at last he heard about the plans, what could he say to Julia, who wanted so much to go? She had spent "a lonely winter in South Boston," she had not wanted a fourth child in six years, and a bout of scarlet fever in 1849 had left her weak and depressed.

Dr. Howe consented to the European trip but with a compromise. He would go as far as Germany to "take the waters." Then the Doctor would come home and Julia should have her winter in Rome. There were still a few more difficulties to be ironed out before the Ward sisters could embark for Europe, however. As it stood, their party would include seven children, the oldest being the six-year-old Julia Romana Howe. Where would there be any rest for anyone with such a menagerie? It was agreed, therefore, that six-year-old Dudie and five-year-old Flossy Howe should remain at home, while their parents took with them Harry, aged two, and the infant Laura. A seemingly ideal solution was offered. Dr. Edward Jarvis, physician to the Perkins Institute, would be delighted to take the little girls into his own home. He and his wife were childless but his niece, Fanny Jarvis, who taught at Perkins, lived with them and would take especial care of Flossie and Dudie.

The situation seemed ideal except for one small item. Dr. Jarvis, famous for his pioneer work in public health statistics and co-worker with Horace Mann in behalf of the insane, maintained a small school for "idiot children" in his home. The Howe girls were anything but retarded. They did not enjoy the "idiot children," and their father's return from Europe they would hail as a deliverance. Their mother's longer stay they would never entirely understand.

For Dr. Howe, the trip to Europe was doomed, not to failure but to fall short of success. "My heart is heavy with foreboding," he wrote to Horace Mann just before he left. "Its strings will break with my children tugging from this side of the Atlantic." On board ship he wrote to Sumner: "We are dashing off at the rate of 12 knots and shall make Halifax by six o'clock. Had I the moral courage, I should land there and wait for the next steamer and go back to my dear nest in South Boston."

In Paris, Thomas Crawford joined the party according to his promise. Success had followed him across the Atlantic and now, in addition to the Richmond and the Washington, D. C., commissions, he was to do a full-length statue of Beethoven in bronze for the Music Hall in Boston. "Crawford is in high feather because of high health and successful *carrière*," wrote Dr. Howe to Sumner with just a trace of understandable envy. "Did you observe how he begins to develop a *belly?*" [1]

By the first of September, the Howes were on the Rhine enjoying at last the vacation which they both really needed. Even the Chevalier admitted in letters home that there was "nothing like the Rhine for beauty." He confessed that his "besetting sin" was "always to be in a hurry" but now he had slowed down long enough to "take walks with Julia." Of course it was too much to expect to find him completely satisfied. "The water . . . " was "not the best, not so good, I think, as at Brattleboro," he said. "And as for the physician, he is nothing. . . ." Nevertheless, Dr. Howe had himself wrapped in wet sheets, he had water poured on him from all angles and he drank water by the gallon. By September 27 he was able to say, "I can eat my weight in anything edible, climb the steepest crags and warm up a wet sheet in a very few minutes."

But Julia, the children, the Crawfords and the Mailliards had gone. "Parting from Julia and my children and being left alone in the world, as it were, so affected me as to bring on a *crise de nerfs* and to prostrate me," Dr. Howe wrote to Charles Sumner. He sailed from England aboard the *Asia* on October 12 and in South Boston two little girls were waiting for him who would be their father's allies forever.

It was as well for Dr. Howe that he went home "improved in health and vigor" rather than attempting the fantastic coach journey from the Rhine country across Switzerland, a corner of France and then by boat from Marseilles to Ostia, the port of Rome. The Ward sisters had married men who were curiously alike in certain ways. Each was tall and strikingly handsome — each masterful to a degree. Adolph was the most princely with his careless attitude toward mere money and his way with a retinue of servants. Crawford was the most hasty-tempered. Dr. Howe was born to be obeyed, but even he, with his executive ability, could hardly have organized two equally masterful men plus a coach full of women, babies and nurses with their mountain of baggage. In after years, Julia laughed over the way her own temper flared, sparked off by Thomas Crawford's. And finally Louisa cried with fatigue, although "rejoicing over her prospects" — for she was expecting a child. It was Annie who cheered them all when they waked in the night, by telling funny stories of old days on Bond Street when the Ward sisters were children together "keeping each other in mischief" in the nursery. And it was the good German beer which Adolph and Thomas Crawford (who rode outside the coach) brought to the girls at diligence stops along the road which refreshed their spirits and made them all philosophical over troubles which had before loomed so large.

Years later, Julia wrote of her arrival in Rome on this second journey. "After the privations entailed by maternity, the weakness and physical discomfort, the inevitable seclusion . . . I found myself free and untrammeled. . . . I was absolutely intoxicated with the joy of freedom and used to dance across the great salon in my sister's apartment, singing 'Liberty, Liberty!' "

Every morning, Thomas Crawford repaired to his studios in the Villa garden with the regularity of a New York businessman. Adolph Mailliard also had work to do. His father's sister by blood, the Princess Zenaïde, was in Rome and she summoned him to almost daily conferences, in the course of which she urged him to invest her American funds so that they would yield more money. Her husband, the Prince of Canino, was in Paris spending her income, and she also wanted Adolph to send her cash direct before her husband could get his hands on it.[2] Adolph could only assure her that the firm of Ward and Price, where most of her funds were placed, was dedicated to the

policy of making money as rapidly as possible. As for the Prince —
he had the law on his side when he squandered his wife's income but
Adolph said he would see what he could do. It was not surprising,
however, that Adolph soon left Rome assuring the Princess that he
would see her royal relatives at the race tracks where he was going
with an eye to his own business — the Bordentown stables.

Now the Villa Negroni became a very quiet place, with Adolph
away, Crawford hard at work — and Louisa increasingly in seclusion
because of the coming child. Annie was content to sit with Louisa and
sew a fine seam. But the gay and sociable Julia had not come all the
way to Rome just to wander alone in the villa gardens or attempt fine
sewing, which she hated. Very sensibly, she took a small apartment
of her own; bought a donkey-load of firewood; hired a grand piano
— and moved there with her children and their nurse.

Julia Howe's capacity for friendship was remarkable; but to her it
was the most natural thing in the world to gather together a choice
group of people in whatever strange city, wherever in the world she
might find herself. She entertained in her own delightful fashion, with
music, with modest repasts — and with witty conversation. Julia loved
all kinds of people, and never forgot a name or a face — this gift becoming increasingly miraculous as time went by and her hosts of
friends increased. Under the influence of Mrs. Howe's friendliness,
strangers expanded and told their life histories before they knew what
they were about. Julia listened and remembered. Years later, she would
startle a former acquaintance by quoting something said long ago and
the effect was flattering, to say the least. This gift of Julia's was the
more remarkable because her own remarks were highly quotable.

Old friends from New York turned up in Rome constantly, for a
Roman winter was the fashion. At a Christmas party at Louisa's, arranged by Julia for the whole English-speaking colony in Rome, there
was Horace Binney Wallace of Philadelphia and New York. "Do you
still ridicule Boston society?" Mrs. Howe asked him. And with a
start of amazement, Wallace realized that he and Julia had been members of a Philadelphia wedding party eleven years previously and that,
at that time, he had championed Philadelphia over Boston, she taking
the side of both Boston and New York against him. He had changed
a great deal, he said. But he was still red-haired and was now promoting
the theory that all "Rossos," as he called red-haired people, were especially gifted — like himself.

Wallace, a mathematical genius at fifteen, was now a lawyer and a writer on law subjects. He had never married, was independently wealthy and was now upon a European tour to study art, to try a new line of writing and to collect "Rossos," as he solemnly assured Julia Howe. Julia's hair was still just as red as it had been when first they met, when she was twenty and he twenty-two. Horace Binney Wallace could only tell her now that she was the most charming "Rosso" of them all.

Horace Binney Wallace was "an exhilarating companion," Julia said. She never forgot "the silvery timbre of his rather high voice, nor the glee with which he would occasionally inform me that he had discovered a new and remarkable 'Rosso.' This was sometimes a picture, but oftener a living individual. If he found himself disappointed in the latter case, he would account for it by saying that he had at first sight mistaken the color of the hair." Mrs. Howe's wit stimulated Wallace's so that perhaps it was not surprising that the essays he was writing, "Art, Science and Philosophy in Europe," were considered among the best things he had ever done.

This is not to say that Mrs. Howe and Wallace agreed on all the subjects they discussed. Far from it. Wallace was a leader in a new school of thought called Positivism. Directly opposed to Transcendentalism, with its religious overtone and emphasis on individuality and the divine origin of the soul, Positivism substituted organized society for God. This was the last thing an ardent individualist like Julia Ward Howe could agree to and fierce must have been the arguments. Wallace interested Mrs. Howe in philosophy, however, and her subsequent delvings into Kant and Spinoza were partly the result of his influence.

Julia Howe's apartment was on the Via Capo le Case, and on the floor below "Mrs. Dudley Field and her children" were settled for the winter, David Dudley Field being in New York furthering his career as counsel for Jay Gould and James Fisk. Upstairs lived the James Edward Freemans, the husband a British artist and his wife Augusta a sculptress, the chubby baby cherubs with which she ornamented overmantels and christening fonts having made her famous. She was "a friendly little person, partly Italian by birth but wholly English by education" — and she was also one of Louisa Crawford's dearest friends.

"When Mrs. Field entertained company, she was wont to borrow my large lamp," Julia said. "When I received, she lent me her tea cups." And Augusta Freeman "willingly became" Mrs. Howe's "companion and guide" on her walks about Rome, "which were many and long." For serious occupation, Julia had her singing lessons and her lessons in Hebrew "with a learned Rabbi." Taking lessons, "receiving" friends, chatting daily with her sisters and sight-seeing in Rome — such was the innocent, happy life which Julia Howe planned for herself. Her tastes were intellectual, but like Madame de Staël (and Elizabeth Peabody) she believed that "there is no sex in intellect." It was not her fault that she was much prettier and more attractive than most intellectual women and perhaps she never noticed how many men flocked to her little parties.

Every time that Horace Binney Wallace called, he brought Julia a bunch of violets, bought from the flower-vending woman in the Piazza at the end of the street. This tribute Julia accepted with pleasure but it was with only friendly regret that she said good-by to him when he set out on his further European travels. She invited him to visit her in Boston, where she would be sure to have some Transcendentalists to meet him. Boston Transcendentalists could stand up even under the pyrotechnics of his wit as he championed Postivism, she assured him, and he laughingly accepted the challenge. But Wallace was "haunted by the fear of becoming insane," [3] as Mrs. Howe told afterwards. In London in 1852, after "visiting a friend whose mind was impaired, he took his own life." Mrs. Howe never forgot the friend who sparked her own philosophical inquiry, and to Horace Binney Wallace she wrote one of her most charming poems:— "Via Felice."

On June 8, 1851, the event which Julia and Annie waited for occurred. Thomas Crawford's personal servant came hastening through the streets to Mrs. Howe's door and he was all smiles for the news was good. Mrs. Howe must come at once, for the expected child was born. Francis Marion Crawford the baby had been named in advance and in memory of the youngest of the Ward brothers. But the name would have to wait, because the baby was a girl. Mary, they named her, for her father's mother; her father calling her May, but as she grew up she was "Mimoli" to everyone else. This was a name composed from French, English and Italian which somehow suited exactly a temperamental little girl whose hair was red and whose gifts in some ways resembled her Aunt Julia's — whom she did not care for. All the Crawford children came close to genius — the long-awaited boy, born four years later, would achieve fame. But Mimoli had a way with words, and when she grew up to write of her Roman home and her foreign-seeming aunts and cousins, her brother F. Marion Crawford could not quite equal her.

American visitors wintering in Rome had all flocked homeward now. Still Julia Howe lingered, finally taking passage with Annie and Adolph on "an old-fashioned packet," one that combined sail with steam and made a month-long voyage. All light and gaiety seemed to go out of Julia as she left Rome. "Pain, almost amounting to anguish, seized me," she said. But it never occurred to her until later that people watched her, noted how happy she had been and then how sad — and gossiped maliciously.

Julia would not have been going home if she had not still loved the Chevalier. But she was by no means sure what reception awaited her. At the time of his death, the Chevalier asked his wife to burn all the letters they had written to each other during 1850 and 1851 and his correspondence with Charles Sumner of the same period. This she did reluctantly, although many passages "gave me pain," she said.

There is of course no means of knowing what these letters said. But letters do remain, from people outside the family, containing stories of Mrs. Howe's life in Rome that winter and these tales could easily have reached Dr. Howe through some of his overzealous friends. It shocked one woman to discover while in Rome that Mrs. Howe "did not live with her sisters but in lodgings" and that "she was happy and gay as a lark there, giving elegant parties every week, *until* she decided to come home. . . . After that, she was very melancholy and lost all her gaiety." One would almost suspect that this lady had not been asked to the parties. The gossip in her letter home continued. While in Rome, Mrs. Howe "was always attended by a hunchback artist . . . who was fool enough to be pleased with her allowing him to follow her." But even this uncharitable person admitted that Mrs. Howe never in any way encouraged the unfortunate man, but tried to send him away.[4]

Far more generous was Fanny Longfellow's comment, but even she failed of complete sympathy. Dating her letter September 3, 1851, and writing to her sister, Mrs. Longfellow said, "I see by the papers that Julia has returned. I hear she was much admired in Rome and her soirees much courted. With her resources of languages and clever conversation, I can imagine how attractive she must have made them, where people love society for its own sake. How dull she will find it in South

Boston — she is not to be satisfied with the society of husband and children and a social nature like hers requires much more, not to consume itself." [5]

Julia's nature did not consume itself, however — although Mrs. Longfellow forgot that Julia's husband was away a great deal and that South Boston was not Brattle Street, Cambridge. During the long voyage, Julia had made certain wise resolutions. She would "get on quietly and better than of old." She had "acquired a little firmness and independence during" her "year of freedom" and now she would "no longer quiver at a cold look or weep at a sharp word." Books would continue to be a solace during lonely evenings and writing had assumed a new importance. Julia Ward Howe had published a poem or two in English language newspapers in Rome, and she had brought home a notebook full of new verses written while living in her own version of "Casa Guidi." She would get her work published if she could.

In a letter to her sister Annie, Julia told of her arrival in South Boston, which was always a place of exile, good resolutions notwithstanding:

"After a very dusty, dirty journey, I arrived at Green Peace at six o'clock, Saturday evening. Two children whom I should not have known for mine ran out to meet me, and after some little show of shyness, hugged me heartily. I found the house in perfect order and the place wonderfully improved. Everything was calculated to make a pleasant impression on me. My husband is very kind and seems to wish to make me happy.

"As first I was quite overpowered at the newness of my position after so different a life, but I already begin to feel at home. . . . I ought to do many things for the elder children — they seem to me very petulant and a little coarse-mannered, I mean given to loud and quick talking, contradicting each other etc. They are in good health but constant exposure to the sun has injured the beauty of their complexions. Julia is freckled and Flossy is badly tanned. I cannot help a feeling of disappointment at finding them so, they were so fair when I left — their voices too have a harshness of tone most unpleasant to me, who esteem too highly grace of speech in a woman. Still there is ample time to reform all these things if their father is willing."

Theodore Parker had already come to call and to welcome Mrs. Howe home when this letter was written. He came often during the winter and "was admirable in conversation." Mrs. Howe took some of the credit for this herself, because, "He has to talk his best when I am with him," she said — otherwise, she would "trip him in dialectics." Although Theodore Parker was one of Dr. Howe's group of reformers, he differed from both Howe and Sumner on one point. He saw no reason why a woman should not be a writer if she wanted to go to all that trouble and do the hard work good writing required. He was one of the few friends to whom Mrs. Howe showed her poetry written in Rome. Without stretching the truth, he could not tell her that it was great poetry, but he could sincerely say that she wrote pleasant verses with here and there some fine lines which lifted them well above the average. He could say that he saw no reason against publication — provided she could find a publisher. Julia must have hesitated to show her poetry to Longfellow. He had already gone on record against her publishing anything — possibly to save her from what he must have feared the critics would say. But he seems to have been consulted about the title of her book.

In February, 1852, the Longfellows "dined at Julia Howe's" with "after dinner a game of bowls." Dr. Howe had recently become a total abstainer. "We had no wine," Longfellow said. "The Dr. does not mean to do penance alone." But Longfellow had been pleased to hear more of the way in which "Mrs. Goodwin," a teacher at the Institute, "was reading 'Evangeline' with her fingers to Laura Bridgman."

The Longfellows shared Mrs. Howe's love of the theater and often shared a box with friends at current performances. But their efforts to include both the Howes were not always successful. A letter from Mrs. Howe to Longfellow, dated March 12, 1852, tells a sad story. "I am sorry to tell you that Chev will not be able to go to the Theater tomorrow evening. He went, on Tuesday evening, to see Lola Montez, and was very sick all of yesterday in consequence." This lady who had proved too much for the Chevalier was an Irish-born dancer, ex-mistress of the King of Bavaria, ex-Countess of Lansfield, now touring the United States in a play called *Lola Montez of Bavaria*. But Mrs. Howe had enjoyed the play and was ready for another. "I shall secure tickets for you and myself in a private box," she wrote. She hoped it would not be too much trouble for Longfellow to stop at Chev's office in Bromfield Street and she would promise to be there early.

Out of the pleasant social exchanges of this winter came the idea that the Longfellows and the Howes go to Newport together during the summer of 1852 and stay at the same modest boardinghouse. Long-fellow himself attended to the arrangements for rooms at "Hazard's house" — although he grumbled a trifle at having to take time from his writing to make a special trip. Fanny described the place as "comfortable and clean." It was "on the cliff, half way to the beach," with a "beautiful outlook on the sea and the clover-scented cliffs, most accessible for walks and dreamings on the rocky ledges, far from the dust and noise of town."

Early in August, Mrs. Howe arrived. "Julia Howe is a great acquisition," wrote Fanny Longfellow. Julia was "so full of spirits and every variety of talent — her wit rouses us out of the languor this climate induces and her singing (greatly improved since Italy) is a perfect delight."

Longfellow took up the story a week later in his diary. The Doctor had come with Julia, was "as restless as ever" and had left. "They have given us a new name in the town: the 'Hotel de Rambouillet!' That will do very well, Julia Howe being our Madame de Sévigné."

Julia herself continued the tale, painting the scene at Newport for Louisa, so far away in Rome. Tom Appleton, Fanny Longfellow's brother, and George Curtis, famous for his "Nile Notes," had joined the party at Hazard's House. "Imagine Fanny Longfellow and myself, playing Puss-in-the-Corner with George (Howadji) Curtis, John da Costa of Casa Dies memory and Longo," Julia wrote. "Fanny's long hair fell down her back and she looked finely."

Dr. Howe shuttled back and forth between South Boston and Newport and one evening in Newport he "illuminated all the front of the house" for an impromptu party the guests gave. It was "amusing and gave the party something to talk about," Longfellow said.

And one day, "as restless as ever," Dr. Howe explored the country-side and discovered a most beautiful country property for sale, "six miles from town." It was called "Lawton's Valley." An old farmhouse stood close to the road, while behind it fine meadows sloped away to Narragansett Bay which could be seen, shining blue in the sun beyond a green sea of meadow grass. To the right, as the Doctor faced the house, the level acres gave way to a deep wooded valley through which tumbled a brook. An old mill, long since abandoned, added a picturesque note and had even a few usable rooms. Falling in love with Lawton's Valley, Dr. Howe bought it and Charles Sumner, making out the deed, put the whole property in Howe's name. This was "an error" which had later to be explained with some embarrassment to Julia's Uncle John — since the money paid was hers. But the error was not corrected.

Julia loved Lawton's Valley just as much as her husband did, but with this difference. Where he saw it as a fine investment to be sold someday at a profit, she gave her whole heart to it and wanted to keep it forever as a summer home. Julia's house on Mt. Vernon Street, which her husband had given her, had been sold. She thought perhaps she could keep this one.

Returning to South Boston much refreshed by her weeks in Newport and by the prospect of a happy summer there next year, Julia put into effect a daring plan. She arranged her poems for publication and sent out a few to magazines. After all, although Dr. Howe was still sternly set against a woman's appearing in print, he had put Julia's "Roman Beggar Boy" into Braille "in a book for the Blind," anonymously, of course. She was "*so* gratified," she said. Why not just go round to Ticknor and Fields? They had once refused the poems of Julia Ward and what could they do now but refuse Mrs. Julia Ward Howe?

In February, 1853, Putnam returned a poem "with a short letter saying that 'people watch very narrowly the tone of his magazine'; that his editors thought 'there were some lines in the poem which made it inexpedient to use it.'" Julia was angry to the point of tears! "The implication of some impropriety of thought or expression was what especially vexed me," she said. She had not actually given Putnam the poem, he had seen several and "he selected it." And now, "I should like so much to write a squib entitled 'How to Write for Putnam's'" Julia added — and it is a pity that she never did, for she could be very sarcastic indeed when she was angry and it is hard to see where her perfectly proper poetry could have offended anyone. But defeats often lead to victories and Mrs. Howe took her rejected poem along with the others to Ticknor and Fields.

To her surprise and joy, Ticknor and Fields took a different view of her poetry now. In 1847, she had been included in *Griswold's Female Poets of America* — thus satisfying an ambition to follow in her mother's footsteps. A surprising number of the poems in this new collection had appeared anonymously in different periodicals and returning American tourists reported seeing Mrs. Howe's poems in an English language newspaper in Rome. They recognized scenes such as the Brownings' apartment and the Crawfords' Villa Negroni — called "Villa Massimo" for the sake of the metre. Mrs. Howe's reputation as a hostess in Rome was not forgotten and Ticknor and Fields thought they could sell a small edition.

Hope deferred had triumphed at last, and Julia went home in such a state of happiness that the jolting South Boston omnibus seemed drawn by Pegasus himself instead of the usual tired old nags, and all the cobblestones were clouds. Surely the Chevalier knew how it felt to have a cherished dream denied — then granted at long last. That evening, Julia approached the subject warily.

She found that Dr. Howe still disapproved of women writers and that he was ably supported in his view by his dear friend, Charles Sumner. There was no use courting an outright refusal. Julia decided not to tell what she had done.

Mrs. Howe went back to Ticknor and Fields with the news that they must publish her poetry anonymously. Probably they would refuse, and there would be a rude awakening from her dream of holding in her hands a book of her own that she had actually written. But Ticknor and Fields agreed willingly. There was good publicity in secrecy — provided the secret were not too carefully kept, although this they probably did not tell her.

Next came the conferences concerning title. The "Passion Flower" with its symbolism associated with Christian religion, was much in vogue among mid-nineteenth century writers — especially for women's magazines. "The simple title, 'Passion Flowers' was invented by Scherb and approved by Longfellow," Mrs. Howe wrote Annie.[6] The editors leaped upon the idea. The title would prove all too good a choice. *Passion Flowers* appeared on December 29, 1853. On November 30th it was in unbound sheets at the publisher's and already the secret of its authorship was beginning to come out — not slowly but like water through a sieve.

Ticknor and Fields were amazed at the success of *Passion Flowers* and they very soon ordered a second edition. Julia proudly wrote that she had made two hundred dollars and had furnished her Lawton's Valley home. This was the largest sum of money she had ever earned, and although long later, when she was thrown upon her own resources, she earned much more, no check would ever again look half so handsome. Overnight, Julia found herself famous and she enjoyed it thoroughly — until some of the reasons for her fame came to her ears. There were people who thought *Passion Flowers* too passionate. And to Annie, Julia wrote that "one bitter drop poisoned all" her pleasure. "Chev took it *very* hard." Some kind friend had pointed out that a certain merely playful poem in the volume, called "Mind versus Millstream," satirized his efforts to make his wife obey him.

CHAPTER SEVENTEEN
Back to the Gold Mines

SAM WARD made his "quarter of a million" in California in six months. Before his sisters had returned from their Roman holiday, he had lost the money and one year and three days after his triumphant arrival in New York he was on his way back to California in search of another fortune. The New York firm of Ward and Price had been wiped out by a disastrous fire in San Francisco.

Again it was not really poor Sam's fault, at least in the eyes of his family, and this time the San Francisco McAllisters wrote to Julia Ward Howe to make excuses for him. "His late partner has been more to blame than he in their late troubles," went the letter. But as usual, Sam had taken outrageous risks and the real estate he thought of as his was held on the narrowest of margins. Again the penitent Sam told of the hard work he meant to do with pick and shovel to restore his own and the fortunes of others he had lost. Only this time, fate took him at his word and he really went out to the gold mines.

With his capacity for dramatizing a situation, Sam Ward spoke of himself as a soldier of fortune; a hero among three musketeers. As a matter of fact, he was one of three "companions" but while they talked of pick and shovel, what they actually had in mind was to buy a gold mine and later organize a company to pay for and operate it. The two "companions," encountered during the journey from New York to San Francisco, could soon see that Sam Ward was their man when it came to selling stock in a gold mine. They set out from San Francisco for Stockton in the steamer *Sophie*. And once in Stockton, Sam's infallible technique paid off. "A couple of days were devoted to friends who had colonized that town," with the result that an army major gave the three adventurers the use of "an army vehicle" as far as the Stanislaus River. Here there was a ferry, an ale house — and the end of the road. Here contacts were of no further use and Sam Ward and his friends got into the saddle and set out up a trail on hired horses, "twenty miles to breakfast" which they hoped awaited them at a ferry on the Tuolumne River.

They were now not far from the present Yosemite National Park and it was understandable that they "lost their way several times." Said Sam, "It was nearly noon ere we broke our fast" and this was certainly not the first time that Sam Ward had breakfasted late — but under different circumstances. Before they reached the next stopping place it was past midnight, and fortunately for all of them the horses knew the trail better than they did.

Although short of stature, Sam Ward was proud of his muscular strength and his horsemanship. But the fifty-mile saddle journey he had just ended proved a different matter from a brisk trot around Washington Square at home in New York, or even a canter around the lake in that country district to be known as Central Park. "The fatigue resulting from our first experiment in the saddle . . . and possibly the remnant of a small cask of very tolerable claret placed at our disposal (the mercury must have been 90°) tempered our ardor to reach the Eldorado beyond," Sam said, "and overcame our resistance to the invitation to rest for a couple of days upon the 'River of Grace.' " Sam's mood of repentance gave way rapidly to his unquenchable love of adventure and his delight in his fellow man (and woman).

The Merced River, or "River of Grace," had been rich in gold although now almost panned clean. Sam remembered mournfully the gold nuggets he had seen in San Francisco in '49 — and now there were no more. But just as Sam and his companions arrived on the Merced a new pocket was discovered and at least two hundred Indians arrived to work it. There they were, men, women and children, wading into the water, then "kneeling in the river and huddled together" looking "for all the world like Baptists at an immersion ceremony" — except for a lack of costume, which suggested some rite of "the Dancing Dervish of India." The "shouts of enthusiasm and satisfaction" when some of the Indians panned out flakes of gold "would have made an impression even upon a Methodist Camp Meeting," [1] Sam said.

"On the morning of the third day" — the claret being all gone — on went Sam and his fellow adventurers. They headed for the "little town of Quartzburg, which lies at the termination of the spur of the first range of rising land." The village "consisted of about a dozen large tents, most of them stores, one blacksmith's shop, a ten-pin alley, two boarding houses and a number of unoccupied cabins." Sam and his party went at once to visit Colonel Thorn, a Texas pioneer who had come with his family and his family of slaves to California in '49. The Colonel had "an old-fashioned log cabin" with additions built of sawed lumber where "the wayfarer found a well furnished store, a clean bunk, a tidy supper and the luxury of milk — then a great rarity in all California." Colonel Thorn also knew of several gold mines for sale.

The "Washington Vein" was discovered in 1850 and "had already yielded highly remunerative returns to its discoverers, who had worked it after the primitive Mexican fashion, with arrastres, a slow but inexpensive process which may be compared to the grinding of corn by a single mill-stone. . . ." Sam and his partners bought into the "Washington Vein," proposing to put in what was then "modern machinery."

Actually, tenderfeet though they were, they had not been led astray as might be supposed. They had acquired a very good property; a vein which produced about two million dollars' worth of gold before the end of the century. The proprietors offered to Sam Ward and his friends, "one half of the mine for fourteen thousand dollars to be expended in its development." This they accepted.

Then on went Sam, for he had developed a passion for exploring the gold country and observing its people. There was "Quartz Johnson," the man who knew where there were three hundred veins of gold and would sell half of any or all of them for machinery to work them. Quartz Johnson lived in a log hut in Bear Valley surrounded by "scores of bags and heaps of ores in newspapers, each labeled with some hieroglyphic" which told where the gold came from — in a code known only to himself. In 1850, John F. Johnson had discovered the "Great Johnson Lode" and it was said that he tried to build his own quartz mill, run by steam. As soon as the "Washington Vein" should make Sam Ward a new fortune, how easy it would be for him to multiply it — three hundred times over!

The gold seekers of the Mariposa differed greatly from those on the Merced. In the Mariposa, Sam's path "lay over the dividing walls of square pits, eight to ten feet deep and about the same width." These were worked-out claims which looked to Sam like a huge cemetery of opened graves; a sort of day after the Last Judgment day. Farther on, the claims were still being worked, not by Indians but by white men, "sallow and bearded." It was heavy labor with pick and crowbar and "but few panfuls of earth rewarded their daily toil," the gold, when it was found, "being coarse, silver its principle alloy." This sort of thing was not for Sam.

Sam completed his round trip of exploration of the Yosemite Valley region by returning to the Merced River, where he found that the Indians, in his absence, had made a "ten-strike" — finding another gold pocket in a bend of the river. They had cleaned out the shelves of the trading post, spending their gold as fast as they got their hands on it. The proprietor of the trading post was the man who really panned the gold on the Merced River — without so much as getting his feet wet. Sam returned to San Francisco to help organize the company to exploit the Washington Vein; to get himself appointed to keep an eye on the operators of the Quartzburg property — and to run the store on the Merced River.

Seated in his tent on the Merced, Sam Ward wrote a long letter to his sister Julia, dated February 7, 1852, and describing his life in the gold fields. He was "isolated . . . from all mankind," Sam said, "living here near mountains of snow, 200 miles from San Francisco, surrounded by 600 Indians without a civilized being near." He was "in the saddle from morning till morning; at times digging and washing gold and mostly alone. . . . Each morning throughout the winter I have plunged into the snowy stream which skirts my tent and am as hardy as an Indian," Sam said. "I do not know what *avenir* Fate has in store for me, but I am growing strong, bracing my nerves to every kind of physical danger. I may now say from experience and actual test, that I fear neither man nor beast. When I first came, I suffered greatly in the ascent and descent of the steep mountain passes, when a misstep of my mule would have brought the Life Insurance companies in debt and made poor Medora a widow. Now I gallop up and down like an Indian. . . .

"I have learned the Indian language and now speak Spanish as fluently as French. The former, I mastered in about a month. I can now make a good Indian speech." And Sam was continuing his Indian language studies. "Having mastered Potoyeuse, I am now imbibing Chanchichee. . . ." Sam wrote down a few Indian words for his sister Julia's edification and added, "As is natural, I am a favorite with the Indians." [2]

But there were other versions of the story of Sam Ward's learning Indian tongues. He had "made a bet that he could learn the Indian dialect of that region in three weeks," it was said. "He shut himself up with an Indian for that length of time, and by plying the savage with whiskey, kept him talkative and good-natured." A further footnote to the tale questions whether Sam's Indian teacher were a brave: the "savage" might have been a squaw. In any case, and in spite of long passages in Sam Ward's letter to his sister concerning lonely evenings spent reading Horace and Virgil, Sam's life upon the Merced was not entirely austere.

Stories about Sam Ward had a habit of growing tall. His reputation as a gourmet was established by this time perhaps, but his skill at discovering and fostering latent genius in a chef would have to await his Washington days as King of the Lobby. Nevertheless, it was said that he "taught the Indians" on the Merced "to cook dog so lusciously that they elected him chief of the tribe." [3]

Whatever the tall tales, Sam Ward was really a good friend to the Indians. The store which he ran for Belt and Company was an honest one and Sam's only difficulty was with his own Government. He supplied the Indians with stores allotted to their reservation and then had to go to law to collect money owing him by the Government in Washington. This was a bill which was long overdue before it was finally settled.

The new and "modern machinery" to grind up quartz and release gold arrived late in the summer of 1851. And it was late autumn before the result of the first week's mining was ready to be judged. Sam Ward was on the spot. The stamp mill had been shut down and "the clattering stampers were silent" when he arrived, the "engine was cooling off." An old-fashioned "arastre" was something like a huge orange squeezer with a beam for a handle and a mule to turn it. A stamping mill stood up in the air with chutes like organ pipes to take in rough-broken quartz and iron claws operated by belts and pulleys to grind the quartz while water washed out the gold into "amalgamating tubs" below. "The water had been let off the amalgamating tubs," leaving quicksilver in the bottom when Sam arrived — and in the tubs there was also gold — he hoped. The gold, released in particles, filtered through mesh wire into the tubs to be taken up by the hungry mercury, Sam said and he watched the mine superintendent "scooping into an iron pan the mercury graced with yellow promise."

The "five or six stockholders" went into a roughly partitioned-off anteroom to watch the final process. The gold-loaded mercury was poured into a piece of buckskin which was then picked up at the corners to form a bag and squeezed. The mercury came through the buckskin and "what remains is gold." Miners were "generally satisfied when the residium which refuses to pass through the 'chamois' is no bigger than a hickory nut," Sam Ward said. "An English walnut brings on palpitation of the heart and any larger mass brings on delirium. *Our first ball was the size of a pippin!* The next five showed no diminution — and even the mercury from the six lower tubs (for the miners had tried the experiment of filtering twice) gave us many filberts." When the first day's mining results at the "Washington Vein" were weighed "the grand total was 316 ounces — equal to five thousand and sixty-four dollars at sixteen and a half dollars per ounce!" Sam left the scene quietly, it having occurred to him to "anticipate the rise in Washington stock."

Pretending to ride up into the hills to visit a prospector friend, Sam circled instead and made for his store and the ferry on the Merced "by an Indian trail" he had "noted on" his "frequent shooting excursions." Before dawn next day he was on his way to Stockton and San Francisco. While waiting for the steamer *Sophie*, he bought "150 more shares at the price which our party had been 'let in' to the enlarged company." In San Francisco, he got hold of fifty more shares before letters from the mine superintendent tipped off the news and the stock rose from fourteen to thirty-five dollars a share. Sam then sold his newly acquired shares and the operation gave him "a pocket full of rocks for many a week" as he put it. But he lost faith in the mine much too soon. "The deposit in our tubs that famous week came from a pocket, not a vein," he said and the stock he had kept for himself he soon believed to be worthless.

In the Washington mine, "pay rock" was "usually found in bunches, generally separated by large bodies of slate which have occasionally confused the owners," according to the *Mariposa Gazette* in an article written much later. Sam Ward was one of the disheartened stockholders at a time when machinery was still too primitive to operate at a consistent profit. Sam's gold mine, like so many other ventures in his life, was really a good thing if he had been content to go slowly and hang on a long time.

But if ever there was a man in a hurry to be rich, it was Sam Ward. He left the Merced River in the early part of 1852 and went back to San Francisco and his real estate business. Prices were depressed. It was the time to buy. Letters must have been dispatched by Sam to his favorite brother-in-law, Adolph Mailliard, about the time when the Washington Vein was in brief bonanza. The "pay rock" was probably exhausted when Annie lovingly packed Adolph's saddlebags and said farewell. She was expecting her second child and Adolph had been "so kind," never "leaving her alone" while her first child was on the way.[4] Now he would be far across the continent when their much-longed for baby was born — but Annie was brave. She was "in better health than for some time" and "looked prettier than ever before" as she assured her husband that all would be well. Julia was coming to mother her and perhaps there would be a little son waiting for Adolph when he returned with some of that gold brother Sam was raving about.

When Adolph arrived, Sam's enthusiasm was all for land again, and the thing to do now was to buy a ranch, stock it with cattle, and grow rich supplying hungry San Francisco with beef and dairy products. Land was available the size of a European principality and the princely Adolph could imagine how delightful it would be to stock a few fertile valleys with his fine Jersey cattle, and live at his ease. But there was no hurry about all this. San Francisco offered many attractions and Adolph had been ill — he needed a rest.

San Francisco was swarming with adventurers. The majority were Americans but almost all nationalities were represented, with a large colony of Frenchmen living in French boardinghouses, frequenting French cafés and keeping very much to themselves, as French expatriates were apt to do. But Adolph Mailliard, though American-born, was of pure French (and Corsican) descent with personal charm that was all French. Sam prided himself on his ability to pass as a Frenchman whenever he pleased. These two boon companion brothers-in-law were welcome in the San Francisco French colony and doubtless they recognized some of the ex-nobility they found there.

When Sam first came to California in 1849, the Marquis Charles de Pindray [5] had been the leader of the French colony. Not that he was always in the city — but when he did arrive his exploits were spectacular. The Marquis, having gambled away a family fortune, fled to the United States and came over the Rockies during the early days of the Gold Rush. He soon tired of mining, observed that meat sold in San Francisco for five and six dollars a pound, and turned bear hunter. His bravery as a hunter was legendary and so was his defense of his reputation whenever he turned up in town with a cartload of bearmeat. But what might be termed *local* bears became scarce and the

Marquis made a deal to go to Los Angeles for cattle. He was paid in advance for the cattle he was to buy but lost the cash while gambling. The Marquis recouped his losses, not by bear hunting this time but as a result of a man hunt. Tracking down two notorious bandits, Joachim Muretta and a man known as "Three Fingers," he killed them, received the bounty — and their heads were displayed in a Los Angeles drugstore.

When Adolph Mailliard reached San Francisco, there was a new leader in the French colony. He was Count Gaston de Raousset-Boulbon, a friend of the late Marquis de Pindray. The Marquis de Pindray led a filibustering expedition into Mexican Sonora and fired the Count with his tales of new gold mines and a new overseas empire for France. However the Marquis de Pindray died by an assassin's bullet within sight of his goal, and Count Gaston de Raousset-Boulbon took his place.

Quite probably, Count Gaston de Raousset-Boulbon already knew both Adolph Mailliard and Sam Ward. He had been a close friend of Prince Demidoff, the Russian who had ordered "Heracles and Diana" and other works of Thomas Crawford. In Paris, the Count's black horses with silver-mounted harness, his houseboat on the Seine and his lovely mistresses were famous — but he had gone through his property at the gaming tables, had acquired a new stake in California and also a dream of empire. Sam Ward had gold mining stock and real estate for sale but would buy and sell almost anything. Count Gaston wanted to buy rifles.

California had been so recently acquired that no one had forgotten the "Bear Flag Rebellion" whereby colonists, certainly with a grievance, had "liberated" themselves from Mexico, their territory subsequently bought by the United States from a crumbling Mexican Government only too glad to take the money and be rid of a trouble spot. To the southward, bounded on the north by Arizona and on the west by the Gulf of California, lay Sonora, one of the largest states in what was now the Mexican Republic. Here a few unhappy colonists also had a grievance. They were beseiged by Apache Indians and would surely welcome a military force sent for their protection. Or so reasoned Count Gaston and his French adventurers. It just so happened that the Sierra Madres of Sonora were said to be full of gold, the "gold and silver mines reported richer than California."

Count Gaston went to Mexico City where he found President Arista briefly in power. The president promised 60,000 piastres; pay for 200 soldiers to keep the Apaches under control in Sonora, and "property, half in lands, mines and placers," wherever the Count de Raousset-Boulbon should "plant his flag" — all this secured to him and his "companions by title deeds." The Count's part of the bargain was to reach the Sierras and work the mines — for which he would receive half the gold.

With some of his Mexican money in cash rather than promises, the Count returned to San Francisco and raised a small private army of 160 infantry, 40 cavalry, 3 officers — and equipped them with rifles and two cannon. It was all very expensive, but Count Gaston borrowed money on his prospects — and with President Arista's smiling sanction, the expedition was not illegal. It was said that the Count tried to persuade Sam Ward to go with him to Sonora.

No sooner was Count Gaston's back turned than the Mexican Government set up its own Sonora mining company. A British company put in a bid for Sonora mining concessions and there were also American firms interested. President Arista was overthrown by Santa Anna in 1853, which made it a simple matter for the Mexican Government to repudiate the agreement with the French adventurers. When Mexican support failed him, the Count was obliged to turn back with the famed Sierra Madres in sight and with nothing to show for his expedition save a beautiful Spanish girl, María Antonía, who left her father's hacienda to follow him.

Back to Mexico City went Count Gaston — taking his María Antonía along. Santa Anna offered the Count "an annuity of 60,000 piastres to maintain Sonora as a colony for French people," but "refused him the title of governor" — a curious proposition, surely. Count Gaston plotted against Santa Anna, was discovered and fled — leaving María Antonía behind. Back in San Francisco, he organized another expedition of 800 men and his señorita, escaping from Mexico City, joined him in time to go back to Sonora. Once more, it was said, both Sam and Adolph were urged to go with the Count to Sonora — and acquire a small kingdom for themselves, rich in gold.

But Adolph had every reason to return home to Bordentown. News of the birth of his first-born son, Joseph Louis Mailliard, had finally reached him. This was " 'Poleon," the baby with big dark eyes and a funny little air of command — so like the Bonapartes. The boy's father had bought a ranch of ten thousand acres near San Rafael, California, and not far from San Francisco. It had been "taken over by Ward and Company for a bad debt" and Adolph got a bargain.[6] There were redwood forests, running brooks, open glades and pasturage. This was a handsome heritage to be bringing to a little son called " 'Poleon" — and this was not all. Adolph was certain that on his ranch there was a gold mine, rich beyond the Washington Vein in bonanza. He had but to develop it when he chose. No one seemed to know just who gave Adolph this idea or showed him the rich samples of gold taken from a certain hole between rocks on his land. But most certainly he believed the story.

Sam Ward, though never cautious, continued also to resist any temptation to go filibustering to Sonora — although the romantic adventure was just his style. And then, early in 1854, Jefferson Davis, Secretary of State, ordered Major Wool, military Commander of California, to "maintain international obligations by preventing unlawful expeditions against the territories of foreign powers." Orders were given for the arrest of the French consul in connection with Count Gaston de Raousset-Boulbon's second expedition. Four hundred of the Count's eight hundred men were taken off his ship, and he was arrested just as he was about to sail for Guaymas, the port of Sonora. Unfortunately for himself, he escaped — to fulfill his tragic destiny. He and his little army were defeated in Sonora and he was taken prisoner along with the routed remnant of his men. María Antonía joined him in prison.

And now at last it looked as if Sam Ward would actually make an expedition to Sonora. He was retained — he did not say by whom — to negotiate for Count Gaston's release and the release of the other prisoners. But the Count, like some tragic hero on the operatic stage, proudly refused to make any compromises or come to any terms and he was executed in Guaymas before Sam Ward could get there. María Antonía went into a convent.

Santa Anna ordered the other prisoners brought to Mexico City that they might march past him, "heads bowed, their limbs in chains," like prisoners of a Roman emperor. Sam Ward's commission now became more official though no less confidential as he hurried to Mexico City to prevent the public humiliation of the prisoners — some of whom were citizens of the United States. This was the beginning of Sam Ward's secret diplomatic career, which he loved to hint at, his stories losing nothing in the telling.

The prisoners were put aboard a ship at Guaymas, on the Gulf of California, and freighted around to Veracruz. From there they made a painful overland journey through steaming jungle country, then high over mountain passes where a flint-paved muletrack was considered a road. They were following in the footsteps of Cortez the conqueror but — white men though they were, and free born — they knew how it felt to be victims of conquest. Dark-skinned descendants of conquered Mixtec and Aztec peered at them from rocky hillsides. Their progress was pitifully slow but secretly the word had been passed among them to cause all possible delay. Time was in their favor. Sam Ward needed time.

Although Sam Ward did his best to reach Veracruz ahead of the prisoners and then traveled by coach across country to Mexico City, his progress was anything but swift. The overland journey took at least six days and, at first, Sam must have been delighted by the tropical jungle with wild orchids looking like brilliant birds perched high in the trees over the so-called road. Then a mountain wall loomed with snow-capped volcanic peaks in the distance and even coach travelers got out to walk and the horses strained just to pull an empty coach up the steep incline. A chilly night was spent high in a mountain pass at a town noted for bandits.

But Sam Ward was born for adventure. Bandits were the least of his worries and if he were ever taken ill he would later tell how some powerful native remedy, accepted in perfect faith, had cured him. At hostelries when the diligence paused for refreshment, barnyard animals mingled freely with the guests and the odor was strong if not sweet.[7] But Sam enjoyed it all. He peered into open earthen pots which bubbled slowly over charcoal braziers and never doubted but what the all too recognizable portions of animal anatomy, feet, ears or tails, would soon become delicious morsels. Sam was not disappointed, as pungent herbs competed successfully with the barnyard smell, and he hunted up the cook to pass compliments upon a delicious meal. What did it matter if Sam spoke Spanish and the cook only an Indian dialect? — A rapport was established through Sam Ward's friendly smile.

Once in Mexico City, Sam needed all his remarkable gifts as a "promoter of good feeling and friendly relations." He called upon Dano, Secretary of the French Consulate, and learned that Santa Anna was not in town — that he was at Tucabaya, his "regal estate." Somehow, by means of his fluent Spanish and his tact and charm, Sam got himself and Dano invited out to Tucabaya for a visit. The place, though spoken of as in the country, was not far from Chapultepec Castle, but Maximilian had yet to appear upon the scene to build a broad avenue to castle and royal park. Santa Anna lived regally none the less, surrounded by an army of retainers who could literally become an army at any time; and Sam Ward had the seemingly impossible task of persuading a dictator not to behave like a Roman emperor.

Sam Ward was "so quick of apprehension and so versatile . . . that he could not fail," it was said, even by people who did not approve of him. This time, he succeeded in a delicate and even dangerous mission, rendered all the more difficult because he served in an unofficial capacity. The prisoners were granted amnesty and spared humiliation — if not exhaustion and disease. Moreover American mining interests did not suffer from Sam's expedition to Mexico, if his joyful mood on his return were an indication. Still stronger proof of prosperity was his stopover in New Orleans to see Medora.

On June 10, 1852, George Templeton Strong, the indefatigable New York diarist, had written; "Mrs. Samuel Ward who's living in Paris while her husband's in California, said to be the mistress of a Russian prince." It was not necessarily so. Medora's beauty had made her the subject of gossip many times before. But Mrs. Grymes had indeed taken her two daughters, Medora and Athenais, to Europe, where, especially on the Riviera, their striking good looks and their magnificent wardrobes caused comment. There was just one person in the world whom the generous Sam Ward really hated — and that was his mother-in-law.

But on December, 1854, Sam found his Medora in New Orleans and dressed in deep mourning for the recent death of her father, whom she had been attending during his last illness. Mourning became her. Sam never saw her looking so beautiful before; they came back to New York together and during the summer of 1854 the two of them visited Julia Ward Howe in Newport. "Medora looked most beautifully," Julia said. "And Sam won for himself golden opinions from many people, prejudiced as the world has been of late against him."

Shortly afterward, Sam and his Medora set out for Europe together, taking with them their two boys, Sam Ward, Jr., now ten years old, and John Randolph Ward, two years younger. The boys gave their pony, their pony cart and the silver-mounted harness to the Howe cousins.[8] Doubtless their father had promised to buy them real saddle horses in England or whatever else their hearts desired — for as usual, Sam Ward was off on a big deal with a vast fortune at the end of the new rainbow.

CHAPTER EIGHTEEN
End of an Eagle's Flight

THOMAS CRAWFORD received his commission for the Richmond monument in 1850, but six years went by before he returned with his family to his native land to supervise the setting of the first bronze figures. To the layman, this might seem a long time; but actually Thomas Crawford worked as rapidly as possible and with great intensity. There were those who said that he worked as though he realized his days might be numbered. "Fashionable crowds flock to the Palazzo Negroni," said Thomas Hicks, noted New York portrait painter and friend of Crawford's. Everyone came to see "the colossal equestrian statue of Washington" for it was just as Louisa had observed during the early days of her marriage — a commission for an equestrian was the sculptor's badge of success in Rome.

The equestrian Washington had been designed for marble and would see the light of day in bronze, only because the Richmond city fathers so desired. Bronze was a new medium for Crawford, expressive of a new age where metals were supreme. Another new experience was in store for Crawford when he went to Munich to see the equestrian cast. In the huge, murky foundry, workmen, stripped to the waist, handled molten metal which shed a ruddy glow over swelling muscles of arm and chest — gleaming wet with sweat. It was a scene to delight a sculptor's eye even while he held his breath with anxiety — for one slip on the part of the workmen could cause a year's delay with casts and molds to be made all over again. But Munich's foundries were justly famous. All went well as section after section of the huge statue was cast.

On the last day, Crawford returned to see the work finished. When he arrived, the foundry was dark and seemingly deserted. His heart sank as the director came to him and he waited to be told of some dreadful accident — a crack in the metal — some last-minute flaw requiring months to repair. Then suddenly torches flared and there was a sound of music echoing through the vast stone building. The workmen were singing. And there in the torchlight towered "the magnificent horse and rider," in bright new bronze and gold. It was a scene only the Bavarians could have contrived, and if Thomas Crawford's eyes filled with tears, no one could have blamed him. In fact, he would have broken the hearts of these craftsmen "who called him brother" if his emotion had not matched their own.

Although the equestrian was designed for marble, Crawford modeled the Beethoven for the Music Hall in Boston with bronze in mind. The subject suited him and restrictions on the part of Charles C. Perkins, who commissioned the statue, were few. Crawford was free to do as he pleased and music was his second love, after art. In his Roman villa, musical evenings had been his especial delight, musical guests most welcome. Louisa herself played very well but as in girlhood she always relinquished the piano to Julia, so now she lured her guests into performing for her and it surprised and pleased her to have her husband say he liked her music best. The Beethoven statue took form in Crawford's mind during his most happy hours. It was perhaps his finest work.

When the Beethoven was cast in Munich, it was "so grand and noble" that Lachner, conductor of the Royal Symphony Orchestra, gave a symphony for it. A six-foot pedestal was made and a green velvet background supported by gold columns. The statue was placed in the Munich Concert Hall and "King Maximilian and his Queen attended a Beethoven program, presented by three hundred musicians and singers." It must have been a happy moment for Thomas Crawford and Louisa as they were shown into the special box prepared for them. "The splendor of the fete surpassed anything ever given in Munich," Thomas Hicks said — speaking as though he had been there. Crawford was made a member of the Royal Academy of Art in Munich; was equally honored in St. Petersburg and by the Academy of St. Mark in Florence, Italy.

When the Beethoven was received in Boston, enthusiasm ran just as high. A concert was given at the Music Hall, at which not crowned heads but Beacon Street aristocracy was present and William Wetmore Story, himself a sculptor of high repute, read a poem he had written in generous praise of his fellow artist. The Beethoven had great simplicity. It showed what Crawford could do when his public let him alone — but all the critics of his day spoke of it as too severe. Before many years had passed, the plain white wall against which it was designed to stand was covered with a Gothic monstrosity housing a new organ and the "too simple" Beethoven was put outside the door.

The son whom both Louisa and her husband so ardently desired was born August 2, 1854. His name had been selected years before, to honor Francis Marion Ward, who had died in New Orleans at the age of twenty-seven. He was always Louisa's favorite brother and it was he who had helped her when her Uncle John opposed her marriage. Almost too beautiful to be real flesh and blood, Francis Marion Crawford — or "Frankino" as they called him — was soon almost too spoiled to live with. Like his father, he would achieve remarkable success. He would be F. Marion Crawford, the novelist. And as in the case of his father also, popular taste would turn against him, but not before his early death.

Frankino was born not in Rome but in Bagni da Lucca, a favorite mountain health resort since earliest Roman times. "My father was beside himself with joy," little Mimoli remembered. He "showered presents on all of us to make us understand and share it." Mimoli, her father's darling and hitherto the youngest child, entered completely into this sharing of joy so wisely offered. She gathered up her dearest treasures, a "woolly parrot" and a pair of little white shoes, to give to the baby. Even the shining silver dollar which her father had just given her, she added to this loving offering, and her devotion to her brother increased as he became her only playmate.[1]

Annie, the Crawford's oldest child, was now eight years old; and with her, the attitude of shared delight did not succeed. Annie was dark-browed and passionate, feared by the servants and even by her own mother for she had discovered that her temper tantrums raised her temperature and she could become ill almost at will. Her sister Jennie, only a little over a year younger, was considered much prettier and she was certainly pleasanter to get along with. Distinction in appearance would come to Annie, and a kind of arresting, tragic beauty as she grew up to her clear-cut features, now too sharp to be pretty in a little girl. Annie lived in a private dream-world of her own, Italian peasant servants providing her with strange material for her fancy to feed upon. At present, she obeyed no order — not even a kind request — without first consulting invisible, imaginary playmates she called her "friends from China." If the Chinese friends agreed, Annie would do as told — not otherwise. In later years she wrote stories as good as if not better than some of her brother Francis Marion's.

"The wild Crawfords," Julia Ward Howe called her sister Lousia's children. But Jennie, the second child, born in 1847, was at least a happy contrast to Annie. She harked back to no dark Celtic ancestor, half fey and gifted with second sight, but resembled her mother's famous ancestor, Governor Ward — with golden hair and sunny smiles. "Piccola" they called her — a pretty Italian pet-name for a very feminine little girl who played the piano unusually well and danced the tarantella.

"Beauty was everywhere," wrote Mimoli, the youngest of the Crawford daughters, recalling her enchanted Roman childhood and especially the years just after her brother Francis Marion was born, when her father's career was at its height. Colossal statues crowded his studios and visitors flocked to the Villa Negroni to see the great Thomas Crawford. Mimoli described her mother who was thirty-one and whose beauty, instead of fading, only deepened. Louisa was dressing for a Christmas party and Mimoli recalled her mother's "perfect oval face, the dark, sweet eyes, the camellia whiteness of the bare shoulders framed in old Venetian Point that lost itself in the folds of her tea-rose moire gown, just the tint of her cheeks. She had big pearls in her ears and a silver girdle knotted around her waist and falling to her feet." The little girl took hold of the ends of the long sash and held them tight. She told how she had suddenly feared that her mother might escape her — fading as visions of saints faded away never to return, according to the legends her Italian nursemaid told her.

Although none of the Crawford children became artists, there was a great deal of the artist in each. Beauty was indeed everywhere within their home, with its walls covered with paintings — some of them old and rescued from oblivion in the corner of some junkshop; some of them new, the gifts of fellow artists or purchased of contemporary artists by the Crawfords, who were generous in helping the less fortunate. The doorway to the villa, "wide enough for a coach and four to pass through," led to gardens and ilex groves as old as Rome itself. And in the city, each changing season had its own church pageantry, rooted deep in the pagan past — growing in splendor through the Middle Ages and flowering in Papal glory before their eyes. Holding fast to the hand of an Italian nurse, and listening to her simple, soft-voiced explanations, the Crawford children responded to the color, the music and the scent of incense. By the time Francis Marion was born, Annie and Jennie had an English governess and regular classroom hours. The gates of Paradise closed for them a little, although their lessons were easy, being for the most part in languages none of which were really foreign. Mimoli and Frankino were still free to wander in the sunshine a while longer.

Frankino was carried in his nurse's arms, that remarkable invention, the baby carriage, being unknown in Rome. The baby was "so beautiful that . . . our nurse was constantly stopped in the street to answer questions" as to whose child it was, said Mimoli. Frankino's father's famous name brought smiles of recognition. Among the dark Italians, the blond, blue-eyed Frankino looked like one of those Anglo-Saxon children who inspired Saint Augustine to exclaim, "Not Angles but angels!" and forthwith to travel to Britain to offer salvation.

On January 21 came the Roman feast of Saint Agnes, which no child would want to miss. This was the day when the shepherds from the Campagna brought in the newborn lambs, "all curled and beribboned," to the church of Saint Agnes Fuori Le Mura, where the "blessing of the lambs" took place. An English nurse had just been installed for the infant Francis Marion. Mimoli led the new nurse to the church outside the walls — the nurse carrying the baby in her arms, of course. "That day, the officiating Cardinal was a very old man and his sight was very dim," Mimoli remembered. "The English nurse, curious to see everything, pushed forward with Marion, a bundle of fluffy whiteness, asleep in her arms."

" *'Che bell' Agnellino!'* " exclaimed the old Cardinal, blessing Francis Marion Crawford by mistake for a lamb. But even his sister Mimoli, while maintaining that he was beautiful, never claimed that her brother was a little lamb. "He had a most imperious temper combined with a stubborn resolve to do nothing for himself that other people could be coerced into doing for him," she said, and she could not have summed up F. Marion Crawford more concisely — at least for some years to come. She was one of his slaves and she knew it. His mother was another, and eventually his Uncle Sam Ward was entirely at his command. Only his Aunt Julia Ward Howe proved impervious to his charm — but she loved him none the less and eventually she helped to make a man of him — and a writer.

The future F. Marion Crawford absolutely refused to learn to walk and by the time he was a year and a half old he was too big for even the strong English nurse to carry. English Mary did her best but "if she let him down for a moment his wrath broke loose." His sister Mimoli remembered "the most humiliating day" of her life when she and the nurse were "climbing the Via Quattre Fontane" on their way back home from the Pincio Gardens. Completely out of breath, Mary paused and "stood Master Marion on his feet for a moment. He immediately sat down in the middle of the street, roaring with rage, and a friendly policeman had to pick him up and bring him home, fighting and struggling all the way." Mimoli "followed in deep abasement, sadly carrying a shoe he had kicked off."

Mimoli spoke of her father as always ready to play with his children. He had taught her to walk by rolling oranges along the garden path for her and, now that she was older, he gave her a bit of clay to model when she came to his studios, where she was always welcome. When nurses came looking for her, he would lift her high inside one of the sections of the huge plaster cast of General Washington's horse, so she could hide. Then what about the spoiled little son, so much in need of a spanking? Perhaps Thomas Crawford saw himself in the boy who looked so much like him — and remembered his own stubborn, passionate will and the unhappy scenes in his home, where the rod was never spared.

Brought up an Episcopalian, and remembering with nostalgia the well-filled Ward family pew at Ascension Church in New York, Louisa took her children to the English Protestant Episcopal church in Rome. Faithfully she taught them their catechism, marveling at Francis Marion's quick memory — once he made up his mind to learn. The familiar words of the Episcopal service always carried Louisa back to her childhood and she thought of her sister Annie, saying those same words across the sea.[2] It had rather saddened Louisa that her sister Julia should become a Unitarian, but she supposed her own children would somehow inherit her love for her own church. But Episcopal services in Rome were held in a remodeled barn outside the city walls and Louisa did not realize how bare and poverty-stricken the place looked to her children — compared to other Roman churches they often entered, all alive with gold and lights, painted images, far-off voices and solemn music. The Crawford children fidgeted through uninspired sermons in their mother's church, delivered often by clergymen whose chief qualification to preach in Rome had been the need of a good rest in a warm climate. These were nice old gentlemen and it never occurred to Louisa that her children might need stronger religious fare if they were to achieve a personal Protestant Reformation and resist the Church of Rome. Against the possibility of such a thing was the very air they breathed and the beauty that they loved.

Mimoli was still "a very little girl," she said, when she saw Pope Pius IX borne up the long aisle in St. Peter's in the Pontifical Chair. She saw the "dazzling procession of cardinals, bishops and nobles in seventeenth century costumes." It was Easter and as "the long high mass" proceeded, splendid voices answered to a voice. Suddenly, far overhead in the great dome silver trumpets rang out. And "when the music ceased, I found myself kneeling on the pavement, crying helplessly," she said. The Scotch nurse, recently installed, pulled her to her feet. "You are not to kneel," she whispered angrily to a child who would never forget the silver trumpets.

Permissions were even harder to understand than prohibitions at times. On Easter evening, the whole Crawford family "climbed the long twisting stairs leading to the tower terrace and stood under its open arches in the soft April darkness," to watch the illumination of St. Peter's. Far out across the dark city, St. Peter's was already outlined in tiny twinkling lights: portico, dome and cross. The whole city waited in breathless silence, and beyond the Campagna, from the mountain hamlets overlooking Rome, peasants waited and watched. Then from the Castello Sant' Angelo a cannon boomed. Instantly the cross on top of St. Peter's dome "flamed into molten gold which ran in a torrent of glory down, down, from dome to roof, from roof to pillar and from pillar to colonnade. . . ."

The miracle of light was wrought first by means of candles which, at the signal, became torches and "the task of changing the top-most light on the towering cross, four hundred feet above the ground," was so dangerous that "a condemned criminal" would be pardoned if he attempted it and lived — being given absolution before he made the climb. The little Crawfords, going to their nursery beds, "held hands tightly" and asked each other, " 'Did he get down?' "

The proportions of his "Armed Liberty" were "derived" from the cross on St. Peter's in Rome, Thomas Crawford had said. It was all very well for a grown man to "derive" and draw his inspiration from life in a foreign country; but when two of the "pedestrian statues" for the Richmond monument were done and shipped overseas, and the children were told that they were all going "home" to the United States, this "home" was a place only two of them had ever seen and none of them remembered. It approximated heaven if all their parents told them should be true. "I am an American," little Francis Marion had learned to say as soon as he could talk. Later, he would concede, "Perhaps my nose is Roman," and wonder why the grownups laughed. Children born and brought up abroad always have a hard time finding themselves in their parents' native land, and perhaps the Crawford children found the adjustment harder than most. Their clothes, charming by Roman standards, looked queer to their American cousins in Boston. Their speech, though perfect English, had a faint foreign intonation laughed at in Bordentown — while not a cousin understood the sort of Italian that ten-year-old Annie Crawford flung about her with such effect. "Back home?" Where was home, but Rome?

Louisa was too happy to be with her sisters to understand much of what went on among the children. She only wished that her four would behave better. No use to say that they were worse while visiting — who would believe it? But Adolph had the perfect solution, at least for the comfort of the parents. He built an addition to Spring Villa especially to house the children: Louisa's four, Julia's five when she came bringing them all — and his own only child. For Annie and Adolph's little " 'Poleon" had died.

Leaving the sisters together in Bordentown, Thomas Crawford was off to Richmond. His two pedestrians, Patrick Henry and Jefferson, were in place but he had not seen them since they left the foundry in Munich. It was typical of Crawford that he had decided to make his statues twelve feet high instead of nine, "thus causing an extraordinary increase of expense" with which he "had no intention of bothering" the Richmond committee. The equestrian had "become 21 feet instead of 15" and the bas reliefs were all increased proportionately.[3] Like any good artist, he was more interested in having his work look the way he wanted it to than in making a maximum amount of profit on it. But the stone "star-shaped pedestal" had to be altered — a matter too difficult to explain by letter. Crawford found much to do in Richmond and he had to be a mechanic as well as a sculptor for "the arm of Patrick Henry" had to be "cast so that it could be removed," placed in the packing case separately, then locked in place when the statue was set up.

Confronted with the one-armed Patrick Henry, the Richmond workmen had been dumfounded — like children who receive a fascinating mechanical toy at Christmas but with no idea how to make it work. Crawford arrived to clear up all difficulties.

To see their work under the sky and in the light of day — that was the ambition now of all the sculptors who began, as Crawford did, with parlor pieces and portrait busts. It must have been a great moment for Thomas Crawford, as he walked along the streets in Richmond, came out upon the square and saw his Thomas Jefferson and Patrick Henry — not as today, in a crowd of dingy statues all too German in their excessive realism — but standing bright and new, a miracle of metallurgy and a symbol of an astonishing new world. In his mind's eye, Crawford could see his great equestrian Washington riding high. Faith in the future was part of Crawford's creed, together with a boyish enthusiasm for his country's heroes which maturity had never dimmed. Thomas Crawford was forty-three years old. He realized that it would take years more to complete the Richmond monument, but he never doubted that it would be a great and enduring work.

Crawford returned to Bordentown to say good-by to his family. It was now July, 1856. Picking up his little daughter Mimoli and swinging her high into the air the way she loved so much, he gave her a last tight embrace. He would be back soon, he assured her. She clung to him, begging him to take her to Rome with him — but she remembered that he did not like to see her cry.

Thomas Crawford wrote to the Richmond committee concerning the crating of the equestrian statue. The total weight, he said, would be 30,000 pounds. The packing case would be 22 feet long, 16 feet wide and 8 feet thick. The statue would "arrive in one piece with the exception of the horse's tail" which was arranged "to be assembled in Richmond with the same facility as the Arm of Henry was." And Thomas Crawford reminded the Virginians that the United States Government had sent a vessel for the "Perisco statue," so why not for his? What Crawford wanted was "a first class ship of war" and the Richmond committee thought there was every good reason why the Government should send "the steamer *Merrimac*." But the statue, in its crate, would have to be lashed to the deck because it "would weaken the ship to have a hole cut in the deck" big enough to get the crated Father of his Country into the hold. Crawford was now certain that all arrangements were complete.

Louisa and the children had arrived in the United States ahead of Thomas, and when he came he found his family established at Bordentown. "On meeting" her husband "after an interval of four months (from April to July, 1856)," Louisa saw "a slight protrusion of his left eyeball" that had increased, amounting now "to a slight disfigurement." She had noticed this condition for the first time about six

months previously, but her husband assured her that it was just because of a slight cold. Now she was beginning to be alarmed.

Upon her husband's return from Richmond, Louisa saw that the condition of his eye was worse. Anxiously, she questioned him. Had he been lying on his left side and reading late at night the way she had begged him not to do? He had kept all his promises to her, he said, even giving up sketching at night. And much as he loved his books, the classics in translation, the American history which so fired his artistic imagination — he would not read until they were all at home in Rome again and Louisa could read aloud to him the way she loved to do. Reluctantly Crawford admitted, however, that the headaches from which he had begun to suffer in the spring were increasing.

When Crawford arrived in Europe, the pain behind his eye was so intense that he stopped over in Paris to see a famous specialist who urged him to stay on and take the "medicines prescribed for internal and external use." But in Rome the statues of John Marshall and George Mason were awaiting the final touches before being sent to the Munich foundry. The bronze doors for the Capitol in Washington were still on paper. "The Life of George Washington" was the subject chosen for the doors, and Crawford delighted in working on them. He hurried on to Rome.

All known historical figures for the doors, Crawford modeled as much like miniature portraits as he could. But there were many other figures in his design whose appearance was not a matter of record or who were merely onlookers at a famous scene. Thomas Crawford took pleasure in making these people portraits of the Ward family, as he had known them! Here was Grandfather Ward — whom Crawford could have seen and who was certainly familiar through family paintings. Colonel Ward had every right to stand in a group surrounding Washington. But here also was Samuel Ward the banker — an American of the old school surely, if not of Revolutionary fame — and Aunt Eliza Cutler, who would have been a peppery Patriot, if she had lived in her mother's time. There was Crawford humor behind this idea — but genuine admiration also. Not until years later did Julia Ward Howe discover the gallant pleasantry — exclaiming, "Why here are portraits of my whole family!" [4]

This last affectionate tribute by a man of Irish parentage to a great American family, now proud to accept him as one of them, was done at great physical cost. An exploratory operation was performed in Rome in the vain hope of giving him relief from pain. Dr. Gibson, an

American surgeon working in Rome, hoped to find a sack containing fluid behind Crawford's left eyeball — but found instead a tumor. It was so small a thing — surely it could be cured. With a much-loved friend of the family, an American artist by the name of Luther Terry, Crawford went to Paris. Louisa was sent for.

Louisa was in New York, having gone there from Bordentown just after Christmas. "Please ask Elizabeth to have the fires made up in our rooms," Louisa had written to Uncle John Ward, for she planned to spend the winter at Number 8 Bond Street, which was still very much her home. Uncle was to see if there was not a large nursery fender in the garret, brought there after the Ward house at the corner was sold and surviving the days when Louisa and her sisters were children. Or perhaps Aunt Eliza Cutler Francis had the nursery fender, for her own children had come along after most of her sister's children, whom she had mothered, had grown up. The Crawfords would come by the steamer *John Potter* unless the ice should be too heavy, in which case, they would have to take the mail train.

It was February, 1857, when Louisa got word of her husband's illness. She hastened to Boston because the Cunarders were still sailing from that port. Her ship was frozen into the ice in Boston Harbor — and she never forgot the anguish of that delay. Yet, "strong and full of hope," she arrived in Paris; and despite the doctor's opinions, she believed that "tender nursing, combined with so vigorous a constitution" as her husband's "would overcome the evil."

At first there was improvement. "Certainly the worst symptoms did for a while disappear" and there were days when Thomas Crawford and Louisa talked happily of future years. He must never work so hard again. They would take time to enjoy each other and the children — to sit in the orangery in the old Villa gardens. The good Luther Terry, with his plain-featured, almost ugly face and homespun air, would look at his two dearest friends — both of them so beautiful — and tiptoe out of the room to leave them to their dreams. It was almost as if they were young and in love with all their happiness before them.

But Thomas Crawford had cancer of the eyeball. In a hopeless search for a surgeon who could perform a miracle, the Crawfords went to London. And in the end, even Louisa lost hope — and she was glad to see the man she loved released from pain. Thomas Crawford died in London, October 10, 1857.[5]

Her family always said of Louisa that she was weak. She now proved

herself to be strong, for she had work to do in her husband's name. She must send the colossal equestrian statue from Bavaria, where it was in storage, to Richmond, Virginia. The Government had decided not to send the *Merrimac,* and the difficulties facing Louisa would have defeated a weak woman at the very start. Negotiations had been going on during Crawford's illness and were carried forward by Louisa. A sea captain was found, owner of a small sailing vessel. He was willing to cut into the deck of his ship, and intelligent enough to figure out stresses and strains, to reinforce his timbers, and to ballast properly. While Thomas Crawford was too ill to dictate letters, Louisa instructed her captain. News of Thomas Crawford's death arrived in the United States at the same time as the safe arrival of his equestrian Washington.

Crawford was buried in the Ward family tomb in Greenwood cemetery. Louisa endured the huge funeral, the "eulogies" — then returned with her children to Europe to continue her husband's unfinished business and attend to the shipping of his other works. Annie Mailliard wrote anxiously to her husband's father at Mortefontaine, just outside of Paris. And the old man, though rarely going into town now, went at once to the Hotel Holland in Paris to offer his services. But "dear Mrs. Crawford," though pleased to see Monsieur Louis Mailliard, needed no help. She "shows courage," the old man said. "She places great faith in her captain."

The bronze doors, finished by Crawford's pupils and workmen, were sent in plaster to the United States and cast in bronze in Chicopee, Massachusetts. "Armed Liberty" was also cast in this country by the self-taught artist Clark Mills, who built one of the first American foundries on the strength of this and other commissions. Thomas Crawford, whose story was so similar, would have been pleased at this typical American enterprise.

But in April, 1859, the clay models of the bronze doors were still in Rome. "General Pierce . . . made a visit to the studio expressly with a view to satisfying himself about the condition of the panels, in the completion of which he seems much interested," Louisa wrote her Uncle John. General Pierce had been pleased. But Uncle John feared, with reason, that the Government might refuse the doors on the grounds that Crawford had not been able to finish them.

Crawford's friends prevailed and the doors were cast and installed. One would have supposed that Charles Sumner, Crawford's first patron, would have helped to set this final piece of work in place. Apparently such was not the case. Writing in her diary in 1872, Mrs.

James T. Fields told of being taken by Senator Sumner to see the sights of Washington.

"He showed me all the wonders of the place, not forgetting the doors which Crawford never lived even to design in clay altogether, but which his wife, desiring to have the money, caused to be finished by her husband's workmen and foisted upon our government. They are poor enough. Sumner opposed her in what he considered a dishonest attempt to get money, but of course he could not make an open opposition of this nature against a lady, the widow of his friend." [6]

Granted that the doors are not Crawford's best work — neither are they poor. As to the authenticity of the modeling — the portraits of the Ward family bore testimony in Crawford's favor. And as for Louisa's grasping attitude toward money — the rest of her letter to her Uncle John shows just how selfish she really was. "Mr. Grinnell of New York" had been to Crawford's studio and "expressed a desire to buy the beautiful Peri." But he bought instead "a statue by Mr. Dorr — a very nice work of art — and considering the artist's real necessities, I was infinitely more pleased than if (since Mr. Grinnell had but a certain sum to expend) it should have gone in this direction."

Uncle John urged Louisa to come home to live with him on Bond Street with her four little children. She would come, she said, as soon as she had sold her late husband's work, with the exception of a few pieces she hoped to keep.[7] But, "We are all so much happier here than we ever were on the other side of the water," she confessed. Rome had become her home.

CHAPTER NINETEEN
Sam Ward, King of the Lobby

IN 1855, Sam Ward was in Newport, winning "golden opinions" for himself. Or so said his sister, Julia Ward Howe, who certainly did not share the "world's prejudice" against him. In 1858, Sam went to Paraguay in behalf of the United States and Paraguayan Navigation Company whose Rhode Island stockholders had raised one hundred thousand dollars which they had now written off as a total loss. There were also Rhode Island citizens who had become settlers in Paraguay, buying land in good faith which now the dictator, Carlos Antonio Lopez, had confiscated. Sam went to see what, if anything, could be salvaged and perhaps he really did deserve golden opinions in Rhode Island, for he had *not* been the promoter of the scheme! [1]

The promoter was Edward Augustus Hopkins. Son of an Episcopal bishop, former Navy man and an enthusiast concerning opportunities in South America, Hopkins agreed to a small salary and a large block of stock in the company — promising to make his own and everyone else's fortune. Among his mistakes was his reliance upon the promises of Dictator Lopez. A religious upbringing should have educated him to the danger of putting his trust in princes — or worse still, dictators. But Hopkins was at first in high favor with Lopez, who wanted recognition from the United States. His company was granted a generous charter and Hopkins "loaded a steamer of the best construction" with "steam engines, road scrapers, paper cutting machines . . . a saw-mill and many workmen." The steamer foundered off Brazil but much of her cargo was salvaged and Hopkins arrived at Asunción and began operations at once. On a large grant of land ten miles from the capital, the sawmill was set up, bricks were made and tobacco manufactured into cigars for export. In less than a year the new enterprises were doing all too well and Lopez decided that he might as well take all the profits. Trumped-up charges were brought against Hopkins. For example, a painted sign at the cigar factory read that Hopkins was "General Agent" of the Navigation Company — and there could be only one "General" in Paraguay — the dictator's son. The charter was repudiated; land purchased by the settlers from Rhode Island, and all other property, was confiscated.

The United States and Paraguayan Navigation Company complained loudly to the United States Government in 1854. Their ten-year contract with the dictator had lasted ten months. But no one in Washington would listen until 1858 when a United States naval vessel, the *Water Witch*, was fired upon. She was a 400-ton experimental side-wheeler, a pretty craft with sails as well as steam and looking like a racing yacht wearing paddle-wheels and smokestack for a disguise. While Hopkins was in favor and when Lopez had wanted recognition from the United States in his quarrel with Brazil, the United States Navy was given permission to explore and chart the Paraguay River and its tributaries. The *Water Witch*, Lieutenant Thomas Jefferson Page commanding, had been sent to do the job. When the star of Hopkins set, and Brazil seemed no longer a menace, Lopez told Lieutenant Page that he had sailed too far up the Paraguay and had explored forbidden territory. The incident of the *Water Witch*, and the death of a helmsman was blamed entirely upon Lieutenant Page's "indiscretion."

The United States Congress took a different view; and on October 17, 1858, James B. Bowlin sailed from New York for Paraguay with twenty-five hundred men and "a score of warships armed with two hundred guns." The affair of the *Water Witch* must be settled and indemnity paid — and the business of the United States and Paraguayan Navigation Company might just as well be looked into. Aboard the frigate *Sabine* was Sam Ward, "in the official capacity of Secretary of Legation," he said.

The usually irrepressible Sam Ward was in low spirits. Medora had left him — this time for good. Although he blamed her mother, he was through with her; and he felt certain that he would never take her back "even though she should beg for reconciliation" — which was unlikely, since it was he who had gone to her every time so far. She had taken both their children and was living abroad. Yet on board ship after "a jolly dinner with the commodore" Sam could not help dreaming of Medora in his bunk at night. "Dreamed that I was again in love with Medora," he wrote in a journal he kept of the voyage. "Reflected on waking that her indiscretion in communicating to others my affairs has been ruinous. Instead of sending for advisors, why did she not come to me? This she never did, save to ask questions and to scold, and to raise the devil. All vanity, some pride, more haughty than self-respecting and not a bit of heart. . . . A complete sell from A to Z." [2]

Sam did not say just what secrets Medora had betrayed and which loss of fortune she had incurred — surely unwittingly, for she liked a fortune just as well as he. But he could not hold out against her in his thoughts even now. "The loss of fortune which I have several times experienced never gave me one tenth the sorrow I have felt at having lost a woman's affection," he confessed.

Medora was not easy to forget; nor was Sam the only man who ever tried to forget her. But in Paraguay Sam found much to console him. President Lopez received the delegation in a brilliant uniform and cocked hat trimmed with gold lace and ostrich plumes. Madame Lopez and her daughters were "ladylike," and the girls, "like all women of the country, were extravagantly fond of dancing." Sam Ward was said to have taught the Paraguayan girls some new dance steps.

For once, Sam Ward's gift for entertaining at charming little dinners was wasted. In Paraguay, dining out was simply not done. Other sufficiently interesting customs prevailed, however, and Sam was soon adept at all of them. In the afternoon, the gentlemen got into carriages to go calling upon the ladies. At every house, maté was immediately served or *panales*, little cylindrical cakes that looked like honeycomb and were to be dipped into the goblet of water the servant presented. The *panales* "dissolved immediately making a delicious and refreshing drink." Sam was still more intrigued when the servant brought long, slender cigars for everyone — "including the ladies." With what "gravity and gusto" the pretty little Spanish-looking señoritas "puffed away at their cheroots!"

It was the custom, when gentleman callers got up to go, to present them with a large bouquet of flowers. And it was not good manners to appear at a second lady's house bearing the flowers received at the first call. But Sam Ward would know this by instinct. He would know that custom allowed him to stroll in the garden while a lovely señorita picked flowers for him, and he would know how to tell her that her beauty surpassed the fairest bloom. It was remarkable, Sam said, what progress he made in Spanish during his three months' stay in Paraguay.

The progress of negotiations concerning the property of the United

States and Paraguayan Navigation Company could not be said to keep pace with Sam's Spanish. Paraguay finally agreed to pay ten thousand dollars' indemnity to the family of the helmsman of the *Water Witch* The charter permitting the company's use of the Paraguay River was renewed, but Lopez denied that he owed anything for confiscated lands and equipment. The company demanded forty thousand dollars' damages and Sam could say with truth that he had been successful when Lopez agreed to twenty thousand. This money was never paid, which may or may not have been a surprise to Sam Ward.

Sam came home with souvenirs. He had "Jessamine," given him by what señorita he did not say. "Their leaves dropped off after the first few days. They had been wetted by salt water on reaching the Frigate, and the chilly blasts nipped them in the bud. But with care and sunshine and the tender influence of *eau douce* three of them have survived, two of them have put forth new leaves, and one has three flowers. Another has thick promise of buds. Like some stout heart that has kept warm through the storms of adversity, the roots which lie in the congenial earth have furnished new life and sap to these victims of inclemency."

It sounded very much as if Sam referred to himself, with his simile of a stout heart and new life.

Sam Ward had found his niche at last. He was a negotiator. Of course he had practiced the art almost all his life, letters from boarding school being full of convincing arguments concerning lost items of clothing (not his fault) and a need for additional allowance. But he now discovered that the climate of Washington agreed with him, and that Washington, D.C., was the place where negotiation really paid off. He became a lobbyist.

The British had a dignified name for lobbyist — Parliamentary Agent. And Sam's first client had been a British firm. It was probably for this firm that he had gone to Europe in 1855 or 1856 and had spent several months or a year. But affairs had gone badly and perhaps it was at this time that Medora had been indiscreet. In any case, that phase was over, and Sam Ward, in 1859 and upon his return from Paraguay, took a house in Washington. He had arrived with more than flowers, evidently. "I have my own crockery and a set of silver marked 'S.W.' which I have earned with the sweat of my brow and the oil of my tongue," he told his sister Julia. One of his Paraguayan souvenirs he sent to Julia; a "graceful silver flagon and a maté cup and tube" which he said he had won "in shooting matches in Asunción." Exactly what sort of "shooting matches" Sam did not say.

The most important member of Sam Ward's new household was his cook. There was never any doubt in Sam's mind but what the best cooks were men and that the French were the best of all men cooks. Among his friends in the French colony in San Francisco had been cookstove artists and among them he found the man for his dinner hour. Once a chef was hired, however, only the foundation of fine dining was laid. Money could hire a French chef but only sympathy and appreciation could keep him.

Ward McAllister, who gave dinners "patterned after" his "distinguished cousin's," described Sam's method. "My distinguished cousin . . . would bury his head in his hands and (seemingly to the chef) rack his brains seeking inspiration, fearing lest the fatal mistake might be made of letting two white or brown sauces follow each other in succession, or truffles appear twice in the same dinner. The distress that his countenance wore as he repeatedly looked up at the chef as if for advice and assistance would have its desired effect on the culinary artist and *his* brain would at once act in sympathy." [3]

One of Sam Ward's associates, whose comments about him were not always the most friendly, nevertheless paid tribute to his dinners. "His own dinners were not merely so many courses of seasonable dishes, they were compositions. In making a bill of fare, he considered the guests, the occasion, the theme. The dinner was in harmony." Invariably, of course, a client of Sam's, on looking around the table, would see the men he wanted most to meet — men to be encountered nowhere else save on the floor of the Senate or in the noisy lobby of the Willard Hotel. Yet no one, invited to Sam Ward's to dine, felt trapped because of Sam's ulterior motives. Invitations were ardently hoped for — because of the pleasure alone.

Sam liked "to shoot pool" and liked rather too well to play cards. He was "not a winning player," according to his critical friend. Sam also dearly loved horses and there was one other important member of his household in Washington — his "secretary," Jim Valentine, also known as "King of the Turf."

Jim Valentine was Sam Ward's secretary in Washington for years and "during the most severe congressional campaigns," Sam said. Regardless of the severity of the campaigns, however, it was observed that Sam never failed to appear at "every race track in the north, from Baltimore to Saratoga . . . attended by his faithful, original, shrewd and experienced ally and squire." Jim Valentine had crossed the continent to California before the gold rush. There was little he did not know about games of chance and about billiards — having studied billiards at "Fred's," a place on the corner of Reade Street and Broadway where "all the Columbia College boys of the period" assembled. Sam Ward was an alumnus of this same collegiate billiard parlor — all unbeknownst to his father of course. Although Sam did not say when he met Jim Valentine, it might have been at almost any time during Jim's varied career — even when Jim was a sports writer for the New Orleans *Picayune*. Jim's descriptions of famous races made him famous in turn, and in 1855–1856, when the Fashion Course was opened on Long Island, Jim Valentine was manager.

Who but Sam Ward would pick such a secretary? But Jim Valentine was "the sunshine of the banquet," Sam said. Jim's "exuberant humor" made him "the joy of the stable and the course." Sam Ward and Jim Valentine were birds of a feather as well as boon companions, and racing was the thing — in spite of railroads that now rapidly spun their iron webs across the country, it was a horse-drawn world that Sam Ward knew and loved. Most of Sam's clients were to be met with at the race tracks, and Sam chose well in acquiring the versatile Mr. Valentine as "ally and squire."

Poor Jim Valentine's ultimate fate was sad. He was knocked down by "a butcher's cart, which was being driven rapidly through Broadway," and before he could get up, he was "run over by both wheels of a passing omnibus." Both ankles were broken and the injuries "led to his death," said to be from "gout." The horse-drawn era took its toll of the "King of the Turf," but sad endings were not yet in sight and Sam Ward was a happy man in his Washington establishment.

A self-styled "familiar friend," who signed himself J. E. Lewis in a newspaper article, told what went on in Sam Ward's house in Washington after dinner. When the "real business began" it was "time to send Sam Ward away. He had no business qualities, no convictions or fixed beliefs, he could not contend for anything or dispute the opinions of others; he listened to arguments and disputes with patience but never took part in them." What escaped J. E. Lewis was the fact that Sam Ward was often paid by both parties to a business deal just to arrange a meeting. Often he had no interest whatever in the purposes of the conference and sometimes, doubtless, the purposes were so shady that even Sam's elastic conscience might have suffered — had he not gracefully withdrawn. Occasionally, Sam was paid to prevent a deal; in which case, he kept someone too long at table. J. E. Lewis had just described elements which made Sam Ward a great lobbyist.

Sam described his own methods once, when called before a Senate investigating committee in connection with "nearly one million dollars" missing from the till of the Pacific Mail Steamship Company.[4] It was suggested that this money might have gone to lobbyists to promote a subsidy for the company; and Sam, after describing his own services, was asked if they didn't come a little high. "There is nothing in this world so excellent as entertainment of a refined order," Sam replied, considering any money well spent in his behalf. "Talyrand says that diplomacy is assisted by good dinners. But at good dinners, people do not talk shop but they give people who have a taste in that way a right, perhaps, to ask a gentleman a civil question and to get a civil answer; to get information . . . that can be properly given. Sometimes a railroad man wants information; sometimes a patentee wants his patent renewed — that is a pretty hard fight. Sometimes a broker wants to know what the Treasury is going to do about a certain measure. Sometimes a banker is anxious about the financial movements in Congress, or a merchant about the tariff. All these things we [the lobbyists] do constantly, and we do not make any charge for them. We keep up a circle of friends and once in a while an opportunity comes of getting something that is of real service and for which compensation is due and proper. But the entertainments are proportioned to the business of the sessions [of Congress]. Where the business is good, so are the entertainments. . . ."

Sam now launched into a long story which he credited to Washington Irving. It was about a "King of Spain" who got lost out hunting and for whom a grandee had unexpectedly to prepare a meal when there was nothing to eat in the castle. The cook, surely a resourceful man, cut off the ears of fifty-two pigs and served them in many different and delightful ways — keeping the King waiting only an hour. The King of Spain was supposed to have told the cook he should be "governor of a Province." And the next day a Washington newspaper carried a cartoon of Sam Ward, wearing a chef's cap and cooking pigs' ears.

But at the investigation, one of Sam's questioners twitted him. "You got much less than the others," he said, for Sam had testified that, for his services in the steamship subsidy case, he received five hundred dollars by check and three thousand five hundred "in bills" and "went to New York that same night."

But Sam said he had done little or no work and was satisfied with the fee. "I was retained, I suppose, because the 'King's name is a tower of strength' and I am called 'King of the Lobby,' " Sam modestly reminded the investigation committee.

The King of the Lobby was finally asked, "Is there not a great deal of money wasted on good dinners?"

"I do not think money is ever wasted on a good dinner," said Sam. "If a man dines badly, he forgets to say his prayers going to bed, but if he dines well, he feels like a saint."

Sam Ward made a magnificent witness in this case. Although he chatted genially and at length, he sidestepped every catch question, proving that his relaxed air was most deceptive. Congress finally decided that members had taken no bribes but that a man who had become president of the company "by a stock combination" had lost the money trying to "bull and bear the stock" — or, in modern parlance, the Pacific Mail Steamship Company was "raided."

Sam Ward "had wonderful skill at bringing out other men," admitted Mr. Lewis. "It was an instinct with him to know the best thing in a guest; his exactest knowledge; his finest quality — and opportunity was given him to shine in the most natural way." Sam "never monopolized a conversation, but gave each man a fair chance to be heard." And Sam was "never seen drinking at a bar." He was a connoisseur of fine wines, proud of his ability to tell by taste and bouquet the year and origin of any quality wine that might be served. He took great pains to serve the right wines with each course at dinner, but he himself never drank wine to excess. He was afraid of spoiling his palate. "Though so noted for dining, he was a light eater, also."

Later, Sam said that there was just one of his works of art which he hoped might endure. "Lay the thin peel of a lemon around the inside of a glass," Sam directed. "Fill the glass with cracked ice and pour yellow chartreuse over it." You could order this drink at Delmonico's in New York. It was a "Sam Ward." [5]

Sam was well paid, if one of his favorite anecdotes gave a fair sample of fees received for services rendered. Writing to Longfellow, toward the end of his lobbying career, Sam said: "When I see you again, I will tell you how a client, eager to prevent the arrival at a committee of a certain member before it should adjourn at noon, offered me $5,000 to accomplish his purpose which I did by having his boots mislaid while I smoked a cigar and condoled with him until they would be found at 11:45! I had the satisfaction of a good laugh, a good fee in my pocket, and of having prevented a conspiracy."

There were flaws in Sam's happiness, of course. He could not help realizing that his family was anything but proud of his lobbying activities and that he had failed to fill his father's shoes — to put it mildly. He gave his family lavish gifts; a fine jewel for a pretty niece, French hats to young girl cousins and eventually a house on Beacon Street for his sister Julia who, more than anyone else, was a symbol of conscience to him. Knowing that Julia had forgiven him more often than seven times seven, Sam turned to her whenever he thought (or hoped) he had done well. When he failed to win her approbation he was truly, if only temporarily, cast-down. And now war clouds were gathering over the United States and Julia Ward Howe was an ardent Abolitionist. Sam Ward was a Southern sympathizer!

In the spring of 1861, William Howard Russell was sent by the London *Times* to the United States to see what, exactly, was going on in connection with antislavery.[6] Mr. Russell had already won fame by reporting the Crimean War, not romantically but truthfully, thereby shocking many who preferred to live in a dream world. But he did not suppose that he had come to the United States as a war correspondent, because Lincoln had just been inaugurated, Fort Sumter had yet to be fired upon — there was as yet no war.

William Russell first met Sam Ward in London. It was about 1860, he thought, although it seems probable that it was earlier. In any case, a ring at his door late at night disturbed him. "Not at home," Russell told his servant, but "the door was already open and a voice I loved dearly cried, 'Only five minutes, William. I have brought an American friend to see you.'" The well-known voice was Thackeray's, and the American friend was Sam Ward. They talked till early morning.

On March 16, 1861, William Russell arrived at New York, feeling cold and dismal. Sam Ward had prepared him for his trip up New York Harbor, with its glimpses of Staten Island, that summer resort where his and Medora's mother's villas could still be seen. But it was "difficult to distinguish through the snow the villas and country homes said to be so charming in summer," Mr. Russell found. He was impressed with New York's defenses, however, now "being rebuilt or remodelled. Even now, it would be hazardous" for a hostile fleet "to run the gantlet of the batteries, unless in powerful ironclad ships, favored by wind and tide," Mr. Russell said. "Against a wooden fleet, New York is all but secure."

The snow melted into deep slush next day, and William Russell had nothing good to say about New York streets. But the cheerful Sam Ward had given him a warm welcome and it was good to meet Sam at several functions arranged for the visiting London correspondent. Mr. Russell accepted with pleasure Sam's invitation to dine in Washington.

Washington received an even blacker mark in William Russell's book than did New York. The train rolled into the nation's capital "at street level" and Mr. Russell "looked out and saw a vast mass of white marble towering above us on the left . . . surmounted by an unfinished cupola, from which scaffold and cranes raised their black arms." The cranes were waiting to hoist Thomas Crawford's "Armed Liberty" to the top of the Capitol Building, as Sam Ward could have told the London press correspondent. But now Mr. Russell was looking out of the other side of his train at "a cleared space of mud, sand and fields, studded with wooden sheds and huts, beyond which again could be seen rudimentary streets of small brick houses." They reached the railway station at last, and "emerging . . . found a vociferous crowd of blacks who were the hackney coachmen of the place."

Like every other visitor, Mr. Russell went straight to Willard's Hotel, which he considered "a great pile" all of "six stories high." If he had any doubt of the value of Sam Ward's dinner invitation, one visit to the hotel dining room increased his gratitude to Sam a thousand-fold. "Not less than twenty-five hundred people dine in the public room every day," Mr. Russell estimated. The dining room was "on the kitchen floor" — another form of barbarism, for all proper London kitchens were in the basement with the dining room up a steep flight of stairs. It was a "vast apartment, a hall without any carpets or any furniture but plain chairs and tables which are ranged in close rows, at which flocks of people are feeding, or discoursing, or from which they are flying away. The servants never cease shoving the chairs to and fro with a harsh screeching noise over the floor so that one can scarcely hear his neighbor speak."

Of course Mr. Russell would never need to dine often at Willard's. He was at the British Legation on Easter day, the guest of Lord Lyons with "members of the legation and Sumner." General Winfield Scott had "modest lodgings which however were in the house of a famous French cook," he said. It was while dining with General Scott that William Russell formed his opinion of the Union Army. A few of Scott's men gathered outside the house to shout and cheer. The General went out on his balcony and waved genially in response. But the British war correspondent was horrified. It was an undisciplined, unmannered crew of raw recruits that Russell saw out there in the street; they were wearing muddy uniforms with unpolished buttons — and they had obviously been drinking.

At Sam Ward's house, Mr. Russell's spirits rose and his mood mellowed slightly. Already, his caustic comments upon New York and Washington had been sent to *The Times* of London, in due course to return in print across the Atlantic and infuriate such pleasant gentlemen as Philip Hone, who had entertained the Britisher. But Mr. Russell had not really seen the United States, Sam told him — how about a trip through the South? Sam, who had business and family connections in the South, would be his guide. Mr. Russell readily agreed, and Sam set out ahead of him — perhaps to set the scene.

Sam arrived in Charleston, South Carolina, at a moment in history when William Russell would most have liked to be with him. All Mr. Russell could say was, "On arriving . . . found Mr. Ward whom I had already met in New York and Washington and who gave me an account of the bombardment and surrender of the fort!" It was Fort Sumter to which William Russell referred.

Sam Ward introduced Mr. Russell to General Beauregard, "a small, compact man" with "a good deal of the Frenchman in his manner and look." The appearance of Southern "senators and governors turned soldiers" pleased William Russell as much as the Yankee soldiers had disgusted him. He liked the Southern "blue frock coats with upright collars and shoulder straps trimmed with lace" and he said he thought the South ought to win the war. Later, he was accused of saying that the South *would* win.

After visiting Fort Sumter, Mr. Russell went to "Mr. Pringle's plantation, above Georgetown on the Peedee River. Party; Mr. Mitchell, an eminent lawyer of Charleston, Colonel Reed, a neighboring planter, Mr. Ward of New York — and our host." It will be remembered that Sam's grandmother had been Sarah Mitchell Cutler of Georgetown. She had brothers who married and lived in the vicinity and Sam had always been fond of these Southern kinfolk.

Just as Sam designed a dinner to produce harmony and a mellow mood, so he planned a tour of the Confederacy to make a favorable impression on William Howard Russell of the London *Times*. Choosing with care among the great houses that he knew, Sam led the way to White House Plantation where everything was certain to be perfection — from the old Negro valet who gravely bade Mr. Russell welcome and unpacked his bag, to the tiny Negro child fishing for catfish in the river. Host and guests were cultivated gentlemen, quoting their Latin and conversing over their wine with old-school elegance. For Mr. Russell, the climax came when "Madeira was brought downstairs cautiously, as in the days of Horace and Mæcenas, from the cellar between the attic and the thatched roof."

Southern planters lived in the tradition of the English nobility. Mr. Russell could not fail to observe this and it was just what Sam Ward wanted him to discover. Sam showed the *Times* correspondent nothing which in any way resembled *Uncle Tom's Cabin*. But Mr. Russell was sharp-eyed. He commented that although the plantation owner knew and loved his household servants, he knew nothing of the field Negroes, who seemed listless and unresponsive. The rice crop had been harvested and there was little work to do, but the field hands neglected their own gardens and their homes were dirty and ill-kept. Children ran away like little animals, frightened and shy, refusing to talk to the reporter. Persistently, however, Sam Ward showed Mr. Russell only the beauty and grace of Southern plantation life. No one could have done a better job than Sam — who loved this side of the picture and shut his eyes to any other.

Sam Ward's "tour of the Confederacy" ended at a psychological moment. William Russell was back in Washington at a time when his instinct for military strategy (which had stood him in good stead in the Crimea) told him that a battle between the Union and the Confederacy would come soon and that it would take place between Washington and Richmond. He received permission to go out with the Union troops on their way to Bull Run. Russell was an eyewitness to the rout of the Union Army, and the day after the battle he filed his dispatch in which he described the behavior of the Northern soldiers as cowardly. Russell was not overkind about Southern military prowess, either. He said in a letter to Sam Ward that "the Union Army ran away just as its victory had been secured by the superior cowardice of the South."

It surprised Mr. Russell to find himself unpopular in the States, whether Union or Confederate. In New York City they called him "Bull Run Russell," and it was no compliment. When it came to running, "Russell headed the race," said George Templeton Strong, who had been appointed to the Sanitary Commission and had met Russell in Washington.

On January 1, 1862, William Russell "dined at the New York Club on the invitation of Sam Ward and others," wrote Strong in his diary. "Bull Run Russell" was now so unpopular that "his presence stirred up a little row outside the dining room." George Anthon denounced Sam for "extending the hospitalities of the club to a man who was writing slanders against us and our cause to the most important newspaper in Christendom." It taxed all of Sam Ward's diplomatic skill, but he succeeded in calming down the club members. As men of violently differing opinions relaxed and began to talk reasonably together, Sam could feel that he was fulfilling an important mission in life.

Sam's close association with William Russell brought unpleasant notice upon both of them from the New York papers. The *Trent* affair, with the interning of Mason and Slidell, was still a hot question when a telegram was unearthed from Russell to Ward and published in the *New York Herald*. It said that Russell had heard the good news and that Ward could now enjoy his dinner. The *Herald* alleged that Russell had used confidential information that the *Trent* affair would be settled amicably, to speculate on the stock market, with Ward's help. Russell was severely reprimanded by his paper and nearly lost his job. There was just enough probability, because of Sam Ward's reputation as a stock speculator, to make the story widely accepted. But for once, it might seem as if Sam Ward was as misunderstood as he so often claimed to be. He was the most peaceable of men and the prospect of a war with Great Britain would really have disturbed him. It might *really* have spoiled his pleasure in dining.

With all the zest of a man who loves his work, Sam labored on at lobbying in Washington. Many of his clients were Californians with land-title and gold-mining troubles, whom Sam delighted to help. He was well rewarded, sometimes with mining shares, and this was infinitely better than personally digging for gold under the broiling sun. Sam had reason to believe that he served his clients as well as himself. He had not neglected his family. And confidently he wrote to his sister Julia to know when it would be convenient for him to visit her at Lawton's Valley in Newport. He had fitted up a room for himself over the old mill, but Julia sometimes used it for other guests.

It was a surprised and hurt Sam Ward who discovered that he

would not be welcome and need not come at all. Julia Ward Howe
thought her brother was a traitor.

William Russell had noted that "Southerners" were "exposed to
insult in New York," but that "they may get off better in that respect
than Black Republicans would down South." At the plantation on
the Peedee there had been talk of "duels and of famous hands with
pistols in these parts" and most certainly no one had called out Sam
Ward. He must then have been a Southern sympathizer, it could
be argued.

Sam might reply that if he were a Southern sympathizer he was not
insulted in New York. But that was a matter of degree only, and more
a triumph of diplomacy on his part than anything else. Julia Ward
Howe hung a flag across her door in Boston. Could her brother Sam
pass under it? she asked. The Stars and Stripes or the Stars and Bars
— he would have to choose. And Sam was probably glad that he would
soon be off for Nicaragua.

CHAPTER TWENTY

Lords of the Lash
and Lords of the Loom

JULIA WARD HOWE'S conversion to Abolition was gradual. As a small child, she had glimpsed the best side of plantation life when she went with her mother to visit the McAllisters in Savannah. All the money the McAllisters could earn at law went into the plantation which they loved. Julia's mother, seeing slavery for the first time, expressed pity for the slave yet assumed that a system of bond and free was the will of God.

Writing home to her little son Sammy, young Mrs. Ward reminded him that "We cannot be too thankful that it has pleased God to give us so many friends and so many comforts, when we think of the poor Negro." Sammy was to say over the hymn his mother had taught him, in which he "thanked the goodness and the grace" that on his "birth" had "smiled" so that he "was not born a little slave" but a "happy free-born child." Brought up on hymns like that, it woud take maturity of thought to come to the ultimate conclusion that it was man who occasionally misinterprets God's will.[1]

Julia was probably the favorite among her peppery Grandmother Cutler's many grandchildren. She was the one who listened the most willingly to the tales of old days on the Allston estates on the Waccamaw River in South Carolina, where her grandmother had been a belle. The house of Prime, Ward and King had many Southern clients who visited the Wards on Bond Street; and in Newport, when Julia Ward was a young girl, the summer residents were apt to be either New Yorkers or Southerners.

In Boston, where Miss Julia Ward was herself a belle, the friends who entertained her were those Boston Wards of an entirely different family — but bankers like her father. She met merchants and manufacturers almost all of whom were conservative Whigs. Some of them were less friendly after Miss Ward became Mrs. Howe, wife of a reformer. In 1848, Charles Sumner made his famous speech in Congress denouncing the "conspiracy" between the "lords of the lash and the lords of the loom." It was a bitter phrase which no one could forget. The situation called for Sumner's fire, but to anyone as fair-minded as Julia it must have seemed cruel. She could not possibly picture her gentle Aunt Louisa McAllister's family as "lords of the lash." It was no easier to conceive of Boston friends as "lords of the loom." During the winter of 1847–8, there came to be two kinds of Whigs in Boston — Cotton Whigs and Free-soilers.

This political difference of opinion had one particularly sad result. Julia wrote her sister Louisa about it, dating her letter October 28, 1851. She referred to the Five of Clubs, whose members had taken such an interest in her private affairs at the time of her engagement to the Chevalier. "The Club is completely split up," she said. "Longo and Chev are on one side, Hillard and Felton go for slavery and all the old hunkerisms."

The Free-Soil idea appealed to Dr. Howe because the aim was to stop the spread of slavery. But antislavery was not Dr. Howe's primary crusade at this time, as it was with Charles Sumner. Four years after Sumner's famous "lords of the lash and lords of the loom" speech, Dr. Howe explained in a letter to Horace Mann his reluctance to take the lead in Free-Soil affairs. "I have unfortunately no talent for chalking out their course," Dr. Howe wrote in 1852. Failing of election as Free-Soil Governor of Massachusetts, Mann had become President of Antioch College at Yellow Springs, Ohio, and Dr. Howe's letter reflected loneliness for his fellow crusader.[2] The Doctor felt that he had not many more years of life before him. "Death and I are fencing, not with foils but he with a sharp rapier, and I with but rusty armor for defense," he said. But "there is one thing I want much to do, . . viz establish a school for teaching deaf mutes to articulate." He and Horace Mann had "often talked of it," and he thought that with Mann's help he could succeed.

The fires of Abolition had been lighted but might be said to be smoldering. It was a woman who now fanned the spark. On Sunday afternoon, May 23, 1852, the Howes were calling on the Longfellows at Craigie House in Cambridge. The weather was so warm that they could sit out on the piazza, a fact worthy of note in Longfellow's journal. Talk turned to books and Longfellow had just been reading

Uncle Tom's Cabin. "It is too melancholy and makes the blood boil too hotly," said the even-tempered Longfellow, little realizing how prophetic his remarks would prove to be.

Ten months went by and again Longfellow commented upon *Uncle Tom's Cabin* in his diary, this time from the point of view of a writer. "Mr. and Mrs. Stowe to dinner. Him I have known since my college days; her I never met before. She is a quiet little woman with a low voice and timid manner. But she is shaking the world with her *Uncle Tom's Cabin*. At one step, she has reached the top of the staircase up which the rest of us climb on our knees, year after year. Never was there such a literary coup-de-main as this. A million copies of a book within the first year of its publication!" [3]

The emotional impact of *Uncle Tom's Cabin* could not be measured even in terms of record sales, however. To people who had vaguely felt that slavery was wrong, it came like a flash of lightning illuminating a terrible scene. There were many who questioned Mrs. Stowe's facts, and she replied in a 262-page defense called *A Key to Uncle Tom's Cabin: presenting the original Facts and Documents Upon Which the Story is Founded together with corroborative statements verifying the Truths of the Work*. In spite of the terrifying title, it was almost as gripping a story in itself as the original book. Penmanship copybooks of the era had contained the motto, "The pen is mightier than the sword." A generation was about to learn how the pen causes swords to be drawn; and Mrs. Stowe's pen, although one of the sharpest, was not the only one.

In 1853, Dr. Howe took over the editorship of the *Commonwealth*, a Free-Soil newspaper published in Boston. "Chev is to get $500," his wife told her sister Annie, "so you see, it is a matter of some importance to us." And Mrs. Howe added, "He is so very obliged to me for my small contributions that I do not like to refuse. Indeed, if I were in my former health, they would cost me nothing, being hit off at the stroke of a pen." Of course the Doctor did not allow his wife to sign her columns and when it came to serious matters concerned with the antislavery campaign, he either wrote the articles himself or had a man do them. But there was still woman's work to be done on the paper and Mrs. Howe was always touchingly pleased when her husband praised her for her writing — the one thing she wanted above all else to do well.

Contributions by the editor's wife consisted in reviews of the Lowell lectures, the theater and concerts — which were very good. Mrs.

Howe's musical taste and judgment were remarkable. She wrote reviews not only of books, but also of magazines, including the *Atlantic Monthly*, and while she was generous with praise where she thought it deserved, she had no mercy upon weak writing or evidence of laziness on the part of an author. Some of Mrs. Howe's columns were full of wicked wit and daring criticism of certain sacred Boston personalities, and caused the *Commonwealth* to be a much talked-about paper, if not a profitable one.

Perhaps without realizing at first what was happening, Mrs. Howe found herself not only a Free-soiler but becoming more and more of an Abolitionist as a result of her work for the *Commonwealth*. She often proofread the paper, going over all of the other articles as well as her own. It was a surprise and a disappointment when her sister Annie asked her not to send the *Commonwealth* to Bordentown. Adolph Mailliard was by no means sure, at this time at least, that there was very much wrong with slavery. He could easily have kept several families of slaves busy on his stud farm and even the prevailing low wages paid to grooms and farm hands made it difficult for him to show enough profit on his race horses and saddles horses to satisfy his princely tastes.

"The *Commonwealth* shall be discontinued, my Pet," [4] wrote Mrs. Howe to Annie. "Do not worry, it costs you nothing." She would have liked to have her sister read her "articles on Dr. Holmes's lectures," but this was not enough reason for bringing Adolph's wrath down upon poor little Annie.

There came a day, the exact date of which Mrs. Howe could never quite remember. The scene, however, remained fixed in her mind. Dr. Howe had said to her, "Do you remember the man of whom I spoke to you — the one who wished to be the savior of the Negro race? That man . . . will call here this afternoon. You will receive him. His name is John Brown."

"Thus admonished," Mrs. Howe watched for the caller. "At the expected time," the door bell tinkled and she answered it herself. If she had been living in Boston the neighbors would have been sure to notice this eccentric behavior, she said, but to answer one's own doorbell was "not infra dig in South Boston." She "beheld a middle-aged, middle-sized man, with hair and beard of amber color streaked with gray. He looked like a Puritan of the Puritans, forceful, concentrated, self-contained." Since Mrs. Howe spent her summers in Newport and since winter winds were piercing on the heights of South Boston, it must have been either spring or fall, for Mrs. Howe strolled with John Brown in the garden at Green Peace. Although usually so adroit at bringing people out, she could not get her guest to talk to her. It was a relief when the Chevalier arrived to carry John Brown off for a private conference.[5]

Born in Torrington, Connecticut, John Brown had been brought up in Ohio and had lived in a variety of states. In North Elba, New York, on land donated by Gerrit Smith, he had founded a community for Negroes. But John Brown's mission in New England at the time of his call upon the Howes was to plan a fund-raising campaign and to raise recruits for the emigrant trains heading for Kansas. On many a rocky New England farm, the original acres had been divided and subdivided among sons and grandsons of the first settlers. The pioneering spirit, however, descended in full force and undimmed to the third and fourth generation of both men and women. Kansas land was the lure — but there was more to it than that. In 1854, the Kansas-Nebraska Bill with its proviso that the territories should be admitted as states with the choice of either slavery or antislavery, made it an urgent matter with Abolitionists to find settlers who would vote their way. The descendants of Puritans had inherited another trait along with the pioneering instinct: the desire to do God's will as they saw it. Recruitment was not too difficult, but money was needed to outfit young families well equipped with faith and courage but with almost no cash.

A "Committee for Kansas" was formed, and the list of members was long, including Charles Sumner, John Andrew, F. B. Sanborn, Rev. James Freeman Clarke — and Dr. Samuel Gridley Howe. "Emigrant Aid" societies sprang up in many cities and, although the work involved was considerable, the response was gratifying. The societies were an outgrowth of the New England Emigrant Aid Company in which Amos Adams Lawrence of Boston was greatly interested. Lawrence, Kansas, first of the cities to be founded by the Emigrant Aid societies, was named in honor of the Boston philanthropist. Amos Lawrence sold stock in the company, and it was the company that bought the Sharpe's rifles which were to have an important bearing on John Brown's trial for treason. Dr. Howe collected funds for the emigrants' needs rather than for investment in the company.

In 1856, John Brown and his sons defended Lawrence, Kansas,

against a raid by the Missouri Border Ruffians, using the rifles the land company had provided. Not all the violence was confined to Kansas, that year. It was on May 22, 1856, that Charles Sumner, while seated at his desk in the Senate chamber in Washington, was struck over the head and shoulders by Representative Preston Brooks of South Carolina — who wielded a heavy walking-cane. Sumner managed to rise from his seat but immediately sank unconscious to the floor. To the Howes, the shock and grief of this news was sharp, for Dr. Howe loved Sumner like a brother and he was a constant caller in their home. Although Mrs. Howe's efforts to make Sumner a trifle less austere had always failed, she too admired him. And now he was almost a martyr. Sumner went to Europe to consult European specialists and for two years he suffered agonies under treatment involving the burning of his flesh to prevent paralysis. Hardly anyone believed he would ever resume his public career and Dr. Howe took the burden of much of Sumner's work in Boston.

Toward the end of June, 1856, Dr. Howe wrote to Horace Mann at Yellow Springs, Ohio. "I am in vacation," the Doctor said, "but have fairly broken down, for I foolishly (like the old unwise donkey) undertook to pull the laboring van on the Kansas Aid Committee and had to row boat and all the crew. My family are all at Newport on my farm, and the Lord knows how I long to be with them but I am going to try to get out to Kansas to carry some aid and help the cause." Dr. Howe's dark forebodings about imminent death still obsessed him and it was a pity that he could not foresee the good twenty years still ahead. But action always improved his spirits and his high courage never deserted him. Cheerfully he offered himself to the cause of Kansas and Free-Soil, for "How can one die better?" he asked.

By the end of another month, Dr. Howe was at "Mt. Tabor, Frontier of Nebraska." This time he wrote to Charles Sumner, who must have been avid for news.

"Ever since the 4th of July, I have been on the move in the cause of Kansas," the Doctor said. "I have traversed the whole length of the state of Iowa on horseback or in a cart, sleeping in said cart or in worse lodgings among dirty men on the floor of dirty huts. We have organized a pretty good line of communication between the base and the corps of emigrants who have now advanced into the mountains of Nebraska. Everything depends upon the success of the attempt to break through the cordon infernal which Missouri has drawn across the northern frontier of Kansas.

"The men are all ready for a fight — pity such a man as Lane is at the head," Dr. Howe went on. "We shall have all we can do to keep the bit in his teeth." Speaking for himself, Dr. Howe explained, "I am going to try to get into Kansas by going down the river and passing by the route from Fort Leavenworth to Lawrence."

Dr. Howe's final letter at this time was dated July 31 and headed "Camp of the Emigrants." He was with "the head column," which numbered four hundred, and he was pleased because this particular group had "at least put itself right by getting rid of Col. Lane who has remained behind in Iowa." James Henry Lane led an emigrant train, which he called his "army of the north," into Kansas by August, 1856, however. And Dr. Howe was right in his estimation of Lane for "depredations" were "committed, fully as atrocious as those of the 'border ruffians.'"

Dr. Howe got safely into Kansas and safely he returned home to start out again in 1857. This time, he took his wife and daughter Florence out to Ohio with him "to see the Manns at Antioch." The Manns were so glad to see them they "almost ate us up," Mrs. Howe said. And "Chev exhausted himself in good behavior — he actually smiled till he frightened his whiskers." This was a "huge Western journey" for Julia Ward Howe and the "change of air" did all of them a great deal of good.

But for Mrs. Howe, her first Western journey was soon over because the Chevalier left his wife and daughter in St. Louis to find their way home alone while he went on to Kansas.

This time, the Chevalier bought land in Kansas and planned for the day when he himself might settle there. Whether or not he told his wife, she did not say, but when he returned home she found his moods "wariable." (The touch of family humor in the pronunciation of this word did not stem from Dickens, as might be supposed, but from an elderly Ward relative in New York.)

The course which leaders in Kansas took caused grave concern among the philanthropists who backed the Kansas Emigrant Company and among those who continued to contribute to the various Kansas Aid Societies. Dr. Howe was not the only one who disapproved of Lane. Yet Brown, Lane and others served a purpose for they forced the Government to refuse help to Missouri invaders. "Bleeding Kansas" was the subject of bitter controversy in Congress. Northerners knew that John Brown had been active in the "underground railroad" before he went to Kansas, that he continued the work of aiding slaves to escape to Canada — and of this most Northerners approved. But no one except John Brown himself knew of a more elaborate plan for the escape of slaves which was maturing in his mind, even while he would seem to be fully occupied with Kansas affairs.

The news of Harper's Ferry burst upon Boston Free-Soil leaders like a bomb. On October 15, 1859, when the raid occurred, the news was sketchy but most alarming. Tension mounted as newspapers appeared with word-of-mouth reports from the crew of the "train on the Baltimore and Ohio Railroad" which arrived "six hours late." The train conductor said that "the insurrectionists numbered 200 blacks and whites" and that they had full possession of the armory. He was sure that there were "from 500 to 700 whites and blacks concerned in the insurrection." A wagon loaded with muskets, had been dispatched into Maryland by the raiders, it was said.

By two-thirty in the afternoon "the military of Frederick" had been ordered out and dispatches were received from President Buchanan ordering out the United States troops. A special train was "now being got ready to convey them to the scene of the disturbance." The baggage master on the evening train from Harper's Ferry said that he had been taken prisoner and released after meeting with the leader of the insurrection and seeing in the armory at Harper's Ferry, "from 500 to 600 negroes all armed" and "from 200 to 300 white men with them."

It was true that baggagemaster Luther Simpson had just seen and talked with John Brown. But he had not seen nine hundred or even seven hundred men. John Brown's followers were "a party of 22 persons." And by the time the actual count was made, fifteen of these were dead, two mortally wounded, two were unhurt and three had escaped. Another day passed, and the train was "now getting ready to convey horses and men from Harper's Ferry for the purpose of pursuing the rioters into any state or locality where they may have fled."

Northern reaction to the news of Harper's Ferry was as shocked and angry as any Southerner could wish. An attack on a United States arsenal was treason and no one, not even Garrison in the *Liberator*, called it anything else. There were, to be sure, a few derisive remarks made in the press about the size of the force summoned to put down the insurrection — once the size of the "insurrectionist gang" was discovered. But Garrison himself copied in the *Liberator* an article by a country editor who reminded his readers that a New England town had recently been thrown into a panic by *one* man — an arsonist.[6]

Then details of the behavior of troops, volunteers and citizens began to come out. A young follower of Brown who attempted to swim
the river had been shot, his body filled full of bullets long after he was
dead. The body, propped up on an island, had been used for target
practice by the troops. A flag of truce was disregarded, and the body
of a Negro, fallen in the street, was beaten with sticks by angry
citizens. The dead were partially eaten by swine. It was not a pretty
picture.

During John Brown's imprisonment, two things began to turn the
tide of public opinion: Brown's own heroic behavior and the attitude
of the proslavery press. New York City papers carried articles headed
"Thou art the man," naming Sumner, Giddings, and others as equally
guilty of treason. In Boston, Dr. Samuel Gridley Howe, because of
his activity in aid of Kansas settlers, was accused of actively plotting
with John Brown. And in several newspapers, Brown was pictured
as having planned a march through the South, arming Negroes and
inciting them to murder the white population. The effect of such wild
accusations was to bring thinking people into the ranks of Abolition.

Annie Mailliard wrote anxiously to her sister Julia to know how the
Chevalier was taking all the abuse. "Chev is not at all annoyed by
the newspapers," Mrs. Howe replied, dating her letter November 6,
1859. But Dr. Howe was "greatly overdone by anxiety and labor for
Brown," for money must be raised to hire lawyers for John Brown's
defense. "Of course all the stories about Northern Abolitionists are
merest stuff," Julia Howe assured her sister. "No one knew of Brown's
intentions but Brown himself and his handful of men. The attempt,
I must judge insane but the spirit *heroic*. I should be glad to be as
sure of heaven as that old man may be, following right in the footsteps of the old martyrs, girding on his sword for the weak and oppressed. His death will be holy and glorious — the gallows cannot dis-
honor him — he will hallow it."

John Brown's behavior as a prisoner gained more and more favorable
comment. An investigating committee of Senators accompanied by
newspapermen, visited him, finding him suffering from wounds, un-
kempt, uncared for. "Who sent you here?" they asked.

"No man sent me here. It was my own prompting."

"What was your object?"

"We came to free the slaves and only that."

"Did you go out to Kansas under the auspices of the Emigrant Aid
Society?"

And John Brown said, "No sir, I went out under the auspices of John Brown and nobody else."

In the beginning, Governor Wise insisted upon his right to hang all the Harper's Ferry prisoners. Then he was advised of an interesting legal angle. If a Virginia Grand Jury, in the course of a trial for treason, named citizens of other states as material witnesses, then the Federal Circuit Court could order the arrest of such persons and have them brought to Virginia. In cases of treason, trial must be held in the county where the crime took place and before a Petit Jury chosen from residents of that county. A person need never have been at the scene of the crime to be found guilty of treason, and in cases of treason, there was no appeal. Every effort was already being made to implicate well-known antislavery leaders and particularly those active in aid to Kansas. Governor Wise now released one prisoner for trial before a Virginia Grand Jury. One was all they needed.

John Andrew, the Boston Abolitionist lawyer, had become the guiding spirit in John Brown's defense. Andrew's advice was now unequivocal. Those men most likely to be arrested and taken to Virginia should leave the country at least for a time.[7] They would only harm Brown if they allowed themselves to be tried for conspiracy in a completely hostile court. Dr. Howe was a man of action whose personal bravery no one ever for a moment doubted. Yet perhaps the bravest thing he ever did was to submit to his lawyer's insistence and go to Canada. First he prepared a statement for the papers:

". . As to the heroic man who planned and led that forlorn hope, my relations to him in former times were such that no man ought to be afraid or ashamed to avow. If ever my testimony to his high qualities should be of use to him or his, it shall be forthcoming at the fitting time or place. But neither this nor any other testimony shall be extorted for unrighteous purposes if I can help it."

"Already the rats are leaving the sinking ship," said the *New York Journal of Commerce*. But the *New York Times* and the *Tribune* both pointed out the legal situation. On December 2, 1859, the *New York Times* announced that "Dr. Howe of Boston, like Col. Forbes and several other persons at the north . . . have taken their departure for Canada." "In the interests of fair play," the *Times* went on to say, "neither complicity in the crime" nor "mere cowardice" seemed to be "imputations . . . warranted by the facts."

On the evening of Friday, December 2, the day appointed for the execution of John Brown, "an assemblage of the people of Boston gathered at Tremont Temple. At seven o'clock, every seat was taken. More than 3000 stood outside." There was no "funeral drapery" inside the building but around the walls, placards had been placed with some of John Brown's sayings printed on them. "I don't know what weakness may come over me; but I don't believe I shall ever deny my Lord and Master, Jesus Christ and I should deny him if I denied my principles against slavery," was one. And another read, "I don't know as I can better serve the cause I love so well than to die for it."

In Canada, "A meeting took place . . . at Bonaventure Hall, numerously attended by colored people. Speeches were made by Dr. Howe and others." Dr. Howe was still unhappy over having gone to Canada. "I am not quite sure I acted wisely in yielding to pressure, but am sure I meant to do the best I could," he wrote to Charles Sumner. "It will be of some use if my expatriation and its cause should draw attention to the infamous act by which Southern slaveholders can throw the lasso over Northern citizens when they are wanted for wicked purposes."

The dramatic events which led to the Civil War seem to have happened in rapid succession. Actually, time elapsed and nearly two years went by, a period of comparative calm, between Harper's Ferry and the firing on Fort Sumter. While the John Brown issue still occupied the press, the *Atlantic Monthly* was running a series of pleasant essays on Cuba by Julia Ward Howe. In February, at the beginning of that eventful year 1859, the Howes had journeyed to Cuba, Theodore Parker being a shipmate on the voyage. And now Mrs. Howe had begun a new form of writing — the travel essay — which was to prove most successful. "Folks say that the last number of my Cuba is the best thing I ever did," she told her sister Annie. "Even Emerson wrote me about it from Concord." The *New York Tribune* promised a hundred dollars to Mrs. Howe for a series of letters on Newport society to be written during the coming summer.

Julia Howe had formed the habit of doing all her writing in Newport, for the peaceful old farmhouse with its glimpse of blue water seemed to give her thoughts new life. Since the publication of *Passion Flowers* she had written and published a second volume of verse called *Words for the Hour*. Again Theodore Parker gave his approval of the project.

"I wonder what you think of Mrs. Howe's poems at the West?"

wrote Mary Jane Quincy to Mrs. Horace Mann. "Of course there are two parties here. I think some of it is splendid poetry and noble thoughts. Some of the 'flowers' are doubtless too passionate. What a pity they were not cut off!" Mrs. Josiah Quincy was speaking of *Passion Flowers* in this letter and the "two parties" of Boston opinion certainly helped the book. When *Words for the Hour* came out some three years later, very little was said about it. A graceful poem called "Washday Rosary" earned for Mrs. Howe the adjective "domestic" — which, poor dear, she was not, much as she loved her home and her children. The best poems in the volume dealt with the everyday tragicomedy of the nursery, and they were good magazine verse. But this time everybody knew who the author was and that she had not been to Rome lately but had been living in South Boston or Lawton's Valley. *Words for the Hour* was damned with faint praise.

Dr. Howe should have been gratified that his wife's work was so innocuous as to pass almost unnoticed — since there was no keeping her out of print and no hope of his enjoying any success she might earn. But any rejoicing on the Doctor's part would have been premature. Julia Ward Howe was not born to pass unnoticed very long. During the summer of 1856, while the Chevalier was off to Kansas, his wife wrote a play in blank verse about a beautiful peasant girl who was wronged by a lordly lover and sought revenge. From the point of view of conservative Boston literary society, this was as wild and daring an act, in its way, as defying Missourians with a dash into Kansas.

Mrs. Howe not only wrote *The World's Own* but, on March 16, 1857, it was produced in New York at Wallack's Lyceum Theater with Matilda Horn as "Leonora, Queen of the village" and the elder Sothern as her seducer, "Count Lothair."

All the Wards had loved the theater, Sam and Julia most of all. Of course Sam's especial interest was in ladies backstage and he was said to have taught Lily Langtry what to wear — pale gold satin to match her hair or black velvet to set off her white shoulders. Julia remembered going to the theater in New York shortly before her marriage and enjoying most of all the stares of admiration from the audience as she appeared "splendidly dressed" in the gaslit box close to the stage. She experienced a much more exciting sensation now as she hurried to New York, "anxious about" her "play." She slipped into a dark, empty theater to listen to a rehearsal, the unmistakable smell of grease paint and canvas scenery lingering in the air must have sent a thrill of pleasure down her spine. At a line well read, surely a flush of pleasure mounted to her cheeks, all unseen in the darkness, and she must have had to fight an impulse to shout corrections to a stumbling passage. The spoken word — what magic it had! Perhaps it was at this time that Julia Ward Howe first began to feel an overwhelming desire to speak her writings aloud to a living audience.

The World's Own seemed at first to be a success. Sam wrote joyfully to his sister to that effect. Then it failed, both in New York and Boston. A storm of protest arose as the strait-laced fraternity awoke to what Mrs. Howe had done. This was an era when Grand Opera was taken seriously, plot and all, and Mrs. Howe might have been excused if her heroine had meekly suffered and repented of her sin like Faust's Marguerite. But there was originality in this play, whatever its faults. Mrs. Howe's Leonora became "the Prince's Favorite," binding him "in a chain of perfumed breath padlocked with kisses" and living in a chamber "floored with amethyst and hung with beaten gold." Her revenge upon her faithless lover is complete before she "snatches the dagger" to die in the last act. The play actually had suspense and Boston took it in dead seriousness, the comment being severe. Even the usually tolerant Fanny Longfellow said that it was "strange so clever a woman" as Julia Howe should have "chosen so wretched a heroine, and should not see that there is tragedy enough in life without descending to vice." The play was printed by Ticknor and Fields as well as being produced and Mrs. Longfellow had a copy. "It is cleverly written," she said, "and the close has a good deal of vigor, but it should never have been published." She thought "the poor doctor must feel it painfully as a thing he cannot give his daughters to read."

Also in receipt of a copy of *The World's Own* was Oliver Wendell Holmes, and he was put to it to know what to write to Mrs. Howe. "I don't know how so quiet a blend as yourself should have such tropical flashes of passion running through your veins," he said. . . . "The only question is how far genius must have its way." It was a nice letter from a very puzzled gentleman to a lady who frightened him, but whom he nevertheless recognized as a fellow author.

During the summer of 1857, while Dr. Howe was again in Kansas, Mrs. Howe wrote another play. At the top of the attic stairs at Lawton's Valley, she set up a table by the north window where the light was good. For a few short hours each day she went there, disregarding the heat, bravely battling the wasps — and making it clear to the children, four girls and a boy, that she must be undisturbed. The play was again in blank verse and called *Hippolytus*.

Hippolytus was taken from the Greek story of the pure youth beloved by Diana and pursued by Phèdre, a passionate princess who was also his stepmother. Mrs. Howe had seen Edwin Booth when he made his first appearance in Boston in 1857. An unknown young actor, Booth had learned his trade in San Francisco and in the mining towns of California, and he was now on the threshold of his great career with Boston his first and most difficult conquest in the serious drama. Booth's famous Hamlet was yet to be created, but the foundation for that triumph was now laid.

Hippolytus was the most difficult thing that Mrs. Howe had attempted but she could almost hear Edwin Booth's beautiful voice reading her lines as she wrote them. The thought of failure never entered her mind and this was by far her best work for the stage. Edwin Booth read *Hippolytus* in 1858 and promised to play it with Charlotte Cushman taking the part of Phèdre.

Miss Cushman was making the second of her farewell tours of the United States. It seems certain, from her letters to Mrs. Howe, that she really wanted to play Phèdre and that both she and Booth admired the play. "Don't attempt to battle with the asses who have pronounced their dictum in regard to *The World's Own*," Miss Cushman advised her "Dearest Giulia." And Miss Cushman promised that "if *woman* can accomplish it," *Hippolytus* would be "read and the music performed . . . in Boston in January . . . on the stage or somewhere and either way with success."

The fate of *Hippolytus* hung fire for several years, however. At last Mrs. Howe was told that her play had been rejected because there was no part in it that suited Booth's manager's wife. Her disappointment was the greater because her hopes had been so high. Of course she had succeeded in shocking Boston again — or rather the Greeks had and Mrs. Howe took the blame.

While writing tragedies, perhaps Julia Ward Howe was the better able to cope with an unhappy situation in her own private life. Surely it was better to shed tears over imaginary heroines than for herself. That there was gossip about her private affairs, she knew well and cared little. But that those close to her might misjudge the situation was a different matter. "I cannot but wish to be understood by the few who really love me," she wrote to her sister Louisa, from Lawton's Valley in 1854 — soon after the publication of *Passion Flowers*.

"Chev was very angry about the book and I really thought at one time that he would drive me to insanity, so horribly did he behave. He has been much less unkind for some time past, and I try to please him as much as I can, but when he is angry he has no control over his own feelings and no consideration for those of others. Indeed, dear Weevie, you may believe all that Annie tells you of my trials on that score — they are sometimes such that I would not endure them for a day, but for the children's sake, but these fits of perverseness come and go and there is generally something like peace between them."

This letter, begun at Lawton's Valley, was finished five months later in South Boston. It was interrupted by the news of the death of Annie's little boy, and "by days of such sadness that I have felt, ever since, unable to go back to them," Mrs. Howe said. By this time, there had been a letter from Louisa.

"I see by your letter that you have learned of a fact of which I could not have written you, that of my approaching confinement," Mrs. Howe wrote. "You ask whether I am glad or sorry. I can scarcely trust myself to speak of it, so bitter and horrible a distress has it been to me. You recommend ether — my dear Weevie, my mental suffering during these nine months nearly past has been so great that I cannot be afraid of bodily torture, however great. Neither does the future show a single gleam of light. I shall not drag this weary weight about with me, it is true, but I cannot feel that my heart will be any lighter. . . . After three years of constantly increasing unkindness and estrangement, no alternative presented itself to me, but that of a reconciliation or a final separation. The latter has been all along in Chev's mind, and was so favorite a project with him that he would bring it up in our quietest hours, when there was nothing whatever to suggest it. His dream was to marry again — some young girl who would love him supremely."

And the Chevalier's proposal was that his wife give him their oldest daughter, Julia Romana, and their son, Harry. "Before God," Mrs. Howe wrote, "I thought it my real duty to give up everything that was dear and sacred to me, rather than be forced to leave two of my children. . . . In this view, I made the greatest sacrifice I can ever be called on to make.

"I am no Fanny Kemble — I can suffer and die with my children, but

I cannot leave them till God calls me from them. I must not let you think, though, that I am wholly wretched. My children are more and more to me every day. Julia has become my constant companion — she shares my lonely walks and is like a young sister to me, something like what Annie used to be. Flossy improves and is very graceful and clever. Harry and Laura are two little angels and love each other dearly. These children and dear Annie give me all the sympathy and happiness I have. My studies help me a good deal — I should sink without them. When I tried to sing, the weight upon my heart would not let me, so my voice lost much. Of late, Julia loves so to hear me sing that I make an effort to recall the melodies of other days."

Just the day before the fifth child, the price of "reconciliation," was born, Mrs. Howe wrote to her sister Annie. As a practical matter and not because of morbid imagination or self-pity, it was necessary to make arrangements in case she died in childbed fever as her mother had done. Annie must look after the children "as much as possible." She was to take care of her sister's jewels and laces "that my girls may have them." But Mrs. Howe was "wonderfully strong."

"I look after all household matters and do it so much better than in old times. Chev seems quite contented for him. He even kissed me tenderly and said that I had grown so kind and patient that he did not know what to do for me in return. I feel so much the importance of the effort I am making, to my children, and through them to myself, that I do not really pause much to think whether things are pleasant or not."

The Howes' fifth child and fourth daughter, born that cold November 9, 1854, was Maud — destined to be one of the most beautiful women of her time. She was much photographed, her portrait often painted, and her praises sung on both sides of the Atlantic. She was also possessed of a violent temper and the will of an empress. Her mother, who had been afraid she could never love this child, became her adoring slave.

The price of reconciliation having been paid, it would be possible to hope that all might be well. Taking her share of the blame and even managing a touch of humor, Mrs. Howe told her sister Annie of a probably quite typical domestic scene. "Then I quarreled with Chev for making Flossy read the Bible with sore eyes. Then he pummeled me till I was black and blue in soul. Then we made peace, fastened up the house, set the watch-dog, and parted for the night as usual, I cursing philanthropy and he probably cursing me. But all this is naughty. I'se reforming, Annie dear, only somehow, I want to begin with Chev and not myself."

Husbands and wives who pretend never to have had a disagreement are either remarkably forgetful or adept at telling lies. But it is the "making peace" afterwards that matters. Mrs. Howe's abiding love for her Chevalier appears again and again in her journals. There was the time when she had been alone in South Boston late at night. She fell asleep but awoke after a few hours certain that her Chevalier was near. There was no one at the door but she got up to make herself a cup of tea and in a few moments he came. She was sure that her husband had summoned her from sleep to greet him. And in Newport one night she heard a strange sound and called out, "Chev!" in alarm — forgetting in her sleepy state that he was still in Boston. Next day he came and told of hearing her speak his name during the night at the very hour when she had cried out for him. These experiences were of importance to her, and she cherished them in her memory.

But in the autumn of 1857, Dr. Howe "again asked for a separation." He gave a different reason. "The ground this time is that there is no unkindness between us and that therefore the present is the time for such a division." Mrs. Howe was entirely unprepared for "this strange and unexpected turn of matters." Overcome not by logic, but by illogic, she was almost ready to give up. But Dr. Howe repeated his previous terms: that his wife give him Julia Romana and Henry Marion Howe; and she could not agree to part with these or any of her children.[8]

During the summer of 1859, while collecting material for her letters for the *New York Tribune*, Mrs. Howe described herself as "navigating around Newport looking like a 74." She was expecting a sixth child. "Would it might be a boy," she said, but added, "God's will be done." On Christmas night her boy was born. He was named Samuel Gridley Howe in honor of his father. Opening the Howe Bible to inscribe the name, "*Dieu donné*," Dr. Howe added to his entry.

CHAPTER TWENTY-ONE
Battle Hymn

"CIVIL WAR BEGUN. FORT SUMTER CAPTURED. FEDERAL CAPITAL IN DANGER. . . THE NORTH UNITED AT LAST." These were the headlines which greeted the Howes when they received their copy of Garrison's *Liberator* for April 19, 1861. Startling though the news might be, it was as though a violent storm had broken after a long period of sultry weather, and at first there was a sense of relief. No one dreamed how long the storm would last nor how heavy the damage would be.

Dispatches dated *Charleston, April 12* told of "indescribable excitement" and then went on to describe that same excitement from "the moment when, with the first boom of the guns, thousands rushed from their beds to the harbor front and all day every available place was thronged by ladies and gentlemen viewing the solemn spectacle through glasses." Charleston men and boys in the land forts were "perfectly reckless of their lives and at every shot jumped upon the ramparts and then jumped down, cheering." Julia Ward Howe, seated in her living room at Green Peace and reading her *Liberator*, could as yet have no idea that her brother Sam had been in Charleston watching the "spectacle." Since Sam Ward was an ardent follower of the turf perhaps he was one of those so fortunate as to have field glasses with him.

For a few months, here was the keynote — that war was a "spectacle"; and as if to support the theory, no one was killed in this action.[1] Later, during the surrender ceremonies, some cartridges blew up by accident killing two men — but this sort of thing happened in country villages every Fourth of July. The Crimean War has been called "the last romantic war"; but the Civil War began in the same unrealistic fashion — with officers' ladies being taken to the front, where they were photographed in silk hoop-skirted gowns, seated before a field headquarters as though at a tea party. The bitterness of the struggle, the Pyrrhic victories with appalling losses on both sides, not only from wounds but by disease, were the more overwhelming to a nation living in a make-believe world of chivalry.

"Whereas the laws of the United States have been for some time past and are now opposed and the execution of them obstructed by the States of South Carolina, Georgia, Alabama, Florida, Mississppi, Louisiana and Texas, by a combination too powerful to be suppressed by the ordinary course of judicial proceedings, or by the powers invested in the Marshals by law . . ." This was a sad sort of message for a newly elected President of the United States to have to write. Abraham Lincoln was calling out "the militia of the several States of the Union to the aggregate number of 75,000." Mrs. Howe saw the Massachusetts Volunteers marching to the railroad station in Boston. The troops were singing, for this was a war during which men sang even when their hopes grew dim. And at this time or very shortly one of their favorite marching songs was a hymn-tune which had been composed by William Steffe — a Southerner from Charleston, North Carolina. But the words which the Northern soldiers sang were new.

> John Brown's body lies a-mouldering in the grave,
> His soul goes marching on.

Sunday School children of Charleston and Northern soldiers alike sang the same chorus:

> Glory, glory, Hallelujah . . .

Julia Ward Howe saw the Volunteers go out and she was present in King's Chapel churchyard when flag-draped coffins of the first Massachusetts men to die were brought in for burial. On April 26, the Volunteers had arrived in Baltimore, en route for Washington. Their train arrived at ten-thirty in the morning at the President Street railroad station, and thirty-one horsecars were drawn up in front of the station to take them across the city to the Camden Street station of the Baltimore and Ohio. Six cars got through. Then a "vast assembly" of men and boys, some with Secession flags and placards, swarmed across the horsecar tracks. At one point, the roads was under repair and "paving stones lying in heaps were seized by the crowds." Amid "cheers for Jefferson Davis and Secession" car windows were broken, the recruits showered with flying glass. When a cartload of sand was dumped on the tracks the Volunteers decided to march. A Baltimore policeman said the first shot was fired from the ranks — the men said otherwise. Only sixty of the soldiers were armed — the rest were recruits.

At the King's Chapel ceremony was the Howe family's good friend, John Albion Andrew, and this was the first time that Mrs. Howe saw him acting in his official capacity as Governor of Massachusetts. She could see "how deeply the Governor was moved."

Ever since the John Brown affair, John Andrew had been a frequent caller at the Howes', and the children always remembered the time when he had taken a part in their dramatization of Thackeray's *Rose and the Ring*. Mr. Andrew's plump, cherubic face and the tight curls around his forehead made him look for all the world like Thackeray's drawings of "Prince Bulbo," but the children dared not ask him to be their Prince for fear of offending him. It was their mother who had the courage, and Mr. Andrew was delighted. Those playful days were over now, but the Governor dropped in upon the Howes often — especially when they lived on Chestnut Street in Boston. Sometimes he was so exhausted that he would sink down upon their sofa for a nap before dinner.

Mrs. Howe returned from the public obsequies at King's Chapel to write one of her first and best war poems. "Our Orders," it was called.

> Weave no more silks, ye Lyons looms
> To deck our girls for gay delights
> The crimson flower of battle blooms
> And solemn marches fill the nights
>
> Weave but the flag whose bars today
> Drooped heavy o'er our early dead
> And homely garments coarse and gray
> For orphans that must earn their bread . . .

Dr. Howe had already offered his services to the Union cause. On the day when news of Fort Sumter reached Boston, he wrote to Governor Andrew:

"Since they will have it so, — in the name of God, Amen! And now let all governors and chief men of the people see to it that war shall not cease until Emancipation is secure. If I can be of any use, anywhere, in any capacity (save that of spy) command me."

Dr. Howe next sent out an appeal for hospital supplies. The "United States Sanitary Commission," forerunner of the American Red Cross, was to be his field.

On April 17, Governor Andrew sent two ships to the Potomac, loaded with supplies for Massachusetts militia. He asked Dr. Howe and Judge Hoar of Concord to go to Washington to check on the arrival of these supplies, to report on health conditions in camp, and list the needs of the men. The troops needed "soap," Dr. Howe found. And at least at present, they needed "washerwomen more than nurses." Also, it was all too clear that the Sanitary Commission was considered as a "fifth wheel" by Lincoln.

While Dr. Howe was in Washington, the supplies he had asked for were piling up at home at an alarming rate with no one to look after them. The obvious solution was to let women do this work. But a woman's place was strictly in the home, and although her duties there were often complicated to a degree, it was assumed that she would be entirely incompetent in any work requiring organization and co-operation with others. On April 15, 1861, the day of the President's call for volunteers, some women in Bridgeport, Connecticut, met; and in Charlestown, Massachusetts, there was another women's meeting — in Lowell another "a few days later." But the Reverend Mr. Henry D. Bellows, President of the Sanitary Commission, remarked patronizingly that these women had " a somewhat vague idea of affording relief and comfort to the volunteers."

On April 19, "the ladies of Cleveland, Ohio, organized an association for the care of families of Volunteers" and to the Middle West must go the credit for recognizing the fact that women were capable of thinking clearly, working together and running their own "Soldiers' Aid Societies." Other Midwestern cities followed suit rapidly but it took the United States Sanitary Commission three months to recognize the women's groups by making them "Auxiliary Branches." By November, eight months later still, Dr. Bellows of New York got around to Boston. "A few ladies met in a private parlor . . . to form a New England Women's Auxiliary Association as a Branch of the Sanitary Commission." Dr. Bellows found his new branch already very much in flower with masses of supplies "already in the hands of Dr. Howe." These were duly turned over to the organization and Dr. Howe was proposed as president. He refused, being by now a member of the national committee and too much involved in the national problem. He became vice-president, however, and reported progress.

"The railroads" were "coming to the aid of the Sanitary Commission in the most generous manner. . . . The obstructions which kept our first consignments in Baltimore have been removed and the rich stream of New England Charity" was "flowing in more bountifully than ever. The huge boxes, the barrels, bales and packages open beautifully and the contents show not only the generosity but the care and forecast of the women in the selection of the articles . . ." Dr. Howe commended the "well-knit mits," and the "thick-ribbed socks." [2]

All the officers of the New England Women's Auxiliary were men, although in Cleveland the "books were kept by a young woman," a matter found worthy of comment years later. In Boston, they took no such chances and although Mary Dwight Parkman was spoken of as "first President" and Abby Williams May as President after the first year and for the duration of the war, this was an error. The presidents were men. The first meeting took place "in a private parlor" and of course it would not be discreet to mention in the annual report whose parlor it was and where located. But it was in the parlor at Green Peace, where Mrs. Howe first organized a group of young girls to work with her own daughters at "lint-picking and pin-ball making." Julia Romana was now seventeen, Flossy sixteen and Laura just eleven. The seven-year-old Maud was not necessarily included in these activities, and even Laura envied her sisters' superior skill. Flossy, in particular, could make almost anything; but Laura was like her mother — she had "donkey fingers." The time would come when Laura would find herself again just like her mother — her fingers skillful when she took up a pen.

The year was still 1861 when the Howes moved to 13 Chestnut Street, Boston. Dearly they loved this home on Beacon Hill, not far from the State House and close enough to Boston Common so that little Sammy could walk there every day and hear the bands play. To Chestnut Street came a larger group of schoolgirls to "sew for the Sanitary," on certain days each week. They promised to keep up their sewing circle after the war was over. Everyone repeated that the war would be over in ninety days.

Dr. Howe's reports from Washington were not encouraging, but no one had the sense to listen. Lincoln's first call for 75,000 troops was followed by the call for 750,000; and "a large force reached Washington" with many regiments making the journey in cattle cars and finding on arrival, no preparation to receive them. They stood for hours waiting in vain for rations and shelter. They lay upon straw under shoddy blankets and nobody was willing to enforce the simplest rules of health. Around Washington "the drains were offensive" and this was the Sanitary Commission's polite way of saying that the stench from the camps of the Volunteers rose to high heaven. "Recommendations went unheeded" because it was Secretary of State Seward himself who circulated that story that "the war would be over in ninety days" and everybody repeated and believed it.

Then came the first Battle of Manassas — or the Battle of Bull Run. "Such a rout of such an army — so large, so equipped, so commanded, was never known before on this Continent," exulted the New Orleans *Picayune.* The *Boston Journal,* which in April had talked about peace and thought the Secessionists had had enough, called the first Battle of Manassas "a repulse." But the men on the Sanitary Commission who were in Washington at the time, told the real story of the aftermath of Bull Run.

"It was a hungry mob that raged back into the streets of the capital, a woebegone rabble whose organization was lost in the panic which followed the hard-fought field. Soldiers were grouped about fires in the streets: some were asleep in the gutters and on doorsteps. . . . A reorganization of the army followed. Order, discipline, cleanliness, the policing of camps, the training of officers and men, made a new army." No longer was the Sanitary Commission a "fifth wheel." "Measures which they had urged were now submitted to." The old army medical department was abolished and a new one set up. But "hospital clothing there was none . . . hospital transport was nonexistent." All that was yet to come, and a year later, wounded men were left on the battlefield at Antietam for "four days . . . their wounds undressed, without blankets . . . with nothing to eat."

In November, 1861, Dr. Howe went to Washington to make a survey of the newly organized medical department of the army. With him went Governor and Mrs. Andrew, the Reverend James Freeman Clarke — and Mrs. Howe. This was Julia Ward Howe's first visit to Washington, D.C., although her brother Sam was a well-known figure in the lobby of the Capitol.

As the train pulled slowly into the city, Mrs. Howe caught glimpses of young men in uniform gathered around camp fires, "in the evening dews and damps." They were "pickets detailed to guard the railroad," her husband told her. At Willard's Hotel, the corridors still shook with the tread of officeseekers, just as William Russell had observed eight months earlier and the officeseekers were now reinforced by men with all sorts of goods to sell to the Government for the use of the army. Congressmen and their friends, visitors like Governor Andrew and his party, leavened this otherwise unappetizing loaf. It devolved upon Dr. Howe to write to the children and he addressed his letter to Laura, now nearly twelve years old.

"Your Mama is having a very delightful time; for the weather is delicious: there are expeditions every day, to camps, to objects of curiosity. In the evening there are many people gathered in the Salon of the Hotel and all the people who can appreciate talent and wit and conversational power are sure to be drawn to her. I go about inspecting camps and hospitals and doing what I can to help the cause of freedom. So does almost everybody except the army of office-seekers whose headquarters are in Washington."

The implication that Mrs. Howe did not visit hospitals was not true and was probably unintentional. She went wherever she was allowed to go, struggling hard not to be made ill by the dreadful odors and not to weep at the sight of young faces drawn with suffering. Gangrene was assumed to be inevitable as the aftermath of wounds and amputations were frequent and drastic. People seemed to take delight in showing visitors "the amputation table" and in telling how many boys would never walk again or use an arm or hand. Mrs. Howe felt guilty because, as she said, "I could not leave my nursery to follow the march of our armies." There was another reason why Julia Ward Howe could never have been an army nurse. Miss Dorothea Dix, fearful lest the breath of scandal should touch her first corps of army nurses, was said to have decreed that no one need apply who was not plain almost to the point of being ill-favored. Julia Ward Howe was far too attractive ever to qualify.

Governor Andrew arranged for his party to meet President Lincoln. "The President was laboring at this time under a terrible pressure of doubt and anxiety," Mrs. Howe said. "He received us in one of the drawing-rooms of the White House" with "Stuart's portrait of Washington" hanging on the wall over the sofa where Lincoln seated himself. Most of the conversation was between the President and Governor Andrew, leaving Mrs. Howe free to look about her and to contrast the serene, unlined face of George Washington with Lincoln's deeply furrowed cheek and brow. "I remember well the sad expression in Mr. Lincoln's deep blue eyes," she said afterwards. The eyes were "the only feature of his face which could be called other than plain."

"We have seen it in his face, hopeless honesty — that is all," said James Freeman Clarke upon emerging from the interview. This seemed a curiously unclerical lack of faith in what is so often termed the best policy, but in view of the nation's precarious situation, he had hoped for more. Governor Andrew, on the other hand, was quite confident of Lincoln's ability and pleased with McClellan's new army which paraded the streets in small detachments — to show that they had learned to march.

On November 18, 1861, a picnic was planned for Mrs. Howe and the other members of the Governor's party. They were supplied with a carriage and coachman, a hamper of lunch, and off they went to see a review of the troops which took place "some distance from town." Actually, it was across the Potomac in that territory from which Confederate troops had withdrawn after displaying their flag, for some time, in full view of the city of Washington. Carriage after carriage, filled with gentlemen in high silk hats and ladies in crinolines, equipped also with hampers of refreshments, drove out of town over the bridge and along the narrow road.

No sooner was the review of the troops in progress than Southern skirmishers broke up the show. Mrs. Howe saw "a detachment of soldiers gallop to the assistance of a small body of our men who were in imminent danger of being surrounded and cut off from retreat."

The coachman wheeled the carriage around and set out for Washington at a gallop — which was almost instantly cut down to a crawl as all the other drivers attempted the same thing. The main body of troops was ordered back along the same road. Apparently unaware of their danger, Mrs. Howe remembered that "to beguile the rather tedious drive, we sang from time to time, snatches of the army songs so popular at that time."

> John Brown's body lies a-mouldering in the grave,
> His soul goes marching on. . . .

When Julia Ward Howe sang that, the soldiers marching beside her carriage called out, "Good for you, Ma'am," and they took up the refrain — "Glory, glory, Hallelujah . . . his soul goes marching on."

The Reverend Mr. Clarke leaned forward to speak to Mrs. Howe.

"Why don't you write some good words for that stirring tune?" he asked. Mrs. Howe said that she had often considered the idea, but that no new words had come to her.[3]

Afterwards, Mrs. Howe could not remember the exact date, but Mr. Clarke, referring to his diary, found it for her. It was on the night of November 18 that she went to bed at the Willard Hotel and "as usual, slept soundly." Troops marched in the street below. "I awoke in the gray dawn of the morning twilight," Mrs. Howe said. And as she "lay waiting for the dawn, the long lines of the desired poem began to twine themselves" in her mind. The memory of some of the greatest lines in the Old Testament came to her, together with the picture of the boys' faces around the picket campfires, the sound of trumpets so recently heard — and her own deepening religious conceptions.

"I must get up and write these verses before I forget them," she told herself, and she "found in the dimness an old stump of a pen" and some paper of her husband's with the letterhead of the Sanitary Commission on it.

In the whole original manuscript there were only four words crossed out and amended. A final stanza was discarded because it spoiled the fine climax of the next to the last one, and when the poem was prepared for publication, Mrs. Howe changed only one entire line and throughout the poem perhaps as many as four other words. It seemed to her that the poem had come as a revelation from a source beyond herself, and she had good reason to believe this. Had she not been accustomed to work for many hours upon a poem, counting her syllables, arranging her rhymes? This poem sprang into being without conscious effort on her part and although she felt humble in the presence of this miracle, she did not realize its importance and she gave away her original copy to the first person who asked for it. The first version read like this:

> Mine eyes have seen the glory of the coming of the Lord
> He is trampling out the wine-press where the grapes of wrath are
> stored
> He hath loosed the fateful lightnings of his terrible swift sword
>   His truth is marching on.
>
> I have seen him in the watchfires of an hundred circling camps
> They have builded him an altar in the evening dews and damps,
> I can read His righteous sentence by the dim and flaring lamps
>   His day is marching on.
>
> I have read a burning Gospel writ in fiery rows of steel
> As ye deal with my contemners, so with you my grace shall deal

Let the hero born of woman crush the serpent with his heel
　　Our God is marching on.

He has sounded out the trumpet that shall never call retreat
He has waked the earth's dull sorrow with a high ecstatic beat
Oh! be swift my soul to answer him, be jubilant my feet
　　Our God is marching on.

In the whiteness of the lilies he was born across the sea
With a glory in his bosom that shines out on you and me,
As he died to make men holy, let us die to make men free
　　Our God is marching on.[4]

Still regarding this as a poem rather than a song, and little realizing that she had written the great "Battle Hymn of the Republic," Mrs. Howe sent her corrected version to the *Atlantic Monthly*. It appeared in February, 1862, and was "somewhat praised." The *Atlantic* sent Mrs. Howe a check for four dollars.

Perhaps "The Battle Hymn of the Republic" might have remained exactly that — "somewhat praised" and soon forgotten. But the year 1862 was a bitter one for the cause of freedom. Mrs. Howe was in Newport when the news of the second Battle of Manassas reached the north. She had driven into town with her son Harry, now fourteen. They found the village street lined with "waiting carriages filled with white-faced people intent on — what?"

"They are waiting for the mail. Don't you know that we have had a terrible reverse?" Mrs. Howe was told.

The people in the North were overwhelmed by the failures of the summer campaign, the call for a new army, the first assessment of the war-tax and "the resurging tide of the old army, sweeping up the Ohio and the Potomac, sending its wounded before it, leaving its dead behind." McClellan's Peninsula Campaign was a failure. There was failure everywhere. "The cost of war had not been fairly counted" — so read the report of the Sanitary Commission — "the horror of war had not been fairly seen. It had been entered upon in excitement, almost with a pleasurable fervor." And now the "pleasurable fervor" inspired by *Uncle Tom's Cabin*, for example, must give place to determination and the solemn acceptance of sacrifice.

In the glory of the lilies Christ was born across the sea . . .
As He died to make men holy, let us die to make men free . . .[5]

Stories varied as to the time when the army began to sing the Battle

Hymn of the Republic. Probably it was taken up simultaneously in more regiments than one, but one experience was told by Chaplain McCabe of the 122nd Ohio Volunteer Infantry. He saw the poem in the *Atlantic* and was so impressed with it that he memorized the stanzas immediately. Chaplain Charles Cardwell McCabe had a fine baritone voice, good looks and dramatic ability, so that he might have been an actor. He had a strong evangelical calling, however, and became a Methodist revivalist preacher. He was a poor boy and was never able to finish college, but was later made an honorary graduate of Ohio Wesleyan, where he attended one year, and he was eventually a Methodist bishop. But he was always known as "Chaplain McCabe" because of his Civil War service. Marching along with the Ohio Volunteers, he taught them "The Battle Hymn of the Republic" to the tune he doubtless knew as a hymn-tune, popular marching-song though it had become. One June 16, 1863, Chaplain McCabe was taken prisoner at Winchester while attempting to care for the wounded left behind on the field after one more northern retreat.

In Libby Prison, Chaplain McCabe taught the "Battle Hymn of the Republic" to fellow prisoners who needed the inspirational lift it gave them even more than their comrades still fighting in the ranks.

Chaplain McCabe was exchanged, but not before his health was much broken by fever. He recovered, however, and set about raising money for the chaplain service. Most movingly he sang the "Battle Hymn" at mass meetings, with his audience joining in the chorus. "The effect was magical," Mrs. Howe was told, long afterwards. At a meeting in Washington, "people shouted, wept and sang together . . . and above the applause was heard the voice of Abraham Lincoln, exclaiming while the tears rolled down his cheeks, 'Sing it again!' "

Solemnly taking pen in hand, Ralph Waldo Emerson made an entry in his diary. "I honor the author of the Battle Hymn of the Republic and of The Flag. She was born in the City of New York. I could well wish she were a native of Massachusetts. We have no such poetess in New England."

CHAPTER TWENTY-TWO

War Years

IT always seemed to Julia Ward Howe that her sister Louisa knew nothing about what went on in the United States. It was true that Louisa lived in a different world but nevertheless she had tried all along to explain to her children about slavery in the United States and what their Howe relatives and their friends were attempting to do about it. Mimoli remembered her childish bewilderment.

Mimoli Crawford was just five years old when she left Rome in April, 1856, to come "home" to the country she had never seen. At some time during her visit to Boston, Charles Sumner was "reverently pointed out to" her. "He was a tall, fine-looking man," she said but he struck her as "morose and alarming. . . . From my Howe cousins," she wrote, "I finally learned that he was a friend of the noble and oppressed black people and had been half murdered a few months before, for espousing their cause: also that Aunt Julia nourished the same tender regard for the slaves. These would-be deliverers were called Abolitionists and the cousins said that I must be an Abolitionist too." Mimoli spoke Italian almost better than she did English. "It took me days to learn to pronounce the ugly word, 'Abolition,' and then I boldly took the other side. . . . I wondered how pretty Aunt Julia, with her blue eyes and red hair, could have such fancies, but Aunt Julia was always a puzzling person to me in those days, and, if the term does not sound too ridiculous as applied to the relations of a brilliantly intellectual woman and a very small, ignorant girl, I should say that we did not hit it off." [1]

There were reasons other than Abolition that kept Mrs. Howe and Mimoli from being congenial, of course. Mimoli was a spoiled child, as she said herself. All the Crawford children tyrannized over their mother which was something that never happened in the Howe family

— except later and where Maud was concerned. When Louisa took her children back to Italy in 1859, they had not become as enthusiastic about American ideas as their Aunt Julia could have wished. And as the years went by, Mrs. Howe sometimes reproached her sister for being an expatriate. But the Civil War became a reality to Louisa when, one by one, the young American artists in Rome went home. Sincerely she mourned the boys, some from the North and some from the South, who returned no more. They had found the end and perhaps the answer to all their questions about life and art, but the Roman-American colony would never be the same without them. It was easy for Louisa to remain neutral with sympathy for both sides.

Annie and Adolph had swung strongly to the Northern side, although there were plenty of so-called "Copperheads" in New Jersey if the antislavery papers were to be believed. Much to Mrs. Howe's satisfaction, she was finally allowed to send papers to Bordentown containing some of her writing for Annie to see — without calling down Adolph's wrath upon the political point of view of the *Commonwealth* or the little *Boatswain's Whistle*.

The Civil War was a difficult period for the Mailliards. Racing had been at its peak of popularity around New York and New Jersey just before the war began. Then, one by one, the race tracks closed down and the gay young sportsmen were off to join the cavalry. The Mailliard children's grandfather, writing to them in French from his home near Paris, said, "Your fine cavalry regiment from New Jersey should be a great help in taking Richmond and also Charleston in order to end this wicked and unhappy war which does harm to the whole world." But he added, "It was a long time ago that I wrote that the Confederates would never be beaten so easily."

The Mailliard stables were not noted for the powerful breed suitable for cavalry horses, although probably Adolph sold a few mounts. The army bought horses to haul their cannon and their supply wagons and the Sanitary Commission bought horses to draw ambulances. But these were anything but the sort of animal Adolph raised. He was forced to use his stud farm as a deluxe boarding home for some of the famous race horses — their owners being glad to find a place where they would be cared for properly.

Adolph could not have been exactly happy over pasturing race horses, but the situation had its compensations. He still owned some beautiful imported fillies and by agreement with owners he could use a boarding stallion as a stud horse. Thus Young Eclipse was Adolph's horse by Eclipse, an English stallion brought to this country by Richard Ten Broeck. Young Eclipse with Barbarity sired a line known as the "Barbarous Battalion." In 1864, Monday was Adolph's great stallion, acquired this time from another breeder.[2] The Mailliard farm in Bordentown was stocked with horses ready to become famous — if someone would only buy and race them.

By 1862, there were four children in the Mailliard family, much to Annie and Adolph's joy. Their first child, Louise, but always known as Loulie, was by now fourteen. They had lost a son but Cora, their third child, was born a few months after her little brother's death. In 1857, another boy was born and also called Joseph like the little boy who died — but never " 'Poleon," that name belonging always to the lost baby. On January 25, 1862, came John Mailliard, named in honor of his great-uncle John Ward, greatly to that gentleman's delight doubtless — whether he admitted it or not.

"It seems sad to have left you so long without one token of sisterly sympathy at a time when you so much needed it," Annie's sister Julia wrote her in March. "The lonely days of confinement are doleful, as I have six times experienced, which is too often, let me here record." Julia said that her "days" were "one *cram* of business," and so they were. "My girls don't give me any assistance," she said, "and they do give me a good deal of trouble, Julia being very helpless and Flossy tolerably headstrong." But as soon as she had set down these complaints so familiar to mothers of growing girls, she added, "But they give me great pleasure" — and this was equally true.

"I have had dinner parties the whole winter through," Julia told Annie, "my German cook being an expert in all nice dinner dishes. It is astonishing, dear, how people thank you for a good dinner. I believe the seat of gratitude to be in the stomach after all."

Annie must have seen a newspaper item about which she inquired, or perhaps there was an allusion in another letter from her sister which had puzzled her, for Mrs. Howe explained: "The poem I recited to the newsboys was my 'Battle Hymn of the Republic' — the thing which I repeated to you at Newport when last there. This has been read in many churches and has given me more happiness than anything I ever wrote, I think."

It was almost time now to go to Newport again for the summer and Mrs. Howe went down to Lawton's Valley to open the farmhouse. But there were complications to having daughters in a state of what she called "quasi-outness" in those days when the matter of a chaperone must be strictly attended to. She wrote addressing "My dearest children, Maud and All." "I miss your naughty tormentships sadly. I am so used to my customary tasks of scolding you all and trying to satisfy you all that I seemed in coming down here, to drop out of all interests and all occupations. I would give anything to hear Sammy's 'Upstairs, downstairs' and to make those weary little journeys in which he is the luggage and I the beast of burden." But she must tell them about the tickets, and this part of the letter was for Julia Romana and Florence. "I have taken three tickets for the Amateur Opera at Cambridge — it is for Friday evening at the house of the Misses Parsons, one of whom is engaged to Louis Stackpole.[3] You must find out where the house is and go. You can take Eliza Howe to Matronize you — mind, *Eliza* — Maria is too young."

"Our dancing daughters and our drilling sons," this was the way Mrs. Howe described the younger generation in Boston during the war years. But each year a group of boys completed their drill and marched away — far too many of them never to return. Inevitably it would become the turn of Henry Marion Howe, now, in 1863, in his fifteenth year. Mrs. Howe must have thought she knew how it would feel to see young Harry off on the train for Washington and from then on to fear the very sight of a telegram. "Telegrams" was one of her most often-quoted poems. But no one really knows what grief will be like; and when disaster struck Julia Ward Howe, it came where least expected.

On May 13, 1863, Mrs. Howe took her little son Sammy out for a walk. He was four years old — blond, curly-haired, blue-eyed. It was rather a chilly day, and Julia Howe noticed that Sammy's scarf and gaiters had been forgotten. But surely it was spring — why burden the child with heavy clothing? As he trotted along, he talked to his mother in his own language.

Next morning Sammy seemed "heavy." The doctor said it was croup and Sammy who had had croup before and did not like it, said "I *are* better."

"Diptheretic croup" the doctor called it when the baby's temperature mounted and his breathing became more difficult. Pathetically simple were the remedies: Bryonia — Bella-Donna. Perhaps they did no harm, but certainly they did no good. On Friday Julia telegraphed for the Chevalier who was away on his wartime duties and who "arrived at mid-night." There was never any doubt that these two parents loved their child with equal devotion as they stood together by his bedside. There was never any hope for little Sammy. He died May 17, 1863.

Night after night, his mother dreamed that Sammy was alive again. He was playing in her closet — she was singing to him — "dearest, dearest little boy." She awoke to face the terrible truth and weep for him. "Chev comforts me," she said.

A change was imperative, right after Sammy's death, and, taking Maud and Laura, the Chevalier and Julia went to New York. It was good to see Uncle John, now growing old but just as anxious as ever to make Julia feel that Number 8 Bond Street was her home. But Uncle John's house was filled with other relatives and Dr. Howe stayed at a house nearby. He was taken ill — a lameness returning perhaps as a result of grief and overwork, and Julia spoke of going to sit with him. "I go to see Chev who comforts me." Of all the passages written in Mrs. Howe's journals these at this time were among the most revealing. She felt that it was wrong to grieve. "God have mercy upon me, and restore us to each other in his own good time," she wrote, but she would try to take up her life again and if possible do more for her friends. In the dark days when her husband had wanted to leave her, she had refused for the sake of the children. Now her gratitude to the Chevalier for comforting her came close to being a confession that she had loved him always, and that it was for his own sake also that she would not leave him.

The Chevalier returned to Boston, but Julia went for a short visit to Annie in Bordentown. Now she knew what Annie meant when she said that there was no grief quite like that of losing a child — and that no one could understand it who had not experienced it. Annie comforted her sister with all her loving heart and from Rome came letters from Louisa. If the sisters had been somewhat separated of late, they were brought back together now in mutual sympathy and understanding.

For Julia Howe, the return home was "a sad arrival" with "streets, the Common, the house . . . all full of images of darling Sammy." But Chev, though still lame, "met us at the depot with Harry." Flossy came to breakfast (she had been teaching at the Institute) and "all but Maud and Chev" went to the Church of the Disciples with their mother, where Dr. Clarke preached on "If it were not so, I would have told you" — a text which Mrs. Howe felt was chosen especially for her. More and more, she came to rely on James Freeman Clarke, whose sermons so often seemed to fill a particular need — and on her own reading of the Bible which she took to little Sammy's room in the early twilight. This had been the time when she used to sing him to sleep.

As always, Julia Howe found comfort in putting her thoughts in writing. Just a month after Sammy's death, it seemed to her, "as she lay on his bed in his old nursery," that she heard him say, "I *are* better, Mamma." She finished her "memorial of dear Sammy" a few days later — "my record of my lost Boy — not lost but lent to God." Two months later, she still "dreamed of dearest Sammy, . . . felt his little arms about my neck and his kisses on my left cheek."

The country home in Newport seemed still more dear as Julia Howe sat "with her chicks" under the trees and took them "to bathe in sea water" every pleasant day. As always, summer was the time for creative work and with Mrs. Howe, the morning hours were the best. It was not surprising that she now turned to philosophy. She read Kant and Fichte in German and, inevitably, her readings suggested original thought which must be put down. By the end of summer, Mrs. Howe had written six essays; but now a new idea occurred to her. Instead of sending them to a magazine, she would read them at a series of lectures in Boston, New York and Washington — anywhere that would provide a good audience and pay a modest price for tickets.

It seemed such a wise idea. Expenses were heavy, with children's schools to pay for, and their clothes. Prices were rising and "Beef at .40 a pound" made headlines in the papers. Julia Howe was sure she had found the ideal way to help out. In her journal, she mentioned having "a talk with E. P. Peabody." Here was a lady, now nearly sixty, who could speak with authority on the subject of lecturing. Had she not sponsored Margaret Fuller's "Conversations" at her West Street Bookshop? Miss Fuller profited modestly, if Miss Peabody did not. And times were changing for the better, or so the ever-optimistic Elizabeth Peabody always thought. She herself turned an honest penny giving "Reading Parties" and she was sure Mrs. Howe could do better still.

Julia Ward Howe, now forty-four, at first regarded Elizabeth Peabody as a funny old soul — with her outmoded side-curls and her wild enthusiasms. But when a brash young woman reporter saw fit to make fun of Miss Peabody, Mrs. Howe was most annoyed. She soon grew fond of "E. P. Peabody" and asked her out to Newport. "One of mother's old owls," giddy little Maud Howe called her. Maud was already too pretty to be very polite to elderly schoolteachers. But it must be admitted that all the Howes were convulsed when Miss Peabody appeared without so much as a satchel — wearing her nightgown under her dress and carrying her toothbrush in her "porte-monnae." Miss Peabody was funny — but what ideas she had! Better still, what enthusiasm for Mrs. Howe's idea of giving paid readings in philosophy!

On Sunday, July 20, Julia recorded in her journal, "I finish essay on 'Duality of Character,' 6th of my series." Julia finished in a fine flush of triumph, doing the last lines just as a week-end guest arrived. The guest was "Judge Conway" or Martin Franklin Conway, Free-Soil leader and first congressman from Kansas. He was known as "the silver-tongued orator of the West" and "the Patrick Henry of Kansas." When Mrs. Howe brought him to a large Newport reception, everyone was gratified. In the evening there was time to spare and Julia read her essay to the Judge. He praised it to the skies, and surely she should have been flattered by his "silver-tongued" approval. But Julia Ward Howe was a real artist. She was disappointed in her own work after all. The fire of enthusiasm with which she had written her curtain lines had died out now, and she knew she must go back and do the whole thing over.

Just before leaving Lawton's Valley, Julia finished her essay on religion, "for the power to produce which, I thank God," she wrote in her journal. "I believe that I have in this built up a greater coherence between things natural and things divine. I therefore rejoice over my work and thank God, hoping it may be of service to others, as it certainly has to me." Next day, Mrs. Howe read her new essay to Miss Mary Paddock, faithful friend and part-time secretary. Once more, it was only the author who was disappointed. "I have found the execution of the task to have fallen far short of my conception of it," Mrs. Howe wrote. "I shall try to re-write much of the essay." With infinite patience and perseverance, Julia wrote and re-wrote, never entirely satisfied yet with a shining goal clearly in mind and a determination to reach it by the only possible route — hard work.

Back in Boston in the autumn, Julia Howe wrote in her journal as follows: "Last night Chev declared that I must read my lectures without compensation. I think he is mistaken, but cannot disregard his wishes in this." If this had happened sooner, when Julia was thinking of her lectures for the most part in terms of a means of helping out with family finances, she would have been bitterly disappointed. But in the course of studying and writing, she had received peace of mind after the death of her little son. It would be enough if she could help others through her studies of philosophy and comparative religion — it would be delightful to have small parlor readings at home. Picking up the pieces of her plan, she sent out invitations.

"I went to Mrs. Howe's last evening," said Mrs. Josiah Quincy, one of the guests. "She has succeeded in doing something unique. You have heard of her ethical readings. Last night, it was a sketchy review of the French outbreak of '48 and the statesmen — of Agassiz and Theodore Parker — whom she served up 'couleur de rose' without a shadow — as the Titanic hero — fighting against shame of all kinds, galvanizing a dead church, etc. etc." Theodore Parker had died in Italy, where he had gone for his health, in 1860. He had been Julia Howe's close friend and everything she said about him she truly believed. But Mary Jane Quincy, writing to Mary Mann, November 29, 1863, thought that certain orthodox clergymen present "sat uneasily on their chairs," but that Julia Howe's reading, on the whole, "was very finely done, sparkling and tender too, read in a sweet monotone voice. . . .

"She is a singular woman," Julia's neighbor went on to say — expressing what was probably a fairly common opinion at that particular time. "No one would have thought who saw her overwhelmed with grief at the loss of that boy, that she could have felt like filling her rooms this winter."

There would always be people who failed to understand Julia Ward Howe.

In the autumn of 1863, Julia was being looked over critically but not unkindly by another woman of great importance in literary Boston. This woman was Annie Fields, wife of James T. Fields — Mrs. Howe's publisher and editor of the *Atlantic Monthly*. Annie Fields was fifteen years younger than Julia Howe, being at this time twenty-nine; dark-haired, serene of brow. She was the second wife of James T. Fields; he of the "superb curly black beard." Like Mrs. Howe, Mrs. Fields delighted to entertain, but no children disturbed her serenity; no loss of a child marred her Madonna-like beauty with signs of grief. Unlike Dr. Howe, who restricted his wife's love of hospitality and forbade wine at table, Mr. Fields liked to have his wife entertain constantly and lavishly. It was part of his business. They had now been married nine years and Annie Fields was ever the solicitous wife. At one of their literary dinners, should a crumb get caught in the luxuriant Fields beard — "There's a gazelle in the garden, Jamie," his wife would say.

Mrs. Fields had developed a literary salon of Ticknor and Fields authors who paid her homage — much of which she deserved. She wrote poetry in a modest way. Her greatest gift was to listen and to look beautiful. But in a series of small blue-paper-covered notebooks, she wrote penetrating line-a-day sketches of the people she met. Her Jamie planned some day to write a book about his authors, and Mrs. Fields's notes were to prompt his memory.

Heading her page October 4, 1863, Mrs. Fields wrote: "Passed the evening with Mrs. Howe at her house, where were Prof. Henry of Washington, his daughter, Mr. Alger and the Misses Dewey. We had an interesting talk, Mrs. Howe witty as usual. She spoke of the beauty of character showed by Mrs. George Greene who, still young and with three children, is living in the home of her husband's brother who is not overkind to them and with only the memory left of a very pretty fortune which Mr. G has been unfortunate enough to lose together with his own money." This was that remarkable literary cousin of the Wards', George Washington Greene, who had crossed Louisa's path in Rome twenty years previously — disposing of some of Thomas Crawford's money with equal ease!

But Mrs. Fields continued: "Mrs. H. provoked and sustained a philosophic-scientific conversation with the gentlemen which showed her knowledge of Compte, Spinoza, Kant, Hegel and the like. She said that if shut up with 12 books, Spinoza should be one of them. Homer stood first.

"Miss Dewey made a keen remark. 'Ha!' said our hostess, 'Sheffield cutlery.' She is evidently studying at present and writing. The talk got deep and after it was over she recalled the saying of Mrs. Bell after a like evening when she called for 'a fat idiot.' "

The Fieldses went again to the Howes a short time later to spend Sunday evening. They found "Henry Tuckerman, the essayist" there, among others — and "Miss Elizabeth Peabody." And Mrs. Fields wrote that "Mrs. Howe always impresses us with her conversational skill. I am convinced not many of the French women were more clever at this. Her face will shine and the words will flow . . ." Yet Mrs. Fields thought that "an unobservant" person might never realize that Mrs. Howe was there at all. She drew out conversation rather than dominating it.

It was inevitable that Julia Howe and Annie Fields should be rivals. Both were socially gifted; both attracted interesting people. But because of the position of James T. Fields as publisher and editor, a

Fields invitation had the force of a royal command, at least among writers and aspirants to that trade. People came to Mrs. Howe's, first of all because they wanted to see her, to hear what she would say and to figure out if possible what she would do next. It was sure to be "something unique," as Mrs. Quincy had said. The fact that they met all kinds of people at her house — actors, clergymen, bankers, reformers and scientists — added spice to the occasion. Both women were most successful hostesses, and their rivalry could have remained friendly — but for the affair of the "Ode."

Since the truth must be told, Mrs. Howe was decidedly to blame. The Boston Music Hall, built for Jenny Lind's concert in 1852, was remodeled in 1863 to contain the largest organ on the American continent at that time and one of the three or four largest in the world. An "Ode," written for the occasion, was to be recited by Miss Charlotte Cushman — in Boston on one of her farewell tours. Miss Cushman was happy to memorize whatever poem should be given to her and she was not the only one who supposed that her friend Julia Ward Howe would be the Odist. It is hard to understand why Julia should want to write such a thing — but at that time it was assumed that good poetry could be written to order for any occasion and the "Poet Laureate" idea was popular. Mrs. Howe expected the "honor" and she was among those who thought she was going to get it. The committee decided otherwise and invited another woman to contribute. The "Ode" was to be anonymous, but during a party at the Fields house after the dedication concert at Music Hall, Mrs. Howe discovered the author. The Odist had been Annie Fields.

Mrs. Howe had her column to write for the *Commonwealth* and did so, reporting the dedication concert. First she deplored the changes made in the hall — evidently with justice. Hitherto, the building had been a "beautiful parallelogram" with plain white walls, against which "how nobly the superb statue of Beethoven used to detach itself." Now, "into its place, on the fourth side . . . has walked the façade of a Gothic cathedral" — and Beethoven had been put outside the door. No one could have blamed Mrs. Howe very much for coming to the defense of the statue by her late brother-in-law, Thomas Crawford. And besides, she was right.

Writing in defense of the orchestra versus the organ, Mrs. Howe was at her best. ". . . The organist has but one power and affects us as one, though stops and pedals should make him seem to be one hundred. Commend me to the strings and brasses. I love the sudden zeal of the cymbals, and the prudent, timely interference of the hero with the kettledrums." It was a pity that Julia Ward Howe never wrote a whole essay about music — she did it so well. But it is doubtful if people paid any attention to anything in the column except the short middle paragraph in which Mrs. Howe took care of the Ode and the Odist.

"Judged from the literary point of view . . . ," Mrs. Howe wrote, "the Ode deserves neither praise nor criticism. It has no characteristic of a poem, other than phrase and rhyme. . . ." The Ode had "no stamp of originality." This was true of all its one hundred and eighty-one lines, but unfortunately this could also have been said of some of Mrs. Howe's poetry. Lady poets, like everyone else, should be careful not to throw stones.

The *Commonwealth* "critique" was anonymous — as was the Ode. There could hardly have been a more open secret, however — and Longfellow, who was genuinely fond of both ladies, scolded Julia Howe.

It was a different Longfellow now from the young man with the reddish curling hair who frequented Bond Street. But he was one of the few friends of Mrs. Howe's who called her "Julia." Longfellow's abundant hair was white now and the full beard of the more familiar portraits covered the scars on Longfellow's face. His wife Fanny Appleton Longfellow was dead. On July 9, 1861, Fanny Appleton had been sitting at her little desk by the window in the huge back parlor at Craigie House. She was using sealing wax, and a spurt of flame set fire to her dress. The scars on Longfellow's face were caused by burns received as he tried in vain to beat out the flames and save his wife. He never really recovered from his grief, and his natural gentleness and sweetness of character increased. When he took Julia to task, "This scolding was so genial, one would like to have faults to be so chidden," she said.

And then it was borne in upon Julia Howe that she had "caused pain" and suddenly she was sorry — as she always was after a fit of temper. She wrote a note of apology and sent it to Mrs. Fields by Dr. Bartol, a clergyman who lived near them both. Unfortunately, Dr. Bartol's call interrupted a conversation between Oliver Wendell Holmes and Nathaniel Hawthorne — which Mrs. Fields was enjoying.

In her little blue-covered notebook, Mrs. Fields wrote: "Julia Ward Howe has said and sung her last as far as Boston goes. Her jealousy of the Odist got the better of her better judgment and she has written out her gall for the *Commonwealth*. Alas! Where was her good genius."

Mary Ward, sister of the "good Sam Ward of Boston" and once engaged to marry Mrs. Howe's brother, was now Mrs. Charles Dorr and a lavish Boston hostess. Her rather sentimental girlish friendship with Julia Ward Howe had decidedly dissolved. Mrs. Dorr was hostess at the dinner with "sixteen at table," where Annie Fields soon found herself. "The heat was like the Black Hole of Calcutta," said Mrs. Fields in her notebook, "but the company very brilliant. Mrs. Howe was thoroughly canvassed at table and 'picked as clean as any duck for the spit,' as O.W.H. [Oliver Wendell Holmes] said afterwards to Mrs. Parkman who is a very just woman and who weighed her well in the balances."

It was all too true that Julia Howe's better judgment should have prevailed and that her "good genius" failed her. But Mrs. Fields was wrong when she said that Julia Ward Howe had said and sung her last in Boston. The affair of the "Ode" occurred just as Mrs. Howe's readings were beginning. Her audiences rapidly increased as friends rallied out of loyalty and others arrived out of curiosity. After each lecture, Mrs. Howe wrote in her journal, "audience increases since last time." The fifth essay was read to a "large and attentive audience and at the sixth and last many people" spoke highly of "Duality," with which the series closed.

CHAPTER TWENTY-THREE
Editorial Mrs. Howe

FIRST requests for help made by the Sanitary Commission were pathetically naïve. Would people please bring in old linen which could be made into bandages? They told how long and how wide these scraps ought to be. The soldiers in the hospitals would like to have a handkerchief given them, because so many had lost theirs. Cloth from the ragbag in pieces not long enough for bandages could be cut into squares and "hemmed with loving hands." [1]

And then, during the Peninsular Campaign, McClellan wrote to Lincoln that "this rebellion has assumed the character of a war." [2] Orders to the navy to support McClellan were never given, other plans failed and his advance became retreat with heavy losses. In September, 1863, it was reported in the papers that the death rate among prisoners in hospitals at Richmond was at the rate of 43 a day. The time when the Sanitary Commission could do any good with rags from attics had long gone by. What they needed now was money.

"The Women of Chicago originated and conducted the first of the Fairs," said the Sanitary Commission in their report. But the idea of a Fair in aid of antislavery, at least, was not new to Boston. In 1846, James Russell Lowell in his "Letter from Boston," told his friend James Miller McKim what was going on.

> The great attraction now of all
> Is the "Bazaar" at Faneuil Hall
> Where swarm the anti-slavery folks
> As thick, dear Miller, as your jokes.
> There's Garrison, his features very
> Benign for an incendiary. . .

Music Hall, not Faneuil Hall, was the scene of the "Sanitary Fair" with many of the old friends of antislavery pooling their former experience to make it the biggest thing of its kind Boston had ever seen. The date was December 14 through 21, 1863. Judged by modern standards, however, the only newspaper, (Boston or otherwise) which gave the Fair what could be called "good coverage" was the *Commonwealth* — Dr. Howe's paper, for which Mrs. Howe did all the work of this sort.

Each of the various Sanitary Fairs throughout the country had its "exhibition of antiques and curiosities," for which an extra admission was charged. Most probably, Mr. Sumner had Mrs. Howe to thank for the publicity she gave to his belongings which he placed on loan in Boston. "Through the kindness of Hon. Charles Sumner, several valuable additions have been made to the numerous attractions of the Fair," said the *Commonwealth*. Mr. Sumner was showing his "Album Amicorum, kept at Geneva by Camillus Cordova, a Neapolitan Nobleman, during the first half of the 17th century. It contains what is thought by many to be the most precious existing autograph of John Milton, bearing the date, June 10, 1639." And Mr. Sumner also loaned his "dessert service of gold inlaid with turquoise, formerly the property of the unfortunate Count Bathyani of Hungary." There were "missals" and "autographs," but surely here was the gem of the "antiques and curiosities" show. Admission was fifty cents, the same price as general admission, and the proceeds from the exhibition amounted to a thousand dollars the first day, it was said.

Of course most of the space at Music Hall was devoted to tables with fancy articles for sale. There were also articles for sale by lottery; a grand piano, a "monster washing machine, the gift of the Shaker Colony" — which went for three hundred and fifty dollars — and a "flock of Merino sheep." The backers of the Fair had miscalculated badly on one point, however. They had no idea how popular the thing would be. In the midst of heavy anxiety over war casualties and the trend of the war in general, here was a chance for New Englanders to relax and have a good time. Even the New England conscience could rest, for was not the Fair all in a good cause?

Railroads ran excursion trains. On Wednesday, "Music Hall was thronged as usual and the doors had several times to be closed and hundreds turned away, chagrined at their ill luck and wondering when they could see the Fair." This time, it was the *Boston Evening Traveller* which condescended to report, the Sanitary Fair having proved of interest to a much larger section of the public than the *Common-wealth's* small but ardent group of readers. "The receipts are largely in excess of all preconceived estimates," said the *Traveller*. On Tuesday, the second day of the Fair, general admissions alone came to twenty-eight thousand dollars.

The *Traveller* expressed the general attitude of astonishment that women, or more particularly "ladies," could achieve anything at all outside their parlors. "Accomplished ladies, the leaders of fashion and wealth and intellect, are deeply engaged in arranging the articles of beauty and usefulness upon the various tables." The reporter thought it was "indeed a pleasing sight to see . . . how gracefully hands accustomed only to the requirements of elegance and luxury put in place . . . the rough materials out of which the whole hall" was "converted into a fairy palace." Boston was "crowded with people . . ." the streets "alive with visitors from various parts of New England," who had come to the Fair.

It was a seven days' wonder and then "the Grand Sanitary Fair . . . closed brilliantly . . . its receipts footing up in the neighborhood of $140,000." Under a date of December 25 — Christmas day — it was the *Commonwealth* that reported this. "It can safely be said that the Fair eclipses any similar enterprise ever held in New England, if not in the United States," went on the *Commonwealth* — making a statement calculated to spur other cities to attempt a little eclipsing. The Boston Committee sent the Commission 50,000 dollars, the rest going to buy supplies sent to the troops by the New England Auxiliary Branch. Money came in from the Fairs all over the country. When the totals were all cast up after the Civil War was over, the New England Women's Auxiliary collected and disbursed 315,000 dollars in cash and 1,200,000 dollars in stores and supplies. The national total was 54,000,000 dollars. "All this done by women!" exclaimed the compiler of the figures — as well he might.

In the midst of all the excitement over the Boston Sanitary Fair, a small item appeared in the *Springfield Republican* and was copied by the *Commonwealth*.

"An entertainment, delightfully Bostonian, is regaling the *crème de la crème* this winter. A woman of genius invites her choicest friends to assemble in her parlor for six successive Wednesday evenings and listen to some remarks upon social ethics. Every guest goes, Cambridge professors, poetry, learning, art. At her appointed hour the lady enters and reads an essay of her own production; the philosophers say it is worthy of Emerson, the poets say it is poetry, the theologians, it is religion. 'She has the finest mind of any American woman,' exclaims a Cambridge professor. Ah, now I have betrayed her, which I did not mean to do." So ended the letter by "a Boston Correspondent" and the description fitted no one but Julia Ward Howe at that time, the quotation being dated "Dec. 18, 1863." When summer came, Mrs. Howe went back to Newport to prepare further "Ethical Readings" and to polish up the ones she had just given.

"Philosophy and Religion" was the new general subject and Mrs. Howe drew upon Lydia Maria Childs' "History of Religious Ideas" as well as from books by Thoreau and Emerson to illustrate the contemporary thought of her time. Early in January, 1864, the Reverend James Freeman Clarke asked Mrs. Howe to read her essay on "Duality of Character" at the vestry room at the Church of the Disciples. She was very happy about the invitation, but puzzled to know what she should wear on her head. It would be unthinkable to go into any part of the church bareheaded, but she did not like "to read in my thick bonnet," she said. She decided upon her "white cap" — and a little lace cap became a sort of emblem of Julia Ward Howe as the years went by and she lectured from coast to coast.

She had "quite a full audience" on this her first really public appearance as a lecturer on social ethics, and she was "surprised to see Mrs. Dorr" seated in one of the forward rows. Of course Mary Ward Dorr could have come to replenish her stock of table-talk, but on the other hand it might have been a conciliatory gesture and so Mrs. Howe took it to be. The affair of the organ dedication and Annie Fields's one hundred and eighty-one lines of "Ode" was on its way to oblivion.

In October, 1864, Mrs. Howe received an invitation that compensated for the "Ode" affair. The Century Club of New York asked her to come to the celebration in honor of William Cullen Bryant's seventieth birthday and to "contribute a poem for the occasion." Mrs. Howe at once "commenced to try the poem." It came out with "too short a line for phrasing," she thought, but "in the cars" on the way to Newport she "recomposed the poem," the rhythm of the train "singing a longer stanza." [3]

Oliver Wendell Holmes was Mrs. Howe's "companion" on the train to New York and his "ethereal talk made the journey short and brilliant." But Julia had her moment of private amusement. " 'Mrs. Howe, I will sit beside you,' " Holmes had said, " 'but you must not expect me to talk, as I must spare my voice for this evening, when I am to read a poem at the Bryant celebration.' "

" 'By all means, let us keep silent,' " Julia said. " 'I also have a poem to read at the Bryant celebration.' "

Julia Howe went straight to her Uncle John Ward's house on Bond street as soon as her train reached New York. It was like going back into her girlhood again to find the hairdresser waiting for her and a maid to unpack her dress and carry it off to be pressed. At 8:15, she was driven in Uncle John's carriage to the Century Club, which she found "fast filling with well-dressed women." She was "led to a reception room where those who were to take special part were assembled." And now everything was similar to that New York occasion long ago when Miss Julia Ward attended a dinner for Charles Dickens and was shown into a small room behind the scenes.

But now, instead of waiting in the anteroom and by good fortune managing to slip into a seat not intended for her, Julia Ward Howe was led out onto the platform where stood three imposing armchairs. They were for Mr. Bancroft, Mr. Bryant — and Mrs. Howe.

Julia was delighted to see Mr. Bancroft, her old tutor. She had always been fond of him. But she could have wished his speech which opened the proceedings had been shorter and more to the point. There was plenty of time to look around the hall and plenty to look at, for, "In all directions upon the walls, hung handsome decorations in natural flowers, drapery and gilding — including several quotations from Mr. Bryant's poetry surrounded by wreaths and a harp hung with garlands bearing the letters W.C.B." Or so at least said "a gentleman correspondent of the *Chicago Tribune*" as quoted in the *Liberator*.

Bryant's reply was excellent, Mrs. Howe thought. Then came a musical selection prepared for the occasion and performed by "three little Trinity choristers" to a harp accompaniment. The boys were dressed as medieval pages with "plumed turbans" and sang from a little balcony like a "chamber on the wall." They did well but Mrs. Howe, for one, would have liked the piece better written in a lower key because the song sounded a trifle squeaky.

"Mr. Bryant, in his graceful reply to Mr. Bancroft, named me as 'she who has written the most stirring hymn of the war,' " Julia wrote in her journal that night. "After Mr. Emerson's remarks, I was announced. I stepped to the middle of the platform and read my poem.

I read it well, I think, as everyone heard me and the large room was crammed. The last two verses, not the best — were applauded."

The *Chicago Tribune's* correspondent expressed his own opinion. "Mrs. Julia Ward Howe was next, if I may use such a commonplace expression, 'called upon the stand.' She looks the very embodiment of my idea of a Pythoness. I am sure she would have adorned the tripod if she had been born in that station of life. She has just the pathetic and well-measured voice for oracular manifestations: and while reading one of her own poems, as on this specific occasion, looks remarkably inspired. She was received with much applause." Neither the *Chicago Tribune* nor Mrs. Howe spoke of the poem read by Oliver Wendell Holmes. But presumably he did not actually lose his voice while talking aboard the train.

After two more speeches everybody went out into the dining hall for an elaborate supper. There were "Knickerbocker bowls of Century Punch, claret punch and lemonade . . . oysters, raw, scalloped and stewed, lobster and chicken salad, boned turkeys, Perigord pies and a variety of ices, creams, jellies and pastries, sandwiches, coffee and chocolate." The guest celebrities met members and guests of the club and it was on just such an occasion that Julia Ward Howe's wit always sparkled the most brilliantly. After the supper everybody (except the *Tribune* correspondent, who had had enough and went home) filed back into the auditorium for more speeches. The celebration must have lasted into the small hours.

Julia wrote her own account of the Bryant celebration in her journal, "for her grandchildren." This was, "I suppose, the greatest public honor of my life," she said. But this time Julia Ward Howe was a poor "Pythoness" for she prophesied incorrectly. This honor was not her greatest — it was only her first.

During the winter of 1864, the needs of wounded navy personnel occupied Boston. Mrs. Howe returned home to plunge deep into work for the Seaman's Fair. The object was to raise money to build a National Sailors' Home and the problem, after the huge success of the Sanitary Fair, was a little more difficult. The novelty had worn off. People from inland towns in New England felt less enthusiasm for the seagoing cause and the papers seemed to have nothing to report about any excursion trains going to Boston. As usual, the publicity in the papers was meager and perhaps for this reason all the Fairs published newspapers of their own. In Boston, it was the *Knapsack* which sold

2009 copies in one day at the Sanitary Fair — the New York Sanitary Fair called their paper the *Spirit of the Fair* and in Brooklyn it was the *Drum Beat*. The *New York Herald* rudely referred to this last as the *Dead Beat* and said that women should stay away from the newspaper business. Of course no one paid any attention to the *Herald*, and when the Seaman's Fair was planned, Julia Ward Howe was asked to edit a paper for it.

The *Boatswain's Whistle* [4] was "published every afternoon at four o'clock" throughout the Fair. Contributors were distinguished and were a tribute to Mrs. Howe's tact and persuasiveness. There was a poem by Oliver Wendell Holmes called "The Jubilee" and several articles by Edwin Percy Whipple, a popular lecturer famous for his wit. J. G. Holland contributed a short "Timothy Titcomb" letter, using the imaginary character which had brought him popularity while editor with Bowles of the *Springfield Republican*. Holland used a short anecdote to suggest the idea that Wendell Phillips favored neither McClellan nor Lincoln for the next President because he secretly wanted the office himself. It was the sort of humor Mrs. Howe enjoyed and she never dreamed she would be called on the carpet for it.

Considering who the contributors were, some of the contributions were surprising. The Reverend James Freeman Clarke sent in a pretty little love lyric and a humorous article about the qualifications of a war correspondent. The young "telegrapher" should have the ability to "keep up the courage of the nation by making everything as rose-colored as possible" — a capacity to say nothing in a great many words and to report a crisis made up out of trivialities. For example, "The President is at the War office. A messenger has been sent out for seegars which is thought ominous," a dispatch would read. This would be followed by another: "Mr. Stanton is heard laughing. It is believed that the President has told a joke. The crisis is over."

That humor should lurk behind the bushy whiskers of James Freeman Clarke was something no one would suspect from reading his *Anti-Slavery Days* or the various published sermons he left to posterity. Mrs. Howe found Mr. Clarke a Pastor in the truest sense of the word, as she brought to him her private difficulties and asked advice. It is safe to say that if they also laughed together this made them completely congenial friends.

Some of the contributions were signed with full names, some with initials and some not signed at all. Bound volumes were supplied by the printer at a nominal cost and when Mrs. Howe gave a copy to Bancroft she wrote in the names of authors wherever needed. The first number carried a poem signed clearly — Annie Fields. Here was the olive branch extended and accepted.

Although much interested in the literary quality of her paper, Editor Julia Howe saw that justice was done to the exhibits at the Fair. She gave space to "the noble white ox, 'General Grant,' given to the President by Mr. Carlos Pierce and given by the President to the Fair." The ox had been "placed in a stall in a passageway opening out of the Lobby, behind the Sewing Machine Department" at the Boston Theater where the Fair took place. The ox weighed 3900 pounds "at present," said the write-up (keeping the statistics strictly accurate), and would be "disposed of by a raffle at $5.00 a ticket."

Along with her daily editorials, Mrs. Howe contributed a serial story to the *Boatswain's Whistle*. This she commended to her sister Annie. It was about a young man who was "Marshal" at a fair and a girl who presided over the fancy-work table for the benefit of "a mission at Pea Ridge" — the "Pea Ridgers" being in a bad way, with "small-pox among the Indians" and their "celebrated chief, Scalp in the Washtub" having "six wives and no religion." This satire gave a perfect picture of a charity bazaar — whether for an imaginary "Pea Ridge" or for soldiers or sailors. Personable young men were always invited to be "Marshals" — their duties being to help set up tables, direct traffic and carry about goods to be raffled. "The raffle business is, I suppose, the greatest humbug of occasions of this kind," Mrs. Howe made her hero say as he staggered about the hall loaded down with horrors for which he was to sell chances. A marshal was supposed to keep the peace between ladies who felt insulted over the location of their booths but Mrs. Howe's hero failed because "people who cannot agree with each other will sometimes agree to quarrel."

A marshal's extracurricular activities consisted of flirting with the pretty young girls who sold goods at the various tables. The story ended properly with a romance aided by a third character known only as "the quiet girl." In the end, the hero, thanking "the quiet girl," asks her why she has been so kind and why she has no young man of her own. She tells him that her lover has been killed in the war, and he sees "a mourning ring on an engagement finger." The real picture, not only of the Fairs but of the times, was reflected in Mrs. Howe's light, satirical story with its serious last lines.

Of course Mrs. Howe also had a table — a "literary table" where she sold autographs, exhibited manuscripts and sold tickets to the

tableaux which were given in the evening. Surely she did her part —
but in her final editorial she reflected somewhat ruefully on the duties
of an editor of a daily paper. "No rash individual should undertake
editorship of any daily journal without first serving a brief apprenticeship in the good old-fashioned pillory." An avalanche of verse had
descended upon the editor and when it could not all be published, without crowding out all the prose, feelings had been hurt. A great deal
of prose had also to be rejected. Moreover, a controversy had broken
out — it would not be Boston if it hadn't — exception being taken to
J. G. Holland's remarks about Wendell Phillips.

"To accuse Mr. Phillips of views upon the White House, after all
the pains he has taken to paint it black, would be incongruous indeed,"
said Mrs. Howe. The author of the article had "hoped that everyone
would see that he was in fun."

But "jokes in Boston are usually detected three weeks after they are
perpetrated, owing to the dilatory character of the city police," said
Julia Ward Howe, and she spoke from experience. "If in our beloved
City, one wishes to abridge this period, it is safest to say honestly and at
once, 'I am about to jest.' "

With her first experience as an editor behind her, Mrs. Howe returned to "readings," and by the spring of 1864 she had plans well
under way to read lectures in Washington and Philadelphia — "for the
Sanitary" if her friends wanted to raise money, or if not, "for my usual
motive — to say my word as well as I can and as often as circumstances call for it." All went well at first and then there was a mysterious setback. Mrs. Howe's journal tells her discovery of what had gone
wrong.

"I have suffered a great deal with relation to my intended readings
in Washington. Mrs. Governor Sprague having been written to on the
subject, gave me a kind invitation to read them at her house. I wrote
thanking her and requesting her to fix the time. Not hearing again, after
long waiting I wrote proposing a certain time." Mrs. Howe received a
strange letter in return. Charles Sumner was again in Washington as
Massachusetts Senator. He had recovered his health and was now at
work in favor of the Negro Emancipation Bill — but he believed in
rights for everyone but women. He considered it disgraceful for a
woman to speak in public or even to a group of friends in a private
parlor. Mrs. Howe found that "Charles Sumner had gravely dissuaded"
Mrs. Sprague "from having readings at her house." Julia wrote him
"a very warm letter."

But as always, Mrs. Howe was sorry after she had spoken sharp words. Her letter had "no injurious phrase as I felt only grief and indignation, not dis-esteem for him," she said. "Yet the fact of having written the letter became very painful to me when it was beyond recall. I could not help writing a second on the day following to apologize for the first. This is a diplomatic fault, I think, but one inseparable from my character. C. S.'s reply, which I dreaded to read, was very kind. While I clearly saw his misapprehension of the whole matter, I saw also the thorough kindness and sincerity of his nature. So we disagreed but I love him." This Christian love notwithstanding, Mrs. Howe found that, as she wrote her "essay on Sex," the thoughts which occurred to her seemed to "run into a treatise of Limitations, as the two subjects run together in my mind." She had just experienced the severe limits men tried to place on a woman's activities, but it never occurred to her to give up her plan to lecture in Washington.

In Bordentown, where Julia Howe stopped en route for Washington, a pleasant group of Annie's friends gathered to hear her on "Equality." Then on went Mrs. Howe "with a resolute but not a sanguine heart." She had "no one to stand for" her, ". . . Sumner against" her, and Channing "almost unknown, everyone else indifferent." The almost unknown Channing was the Reverend William Henry Channing, nephew of the great Unitarian, William Ellery Channing. After a varied career, he had just come to Washington as Pastor of the Unitarian Society there, was Chaplain of the House of Representatives and was active on the Sanitary Commission. He was better known than Mrs. Howe supposed, but gave little enough encouragement. The atmosphere of Washington had changed greatly since Mrs. Howe was there before and had written her Battle Hymn. No one went out to see reviews of the troops now — the troops were fighting. "The whole community is hanging on the fate of this prolonged battle," Mr. Channing told Mrs. Howe, "and no one has the heart for anything else." This was probably the Battle of the Wilderness which began on the fifth of May, with Lee having outmaneuvered Grant. Terrific fighting continued until the eighth when both armies were entrenched facing each other on the road to Richmond.

But Julia Ward Howe had not come to Washington to provide frivolous entertainment. She had come "in obedience to a deep and strong impulse which I do not understand nor explain," she wrote in her journal, "but whose bidding I cannot neglect. The satisfaction of hav-

ing at least obeyed this interior guide is all that keeps me up." On May 12, "Soon comes Rev. Channing with better news. 'I think you may read now, Mrs. Howe — the army news is favorable.' " It is hard to imagine what good news could have reached Washington by the twelfth unless it was just possibly Sheridan's raid of the eleventh when he defeated J. E. B. Stuart at Yellow Tavern. This was only moderately encouraging. Whatever the news, Mrs. Howe went out to buy notepaper. "Parlors had been offered" and she wrote "as many invitations" as she could. The Reverend Mr. Channing and others provided a list of names. It seemed only right to Mrs. Howe to invite Charles Sumner. And it seemed only right to Sumner to refuse.

The reading was well attended, with all the chairs taken and people standing in the entry and on the stairs as the Reverend Mr. Channing "brought in Mrs. Howe," a little woman in a plain black dress and a white lace cap. Name after name she wrote down that night in her diary — remembering all the people she had met, generals, admirals, clergymen, a former minister to China — assorted wives and daughters. Before it was time for the next reading, Mrs. Howe was no longer living at a boardinghouse. She was the guest of Mrs. Eames whose husband was counsel for the United States Navy and whose home was described as "one of the most hospitable and attractive houses in Washington."

Now the tide had turned in favor of Mrs. Julia Ward Howe — by her own account a New York woman, but probably until now looked upon as someone decidedly odd from Boston. Mrs. Howe was now everywhere introduced as the author of "The Battle Hymn of the Republic" as she went about visiting hospitals, and she was surprised to see a smile of recognition on so many soldiers' faces when the song was mentioned. She saw "many painful sights," and she observed that the men "suffered much by the journey from the point where their wounds were inflicted." Her readings provided a contribution to the "Campbell Hospital."

On the last day of the series, Mrs. Eames gave a dinner for Mrs. Howe. Secretary Chase was there, "very fine-looking and rather imposing." Mrs. Douglas "came in her carriage" and would take Mrs. Howe to the place where the reading was to be held. But Senator Sumner, who was among the dinner guests, was the only one not going to the reading afterwards.

"I do not importune you, but you are always welcome," said Julia hopefully to the man who had been a family friend for twenty years.

"He excused himself — and this hurt," Mrs. Howe admitted in the pages of her journal. The audience was large and distinguished, however, "not exactly fulfilling Sumner's prophecy that I had not the ability to interest anyone in Washington," Mrs. Howe said.

Mrs. Howe could not have stayed with her brother in Washington for Sam had given up his Washington home. He had gone to Nicaragua and his huge sapphire ring,[5] recently acquired it would appear, he had given to "Mrs. Barlow" who "took care of" it "for him while he was away." This was not as unwise an idea as it sounds. Mrs. Barlow was the wife of Samuel L. Barlow, New England-born New York lawyer who was becoming a big-time negotiator in the steamship and railroad struggle for power. Sam went to Nicaragua in connection with gold mines but also to further a scheme for a water route to the Pacific. There had previously been a steamship line operating from New York and New Orleans to Greytown (later San Juan de Nicaragua) thence by the San Juan River and Lake Nicaragua, "with only 12 miles of land carriage, a beautiful tropical journey," 1400 miles shorter than the Panama route. This line was closed in 1857, when the captain of an American vessel provoked a serious incident by shooting a native of Greytown. Nicaragua revoked the transit franchise. But it seemed as if the time had come to let bygones be bygones.

Sam Ward was back in New York on April 10, 1864. He called on his nephew John Ward, who set down the following notation: "Sam is very bald. He described the Nicaraguan life in hammocks and spoke of a yellow parroquet found on the Paraguay River." Sam showed his nephew "a superb sapphire" — so evidently it was new — told about Mrs. Barlow's keeping it for him — and recommended that John "go to Nicaragua." He himself would shuttle between New York and Washington for a while.

Before Julia Ward Howe left Washington she dropped in at the Willard Hotel to see Sam. He was already "King of the Lobby," although it would be a few years before he called himself that in court. They greeted each other with delight and Mrs. Howe kissed him. The shocked expression on the faces of some of the other hotel guests must have been a sight to see. Fortunately, before the story spread too far, someone said, "Why, didn't you know? She's his sister!" [6]

CHAPTER TWENTY-FOUR
Louisa's Second Roman Romance

IT seemed to the entire Ward family, and to Uncle John especially, that Louisa would of course return to make her home in the United States after the death of Thomas Crawford. But Mrs. Crawford engaged no passage for New York or Boston. She must first dispose of as many of her late husband's sculptures as possible and sell furnishings suitable only for a Roman palace. When Uncle John failed to send her money, she reminded him that it cost her only a little over five thousand dollars a year to live in Rome and that her income was seven thousand. Uncle John had to face the fact that his gentle, pliable Louisa had grown up. Before long, there were those who thought they knew why Louisa's return was indefinitely postponed. Charles Sumner, who had so unlucky a capacity for getting in trouble with Ward sisters, received the following letter from Louisa Ward Crawford, headed "Villa Negroni, Rome" and dated March 7, 1860.

"I was both surprised and distressed yesterday, by a report nearly concerning Mr. Terry and myself, which has reached me from the other side of the Atlantic and which is clearly traced to you. I am informed that you carried it home from Rome last year and must ask who is your authority for that report, giving you *mine* in exchange, to contradict it. You of course understand that I refer to the supposed engagement between Mr. Terry and myself. I have to request that you will be at the same pains to retract, as you may have been assiduous in circulating, such report." [1]

Most extremely beautiful women know all too well how attractive they are and take it for granted that men must fall at their feet. Although Louisa had plenty of experience along that line during her girlhood, she never thought of herself as irresistible. When she reached Paris after the news of Thomas Crawford's illness, she found Luther

Terry there, taking care of her husband. Terry stood by her faithfully in all the difficult times to come. He was her friend, and that was all.

Luther Terry was born and brought up on a farm in Connecticut where his family had lived since early days in the colonies before the American Revolution. Some of the Terrys were Protestant ministers — Luther had a brother named Calvin, their parents being evidently impartial in their admiration of Protestant reformers. Some of the Connecticut Terrys, when not preaching and not farming, were handy with clocks. Luther was twenty years old before he escaped from Connecticut to go to Rome to become an artist. He had been in Rome since 1833, and Ada Shepherd — governess to the Hawthorne children in Rome in 1858 — told of Mr. Terry.

"We also went to the studio of the young American artist, a Mr. Terry who showed us several beautiful paintings. There were two Italian peasant girls clad in their rich and picturesque costumes; one of these was exceedingly lovely, with a world of passion in her dark eyes.

"Mr. Terry has a pleasantly situated studio. In front is a little garden with two rustic arbors and a court filled with fragrance." He had given pretty Miss Ada Shepherd some violets out of his garden and evidently her fiancé, Clay Badger, back at Antioch College, wrote anxiously to know just how much this bachelor artist meant to his Ada!

Ada was most reassuring. "Mr. Terry is old enough to be my father," she declared in a letter written two months later. He was "decidedly ugly and not at all a ladies' man."

Luther Terry was fifty-three years old in 1860 when Louisa wrote so indignantly concerning rumors of romance. She herself was thirty-seven. There was no gray in her dark hair and if she were a little thin this only served to bring out her fine eyes, now filled with sorrow and loneliness. In 1860, Louisa was ill and went to Paris in search of a good doctor. It gave her "great pain and fatigue" to sit up at a table to write a letter to Mr. Terry, who evidently feared that she needed an operation. The difficulty, however, seems to have been arthritic or rheumatoid as was the case with her father and various other members of the Ward family. She was helped by "taking the waters" and especially by treatment at the "hot springs" which doubtless reduced tension as she relaxed daily in sulphur baths.

Faithfully, Luther Terry visited the Crawford children, left alone at the Villa Negroni with their governess, a Boston girl. He wrote almost daily to their mother reporting their good health and safety. "They welcomed me with shouts of joy the other evening," he said with evident satisfaction. But he was not to be deceived. "Annie of late, shows very considerable cordial feeling towards me. No doubt she hopes for my influence in some of her schemes."

In letters reaching Louisa every few days, Terry told of his work, evidently sure of her interest. He had finished "Chapman's portrait" and he thought it had come out well. Then there was the picture he thought Louisa did not like — he had improved it. But none of his work was so important that it could not be dropped if Louisa wanted him to bring the children to see her. And Luther Terry could not help revealing all too clearly his state of mind concerning the beautiful Louisa — for all he so carefully addressed her as his "dear sister."

Terry's choice of words was as Victorian as the novels which Louisa was now reading to while away her loneliness at the health resort in Austria where her Paris doctor had sent her. "How much sweet enjoyment of the finest sentiments of our nature have we had during the year now completed," Mr. Terry wrote. "Life would be too full of happiness if it were all like the happy part of the present year. It has also had its great pains and trials; great indeed for you, dear sister, and great to me through the love and affection I feel for you and yours. May He who is all wise and all merciful raise the cloud which now hangs over the future and reveal a clear prospect, all the more beautiful and bright for the thick darkness which has hovered over your — and I will say also *my* horizon.

"Goodbye, dearest sister. I love you tenderly, think of you constantly and pray for you earnestly. . . . "

This was no fiery, impetuous Crawford to sweep Louisa off her feet with passionate love making. Luther Terry loved Louisa, none the less. No one could have made her forget her first love, so that it was as well for Terry that he was so different. By September, his patience and devotion were rewarded. He now dared to call Louisa "my sweet little girl" and tell her again and again how "tenderly" he loved her.

But Louisa's problem was not entirely easy. When Mr. Terry returned briefly to the United States, the Wards had not particularly liked him — being inclined to find him something of a rough diamond and to compare him unfavorably with Thomas Crawford. They seemed to have forgotten their opposition to Crawford but they should have known that Louisa would never choose a man-about-town as exemplified by certain of her cousins. The Ward opinion was of no great consequence. Louisa was a mature woman and had been making her own decisions for some time. The real difficulty lay with her Crawford children. They had liked "Mr. Luther" as a sort of uncle who came by to see them when their mother was away. It would be a long time before they could accept "Paterno," as they eventually called him. Annie Crawford was the most passionately jealous, and F. Marion was extremely difficult for a stepfather to cope with during the years immediately ahead.

Louisa and Luther Terry were quietly married in Rome, September 21, 1861. Louisa now owed poor Charles Sumner an apology — he had not been wrong but only premature. They were quietly, serenely happy just as they deserved to be — except for occasional upheavals caused by the "wild Crawfords" — and except for financial difficulties for which Louisa was unprepared. There were ten prosperous years, however, for which she never forgot to be grateful. On August 6, 1862, Louisa Margaret Terry was born — to her parents' great delight. They called her Margaret which in turn they translated into Daisy. On December 25, 1864, Arthur Noel Wurtz Terry was born. Like her sister Julia, Louisa also bore a son on Christmas day.

As a painter, Luther Terry was good but not great. Thackeray had once exclaimed while looking at Terry's draftsmanship, "By Jove, I wish I could draw like that." Not only was Terry's drawing sound, but his color was rich and warm. He was not particularly original, however, and he lacked showmanship with which to eclipse his rivals and dazzle his clients. One of his most successful paintings (it almost goes without saying) was a portrait of Louisa. There she stood, straight and lovely. She was matronly in this portrait, with fine high coloring — a full-blown rose of a woman with Madonna eyes. It was remarkable how Louisa Ward brought out the best in the two artists who loved her.

Before her marriage to Terry, Louisa had sublet the Villa Negroni. She wanted to cut down on her expenses and besides she was far too lonely there. From the twelve studios in the garden, the ring of chisel on marble was no longer heard and there was no sound except the wind in the cypresses and the plash of water in the fountains. The Villa Negroni was so far out of town that at night the little foxes came from the Campagna just beyond and drank at the fountain in the villa garden.

Louisa took rooms at the Casa Dies, close to the Pincian gardens. It was a pleasant apartment but the Crawford children felt like exiles from Paradise and they went back to their lost garden, where the new tenants let them wander at will. It never occurred to them that their mother might be hard pressed to pay for their governess and the tutors in French, German and Latin who came daily, and the piano teacher who praised their talent so highly. Annie Crawford fiercely declared that she detested Mr. Terry but she was somewhat mollified when the Terrys moved to the Palazzo Odescalchi.

The Palazzo Odescalchi [2] was on the Corso. It was a huge three-story building looking, on the outside, like a public library in classic style. Within, a broad white marble staircase led to a formal drawing room hung with panels of "deep oleander-pink brocade with silver-gray flowers." An immensely high vaulted ceiling was ornamented in low relief with Bellerophon riding his winged horse against a sky-blue background, slaying white chimeras — for another gifted daughter of Louisa's to dream about. It was Daisy Terry, rather than Mimoli Crawford, who described the new palace and a beautiful mother who was a sort of much-loved fairy princess. Her mother's room, Daisy said, was "all painted in flowers and light colors and smelling of orris root and violets" which her father brought every day from the Piazza di Spagna, on his way home from his studio in the Via Margretta. The violets were "placed on her dressing table" and the room, as her daughter remembered it, was "inseparable from their fragrance." Louisa's dressing table was "a sweet creation of pink silk skirts and overflounces of lace-trimmed lawn" and everything surrounding Louisa was feminine in the extreme, chosen for her by an adoring second husband who painted her picture in gifts as he had painted her in oil on canvas.

Going to Paris on business just a year after their marriage, Luther Terry returned with a surprise for Louisa. First, he brought out gifts for the baby — "socks, mittens, etc." Then he explained that he had been too busy to buy anything for Louisa except a trunk — since he had noticed that she needed a new one. She took this quite seriously and was pleased when he showed her the trunk and handed her the key. It was a very nice present, she thought.

Then "Imagine my surprise," she said, when she opened the trunk and found it "filled to the top with everything that was elegant and appropriate" for the coming season. Luther had "hunted up" Louisa's dressmaker in Paris, and everything was made to measure. There was a brown silk with gold dots. There were embroidered "collars and sleeves" to go with different dresses and there were "cravats, boots, quilted shoes. Most beautiful was a gray poplin with black stripes and plain gray coat to match" and "finally, *such* a bonnet, gray velvet with a pomegranate flower" under the brim and outside a "black lace flower and two leaves of real Chantilly lace." It was a "grande toilette" and Louisa said she had no excuse now but must go calling. Always anxious to present her daughter Annie Crawford in the best light, "Nannie was in ecstasy with all my presents," Louisa said, "and was rewarded for her disinterested enjoyment by a handsome gray poplin in which she rejoiced as the very thing she wished for."

The group of friends which surrounded the Terrys was different from those who frequented the Crawford villa. There were fewer sculptors and more painters, as was only natural. But also there were more writers, attracted to Luther Terry perhaps because his approach to his work was somewhat like that of an illustrator. Louisa read aloud constantly, with Roman history as one of their shared enthusiasms.

One of the most frequent visitors to the Palazzo Odescalchi was Augustus Hare. He was a retired British clergyman, spending his winters in Rome and rapidly acquiring a reputation as a writer of medieval Italian history and folklore. Hare's *Walks in Rome* would soon be in the hands of most English-speaking tourists and the delighted Mr. Hare would find the hobby of his retirement becoming a fascinating new occupation. He had another perhaps greater gift than that of writing. He told ghost stories.

"It was not a case of listening but almost of actual experience," Daisy Terry said, recalling the "dapper little man with a narrow aquiline nose and rather beady, penetrating eyes," who had an uncanny gift for becoming an actual character in his tales of horror, all of which "seemed to have happened to members of his own family."

Mr. Hare insisted upon having the scene properly set. The lights were turned low and Louisa put aside her tapestry needlework. The doors were locked and the servants told not to try to enter to put wood on the fire or for any other purpose. Then the story would begin in Mr. Hare's "curious, rather nasal voice." As the climax approached, the voice "would tremble and break and rise almost to a shriek," while Mr. Hare "writhed in his chair, twisting and wringing his hands — tortured, it seemed, by the horror of his tale."

At last the story ended, the lights were turned up, the fire "poked into a blaze" and the "servant came in with mulled wine." The grownups would laugh and talk in normal voices as they discussed the Italian political situation or the latest arrival from the States to the English-speaking colony in Rome. Once, Maud Howe, Louisa Terry's beautiful young niece, was a new arrival. At the climax of one of Mr. Hare's stories, she fainted dead away. When they brought her around she said she had actually seen the demon that Mr. Hare was telling about spring from his mouth! The Reverend Mr. Augustus Hare couldn't have been more flattered.

It seems as though Louisa, devoted mother that she was, should have realized that Mr. Hare really frightened her children. But she remembered only her own very normal Bond Street childhood and she forgot that her children lived in a strange Italian palace full of empty rooms, where there were "strange noises and unaccountable happenings." At the Odescalchi "the carpets were laid over a thin layer of straw which rustled a little at every footfall." When Mr. Hare's story was over, the children set out along the dimly lighted corridors to their "shadow-crowded bedroom" where the imaginative Daisy "lay for hours in an ecstasy of fear." The straw under the carpet rustled softly though no one passed and she was "sure of ghostly presences." The great high windows rattled, and who could get in but the vampire bat Mr. Hare had been telling about? In defense of Louisa, it should be said that she took away the story of "Cock Robin" because she found little Daisy crying over it. Daisy knew very well the price of admitting her fear — no more listening to Mr. Hare!

Fortunately, another family friend was more suitable for the younger members. This was Edward Lear, encountered for the first time while Louisa and her children were passing the summer in the Maritime Alps near Turin. He was a "rosy, gray-bearded, bald-headed, gold-spectacled little old gentleman." He took walks with the Terry children and as they went along he sang his own poem, "The Owl and the Pussycat" to "a funny little crooning tune he composed for it." When she first saw Mr. Lear, Daisy had whispered to her mother that she would like him for an uncle. Louisa told Edward Lear, who was, of course, delighted. Every morning "Nonsense Verses" written especially for Daisy Terry appeared at her breakfast plate, signed "the Dopty Duncle." Edward Lear had been drawing master to Queen Victoria's children and, like Augustus Hare, his health had sent him traveling. His famous "Limericks" had brought him recognition which his serious work in history had not.

In 1862, Louisa sent her Crawford daughters, Jennie and Mary (or Piccola and Mimoli as they were called) to England to boarding school.

Many were the affectionate letters their mother wrote them — differing only in detail from the letters mothers must always write to little girls away from home, no matter what the period. The girls declared that their clothes were all wrong — not like the clothes the other girls were wearing. Louisa was "really sorry if there was, as you seem to think, anything outlandish" about the clothes she had given them. They could each have a dress made. Their mother was "quite pleased" that they "should conform to the fashion" of their "present surroundings" — even to having "Mimoli's dress fastened up before instead of behind. The Garibaldi jackets, skirts, or whatever they are called will, I doubt not, be very pretty."

Louisa and Luther Terry agreed that the thing to do was to send F. Marion Crawford, now called Frank, to school in the United States "to make a good American out of him." The phrase was Mr. Terry's and it irked Frank considerably. Frank was thirteen when this decision was reached; he had outgrown his nursery governess and the French lady retained to teach him her language had become violently jealous of the German Fräulein who came daily to teach German. They vied with each other to perfect him in their respective languages. Each claimed success but the male Latin teacher was not as impressed with Frank's prowess though agreeing that he had a most brilliant mind. Dressed in a sort of comic-opera version of an Eton schoolboy's outfit, top hat, starched collar and sharply tailored trousers, Frank was sent to conquer the New World. "Dearest Aunt Annie" was elected to receive him in Bordentown until it should be time for him to enter St. Paul's School. But in Bordentown, the boys threw mud at Frank's top hat and F. Marion, named for a Revolutionary hero and half Irish besides, retaliated. Many escapades were credited to Francis Marion Crawford and his gentle Aunt Annie was in despair.

Frank's Uncle Sam Ward was delighted with the boy. Before long, Sam would be ordered by all three of his sisters not to give Frank any more pocket money.[3] And meanwhile Aunt Julia Ward Howe took a hand. So for three depressing, bewildering years, F. Marion Crawford endured St. Paul's School and the land which people called his home. He was passed from relative to relative during vacation, until at last he was allowed to go to Rome again, the real home where he was properly appreciated at least by his mother — and to an astonishing degree by his sisters as well.

F. Marion Crawford, at the age of fifteen, was six feet two, broad-shouldered and immensely strong. It was not his fault that he was so handsome that he was often compared to a certain bas-relief of Antinoüs and called "godlike" to his face. It was not his fault that he so much resembled his father that his mother and sisters were almost overcome when they saw him again after a three years' absence. The wonder was that the admiration he aroused went to his head no more than it did.

The family was spending the summer at a villa near Siena when Frank returned. Visiting, and under Louisa Terry's chaperonage, was a remarkably beautiful girl, Lily Conrad — "tall, slight, with hazel eyes and an abundance of wavy blond hair." Her mother was the widow of a Confederate officer. Lily Conrad now had a stepfather, the Marchese Cavaletti, a member of the Pope's Guarda Nobile. And Lily's future had been carefully planned — she too was to marry a Marchese. But poor Frank Crawford fell madly in love with Lily Conrad and persuaded his mother not to send him back to the United States. He spent the winter in hopeless adoration of Lily — going to all the balls where he might expect to see her. The heroines of his future novels would most of them be "tall, slight, with hazel eyes" and a great deal of naturally wavy blond hair. When, as a grown man, he finally fell in love, his choice was a small blond echo of Lily Conrad.

"The Crawfords were *different*," said Daisy Terry, summing up her half-brother and sisters. Her father, earnestly trying to be a good "Paterno," found them not only different but difficult. After observing Frank's winter of so-called tutoring in Rome, Luther Terry decided that the boy must be sent to England — if he would not go back to America. It was a hard decision for Louisa to accept. She had sent Jennie and Mimoli to school in England and in 1866 Jennie — her dearest "Piccola" — had died there! Jennie's lungs were delicate, they said. She was not ill very long.

Louisa had known great grief when Jennie's father died. But Thomas Crawford's illness had been severe, his death a release. Jennie was only nineteen. She was gifted in music but farther from genius than the other Crawfords and closer to a happy medium. Louisa lavished still more love upon her other children and felt anxious about Francis Marion, sent away to that land so far from the Italian sunshine which he loved. Frank went to study with a clergyman in Essex. It took F. Marion two years to prepare for Cambridge and he also acquired the background for a novel, *A Tale of a Lonely Parish.* "Anything could happen in those lonely old country houses lost in a dip of the moors, miles away from the beaten roads," he said. And with a certain sympathy for the unnamed British clergyman, it is possible to wonder what *did* happen when the Italian-bred schoolboy of Irish-American parentage burst upon him!

F. Marion was a student at Cambridge University for one year and "managed to get through an examination," he said. He also created a sensation in a manner which suddenly recalls the fact that he was the nephew of the spectacular Sam Ward. "He hunted round for the biggest trotting horse that he could find, had a towering dog-cart built, dressed himself in checks a foot square and of outrageous colors, and thus equipped, paraded the dignified university town. He had a clock . . . exactly imitating a watch, and, having instructed his tailor to make a pocket large enough to hold it, he attached it to a big dog-chain, the links of which dangled outside his waistcoat."[4]

All this exhibitionism was paid for by his mother of course. Money was something supplied to him whenever he wrote for it and he gave no more thought to its source than he did to the air he breathed. To be sure, there were stern letters from Paterno, but who ever paid any attention to a stepfather? Only extremely serious financial reverses finally convinced the young man that he would ever have to earn a living.

After his year in Cambridge, back to Rome came F. Marion Crawford — like a young prince who finds his kingdom overthrown. This time it was not Sam Ward but Charlie Ward, a cousin of his mother's, who had wrecked the Ward family investment house which he had been running with his (and Louisa's) Uncle John. Francis Marion probably understood nothing of what had happened, but there was good stuff in him although at times he seemed bent on proving the contrary. He tried various jobs that occupied wellborn young men in Rome not possessed with a fortune, such as clerking in a bank and translating. The trouble with F. Marion Crawford was that he was too gifted. He could have been a painter or a sculptor. For a time he was sure that he would be an opera singer for he had a magnificent baritone voice, was excessively handsome, and certainly had a flair for the dramatic.

But after wasting a good deal of his mother's fast-dwindling resources on singing lessons, F. Marion was obliged to give up his favorite dream. He had a faulty ear. His Aunt Julia was almost equally disappointed. No member of the Ward family ever had a faulty ear before, she exclaimed.

It was typical of the odd Crawfords that F. Marion should find a Sanskrit grammar among his sister Mimoli's belongings. She had now abandoned Sanskrit in favor of falling in love and Frank, about to take a walking trip, picked up the volume without noticing what it was and stuck it in his knapsack. Finding himself alone in the Italian hinterland with no book but this, he learned Sanskrit — took lessons on his return and studied Sanskrit intensively at the University of Rome.

It is easy to imagine Luther Terry's despair over a young man who needed to prepare himself to earn a living — and who devoted himself to Sanskrit! But Francis Marion Crawford was at last on his way. He took a job editing a newspaper in India, the *Indian Herald* at Allahabad. While in the Far East, he met and learned the life story of a man named Jacobs, a diamond merchant.

F. Marion Crawford next made his appearance on his Uncle Sam Ward's doorstep in New York. He was greeted with enthusiasm, for Sam loved the "wild Crawfords." F. Marion, fresh from a really rugged time in India where good pay was not as easy to find as hard work, had come to the United States with the idea of studying Sanskrit at Harvard.

But one night at dinner, he told his Uncle Sam's guests the life history of Mr. Jacobs, the diamond merchant. "You must make a novel out of that," Sam declared.

And then, after all, it was Aunt Julia who ordered her nephew F. Marion to sit down at a table in her little garden in Newport and write at least eight hours a day until his novel was done. It was always a shock, to Crawfords and Terrys alike, when they came to the United States, to discover that their gentle mother and their sweet little Aunt Annie had a fabulous brother like Uncle Sam Ward and a formidable sister like Aunt Julia. Aunt Julia Ward Howe was the most to be reckoned with, because she was so pretty, so gay and so much fun. But she believed in hard work!

Mr. Isaacs, by F. Marion Crawford, was an instant, meteoric success.

Annie the Pioneer

WHEN Julia Ward Howe, on her way to give her first Washington lectures, stopped over in Bordentown, she was not surprised to find that Annie had planned everything perfectly. Annie's rooms were beautiful, the tea she served elegant. This was no longer the self-effacing youngest sister doomed to have "little" forever coupled with her name. If Adolph still ordered the dinners (a prerogative which sister Julia was not sure belonged to him) it was because Annie liked to see her husband enjoy his home in his own way.

Annie always enjoyed Adolph's peculiar brand of humor — even when it shocked her. Surely he should not have laughed in church that day and whispered to Annie (rather loudly) that the clergyman was an old gray parrot. He should never have pretended to lose his coin for the collection up his coat sleeve! And once Annie had to come to the rescue of an uninvited caller — a young French artist who wanted a commission to paint her portrait. After seeing an example of the young man's work, Adolph had offered to let him paint a portrait of Bonnard, his prize bull — but not Annie!

This is not to say that Annie's life was all fun and laughter. She had sorrowed over the death of her first little son and because of her health she had waited a long time to have the complete family she wanted. Her son John was born after she had been married sixteen years. All the children were born in royal Bordentown, but Joseph Bonaparte's great white stuccoed palace had long since been sold and all that remained relating to Bordentown's royal past was Annie and Adolph's villa — and the Princess Zenaïde's pleasure pond.

During the winter of 1864, seven-year-old Joseph Mailliard "went on the ice with Papa. . . . There were 300 on the lake and I saw ten of them fall on the ice, it did not seem to hurt them, I wish I had a pair of skates, don't you think I am big enough to skate, Mama?" he wrote. It took a long sentence to express so important a request. He had never seen his great-grandfather, the former King of Spain and Naples, coming to the lake to toss pennies across the ice for the children. But Joseph Mailliard had "3 cents and can get as many gumdrops as I want with them," he said. Ex-king Joseph Bonaparte had never been so rich. Soon even the Mailliards would be far away and royal Bordentown but a memory — even for them.

Sam Ward and Adolph Mailliard were the most congenial of brothers-in-law, often recalling days in California — often meeting California friends. There was James R. Keene, a California racing enthusiast. He had come from England as a young man, had made a fortune on the gold coast and was now looking for ways to spend it. He would like to own some race horses that would win in California. And Adolph Mailliard's ten-thousand-acre ranch was just north of San Francisco — waiting for stock!

On January 7, 1868, friends were saying farewell to the Mailliards. Charles Sumner, whose sister, Julia, had married and was living in California, wrote cordially to Adolph. "Accept my best wishes in the new career which you are beginning. I cannot doubt that you will find . . . an opportunity for your agricultural knowledge and taste and a congenial climate." His sister would "receive Annie with open arms." [1]

Whatever his "agricultural knowledge," Adolph Mailliard's courage was undeniable as he considered sending thoroughbred horses to California. Young Eclipse was to go, and Monday, and the mare Hennie Farrow, to name only a few. From Monday and Hennie Farrow would come one of the first famous California horses: Joe Hooker. Adolph also knew that dairy products were still at a premium in the San Francisco area, so before he had the horses shipped the pure-blooded Jersey cattle went West. Mailliard horses and cattle would be California's first blooded stock. They would not be registered as Adolph's alone, however. They were registered by Annie and Adolph Mailliard, together.

If Annie Ward Mailliard had really been timid, she would have been in tears at the thought of the journey before her. She *was* tearful at parting with her sister Julia and at separating herself still farther from Louisa. She begged them both to write. But the adventure filled her with joy. She was now Annie the pioneer.

Spring Villa was sold and Annie's problem of packing its contents was enormous. Adolph would not consider leaving very much behind, so into a crate went the life-size portrait of himself and Prince Joseph — Adolph seated and the prince standing; each a sartorial dream in canary-colored trousers and black frock coat. The fine portrait of Joseph Bonaparte went to California and those of Annie's family: her mother who looked out with dark eyes resembling Annie's from a large and gracious portrait "attributed to Charles C. Ingham"; Brother Sam painted by von Vogelstein [2] in Europe — and sister Julia as a chubby child with an improbable cat painted by Aunt Anne Hall. The Crawford bust of the beautiful Louisa would look strange in Annie's California home but she would not for the world have parted with it — nor would Adolph have expected her to. With tender care, Annie packed her mother's silver tea-set, pure Georgian in design, and given to the child who had caused her mother's death. Annie, having experienced childbirth five times, now realized how blameless she had been; and she could think of her mother and cherish her mother's silver without a sense of guilt.

The Mailliards left New York "by steamer" about January 11, 1868, and they arrived in San Francisco on February first or second "making a run of 22 days." Brother Sam had prepared Annie for San Francisco Bay but now she found that no one could really tell another what it was like. Bordentown had been pretty in a gentle sort of way — California was dramatic. Annie Mailliard never stopped admiring California sunsets which she described at length in her letters, and she never stopped commending them to her guests as long as she lived. She was destined — foreordained, it seemed — to be a Californian.

Not but what there were difficulties. The whole tribe of Mailliards, father, mother, four children and governess, became guests of the McAllisters — Annie's relatives on her mother's side. The cattle, coming around Cape Horn, probably, must be waited for. After the livestock arrived the Mailliards somehow wore out their welcome at the McAllisters and they moved on to the United Arsenal, of which a cousin of Annie's, Julian McAllister, was Commandant. Ten months after their arrival in California, they had a home — in San Rafael, not far from San Francisco.

On November 11, 1868, Annie managed to find time to answer her sister Julia's letter, written October 4. She had brought with her all of the books written so far by Julia Ward Howe and she was re-reading them with "renewed pleasure in this distant land." She spoke politely of Julia's "world of action," but without envy. Her own world was not entirely static.

"Earthquakes, darling, are not nice," Annie confessed. "The first shock found us at the breakfast table and its beginning sounded like a vigorous storm overhead. In a few seconds, however, the windows rattled angrily and the house began to rock. At this crisis, Mrs. McAllister, who was with us, exclaimed, 'An earthquake! Run!' and rushing out of doors, fell insensible on the ground.

"The rest of us were calm," Annie said, "with the exception of poor Cora," her little thirteen-year-old daughter, to whom they dared not mention earthquakes any more. There had been fifty-two shocks in three days, the papers said, so that Cora's state of nerves was understandable. But Annie declared that "of the ensuing shocks" they had really felt only two. She was already loyal to San Rafael, where her husband had recently taken her. "In San Francisco, the panic was very great and still continues to be so," she said. "In a frame house in the country, we feel comparatively safe." Adolph bought 110 acres in San Rafael and built the largest house in town and a stable for his horses. According to his son Joseph's recollection, the race horses were not brought to California until the railroad was completed, which was in 1869.[3]

Annie at once learned to speak a new language of health and optimism. Adolph's neuralgia had "entirely yielded to this milder climate," she declared. "These long droughts enable us to spend much of our time in the open air and on the 11th of November I write to you by an open window, my room heated only by the bright, pleasant sunshine which fills it."

In 1871 or the following year, Adolph sold his race horses at auction — or so his son Joseph remembered. He also sold the San Rafael home and "gave my mother twenty-four hours to decide whether she would go out to the Rancho San Geronimo to live, or to Southern France." Annie chose California. When at last her sisters visited on the ranch they pitied her because of her isolation. Not even Louisa, who was closest to her, ever realized what peace and happiness Annie had found.

It was just as remarkable that Adolph, so sociably inclined, should be happy so far from anything resembling Europe or New York. Perhaps at first he regretted having left the decision to Annie. But the ranch (bought in 1866), although a long dusty carry-all ride from San

Rafael, was actually only seven and a half miles away. The ten thousand acres of forest, deep valley, intervale and pastureland cast their spell over Adolph as well as Annie. "The beautiful ranch," both of them always called it — they could not refer to San Geronimo otherwise. Adolph built a large boxlike wooden house in the heart of their domain, and brought his family to live in it as soon as it was ready. "The house of tomorrow" it could have been called when it was built in the 1870's, for it was high-studded with a deep porch that ran all around it; and within, the floor space was cut up into too many rooms from whose high, narrow walls the family portraits looked down with an air of faint surprise.[4]

A huge rock, standing alone in a meadow a few hundred yards from the house, became a family gathering-place in the cool of the late afternoons. The little boys dared each other to climb it. The two girls sat at its foot with their needlework while their mother read aloud from the many books she had brought with her and from the new ones that arrived for them each Christmas. The Mailliards loved the shadow of this rock although California was not a weary land.

But if it were not a weary land, neither was California the land where Adolph could realize those princely dreams of his. Everyone who has ever loved the land, from Western ranch to small New England farm, knows that it has a way of absorbing riches rather than producing them. The return, for those who love the beauty of forest and meadow, mountain and valley, is actually beyond price — and Adolph, with his curiously combined traits of artist and husbandman, found himself exactly fitted for his new life.

Adolph was the princely tyrant when it came to managing the farm hands. They were "Azorean Portuguese" during most of the time when he ran the ranch as a dairy farm, and were found by nature and training to be natural born dairymen.[5] They understood the lordly Mr. Mailliard and obeyed him properly. But when it came to selling his wonderful butter, of which he was so proud, Adolph did it himself, like the French farmer who haggles and bargains on market day and has his own personal pride in his product. If there had been just a little more of the Corsican strain in Adolph he might even have made ends meet. But of course there was the huge barn to build, about a quarter of a mile from the house. There was the good table to provide and house servants to acquire and train, for although Adolph might be a pioneer he knew how he wanted his venison cooked. Adolph never kept any books and when, for some mysterious reason, his ranch did not seem to show a profit, he could always sell some timber. There was never any need to worry about money, Adolph would have said. He had also his gold mine.

Once in a while, Adolph Mailliard would ride along the valley road, then down a path to his mine. On the surface of the ground a few curious gray rocks with quartz outcroppings lay about as though a giant child had picked them up to play with and then tossed them aside. Somewhere among the rocks a hole had been dug which was now overgrown with grass. But Adolph remembered the day when a man had come up out of this hole bringing broken rock veined with shining yellow streaks. Of course Adolph was no fool. He had taken these bits of rock to be assayed before he acquired the ranch. The yellow streaks and flakes were gold all right. The expert said the vein was 90 per cent gold, 10 per cent silver. So Adolph Mailliard could be fabulously wealthy any time he chose to develop his mine. Meanwhile, though, he was more interested in cows.

The Wards were not as a rule a family to withhold criticism of each other — especially in private. In-laws naturally came in for still more caustic comment, and Adolph Mailliard, referred to as "Uncle Do," was considered a tyrant by the younger members of his wife's family. Uncle William Ward's boys, Charlie and John, loved to go to Bordentown to see "Uncle Do's beautiful colts" and to ride his horses if allowed. Quite possibly their horsemanship was not as good as they thought but in any case they found Uncle Do severe — as did F. Marion Crawford as a schoolboy fresh from Rome. Adolph Mailliard's son John, aged thirteen and writing his letter the day after Christmas, 1875, described life at San Geronimo Ranch and a father who could not possibly have been a tyrant — strict though he doubtless was.

"We had a very funny time, yesterday," young John told his mother who had been given the present of a trip to see her family in New York. Annie must easily have pictured the scene — all of them at breakfast in the narrow dining room at the ranch, when Olivia, the servant, entered carrying a large wooden box addressed to Master John and "placed it by Papa's chair. Of course I immediately wanted to open it," John wrote. "So I got a screw driver but just as I was going to take off the cover I discovered a hole in one end in which I put my finger but soon drew it out as something in the box had bitten my finger; at first I thought it was a rabbit as Papa had promised me some. Then I thought it was a cat as it was black; when suddenly Papa took off the cover and out jumped nothing but a little, wee black pig! Oh, I was so frightened; but soon recovering from my fright, the Dr. and I made chase amidst the shouts and shrieks of everyone else; Joe, stretched on two chairs, laughed till he could laugh no more, while all the feminine gender were perched on the sofa and on the chairs; at last the Dr. caught it in the library when we put it in the box and returned it to its mother, not before its having broken loose in the kitchen, however. The way Papa came to think of this joke was that some time ago I asked him to let me have a pig on which to speculate." Some day, his family would point with pride to John Mailliard and say he was a true Ward. Meanwhile Master John also received several more books by Jules Verne whose style of writing he had already captured.

In 1870, while "Papa" was "having a big stable made," there was also time, nevertheless, to take the boys hunting. This time John, who seemed to be the family historian, was only eight and his brother Joe was thirteen. They set out across an open grassy hillside, when suddenly, "Papa's bull charged right at Papa. But Papa fired at him and so did Joe." According to John, "the bull fell down twice and got up and then ran off" — apparently only a little the worse for wear but with a chastened spirit.

The story current in the family a little later was that when Adolph's oldest daughter began to attract beaux, her father turned his Jersey bull loose to discourage young men! The story might easily be true, for why should Adolph accept a son-in-law less well instructed as to the proper procedure with bulls than his own sons? Loulie Mailliard grew up to be a very pretty girl — fully as beautiful as her first cousin Maud Howe, though far less often praised for it. A sufficiently brave young man never found her, however; no toreador carried her away. She became a lovely and much-loved maiden aunt to her brothers' children.

Adverse comment about her new home and pioneer mode of living far from so-called civilization rarely bothered Annie Mailliard. But when Annie's niece Maud Howe came to visit the San Geronimo ranch, Annie hoped and perhaps assumed that the life would please her. It was a little hard, afterwards, to take certain passages in Maud's first novel, *The San Rosario Ranch*, where the characters were cultured in spite of crude surroundings, enduring such deprivations as straw matting instead of Brussels carpets and afflicted with awkward rather than accomplished servants. It was all very well to call the novel fiction. Annie read and dutifully admired Maud's opus, but she could not fail to be disappointed that Maud had seen ranch life with such alien eyes.

There came at last a long visit from Louisa to San Geronimo. It was blissful for the two sisters who, in spite of their constant letter-writing, had still so much to say to each other. But Annie Mailliard was doomed to have nieces who wrote about her. This time it was Daisy Terry who came to San Geronimo with her mother. The ranch was "two hours drive from San Rafael over rough roads" said Daisy. The house, which Daisy found "roomy and comfortable enough," was nevertheless "bare of ornament" — although photographs of some of the rooms show very little space where any more family portraits, Napoleonic bronze lamps or statuary could have gone. Daisy's complaint seems to have been that "bedrooms and living room were all whitewashed, all carpeted alike." She noted that "on the Mantelpiece in the dinning room stood a bronze clock that had been in Napoleon's room at St. Helena" — but perhaps she did not consider this an ornament.

Daisy was shown "the Emperor's camp dinner service in silver gilt" and this was "beautifully wrought," but Aunt Annie's furniture was "austerely simple, without grace or seduction." Just possibly, Aunt Annie preferred not to be seduced by her tables and chairs, a point that escaped Daisy. And as day after day of the long winter's visit passed, there was one thing which poor Daisy felt she could endure no longer. "The beautiful shadows on the canyon were commented upon after every meal," she said.

Annie never saw this niece's book when it was published. Probably she would have read it with her usual unfailing appreciation, for most of it was excellent. Without doubt, she would have defended the shadows on the canyon, however. They were never the same. No dawn, no sunset was ever quite repeated; and as long as Annie Mailliard should live, the ever-changing beauty about her was her constant delight.

Adolph was in New York that winter of 1879 when Louisa stayed with Annie in California. Neither Louisa nor her daughter said anything of the causes which took Adolph East, but Annie must have known. Probably not even Annie, however, knew the depth of financial difficulties in which her husband was involved.

When Adolph sold his horses at auction, the low prices he received not only shocked him but almost broke his heart. Even so, if dairying were as easy as it sounds, the Mailliards should have had a successful ten years in California. But the original cost of transporting stock and household equipment, some of it around the Horn, some by way of Panama, the cost of building houses and barns and hiring hands, had been staggering. The money received from the sale of Spring Villa had been swallowed up and "a New York bank" had lost the price received for the San Rafael property. The rest of Annie's money was gone, either through the failure of Prime, Ward and King or of Ward and Price, or through the final disaster to Ward and Company — known as "Charlie's failure," to distinguish it from Sam's. Prince Napoleon Charles Bonaparte (brother of Prince Joseph) had a mortgage on the San Geronimo ranch, receiving 9 per cent interest.

Obviously, the time had come for Adolph to "develop" his gold mine. At first he was horrified and incredulous when the "general opinion of the mining engineers" was that he had no gold! Such a thing could not happen to a man who was almost a prince and had always lived like one. He consulted another firm — although the word "gang" might be more accurate. Perhaps these were the same people who had told him that there was gold on the ranch in the first place. In any case, Adolph had at last found someone who would tell him what he wanted to hear, but these so-called engineers wanted a sum to develop the mine that was staggering even to Adolph — who was used to thinking in generous terms.

In August, 1879, Adolph took a job with Keene, agreeing to go to London for the San Francisco millionaire. It must have hurt Adolph's pride because he could not be said to have worked for wages before, unless letting Sam Ward invest the Bonaparte funds could be called employment. But Adolph had lost his heart to his ranch and his cattle. For them, he wanted gold from the mine — and for Annie and the children too of course. He must pocket his pride to raise money for his gold mine.

Richard R. Keene had determined to win every race in England with his string of California horses. His horse, Spendthrift, had just carried off top prizes in the United States and the British-born Keene, now more American than many natives, planned what he called his "British invasion." Richard Ten Broeck was to manage the stables Keene established in England, and Adolph Mailliard was to buy stock for Keene. Adolph sailed for Europe.

On December 11, 1879, Adolph Mailliard received a letter from

Prince Napoleon Charles, evidently dunning him for mortgage money. Adolph had a wonderful idea. He described the gold mine on the property. He had "just received telegraphic dispatches," he said. They "confirmed my predictions and far surpassed my hopes." There was a "50 foot metallic vein, yielding 90 dollars for every 18 square inches and analyzing gold 90%, silver 10%. Naturally, an ore 90% gold is something extraordinary; it is simply fabulous," said Adolph — and never did he use a better word!

"Here in London they are offering to organize companies for me," Adolph went on. "Naturally, I refuse to listen to anyone. I want to see you first, give you full satisfaction and offer you such advantages that it will be difficult for you not to accept them. So please wait patiently ... my great desire is to have you profit, with a few friends, from this return of good fortune." [6]

Prince Napoleon Charles agreed not to foreclose the mortgage but instead, in 1880, he lent Adolph one hundred and twenty-five thousand dollars more for one year at 9 per cent, to develop the mine. But the "developers" spent fifty thousand dollars in "equipment" which, as far as anyone knew, was never delivered. Instead of becoming suspicious, Adolph sought frantically to borrow still more money.

Adolph was in New York in January, 1881, "to take charge of a stud of thoroughbred horses established on a grand scale and to choose a piece of land adapted to the breeding of race horses." He was looking over Kentucky farm land and "working toward an income which would enable" the prince "to await payment of the note" — due in one month. His address was the Brevoort House, he said — the place where Sam Ward always stayed when down on his luck. It was so expensive and gave such a good impression!

"The condition of business in California has been so unfavorable that all my plans have failed; add to this state of things the shutting down of the mines on the property for lack of funds, after spending $50,000 and you have the situation before you," Adolph wrote to Prince Charles. It would cost the Prince "thousands of dollars" to bring suit for nonpayment of the notes due in February and if Adolph were "forced into bankruptcy" he would "be obliged to abandon all hope of helping" the Prince "in the future." This last sounds like a dangerous argument. Suppose the Prince should cast up his accounts and see just how much Adolph's help was costing him? But evidently the Prince cared very little for bookkeeping.

A month later, Adolph was in London again, buying horses for

Keene and full of new schemes for making the Prince's fortune and his own. Statements were vague, sums of money large, and it is not surprising to find the name of "my brother-in-law Mr. Ward" mentioned. Adolph was in London, he said, not only in connection with horses but with "the sale of a *rich* mine of nickel (white silver) belonging to my brother-in-law." And the "third reason" why Adolph left New York "within 24 hours" — or in other words hastily — was "a financial operation which I have been commissioned to put through in London on a large scale through English bankers. This business involves over a million pounds sterling, and I hope to be able to consummate it," Adolph said modestly.

Obviously, Prince Napoleon Charles could not possibly bring suit against a man about to make a fortune and share it. And equally of course, Adolph had to explain why, by July, his big plans had fallen through. It was "the bad faith of the Mexican Congress" — but "next year" he expected "better success" along with "a splendid fortune for my friends and myself."

Richard Keene's invasion of the English turf met with disaster in 1879. Spendthrift failed miserably in England, living up to his name. It is to be feared that both Sam Ward and Adolph Mailliard had placed their faith in Spendthrift and "invested" funds not necessarily their own in this wonderful "business opportunity." In 1881, however, the Keene horse Foxhall won the Grand Prix in Paris. "I am sending you a draft for 200 pounds sterling," Adolph wrote Prince Napoleon Charles — promising more later. "This victory has given a fresh start to our future projects to breed another horse which will win the Derby. . . ."

In 1882, however, poor Adolph had been in Jamaica, "where I have been forced to spend a long period of time to restore my shattered health," he said. He was "burdened with disappointments and thwarted hopes" and his debts were "the result of faults committed by others." If his brother-in-law, Sam Ward, had written the letter it could hardly have sounded differently.[7]

As a matter of fact, Sam was responsible for much of the misfortune that overtook his sister's husband — although of course he too would have said the faults were "committed by others." Sam nevertheless tried to do something for Annie. Uncle John Ward had died in 1886, leaving each of his nieces a handsome legacy. Part of Uncle John's assets had been a mortgage on the Mailliard ranch. The estate was a long time being settled but Sam managed to have the Mailliard mortgage paid off — perhaps out of undivided funds. Annie paid the Prince's mortgage and Sam, certainly in accordance with her Uncle John's wishes, had the San Geronimo ranch put in Annie's name. Little Annie could now step out on her own wide verandas and watch the changing light on the canyon — in comparative security.

Annie, always so thin, had grown plump — "a little woman, round and firm." [8] She was quiet as always and it was assumed that she always obeyed her handsome, masterful husband. But the time came when Adolph wanted to sell the ranch in California and make a new start in Hawaii. No, said Annie. The ranch was hers and not for sale.

CHAPTER TWENTY-SIX
The Chevalier

"RIBBONS for Victory, 40 cents," wrote Julia Ward Howe in her journal. The entry was dated April 10, 1865, and the Civil War was over. "Today we have news of Lee's surrender, with the whole remnant of his army," she wrote. "The City is alive with people. All flags hung out — shop windows decorated — processions in the streets. All friends meet and shake hands. In the newspaper bulletins such plackards as 'Gloria in Excelsis Deo' and 'Thanks be to God.' We call it the greatest day of our lives."

Just five days later came the sharply contrasting entry: "A black day in history though outwardly most fair. President Lincoln was assassinated in his box at the theater last evening by J. Wilkes Booth. . . . Since my Sammy's death, nothing has happened that has given me so much personal pain. The City is paralyzed. But we can only work on and trust in God."

The tragedy of Lincoln's assassination had a double impact for Mrs. Howe. She was a personal friend of Edwin Booth, brother of the man who had done this "atrocious act." When she was in New York immediately after little Sammy's death, Booth had come to her with a strange story. He himself mourned a loss — that of his young wife Mary, who had been an especial friend of Mrs. Howe's. He had just gone to a medium who told, while in a trance, of seeing the dead Mary Booth "leading a little child by the hand." Booth was convinced that the child was Sammy, and although Mrs. Howe could not believe that this was so, she appreciated the loving kindness which prompted Booth's call. She now hastened to the hotel in Boston where she thought Booth must be, for surely he would need to feel that he had loyal friends. He had already gone to New York, however, and Mrs. Howe could only write a letter.

Grief for the loss of Lincoln was gradually replaced by a sense of bewilderment. What was to be done now? Dr. Howe felt the general restlessness keenly, because he had enjoyed his work with the Sanitary Commission. Perkins Institute for the Blind was now so well organized that it almost ran itself, and Dr. Howe, being both a crusader and a pioneer, liked opposition and difficulties. He was like a war-horse harnessed to a plow. Always temperamental, his discontent did not make him any easier to live with.

Mrs. Howe, on the other hand, knew exactly what she wanted to do. She was going to keep just as active and busy as she had been during the war, only now she would have time to concentrate on writing and on her lectures. She had come home from her first expedition to Washington full of elation — as she had every right to do considering how dark her prospects had been when she set out and how triumphantly successful her final reading. She tried to tell her husband something of her doings in Washington, she said. "His comment was that he was glad I was gratified but that all of them here had been much pained." When Chev was displeased, "anxiety of mind seized upon" her and his cold face had "the power of emptying" her "brain of all vitality."

It was a curious and a sad situation. One by one, Mrs. Howe had taken up her husband's interests, from Abolition to prison reform. Her study of religion and ethics was surely a serious occupation and he could not reproach her with the frivolities of the idle rich. With Dr. Howe and Governor Andrew, she had visited the Girls' Reform School in Worcester and, pondering the problem of rehabilitation, Mrs. Howe hoped that education would prove a solution. She thought that the sermons in the prison chapel should not be preached *at* the girls as sinners but should give them hope of finding a better way of life. In 1865, a Boston judge asked her to speak to women prisoners at the Charlestown, Massachusetts, jail and Mrs. Howe had no doubt where her duty lay. She prepared her sermon, which was a product of both study and prayer.

The date was set for April, 1865. It proved "a painful day." When Dr. Howe found out that his wife planned to visit the prisoners — in accordance with an example he had himself set — he was displeased, to put it mildly. "He attacked me with the utmost violence and temper, calling my undertaking a mere display, a mere courting of publicity," Mrs. Howe wrote in her journal. She tried to explain her point of view but the Chevalier "would not hear" her. In the end, she did not go with Judge Russell. It was her wedding anniversary and she still loved her Chevalier. But no one else had remembered the day.

"I feel utterly paralyzed and brought to a stand-still," wrote Mrs. Howe in her journal. "I have been married twenty years today. In the course of that time I have never known my husband to approve of any act of mine which I myself valued. Books — poems — essays — everything has been contemptible in his eyes because not his way of doing things. . . . God help me if I did wrong in not carrying out my intentions, remember that I feared to do wrong in disobeying one who has a husband's authority. God help me, for I am much grieved and disconcerted."

Knowing well that her husband had encouraged Florence Nightingale in her public career — and against the wishes of the Nightingale family — Mrs. Howe thought she had a point in her own favor. But the Chevalier informed her that "if he had been engaged to Florence Nightingale, and had loved her ever so dearly, he would have given her up as soon as she commenced her career as a public woman." When wedding vows were said and marriage bells rang out, then a complete change of personality was expected of a woman. Mrs. Howe *had* changed since the days when, as Miss Julia Ward of New York, she had thought of little else but parties, beaux and poetry. She had become a pioneer and a reformer just like her husband; yet instead of being pleased, her husband still regarded her as an opponent. It almost broke Julia's heart to have her Chevalier against her.

Dr. Howe's discontent was extreme and it was probably Charles Sumner who gave him the hope of a new adventure. A "mission to Greece" was being planned by President Johnson and it seemed to Dr. Howe that he might regain his lost youth if he could be appointed. Mrs. Howe knew that her husband had little chance and she confided to her journal the hope that he would not send her to Washington in his behalf, because if she failed, the disappointment would be the more keen. But when her husband asked her to go she set out at once.

Again Julia Howe stayed with her friend Mrs. Charles Eames. She sent a note to Sumner asking him to call but he refused and also refused to meet her at the Willard Hotel as an alternative. He said she could come to the Senate to see him. At last she managed to arrange for an appointment to see the President on May 10, 1866 — the Attorney General calling for her to take her to the White House for an eleven o'clock interview. She was kept waiting an hour and put in the time in silent prayer — "Let me be not unskillful."

"I found the President not inclined to much speech," wrote Mrs. Howe in her journal. "I made a brief recapitulation of the Doctor's services in Greece and in America, touched upon Laura Bridgman, the idiot school etc., — finally asked leave to show the Doctor's Greek orders and the Prussian medal, which was granted. . . .

"The President said he would see what he could do for us — remarked that I must be much younger than the Doctor." Dr. Howe would be sixty-five in November, and Julia was not quite forty-seven. There seemed an ominous ring in the President's casual inquiry but Mrs. Howe tried not to lose hope. Having done all she could, she went back to Boston.

On Thursday, May 31, Mrs. Howe wrote: "Today the blow fell. A kind letter from Vice President Foster informed me that Chas. T. Tuckerman had been nominated for the Greek Commission. This gave me an unhappy hour. Chev was a good deal overcome by it for a time but has rallied and bears up bravely. The girls are rather glad. I am content but do not see what can take the place of this cherished object for Chev." [1] The opportunity for the Chevalier came early in 1867.

When the Greeks achieved their independence, the Island of Crete had remained under Turkish rule. A "Cretan revolt" had just occurred and failed. There was great suffering among the people of Crete who had no one to help them — unless it might be the United States. On July 7, Mrs. Howe wrote in her journal, "In the evening attended the meeting in behalf of Crete, at which Chev presided and spoke. . . . He was much deservedly glorified by the other speakers and indeed his appearance on this occasion was most touching and interesting. Andrew read the resolution, with a splendid compliment to Chev." Cretan relief was under way. The Chevalier would return.

Julia Ward Howe now set down a description of her husband's personality in a few words — contrasting it with her own. "Chev's is one those characters based upon opposition. While I always seem to work for an unseen friend, he always sees an armed adversary and nerves himself accordingly." Dr. Howe was positively delighted when the Turks forbade him to go to Crete and put a price upon his head if he should land anywhere on Cretan shores. He would indeed land with relief supplies. Here was an adversary worthy of his lance. Using all her experience gathered at Fairs for the Sanitary and for the seamen, Mrs. Howe became the leading spirit in organizing a Cretan Fair to raise money to charter a ship and load it with food and clothing for the Cretan refugees on the Greek mainland.

The Chevalier was not to go to Greece with his relief ship but to sail to Europe and reach Athens overland. Naturally, Mrs. Howe wanted to go with him, taking at least part of the family. The problem was money of course, and Mrs. Howe wrote the *New York Tribune* proposing to report the Paris Exposition in return for a round trip passage plus a hundred dollars each for ten letters, since this last would have to cover living expenses in Paris. This proposal seems not to have been accepted, and the editor of a woman's magazine who had promised a regular salary to Mrs. Howe took this time to inform her that the magazine was not able to pay more than the "Ninety dollars which I have certainly earned," Julia Howe said.

And then, on January 25, 1867, Mrs. Howe received a letter from the executors of her Uncle John Ward's estate enclosing a check for $1428.57, being her "half-yearly" income from her uncle's legacy. This came as a complete surprise, because the Ward sisters had supposed that their Uncle John had never recovered from the failure of Prime, Ward and King. But Uncle John had paid his debts and made a new start. A few years before his death in 1866, he had taken his nephew Charlie into "Ward and Company" and the firm had been prosperous. Charlie built a fine mansion on Broadway and showered his wife with diamonds. But just on the crest of the wave, Uncle John differed violently with his nephew and pulled out of the firm. Charlie was speculating in gold and declared that Uncle John was losing his mind not to go along. He actually inquired of other members of the family to know if there were any insanity Uncle John might have inherited.[2] In the end, of course, Uncle John proved the only sane Ward left in banking. "Honest John Ward" he was still called on Wall Street, and in 1866 the Ward sisters lost the man who had been in every sense of the word their guardian.

When Julia Ward Howe realized that she would have nearly three thousand dollars a year from her uncle's estate, "the largeness of the sum," she wrote, "makes me a rich woman. I am frightened to think how I might waste this money and relax my exertions to make the most of time and other gifts. I pray God I may not do so."

Since this legacy was not included in Julia's patrimony, she was not bound by that promise made more than twenty years previously, to hand it over to her husband. She nevertheless gave the Chevalier her check, hoping he would be pleased. He was not. "A man never wishes a woman to have any [money] which she does not derive from him," Mrs. Howe concluded sadly. This time, however, she was at least told when the money was invested in "B'way R.R.," the stock in her husband's name of course, and she was grateful to be allowed to have a check for $325.57 which was left over after the stock purchase. It would pay for "Laura's school, $66"; for "Julia's dress, $12.50"; and a passage to Europe cost only one hundred dollars. Julia Romana, Laura and their mother could now go abroad with the Chevalier. Truly, to be rich was a wonderful thing.

The family traveled together as far as Paris and then Julia Romana and her father set out for Greece on April 8, 1867. Laura and her mother went to Rome.

Julia Howe had never seen her sister Louisa's new Roman palace, the Odescalchi. She knew her sister's second husband very slightly and was inclined to think little of him, having become fond of Thomas Crawford. But Luther Terry was waiting at the station in Rome and Julia saw at once that he was "most kind." She found Louisa, "unseen in so many years," gray-haired now but otherwise unchanged.

Miss Cushman was in Rome, also the "Coolidges of Boston." As Louisa said of a typical Roman winter, "We have much best Boston," and her sister Julia felt "great contentment" among so many congenial people. But she would have felt untrue to her purpose to "make the most of time and other gifts," if she had let it go at that.

It was at Miss Cushman's villa during an afternoon call that Julia Howe "timidly unfolded" her "desire of reading an essay." Miss Cushman's sister Emma and Mrs. Howe's daughter Laura "talked down" the idea. "I shall, however try it," Mrs. Howe said. She had always received so much opposition from her husband, that she was "in perturbation" about what Luther Terry would say to her plan. She had a room arranged for at the British consulate before she dared to tell the Terrys what she had in mind. And then Luther Terry was not at all annoyed — he thought it a fine idea! And "my sister was perfect." This was "a dear and friendly household."

The whole Roman-American colony turned out to hear Mrs. Howe. There was Mrs. Story, the sculptor's wife, the "Cushman party, Mrs. Tuckerman of Boston, Miss Stebbins the artist — an excellent audience." They were all friends of the Terrys and all interested to have a look at Louisa's sister Julia — author of the "Battle Hymn of the Republic." Mrs. Howe hoped her reading was "instructive." She had yet to learn that some people came just to look at her and went away astonished at the entertainment and instruction she provided.

In June, Dr. Howe wrote from Athens "inviting" his wife to join him and she "resolved to go." So it was "farewell to dear Louisa" and about a six-day journey, part of the time aboard a small steamer stopping at many ports.[3] The Chevalier had gone to Greece expecting to recapture lost youth, but at the port of Syra, on an island in the Aegean, it was Julia Ward Howe's own youth which returned to her in the person of an old friend. A Greek gentleman came aboard the steamer looking for Mrs. Howe. It was Christy Evangeles, who, years before on Bond Street, had loved "Miss Julia Ward with Heaven's purest love."

Christy had not quite realized his boyish dreams of becoming a great leader of his people, but he had done very well. He had established a large school which, in those troublous times, was an achievement. He had married "a good little wife," and when it was discovered that there would be time for Mrs. Howe and Laura to go ashore, he took his guests to call on all the dignitaries on the island, who followed close on their heels to Christy's home — the speed with which a call was returned being a measure of the honor conferred. At Christy's house there was a feast with "native wine of musky flavor" and "Pilaff, made of tomatoes and mincemeat." Christy and his once "beloved Euphrosene," now Julia Ward Howe, talked of Bond Street days.

In Athens, Mrs. Howe found the Chevalier and Julia Romana. Dr. Howe had been greeted everywhere as a returning hero, his wife learned. He had gone to Crete of course, defying the death penalty — and he returned to Athens with his head still upon his shoulders regardless of the price the Turks had set upon it. Dr. Howe had found the mole which he built in Aegina still standing and he had landed there with relief supplies. Men and women he had known pointed him out to their children. Handsome, erect, still the daring horseman — the Chevalier seemed hardly changed and he was everywhere recognized at sight. To the Greeks he must have seemed immortal — like one of the gods.

Arrangements had still to be made in Athens for further visits to refugee camps, and while the Chevalier was happily going about doing his duty, his wife could not be expected to fail in her own. If she had not given a reading in Athens as well as in Rome, she would have suffered severely from a guilty conscience. The Chevalier had been "kind," but "as people began to talk of the lecture, he became more and more annoyed." One might almost suspect that the hero of the Greeks was jealous — but he had married a woman to reform her and he had succeeded perfectly. "I earnestly desire to live in Christian love and Charity with him," Mrs. Howe wrote in her journal — "but not so that my conscience shall be subject to his will." She always left her journal where her husband could read it and he often did so.

The Howes were given a military escort as they traveled to the various Cretan refugee camps on the Greek mainland. And Mrs. Howe found that a new member seemed to have been added to the family — Michael Anagnos, a young man from Epirus, now Dr. Howe's secretary. Michael refused payment for his services. "What are you paid for helping my country?" he asked the Doctor. Of course the answer was that Dr. Howe received no pay. When it came time for the Howes to return to the United States, Michael Anagnos went with them. He became Dr. Howe's assistant at Perkins Institute for the Blind and, after the Chevalier's death, his successor. He married Julia Romana Howe.

The Howe children could be called children no longer. In 1867, just before the journey to Crete, Florence had become engaged to David Prescott Hall, of New York — a connection by marriage of the Ward family. They would have to wait, because David was studying to be a lawyer, but they had faith in each other and plenty of patience. Julia Romana could be married first for she would merely continue to live and teach at the Institute.

Immediately upon her return from Europe, Laura met Henry Richards, a Harvard student from Gardiner, Maine. It was at one of the Boston Assemblies, held at Papanti's Hall, and Laura saw a young man looking shy and awkward but most attractive. Henry admitted that he was not sure of his dancing and had been taking lessons in the "Boston," that gaily springing variation of the waltz suddenly so popular. Only socially eligible young men were invited to the Assemblies and Henry Richards was all of that — being related to the Tudors and the Gardiners, founding families on the Kennebec, and inheriting in his own right considerable interest in Gardiner. He said that Laura Howe was "a vision of loveliness" and that he was "off and away on a whirlwind courtship" after they first danced. But a two-year engagement followed, for Henry Richards had first to find a job as an architect.

1871 was the wedding year in the Howe family. Henry Richards told of his own wedding, at the Church of the Disciples.[4] "I remember Dr. Howe, one of the handsomest of men, smiling delightedly as he walked up the aisle, and greeting all his friends to their great embar-

rassment. I kept my few remaining wits on the ring, which I had safe."
At the reception, "Dr. Howe appeared in his own blue wedding coat
with brass buttons and waistcoat of brocaded silk." After a brief visit
to Newport, the young couple set out for Europe, the bride wearing
a brown traveling dress which her artistic husband described as hideous.

And now it was Florence's turn, after an engagement lasting five
years. There would be no European honeymoon. "I can give her $500
cash and allow her $600 per an." said Mrs. Howe, trying to do her
best to make things easier for a young lawyer and his wife, just
getting their start. Maud was now the only child at home, for Harry
was at Massachusetts Institute of Technology, having graduated from
Harvard in 1869.

Julia Ward Howe was now fifty-two years old and she had just
embarked upon a new phase of her career. Although she continued
to take great pleasure in writing poems for occasions, writing was
not in first place among her interests. There would be no more plays
but the platform superseded the stage. Travel books continued, as Mrs.
Howe sought and found new adventures, but essays became lectures
even though collected and published in book form. A glorious vein of
humor now at last found an appreciative audience. "My dear club"
was the way Mrs. Howe always referred to the group of women she
loved best in all the world — the New England Women's Club.

On February 10, 1868, the New England Women's Club was
founded, and on March 10 they had written their constitution and
elected their President, Mrs. Caroline Maria Seymour Severance. "The
object of the club" was to "organize the social force of women then
working alone or in small circles. Men were eligible to membership
but the club was to be officered and controlled by women." A "parlor
or parlors" were to be hired "in a house on Park Street" in order to
"furnish a quiet, central resting place and place of meeting in Boston
for the comfort and convenience of members." And right at this point
the howl of protest went up — with Samuel Gridley Howe by no
means the only man taking a dim view of the whole thing.

Men were always going to their clubs — it was a divine right and
the best known method of getting out from under. But imagine a
woman, after a hard day's work, going to a club lounge, ordering
something refreshing perhaps — even staying for dinner if she happened to know they were having leftovers at home! The dangers in
the women's club idea were too terrible to contemplate. "Association"

was what women said they had a right to — but "association" was permitted only on the scale of the neighborhood sewing circle. Since early days, single women or women left alone in the world had achieved "association" through religious orders only. Of course an Oriental harem might be termed an association of women — but it was hardly voluntary. Jibes were many. Cartoons appeared showing a husband, in top hat and cane, coming home to cope with his five or six screaming children — his wife being at her club. Women joined in the laughter, since nothing could be funnier than the contrast between the cartoon version of a woman's club and the decorous "parlor or parlors" on Park Street.

It goes without saying that Julia Ward Howe was one of the founders of the New England Women's Club. In 1871, she became President and was re-elected every successive year until 1910, with the exception of two years when she was in Europe. She had a great gift for organization and an almost unbelievable capacity for hard work. According to her journal, she did not think well of herself as a moderator. As mistress of ceremonies, her wit sparkled at its best, whether she admitted it herself or not.

Of course the very thing which the lords of creation prophesied in connection with women's clubs happened, occasionally. Wives lingered too long and arrived home late for supper. Mrs. Howe was very careful because once in the days when she lived on Chestnut Street she had lingered at a wartime meeting and, instead of walking home by way of proper Beacon Street, she had cut across a corner of the Common. A man "clucked at" her, as one does "to make a horse trot faster." She could not help laughing even while she thought how shocked her daughters would have been.

Unconventionalities troubled the Howe young ladies. They remembered how naked they felt when they gave up crinolines. Maud, now not quite fourteen, was the one left at home to be embarrassed by her mother in 1871 and for some time to come. Mrs. Howe had evolved a system of wearing a black dress for which she carried an extra set of collar and cuffs in her purse. She would hop aboard a train with the lightest of luggage and arrive to feel fresh and elegant at lecture time with just the addition of fresh lace at neck and wrists. To Maud, this was altogether too reminiscent of the eccentric Miss Peabody and she scolded her mother for not paying more attention to dress. Maud had yet to read her mother's journal, with its record of expenditures for a pretty daughter's clothes and the contrastingly small sums "to alter bodice of my black silk." While Annie remained in the East, she was always making over her sister Julia's clothes for her, but now a dressmaker must be sent for. "Old Splendid," the dressmaker called thirteen-year-old Maud, who loved beautiful dresses and insisted that they fit — just as her mother had done at her age, if daughters but knew these things.

At about this time Mrs. Howe went to New York, arriving on an early train. She found no one up at her cousin Charlie's house, where she was expected as a guest. She pulled the doorbell again and again, and finally went to the area door where the cook heard her knock. Seeing a somewhat rumpled stranger in black, "Go away, my good woman," the cook said — or words to that effect — "we have nothing for you today." Mrs. Howe loved to laugh over this story, and told it with glee to her friends at the Women's Club — but it was a story a daughter in her teens considered not at all funny.[5]

The New England Women's Club sent Mrs. Howe as a delegate to the first Woman Suffrage meeting she ever attended. She was by no means ready to become a suffragist, but when she arrived at Agricultural Hall she found old friends of antislavery days. Wendell Phillips, Colonel Higginson, James Freeman Clarke were on the platform. Mrs. Howe had hoped to slip in unnoticed — the weather was bad, and she had strayed into the Hall wearing her rainy day suit. But she was summoned to the platform.

It was good to be "among the old Abolition warriors again," Mrs. Howe said. Their arguments were "simple, strong and convincing." Lucy Stone spoke and she had been previously the object of one of Mrs. Howe's "imaginary dislikes." But "here stood the true woman, pure, noble, great-hearted." Her husband, Henry Brown Blackwell, was with her and "ably seconded her work." When Mrs. Howe was called upon to speak, "I am with you," was all she could say.

By an odd twist, Mrs. Severance, whose work for women began with Suffrage, was first President of the New England Women's Club — while Mrs. Howe, whose first love was Women's Clubs, became first President of the New England Woman Suffrage Association.

Dr. Howe was growing much more tolerant! A series of letters to his daughter Laura, now on her European honeymoon, show him as pretty much the modern husband — amused and reconciled to his wife's activities. And moreover getting a good deal of fun out of his little jokes at his wife's expense.

"Mama is crusading in Philadelphia and the adjoining country," Dr.

Howe told Laura in November, 1871. "She is in sublime health and spirits; indeed her spirits are fireproof and there is no danger of purgatory or Inferno for her; because the Devil would not admit her through fear that she would raise a laugh in his warm premises."

And a month later, "Your Mama — old Never-tire, is the most vigorous, active and jolly of that noisy and clamorous group who are now holding a Suffrage Fair in Music Hall. Not content with having all mankind of all ages voluntarily at their feet and serving them, they now want legal power to keep their servants in life-long subjugation. The first act in the new Gospel will be, Husbands obey your wives."

While these letters reflect a wonderfully genial Dr. Howe, he was not of course entirely satisfied. There was the matter of Maud — now seventeen. "Maud is glowing and boiling over with spirits," her father said. "She and Mama arranged a very wise and sober course of domestic habits and quiet life for the winter; and then gaily proceeded to kick it all to pieces, — to enter upon a career of gaiety and excitement which hardly leaves a moment for study or an hour for domestic enjoyment."

Some social engagements met with more paternal favor than others, however. This time it was the oldest daughter, Julia Romana — now Julia Anagnos — who was with her mother "this evening at a grand panjandrum of some sort at the Forbes in Milton. I am glad to have Mama get out of the suffrage drag — and go into decent society," Dr. Howe said — the date being January, 1872.

And for some reason, this seemed to bring up Charles Sumner's marital difficulties. "If you hear any gossip about Mrs. Sumner, let me have it," Dr. Howe wrote. "Charles won't admit that he cares to know where she is or what she does; but I think he is rather interested to know. He does not care for her as a woman but it does concern him that Mrs. Sumner should deport herself ladylike etc. I think he will get his divorce as soon as the law will give it to him, which will be this year." (In 1866, Sumner at the age of fifty-five had married a young widow; but they separated within a year.)

There was one more adventure in store for the Chevalier. President Grant had appointed a commission to investigate the advisability of annexing Santo Domingo, which he was advised would be needed by the United States Navy as a coaling station in case of war. The Honorable Benjamin F. Wade of Ohio, Andrew D. White, first President of

Cornell, and Dr. Samuel Gridley Howe were appointed to look into the situation. In February, 1872, they were sent to Santo Domingo aboard a "government steamer," the *Tennessee*. Soon after the commission left, the rumor went around that the *Tennessee* was unseaworthy. Then came a tropical hurricane and an account was published in the papers of a steamer seen in distress. "The steamer was probably the *Tennessee*, and it is most likely that she foundered in the storm and went down with all on board" — so went the newspaper account.

Days of great anxiety followed. And then at last came the good news. The *Tennessee* was safe in Samana Bay. Now people began to call on Mrs. Howe and letters poured in while only a short time before she had felt utterly alone. She knew that she and her husband had many friends but she had not realized that so many people had been thinking of her. Garrison wrote that he had "shared the grave solicitude" and he added that he "strongly opposed the project of annexation" and was in "full sympathy with Mr. Sumner," who had fought the project from the start.

Dr. Howe did not go along with his friends, Garrison and Sumner. He could not feel that to acquire Santo Domingo would be a form of "imperialism." He saw Santo Domingo as an earthly paradise needing only the benefit of American education, laws and scientific knowledge. The population was a mixture of French, Spanish and Negro, and Dr. Howe longed to share with them the privileges of a democracy. His two colleagues agreed with him.

In spite of the findings of the commission, the measure for annexation failed. Dr. Howe was bitterly disappointed for he had fallen in love with Santo Domingo and wanted to go there to live. If he could be appointed governor of a colony, what an opportunity he would have to put into practice all his theories of education, sanitation, and good government, just as he had done briefly in his rehabilitation colony of Aegina! This was where his genius lay.

The following year, the Samana Bay Company was formed under a charter from President Baez of the Dominican Republic. The project had all too many earmarks of the United States and Paraguayan Navigation Company which Sam Ward had tried in vain to salvage. Dr. Howe, looking not too deeply into the scheme, was delighted to be "strongly urged to go to Santo Domingo by parties interested in the welfare of the island."

By March, 1872 — a year after his first voyage — Dr. Howe was again on his way to Santo Domingo, this time aboard a tiny steamer the *Tybee*. And this time he had with him his wife, his daughter Maud and her friend Lucy Derby, together with two Howe nieces and Miss Paddock from the Institute who would chaperone the girls after Mrs. Howe left for England. Long before the Santo Domingo plans were made, Mrs. Howe had promised to go to the Women's Peace Conference to be held in London and she could not break her word. And long before she left Santo Domingo she wished with all her heart these previous plans had not been made — for she too fell in love with the island.

Mrs. Howe's first move, on arrival in Santo Domingo, was to discover through conversation "with one François, a man of color," that there was "a tiny Negro church in town." The pastor had died, and an elder carried on services as best he could "for a small congregation of very poor colored people, all Americans by birth or descent." Every Sunday evening of her stay, Mrs. Howe preached "from the chancel" of this little church. Not being ordained (as several of her women friends were) she felt she should not enter the "large mahogany pulpit."

Mrs. Howe's second move on arrival was to give a dinner party — next a dancing party. A United States warship was in the harbor, and the young officers were delighted to be asked to a dance at the Palacio National, which President Baez had given to the Howes as a residence. "The fleas in the palace gave us terrible torment," Mrs. Howe said — but having the floors washed and "the use of some native plant" helped. The party was a great success as were all the subsequent parties — except for one thing. It was the native custom to stay till dawn!

Mrs. Howe's last Sunday in Santo Domingo was Easter. The little church was beautifully decorated — "flowers along the rail — flowers in the pulpit over my head," she said. The building was full and people stood outside to listen at the windows, and when the elders thanked Mrs. Howe for all she had done for them, "God knows it has been a great pleasure and profit to me," she said. And in her journals she wrote, "Santo Domingo, how I do love you, with your childish life and your ancestral streets — a grand dame and a babe! . . . God grant that we may come here again."

Only a matter of importance could have taken Mrs. Howe to England at this time. This was her "Peace Idea" which had been growing in her mind ever since she visited hospitals in Washington and saw the effects of war. She had issued an "Appeal to Womanhood

"My Dear New Found"

IN 1874, Dr. and Mrs. Howe returned to Samana Bay. All efforts to annex or to establish a protectorate over Santo Domingo had failed with Charles Sumner almost splitting the Republican Party in his opposition to Grant in this affair. It seems strange that Sumner, the crusader for Negro emancipation and franchise, should have opposed even a protectorate which would have stabilized the government of the Dominican Republic. From a purely economic point of view, however, he was right. The United States could never have benefited very much from half of an island whose natural resources had been greatly exaggerated. Dr. Howe thought only of the plight of the natives under a regime which exploited them mercilessly, and for the first time he and Sumner differed seriously. By 1874, President Baez had been overthrown in a revolution sponsored by "the merchants of Puerto Plata, jealous of the success of the Samana Bay Company," or so said Mrs. Howe. She now witnessed a dramatic scene.

On March 31, 1874, she went "to town early to be present at the taking down of the Samana Bay Company's flag." The new dictator of the so-called Republic had repudiated all contracts. Mrs. Howe "found Chev in the Custom house with the Commissioner . . . and a good many of our people present. Chev read his protest, which was strong and simple. . . .

"We then went out of the building, the employees of our company marched off in their best clothes, their hats stuck full of roses, and stood in order on either side of the flag-staff. . . . Chev got our people to stand in a circle around him and with much feeling made a lovely little address. The old Crusader never appeared better or nobler than on this occasion, when his beautiful chivalry stood in the greatest contrast to the barbarism and ingratitude which dictated

petuosity and zeal for what he called 'construction and repairs.' . . .
He was always busy . . . tinkering here, altering there, improving
bathrooms and replacing closets with wardrobes, quite regardless of
appearances in all this work. He built a bathtub of boards and lined
it with sheet lead and set it just over the narrow front stairs" at Green
Peace. "The house had no central heat . . . and an extra lining of ice,"
formed in that tub in winter "as the water ran out after pulling
the plug."

Dr. Howe went every day from Perkins Institute in South Boston
to his Boston office. "When driven in town in his carry-all, he would
whack the driver's back and say, 'Push along, push along,' whatever
the pace might be. . . . His horses were all named 'Breeze,' 'Blast' and
the like, and were required to live up to their names."

"It was a strange household," the Richards son-in-law said, "with
Grandmother Howe slipping off to lectures and conventions while
Polish and Greek refugees flocked to Grandfather Howe hoping for
employment, which he usually gave them."

Mrs. Howe explained her "slipping off" to her daughter Laura.
She said she learned the system from an old Quaker she met in Abolition days. He had a station on the Underground, and she asked him
how he had been so successful in sending slaves to Canada. "It was
borne in upon me at an early period that if I told no one what I intended to do, I should be enabled to do it," the old Quaker said. Of
course Mrs. Howe always searched her conscience before taking the
Quaker's advice. But the children could never remember whether it
was one of them or their father who first called her "the Swamp Fox"
in honor of her Revolutionary ancestor — when these quiet disap-
pearances of hers proved successful.

CHAPTER TWENTY-SEVEN
"My Dear New Found"

IN 1874, Dr. and Mrs. Howe returned to Samana Bay. All efforts to annex or to establish a protectorate over Santo Domingo had failed with Charles Sumner almost splitting the Republican Party in his opposition to Grant in this affair. It seems strange that Sumner, the crusader for Negro emancipation and franchise, should have opposed even a protectorate which would have stabilized the government of the Dominican Republic. From a purely economic point of view, however, he was right. The United States could never have benefited very much from half of an island whose natural resources had been greatly exaggerated. Dr. Howe thought only of the plight of the natives under a regime which exploited them mercilessly, and for the first time he and Sumner differed seriously. By 1874, President Baez had been overthrown in a revolution sponsored by "the merchants of Puerto Plata, jealous of the success of the Samana Bay Company," or so said Mrs. Howe. She now witnessed a dramatic scene.

On March 31, 1874, she went "to town early to be present at the taking down of the Samana Bay Company's flag." The new dictator of the so-called Republic had repudiated all contracts. Mrs. Howe "found Chev in the Custom house with the Commissioner . . . and a good many of our people present. Chev read his protest, which was strong and simple. . . .

"We then went out of the building, the employees of our company marched off in their best clothes, their hats stuck full of roses, and stood in order on either side of the flag-staff. . . . Chev got our people to stand in a circle around him and with much feeling made a lovely little address. The old Crusader never appeared better or nobler than on this occasion, when his beautiful chivalry stood in the greatest contrast to the barbarism and ingratitude which dictated

the *Tybee*. And this time he had with him his wife, his daughter Maud and her friend Lucy Derby, together with two Howe nieces and Miss Paddock from the Institute who would chaperone the girls after Mrs. Howe left for England. Long before the Santo Domingo plans were made, Mrs. Howe had promised to go to the Women's Peace Conference to be held in London and she could not break her word. And long before she left Santo Domingo she wished with all her heart these previous plans had not been made — for she too fell in love with the island.

Mrs. Howe's first move, on arrival in Santo Domingo, was to discover through conversation "with one François, a man of color," that there was "a tiny Negro church in town." The pastor had died, and an elder carried on services as best he could "for a small congregation of very poor colored people, all Americans by birth or descent." Every Sunday evening of her stay, Mrs. Howe preached "from the chancel" of this little church. Not being ordained (as several of her women friends were) she felt she should not enter the "large mahogany pulpit."

Mrs. Howe's second move on arrival was to give a dinner party — next a dancing party. A United States warship was in the harbor, and the young officers were delighted to be asked to a dance at the Palacio National, which President Baez had given to the Howes as a residence. "The fleas in the palace gave us terrible torment," Mrs. Howe said — but having the floors washed and "the use of some native plant" helped. The party was a great success as were all the subsequent parties — except for one thing. It was the native custom to stay till dawn!

Mrs. Howe's last Sunday in Santo Domingo was Easter. The little church was beautifully decorated — "flowers along the rail — flowers in the pulpit over my head," she said. The building was full and people stood outside to listen at the windows, and when the elders thanked Mrs. Howe for all she had done for them, "God knows it has been a great pleasure and profit to me," she said. And in her journals she wrote, "Santo Domingo, how I do love you, with your childish life and your ancestral streets — a grand dame and a babe! . . . God grant that we may come here again."

Only a matter of importance could have taken Mrs. Howe to England at this time. This was her "Peace Idea" which had been growing in her mind ever since she visited hospitals in Washington and saw the effects of war. She had issued an "Appeal to Womanhood

throughout the world" asking that women work together for dis-
armament and "international justice" without the "fatal mediation of
military weapons" and it was plainly her duty to be at the first
"Women's Peace Congress" in London.

The meetings were not a great success. Mrs. Howe's hopes had been
too high. But she met groups of British Suffragists and their American guests, Dr. Blackwell and Miss Beecher. Her comment concerning
these ladies, told only in her journal of course, was as follows: "The
ladies were as hard as billiard balls, charged with electricity, dead shots
certainly. I like our method much better because it is at once more
cordial and more humane and relieved by a larger aperçus. But I may
be a little nettled by the entire neglect with which I was treated,
altho I was prepared for this."

One bright spot in this rather difficult journey was a glimpse of
Laura and her husband — on their way home now. Miss Elizabeth
Peabody sailed on the same liner and Mrs. Howe had a talk with her
about the Peace Crusade. Then on to Paris went Mrs. Howe, meeting
with obstacles there which have discouraged any other woman. At
the end of July she was home again, "safely and prosperously, thank
God" — more determined than ever to work for "international justice."

The Boston house was rented as was Lawton's Valley in Newport,
so it was back to South Boston — but at least not to the detested
"Doctor's Wing." Julia Romana and her husband Michael Anagnos
were living there now. And Laura and her husband, who were trying
to live on architect's fees, would occupy "the old part" of Green
Peace. There was a new member of the family, Laura's first child,
"a dear little daughter." Julia Ward Howe and the Chevalier were
grandparents and history was about to repeat itself, as Laura E. Richards would soon become a writer — living in South Boston and taking
care of babies all the while.

In the one book which Laura's husband wrote, he described Dr. and
Mrs. Howe as they looked to him. Henry Richards observed that Dr.
Howe "remained" Julia's "Chevalier through life." But he thought
"there must have been many a clash between them. How could they
pull together," he wondered, "when her intellectual striving was so
strong and he, always impetuous, was off and away on some inspired
mission to help humanity." Byron's helmet always hung on the top
of the wrought-iron hat tree in the front hall at Green Peace as if to
remind the Doctor that crusades need never end.

Nothing impressed Henry Richards more than Dr. Howe's "im-

this act." The Company flag was slowly lowered. The Samana Bay Company had ended.

"My heart was full of cursing rather than blessing," Mrs. Howe said, "Yet finding myself presently alone with the superseded flag, I laid my hand on it and prayed" that "I might bless the good effort which has been made here." Later, the natives said that "they would have offered forcible resistance if we had authorized their doing so." [1]

The Howes had reached Samana Bay early in March and Mrs. Howe had written, "In Santo Domingo, glad as a child." She had gone right to a jeweler's and "foolishly bargained for the gold necklace and emerald ring I fancied the last time I was here. The necklace is for Maud." The ring was for herself, and although she scolded herself for having made "so foolish a use of money," she was as delighted with it as though she had been a young girl again. She and the Chevalier took a cottage on a hillside outside of town. They had come to Santo Domingo without daughters or nieces and for the first time in over thirty years they lived alone together. Dr. Howe began to read *Don Quixote* in Spanish and Julia had brought her Greek to study.

By day, they went horseback riding — the Chevalier dashing ahead along winding trails high above the sea and his wife following as best she could. Julia had never been a good horsewoman, much to her dismay, even in the old days when her father's coachman tried to teach her to ride properly around the paddock on the corner of Bond Street and Broadway — before The Corner was built. As a young girl she had been given a far too mettlesome saddle horse and had been thrown repeatedly. But she always picked herself up and rode again and now she tried her best to follow her Chevalier. It was humiliating to get stuck halfway up a steep slope and have to be rescued. But at the same time there was something very wonderful about having the Chevalier rescue his Julia as though she had been young again and he her lover once more. "Chev was very sweet and companionable," Julia wrote in her journal. But she spoke anxiously of his "declining strength." And to her daughter Laura, Mrs. Howe wrote, "Papa has quite an idea of buying a place here; we saw one this morning near San Carlos — all palms and fruit trees."

Here was a dream worth keeping in mind as the Howes returned home. They might some day retire to Santo Domingo. Old occupations were resumed, and Laura's husband described Dr. Howe in his garden at Green Peace . . . "trimming trees in his orchard . . . in an old bonnet of Grandmother Howe's . . . or driving out a hen that had strayed under a rose vine . . . putting a cat into a cage and hoisting her up into a cherry tree to drive the predatory robins away."

The Howes' Newport home was no longer Lawton's Valley but Oak Glen, a smaller farm nearby on another millstream. It would never be as beautiful a place as Lawton's Valley, but the old house required a great deal of Dr. Howe's genius for "construction and repair." Early in August, 1874, he wrote to Laura, "I have been improving the cottage by an ornamental fountain in the little lawn between the porch and the road; much to the delectation of Maud and the admiration of passing farmers."

This was the summer when Maud was nineteen and she was "fluttering and floating over the field of fashion," her father said. She had a remarkable field for fluttering over, because Newport had become fashion's summer capital. All Maud's early promise of beauty was fulfilled, and she was "the decided belle of the season," although her father viewed with alarm her getting "intoxicated daily and nightly by the admiration of silly men, and by the friends of fashion." Of course it was her mother who "has not the heart to restrain her."

But Dr. Howe's understanding and tolerance of women's ways had increased greatly even in the past year. "Mama is in high feather," he said, "and is organizing all kinds of Clubs and Associations, under the guise of advancing the cause of human progress, civilization, woman's rights, etc., etc., but with the appearance of good times at picnics, aesthetic teas, lobster salads, clam bakes, etc. which are to be taken inwardly, while the breath of eloquent exhortation is vented outwardly. *Vive la suffrage quandmème!*"

Grandchildren were a great delight, as Florence with her boys and Laura with her girls made alternating visits to Oak Glen. Mrs. Howe revived her music and every day saw additional tunes improvised for new scenes in the nursery opera, which seemed to grow of itself. There were parts for everyone and no one could forget Grandfather Howe doing the frog dance — nor the wonderful thumping music that went with it. But beneath all gaiety there was a recurring note of anxiety in the words "Chev's declining strength" which appeared, more often now, in Mrs. Howe's journal. It almost seemed that at some time he might have suffered a shock — though slight and unrecognized as such.

By June the following year, there was no doubt about it. "Chev very feeble today at dinner," Mrs. Howe wrote in her journal. "We were much distressed at his condition. It seemed as if the end might be near as he sat and dozed in his chair, eating nothing. A dose of brandy and water and a game of whist revived him." They sent for "Dr. S. W. Francis" who came and "left some degitalis to be administered thrice daily." The Chevalier's condition was now infinitely sad — his passion for playing whist reminding Julia of her grandfather's last years. She herself, now fifty-six, was strong and well — full of active plans. She had never before felt so keenly the difference in age between herself and her husband, who was seventy-four.

"Women should not cut off their first twenty years and then try to repeat them," Mrs. Howe remarked in the course of one of her informal talks at the Women's Club. Some people never take their own advice, but she was the exception to this rule. At fifty-six, she was already well on her way in her new career — that of lecturer. Opportunities were few at first and fees varied. For example, Mrs. Howe spoke in Worcester, Massachusetts, on "Paris" for a fee of fifty dollars. In Ithaca, she spoke on "England as Seen" for eighty-five dollars, and Buffalo paid her a hundred dollars for the Paris lecture. At first the fees did not matter greatly Mrs. Howe was simply making the most of her gifts, as she believed that it was her duty to do. Not but what she could use the money, as the journal entry "Lent Chev $400" indicated. But on October 21, 1875, an inconspicuous item appeared in the New York papers that suddenly made Julia Howe's capacity to earn a living of great importance.

"The upward tendency in stocks yesterday caused the failure of . . . four small brokers. The amounts involved were insignificant." One of the brokers was Charles Ward, and once more the fatal gambling streak had appeared, this time in "Cousin Charlie" — who had charge of all the funds left by his uncle John. That slightly less than three thousand dollars a year which had made Mrs. Howe "a rich woman" had practically disappeared when Charlie sold the gold market short and got caught. The loss might be described as "insignificant" in those days of large profit and loss in stock gambling. To the three Ward sisters, "Charlie's failure" was anything but insignificant.[2]

Mrs. Howe began at once to plan ways and means of earning money. She must make a Midwestern lecture tour that would really help out the family income. Her reputation had been increasing as a result of her leadership in club work and she could command better fees all the time. But her husband's illness, as mysterious apparently to the doctors as to himself and his family, steadily increased. Faithfully, hour after hour, his wife played whist with him while in her mind she tried to plan what she should do in future years if he continued to be a hopeless invalid.

Between games, Julia sat and talked with her Chevalier. At first, the conversation was casual, as the Chevalier told her of his youth and his adventures. Then so much of importance was suddenly revealed that Mrs. Howe's journal must be quoted in full, and word for word.

"*Nov. 23.* I have had some sad revelations from dear Chev about my own sex which greatly astonish me. From these I learn that women are not only sensual but lustful, and that men are attracted, rather than shocked by this trait. The privacy of offices, or at least their remoteness from domestic visitation is eagerly made available by these women for the vilest purposes."

The next entry concerning these intimate talks between husband and wife is not entirely clear in meaning, because of the name which Mrs. Howe omitted.

"*Dec. 7.* A sad talk with —— in which I could not help reviewing the great injustice done me and the other's self by a course of conduct most treacherous and worthy of reprobation. If thought has a grave, may this ghost be laid and appear no more."

"*Dec. 8.* A most touching and comforting talk with Chev, in which I felt once more all the moral beauty which has been my faith and delight in him. I have solemnly sworn never to allude to anything in the past, which, coming up lately, has given us both pain. If my dear Master can by these bitter pangs reconsecrate our lives and make us what we should be to each other, who shall say that so great a good is bought too dearly by those very pangs. Gloria in Excelsis Deo. I have reached the bottom of these years of estrangement, in which there has been fault and wrong on both sides, and we shall begin to rebuild our life in common. My double bed is to be moved into his room in order that we may have the comfort of being near each other in the dark and silent hours. I have followed the frowning face of Duty till it has turned and smiled. Esto perpetua."

The following day, Mrs. Howe had a speaking engagement in Leominster. She was obliged to spend the night away from home, and alone in the strange room she suffered — having loved her husband and being human.

"*Dec. 9.* I had a death agony in my room in Leominster, before I went to bed. I tried to conjure up the image of B to reason with her concerning her shameful conduct and the wrong done me. I wished to see her ghost more than I ever dreaded to see one. I remembered with joy that she died by inches, a painful death in poverty alleviated by the care of friends. And then I felt how devilish these thoughts were, and prayed and so slept. This morning at waking, the spirit seemed to show me my own faults, and it seemed a great comfort to have the burden of offence laid on my shoulders. Strange as it may seem, it was comparatively delightful to me to accuse myself and make my own sins point out the hypocrisy and unkindness of which I have had so long an experience, without the least understanding the facts as they were. All the way to Boston, prayer accompanied me. 'Pray without ceasing' was now the word for me."

But Julia Ward Howe was touchingly human. She needed to reread the Sermon on the Mount in order to be merciful in all her thoughts toward "offenders beyond the reach of reprisals from me." Two pages are cut from the Journal. But the last little note the Chevalier ever wrote his Julia was pasted in. "My dear New Found," he called her.

Dr. Howe died January 4, 1876, "stricken down" by a stroke on his way from Green Peace to the Institute. After the great public funeral was over — with blind children singing — Laura Bridgman being led in — one more ordeal awaited Mrs. Howe. Going over Dr. Howe's papers at the Institute, she "found and burned something which gave me great pain." Her son-in-law Michael Anagnos "would not allow me to read these letters but burned them for me," she said.

The shock of learning the truth about a woman referred to as "B" and her "shameful conduct and the wrong done" Mrs. Howe, seems to indicate that she knew nothing about this woman up to this time. But when, in 1854, her husband asked her for a divorce and spoke of "some young girl who would love him supremely," it must have crossed her mind that he knew of such a person. At the Institute, he was surrounded by women teachers and other assistants of varying ages, most of whom admired him greatly. Upon at least one occasion in Boston, when Dr. Howe had been unusually severe with his wife, she had offered to give up her personal plans and go to the Institute with him, in the hope of pleasing him. He had answered her angrily, forbidding the visit, and she feared there was someone there whom he did not want her to meet.

It is, of course, impossible to know to whom the initial "B" belonged. It could have been a last name or a first name. In a few letters there was mention of a "Becky," who was a fairly frequent visitor at the Institute. She had relatives who taught there. Writing to her sister Annie on November 6, 1859, Mrs. Howe said, "Did I tell you of Becky's visit? She came one P.M. and staid [sic] to tea and I had to send her to the cars for Milton. Then Chev took her on to Newport and cunningly slipped off next morning, finding it not so strange that people could have enough of her. She wore her bosom too low, even for him."

But it would be the merest coincidence if Becky of the low-cut gown were "B." Pages of the journal were so carefully cut and letters burned to such an extent that it is impossible so much as to conjecture as to the identity of this woman.

The decision to take the entire blame for the unhappiness in her marriage continued to bring peace to Julia Ward Howe. Yet such a severe burden of self-imposed punishment was hard to bear, and she formed the habit — not indeed new to her, but now invariable — of turning to God in prayer both night and morning. Her prayers she often recorded in her journals, and also her thankfulness when prayers were answered. "In place of my dear husband, I now have my foolish papers," Mrs. Howe wrote. "Yet I have often left him for them. God accept the poor endeavor of my life."

A woman less severe with herself would have remembered the many lonely hours when the Chevalier was off on one of his crusades and his wife was left alone. Books and papers were her refuge then; hard study, determined self-education, at the high level of German philosophy and Greek poetry in the original, would come to her aid now in time of need. There were mornings when Mrs. Howe "awoke oppressed by financial worries." She soon threw them off, recognizing that "the need to do things" kept her from "brooding over the past."

Dr. Howe's will explains the financial worries. "My wife, Julia Ward Howe having ample means of her own," would, he trusted, waive all claims to anything of his. To his daughters he gave his entire estate to be divided equally. Most of the Howes' real estate had been bought with Mrs. Howe's money, put in her husband's name, and a mortgage signed by him given to her trust fund. A codicil to his will mentioned $69,609.90 now invested in real estate and belonging to Mrs. Howe. It was going to take a long time and cost money in legal fees to untangle the records to find out which houses and which parcels of land belonged to Mrs. Howe and which to her daughters. In the end it made little difference, since the land, at least, was a liability because of taxes. As soon as possible, Mrs. Howe put up her South Boston lots at auction. There were no takers — the bids being so low that the lawyer automatically bid them in for the estate. In Kansas, there were broad acres, untouched, unoccupied and unwanted. Instead of an income, Mrs. Howe's trust fund was producing a deficit — and there was one more shock in store. "I find I am living at the rate of $800 a month," Mrs. Howe said.

The sum seemed incredible; but the Howes had been maintaining three homes most of the time; Green Peace near the Institute, a house in Boston and a Newport summer home. When Mrs. Howe finally "found," with the help of lawyers, that Green Peace belonged to her, she tried to sell it; but the city put a street through part of the property which did not enhance its value and in the end she rented the place, hoping to make it profitable. The horses must go, and Mrs. Howe could hardly keep back the tears as she saw them being led away — they were like members of the family. Since the South Boston land had not been sold, there was only one thing to do — build low-cost housing and rent it to produce revenue. Mrs. Howe went to the bank and arranged a loan for the purpose, her son Harry and the "agent" at Perkins promising to see about building. It would all take time, and no one except Mrs. Howe herself seemed to realize the importance of stopping expense and putting the remnants of her capital to work.

The loneliness of widowhood was lying in wait for Mrs. Howe in Newport. "Oh how we miss the dear Chief," she exclaimed in her journal. "The house at first seems shrunken by his absence. But Maud and I, going about, find many of his little ingenious contrivances and many improvements which made the house comfortable and complete. And would, oh would to God that I had done a thousand times more for him than I ever did. I learn more deeply than ever before, how happy one is in being able to make sacrifices for other people, especially for those to whom we are bound by sacred ties. I thought I made many sacrifices for poor Chev but now I feel I ought to have done more. . . ." Mrs. Howe's first summer's work was "a short sketch of Chev's public life for the bureau of Education in Washington." She next sent the first installment of a much longer memoir to Frank Sanborn — and then she set about becoming the breadwinner of the family, consisting of herself and Maud. With no lecture agent to help her, she planned her Midwestern tour — Beloit; Cleveland; Milwaukee; Chicago. Philadelphia seemed next door to Boston by comparison.

Mrs. Howe was pleased with "a good audience and $50" at the Women's Club in Chicago. When she found no Women's club, as in Milwaukee, she became the missionary of the movement. Friends made in Milwaukee became founders of their club, and always remembered Mrs. Howe with affection. She planned a stop over to look at her Kansas lands and found, at Grasshopper, "various house lots, not remarkably good or bad — and a quarter section well situated enough." A lecture given at Sedalia netted her $31.50, and at Grasshopper she was handed a bill for back taxes.

Mrs. Howe was in Chicago at Christmastime. She went to church and the joyful music made her sad. She "shed tears, recalling dear Chev who was with us a year ago, so touching in his infirmity. On such occasions, my faulty relations to him come back with great regret, yet it is a tender sorrow, too. I cannot be fierce against my human infirmity and the dear God who shows it to me more and more, will I trust enable me to help others through my own bitter lesson."

This was the intimate, private side of Julia Ward Howe's life at this time, yet if it gives the impression that she went about weeping and constantly giving good advice — nothing could be further from the truth. At a party Christmas night at Eastlake Villa Mrs. Howe joined in the children's games, acted in charades and sang "The Muffin Man" amid laughter and applause.

Her sense of humor had by no means deserted her. She saw a sign, "Old Reliable Oysters," and burst out laughing on the street. Mrs. Howe loved to travel, and the sleeping car was a new invention which she put to most sociable uses. She talked to everyone; and sometimes, as evening came and the car rolled along through the dark featureless countryside, she got everyone to singing — old songs and new. She was "in the cars going from St. Louis to Sedalia" when she "woke herself" in the middle of the night to see whether it was 1876 or 1877. "I found my watch," she said, "and by moonlight made out (I think) that the time was 12:20. So I said 'Happy New Year' to myself and dear ones."

Summing up her experiences on this first Midwestern tour, "Kansas is a great state," Mrs. Howe said. "And some of our land, all of it in fact, will be very valuable." She pictured "coming out here to help build up the new state in building up our fortune." And she thought that "Henry Richards is the man, among my sons-in-law, to come . . ."

The difficulty, of course, would be to persuade the beautiful Maud to give up Newport and become a pioneer! "The cities in Kansas are quite gay," Mrs. Howe wrote to Maud — and by the way of extra inducement she added that they "are full of New England people." But "I know that this proposition will be received with derision," Maud's mother had to admit.

So it was "good-bye to the Middle West, to dear Madison, Wisconsin, beautiful, hospitable, warm-hearted," and to Topeka, where she had a wonderful time — "furnace-heated house" — and to St. Louis, where the proceeds of the lectures were forty-three dollars, but would double, she was sure, when her next appearance was advertised properly. Mrs. Howe scarcely counted her earnings before she began disbursing them. "For Harry, $100" and for "dear Flossy," whose husband found the law hard going, "$200." Stopping over in New York, Julia Howe bought for herself "a curious ring, a pawnbroker's pledge perhaps and very handsome." This souvenir of her first lecture tour cost Mrs. Howe ten dollars, and she said, "I am ashamed of the silly purchase, with which still, I am foolishly delighted."

"I have earned my own living without drawing one dollar from my moderate income," Mrs. Howe recorded with justified pride.[3] Gifts to her children had all been earned; but now she must take her daughter Maud to Europe! She heartily wished it were not necessary, but the other daughters had been abroad. In those days of very little opportunity for college, girls went to Europe to obtain a *cachet* of culture if their parents could possibly rake and scrape the wherewithal to take them. And besides — Maud wanted to go.

Sam Ward arrived in Boston to "take leave" on May 5, 1877. John Dee, the Howes' faithful coachman, helped with the trunks — and the *Parthia* sailed. And then "Maud came down the harbor in a steam tug, specially granted for her use and that of her friends." She arrived on board the *Parthia* "like Cleopatra, in great state" — enjoying the drama, the astonished stares of fellow passengers, as no one else could have done. . . . Unless it might have been her mother, who, at Maud's age, always loved the center of the stage.

CHAPTER TWENTY-EIGHT
Gamblers' Luck

WHEN Charles Ward achieved his failure, in 1875, there were no longer any Wards on Bond Street. Annie Mailliard, coming across the continent — her first trip all the way by train — stayed at a boarding house since Uncle Richard, the last of the banker's brothers, had died and hospitable Number 8 Bond Street had been sold. Sam's first cousin Charlie resembled Sam in every way, it seemed. He was "full of amiable qualities and was much loved" by the Ward sisters. Annie found that her loss amounted to fifty thousand dollars, part of which "belongs to Napoleon Bonaparte," she said — referring doubtless to Prince Napoleon Charles. But Charlie, calling on Annie at her boardinghouse, had "wept" and she had forgiven him.

It seemed that also, at some time previously, Charlie had "lost the list of paintings" left to Louisa by her father and kept for her by her Uncle John. The paintings he had therefore distributed as he pleased at Uncle John's death, and the "stately Copleys" which Louisa now needed to sell had disappeared. Louisa's trust fund remained exactly as Uncle John had set it up at the time of her first marriage. She now had nothing but a second mortgage on Hamilton Grange. There was "one chance in a thousand that, at the public sale . . . the property may sell for enough to cover the Emigrant Bank Mortgage which comes first, and my own," said Louisa — and she was right.

Fortunately for Charlie, his wife was wealthy in her own name and her property he had not touched. It seemed a good idea to go abroad and take the children. In Rome, Louisa, who was as forgiving as her sister Annie, was glad to see them.

"Our finances have fallen to a very low water-mark." Louisa confessed, but she did not complain. Instead she wrote to Annie of the pretty little apartment where they lived "in great retirement," having rented the Palazzo Odescalchi. Luther Terry had been very ill, and Louisa had passed anxious days and nights but he was better now — able to sit up and sketch while she read aloud. When Cousin Charlie and his family arrived, it was evident that his children had not been told about their father's failure. Louisa was touched and would not mention her losses. But when she and her daughter Daisy, having sold "horses and carriages," walked to a party given by some of their friends among the Italian nobility, it was a little hard to see Charlie and his wife riding by in their new landau. One would think the Charles Wards might have given the Luther Terrys a lift!

The impact of their mother's loss of income on the Crawford children was as extreme as their temperaments. It was the making of F. Marion, and it was the ruin of Annie, now the Baroness von Rabé. In 1873, Annie had met Baron Erich von Rabé, a Prussian officer wounded in the Franco-Prussian War. "He was tall and rather handsome in a wooden sort of way," Annie's half-sister Daisy thought. Annie, who had refused to learn German when the other Crawford children did, thought Erich's broken French enchanting. "Annie had found her mate — or master," said Daisy, shrewdly suspecting the latter.[1] Louisa ordered an immense trousseau, "piles and piles of lacy things tied together in dozens with pink ribbon" — it had been such a pleasure to Louisa to order embroidery done by some of the patient, needy Italian women she knew. The old Palazzo Odescalchi was decked out for the lavish wedding of an American princess — or so Annie seemed. The bride wore "pale tea-rose satin, bridesmaids in pale blue faille with tea-rose colored feathers in their bonnets," and Daisy was "radiant" in sea-green, with a white cashmere "polonaise." Louisa wrote all about it to her sister Annie but did not say how beautiful she herself must have looked — in "amethyst velvet with Brussels lace."

The following spring came the marriage of Mimoli to Hugh Fraser, a secretary of the British Embassy. The Odescalchi Palace saw it all — but it was all costly. Just as the last of the surviving Crawford daughters was married, their mother's checks from the United States stopped coming.

Fortunately, Louisa had a sound policy taught her by her father and her Uncle John. She always paid her bills promptly — she had few debts. But she had promised a handsome allowance to each married daughter. This could not now be paid and the Baroness von Rabé took it very badly. She demanded money of her mother, whether her mother had it to pay or not, and she reduced the gentle Louisa to helpless tears. In justice to Annie, it should be added that her husband's family put a great deal of pressure on her, for obviously they thought their son had married millions and was now being defrauded.

Matters between Louisa and her daughter Annie had reached a most unhappy crisis in 1877 when Julia Ward Howe set out for Europe with her daughter Maud. They made the Grand Tour in every sense of the word. In England, they met the Prince of Wales at two garden parties. Mrs. Howe thought Edward, Prince of Wales, was "jolly, fat and commonplace." But Maud's photograph, how obtained no one knew, began to appear for sale among those of other famous beauties.

To France, to Germany, to Switzerland — on went the Howes, mother and daughter. Mrs. Howe spoke at a Peace Conference in Geneva. In Rome she organized a women's club, an almost unbelievable feat where women were never so much as allowed out on the street without at least a servant for escort. Up the Nile went the Howes, meeting Longfellow and his daughters in their dahabeah. And to the Holy Land, where Mrs. Howe rode donkeyback for such long hours that she became almost crippled with rheumatism for a time — although filled with enthusiasm for travel none the less. At night, after a long day's sight-seeing, she wrote travel articles contracted for by newspapers back home. Although "living is much cheaper here than at home," long journeys cost money and the writing must go on.

Maud had been brought to Europe to complete her education, to be sure, but also in search of a husband, if the truth were to be told. With her pure white skin, deep blue eyes and proudly lifted head she looked like a duchess — if duchesses ever looked as they should. But marriageable dukes were few, and most of them were in search of a fortune. Although, by a sort of divine providence, rich girls were rarely pretty — the money dukes must have.

If Maud Howe ever thought it might be nice to be a baroness her visit to her cousin, Baroness Annie von Rabé, soon disillusioned her. Louisa was visiting her daughter the Baroness, and the Howes were invited to meet Louisa and Daisy Terry at Lesnian, the estate in West Prussia belonging to Erich von Rabé. Annie and Erich lived in the Pavilion, which was connected with the main house where Erich's mother lived with assorted relatives. The Pavilion always belonged to a married son and heir, and had the advantage of being haunted. Every night, Annie came to the main house, where her mother had a room,

to rail at her about the loss of her money. Every night, that is, until Aunt Julia arrived and found this out.

"Aunt Julia was a personage. I never met anyone in the least like her," said fourteen-year-old Daisy, now for the first time getting acquainted with an aunt who would also become a friend of hers in later years. Mrs. Howe was "a small woman of no particular shape or carriage," Daisy said — perhaps contrasting her in her mind with Louisa Terry. Aunt Julia's "clothes were never quite taken care of, her bonnets never quite straight on her head; and yet there was about her presence an unforgettable distinction and importance. Her speaking voice was very beautiful, and her face had a sensitive gravity, a look of compassionate wisdom, until a twinkle of fun rippled over it and a naughty imp laughed in her eyes."

One of the first things that Mrs. Howe did was to go out into the town and talk to the Polish people living under German masters. A fine-looking old man, a shoemaker, spoke German and told Mrs. Howe about the serfdom on Lesnian lands. She was shocked. She was next called to account by her nephew-in-law for talking to peasants — something which was simply not done. It goes without saying that Mrs. Howe continued to do it.

And then, one night, Julia walked in upon one of those terrible scenes between her sister Louisa and her niece, Annie von Rabé. Louisa was in tears, begging piteously to be forgiven for something she had not done. "Aunt Julia could upon occasion show temper — her hair had been red," said Daisy, who was there. Now was one of the occasions; and when Julia Ward Howe got through telling her niece what she thought of her, it was Annie von Rabé who ran weeping from the room. It was a penitent Annie who came back next morning to beg her mother's pardon.

Mrs. Howe, her daughter Maud, Mrs. Terry and Daisy left East Prussia to travel to Rome by easy stages, sight-seeing as they went. They were hardly established in Louisa's small Roman apartment before Annie von Rabé appeared, her mood of penitence over. With the help of her husband and her sister, Louisa drew up an agreement which she and her daughter Annie signed. "I do hereby solemnly swear," wrote Louisa Ward Terry, ". . . that my husband Luther Terry has been perfectly loyal to my children . . . that their entire patrimony has been due to his unwearied efforts in their behalf. . . ." Louisa further stated that because of living abroad, she had given Ward and Company power of attorney. Although she did not say so in this document, her Uncle John Ward had required this of her. But here, after John Ward's death, was the way in which Charles Ward had been able to sell his cousin's securities — using Louisa's money to play the stock market.

Louisa agreed to pay her daughter "a yearly allowance of three thousand Italian lira" as soon as the lease on the Palazzo Odescalchi should run out — for the palace had been sublet at a figure which did not cover all it cost the Terrys. One does not get rid of a palace overnight.

Annie signed a paper stating that her mother had "never been guilty of a breach of faith toward" her. Annie von Rabé, "having become by marriage a member of the nobility of East Prussia," used her right of acting independently of her husband when she wrote her name.

This was a sad exchange of documents[2] and Julia Ward Howe, in her journal, was severe with her sister Louisa. "My dear Sister has always been a most fond and indulgent parent. She has indeed been unwise and compliant in many things . . . but her daughter's wholesale condemnation of her today was a thing which could break a parent's heart."

Sam Ward had been involved in Charlie's crash, of course. According to Charlie, Sam owed him eighteen thousand dollars — and apparently according to Sam it was the other way around. Sam had been doing very well as a lobbyist. His California clients had been most grateful and among his fees was stock in the "Gould and Curry and Ophir mines" when they were "in bonanza." Two years later they "petered out" and "split into horses," Sam, it would seem, failing to get out in time. But he knew where and how to meet more Californians.

Not all of Sam's clients dealt in gold mines, land, or stocks and bonds, however. Sam was glad to act as agent and sell anything — even literature. In 1873, he made one of his flying visits to Boston, going out to Cambridge to see Longfellow as he always found time to do. Longfellow had just finished a poem which he read aloud to Sam. It was "The Hanging of the Crane."

"Your poem made music all night in the cars," Sam wrote from the Brevoort House on his return to New York. He thought his "trotting friend, Bonner," might want to buy Longfellow's poem and he would see the Irish-born printer with the passion for fast horses. Starting as a typesetter for the *Hartford Courant*, Bonner had now bought the *Merchant's Ledger* of New York, a drygoods advertising paper, which

he was turning into a popular weekly. Bonner spent large sums of money for fast-trotting horses and he paid what were then fantastic sums for big names for his paper. Sam told Longfellow he thought he could get two thousand dollars out of Bonner for "The Hanging of the Crane."

In the end, Sam got three thousand dollars for Longfellow and one thousand for himself. The transaction took about two months and he said, "I feel I fairly earned my lyrical brokerage." As Sam Ward had sold Longfellow's "Skeleton in Armor" to the *Knickerbocker*, in 1840, for twenty-five dollars, this showed great progress on the part of both poet and agent.

Sam Ward was King of the Lobby for about nine years. Three delegates from Nicaragua and their interpreter arrived in the United States soon after the Civil War and they described Sam Ward's methods as a lobbyist. They were under the impression that they met Mr. Ward by chance on the station platform in Jersey City and they were surprised to find that he happened to be going to Washington, D.C., on their train.

The newcomers looked Sam over. His "mustache and imperial were as white as snow," contrasting with his complexion, which was "brown and glowing with health." On his left hand he wore "a sapphire like the Pope's emerald in size and beauty."

The South Americans approved the ring but not Sam's clothes, which were in marked contrast to their own tight-fitting elegance. Sam was "short of stature and youthfully dressed in clumsy clothing of English make, that did not entirely conceal a figure of immense muscular power." Sam's "dark gray, or brown or blue eyes, for they varied with the atmosphere, sparkled with good humor," his new acquaintances remembered. But if he could have read their description of his bold English plaid coat which he loved so much and the impeccable London tailoring of which he was so proud, it is hard to say just what color Sam's eyes would have been.

"We did not know Sam Ward but he knew us thoroughly, our wants, our weaknesses and our vanities," admitted the intepreter for Don Fernando Guzman and Don Luis Molina. "Our party was Spanish" and Sam spoke Spanish "with fluency and correctness but with a French accent, in his low, husky voice. He led the conversation to Spanish literature and quoted with equal ease from the *Cronica del Cid*, the poems of Góngora and the plays of Calderón."

When the Nicaraguans arrived in Washington, they still thought that they had met the remarkable Sam Ward by chance. They were again surprised when he "proved to be the friend of the men with whom" they had come "to negotiate." They heard Sam Ward called "King of the Lobby." Albeit better acquainted with dictators than with kings, they felt sure they knew how kings ought to behave and Sam was not their idea of royalty, "unless kings move with a bustling rapidity, leaning forward, planting firmly large feet rather splay in their set and with arms of uncommon length." Smugly, the Nicaraguans boasted of selling a charter for a waterway now silted-up and useless. Nobody benefited by their visit to Washington, they thought, except themselves and Welcker, the restaurateur.

It so happened, however, that Welcker was in a way Sam's property and in every way his discovery. Welcker was a German ex-butcher when he and Sam first met. He had a little place on Pennsylvania Avenue where he was trying to run a lunchroom and he was on the verge of failure. Perhaps Sam caught a whiff of good German cooking as he was passing by one day. In any case, he came in, tasted the food, and sized up his man. Welcker kept a clean kitchen, he was not afraid of work and he could cook in a good honest German way. The two men struck a bargain and Sam Ward taught Welcker to cook all sorts of dishes as well as his native German ones. Vintage wines were sent for from the Widow Clicquot, who was running a family business after her husband's death, and "Veuve Clicquot" was soon the favorite champagne in Washington — to be had only at Welcker's — at least for a time.

The hearty food, the genial atmosphere, were far better adapted to Washington at this period than Delmonico's elegance would have been. Sam Ward lunched there every day and there were outsiders who thought that Sam was actually mine host. He was always getting up to greet friends, introducing people and arranging seating as if by chance — but actually for professional lobbying purposes.

When Welcker died, Sam was for the first time tired of Washington. He might lose a patron and win him back — he might lose a fortune, but always expected to win again on the next turn of the wheel. Only God could make a cook like Welcker and even then it required years of work on Sam's part to perfect the creation.

Sam left Washington and took rooms on 8th Street in New York, near St. Mark's Church, "keeping house in a delightful way. He had no business — went to no clubs — but entertained half a dozen friends at 'the Light House,' as they called his place." Sam's sister Julia, calling

on him one day, found him out but saw the boy he kept as his "page" — and who looked enough like him to be his son. She made no further comment.

Sam still went to Washington now and then. He happened to be there in March, 1874, when Charles Sumner died suddenly. The two men never liked each other and after the argument with Sumner, as best man, over Julia's marriage settlement, her brother had reason to feel resentful. Yet resentment was something almost entirely left out of Sam Ward's make-up. He now wrote with great sympathy to Long-fellow, knowing how much Longfellow had always loved Sumner.

"I was in my bath when Williamson, an Amesbury man and a friend of Whittier's, knocked at my door and said that Mr. Sumner had been alarmingly ill since mid-night." Sam telegraphed to Longfellow and then went over to Sumner's house to find that "a vast crowd of freed men, with the gloomiest of faces darkened the street below."

Sumner's sudden illness was aggravated by the news of "his wife's intention to re-marry," Sam thought (though Dr. Howe might not have agreed) "and by the revocation of the Edict of Censure by the Massachusetts legislature." This would seem to have been an "Edict of Censure" against Grant that grew out of Sumner's objection to the "Dominican project." This implacable opposition to both Johnson and Grant and his personal bitterness toward them marred Sumner's great career.

At eleven in the evening "he was heard to fall" in his study. And Sam Ward said that the "last audible words" which Sumner "uttered, with the old ring in his voice, were 'Don't let the Bill fail!' " — and then, in a loud voice, " 'I mean the Bill of Rights,' " Sumner said.

So died a great statesman who fought a brave fight for Negro eman-cipation and civil rights for Negroes. In his private life, Charles Sumner was unhappy. The role he played as friend and adviser to Dr. Howe in his domestic affairs extended his own fatal gift for causing misery to others. Yet now that Sumner was gone, Sam Ward could say that "Sumner's sweet and gracious ways and unvarying sympathy" were what his friends would remember. It might be hard to forget how far from "sweet and gracious" he had been when Julia Ward Howe came to Washington. He had thought she was wrong to come and it never crossed his mind that *he* could be wrong about anything. Perhaps that was the key to his character. It was the nation's gain that Charles Sumner was so right about so many things, so often.

Sam Ward could not help rejoicing that he himself was "so well and hardy at sixty." Soon after Sumner's death he went out to see "dear Longo at Nahant." Longfellow was standing on the porch of his cottage when Sam drove up. "I felt you were on the way. I knew you would come!" Longfellow exclaimed.

Since his wife's death, Longfellow had been a lonely man, and friendships, which always meant much to him, were now still more important. The devotion on the part of two such dissimiliar men as Longfellow and Sam Ward had stood the test of many years and to some people seemed most strange. Almost the only thing they had in common nearly caused their only rupture — Sam also wrote poetry. A phrase in one of Longfellow's letters to him, "the enamelled goblet of life," caused Sam to write a long poem which he recited one evening — telling his parlor audience that the poem was Longfellow's! Gleefully he wrote that he had been believed. And for the first and only time, Longfellow was sharp with Sam. Sam Ward was never under any circumstances to do such a thing again.

At the time of Charles Ward's failure, Sam gave up his rooms on 8th Street and went to live at the Brevoort. There Annie found him when she came east from California to see what if anything could be done about the missing "Government bonds" which had belonged to the Bonapartes. And Sam had one of his inspired ideas. It was just two days before Thanksgiving. Why not spend the holiday in Boston with their sister Julia?

They were driving to the station in a carriage when they "passed a row of houses near Madison Avenue." Sam pointed out one of them. " 'Mr. Astor is dying there of pneumonia,' " he said. Sam's implacable father-in-law had never forgiven Sam for his second marriage, and Maddie Ward had been kept as much as possible from seeing her father.

"Little Maddie" was a grown woman now, however. She was Margaret Astor Ward Chanler, wife of John Winthrop Chanler and the mother of eleven children.[3] Her own mistress since her marriage in everything except the disposal of her money, she welcomed her father to her home in New York. Sam Ward spoke with evident pride of the joyful uproar with which his grandchildren always greeted him when he came to see them bearing gifts.

When Annie returned to New York after Thanksgiving, the expected event had happened. William Backhouse Astor died November 24, 1875. But there was further news which brought real grief to Sam. His daughter Margaret had come down with pneumonia — contracted, it was said, at the cemetery on that grim and blustery day when her grandfather was buried. "As soon as she was taken ill she sent for her lawyer," they told Annie. After the "influx of wealth from her grandfather's estate," and now that she was free to do as she pleased, she "wanted to make a generous provision for her father." She had always loved him, and surely there was never a more loving father than Sam Ward. But when the lawyer came, Mrs. Chanler "was forbidden to make any effort" and he went away again promising to return when she was stronger. Within a few hours she died — not of pneumonia alone, but of the early miscarriage of her twelfth child.

Mrs. Howe came to New York to be with Sam — their sister Annie having gone back to California. Sam had lost both his sons by Medora Grymes, and he was much broken up by Maddie's loss — his only remaining child. It comforted him to have Julia with him during the ordeal of the funeral, and, as Annie said, neither of them dreamed how soon he must go to her to "perform a like service" when she lost her Chevalier.

Maddie's bequest to her father of an annuity of a thousand dollars was a sort of final Astor insult. It was the amount she had been allowed to set aside in her Astor-dictated will. But Sam Ward accepted what he considered mere pocket money. He had by no means given up his golden dreams, and he was right. He had one more fortune to make.

No one was making very much money in 1875, however — as Julia deduced when her brother drove out to Newport to see her, not in his usual glittering style with matched bays and black barouche, but in a "one horse carryall."

"The first evidence of wealth is your equipage," Sam Ward's cousin Ward McAllister said. "A gentleman can always walk but he cannot afford a shabby equipage." Four o'clock in the afternoon was the time, and Belleview Avenue was the place where Newport went riding.[4] "Nowhere in America could so many elegant turn-outs be seen. . . . The quiet though elegant carriages with crests on them" were "Bostonian; the most stylish horse-furniture and matched horses" came from New York. Every afternoon Newport was a horse-drawn "pageant" with "beautiful women and cultivated men, passing and re-passing, mingling and separating, smiling, saluting, admiring and being admired." Sam Ward might be reduced to a one-horse carryall but he knew where to look for money among the horse-drawn set. Keene, the California millionaire, was his man.

James Robert Keene was fourteen years younger than Sam Ward. He was born in Liverpool, England, but referred to his father as "an

Irish gentleman." Coming to this country at the age of fourteen, Keene was a young Jack-of-all-trades turning his hand to peddling milk, editing a newspaper, running a wood lathe, mining — and grooming horses. The Comstock lode in Nevada gave him his first lucky break in speculation and he made ten thousand dollars in silver mine stocks. Taking this stake with him, he invaded the San Francisco stock market as a street broker. He made forty thousand dollars, lost it, and got back into the game again with Nevada stocks. By 1875, Keene was said to be worth five million.

Somewhere along the line, when he was down on his luck, alone and very ill, Sam Ward befriended James R. Keene. When Keene came to New York, it was Sam who showed him how to enjoy spending his money. No one was better equipped than Sam for each role: that of good Samaritan and that of spendthrift. A historian might have explained the few Colonial buildings still left in New York better than Sam could, but Sam was a guide to people.

Keene "became greatly interested in Wall Street and its mechanisms," and who but Sam had more Wall Street experience? The Californian decided to show Wall Street what he could do, but Jay Gould sold Keene out in the pool they formed in Western Union stock. Sam suffered losses along with Keene; but after 1875, with its "Black Friday," its scandals, and its Congressional investigations, Sam rose again with Keene.

At the top of Keene's wild speculating he made nine million dollars, they said. Sam Ward made nothing like as much; but he now had his third fortune. He dealt with it characteristically. First he helped to secure to Annie the ranch that she loved. To his sister Julia Ward Howe he gave a home — Number 241 Beacon Street.

In her new home, Mrs. Howe had a "parlor fitted up as a library" for Sam and his was the bedroom above it. These rooms were promptly claimed, not by Sam but by his nephew F. Marion Crawford, who wrote his second book, *Dr. Claudius*, there. In *Dr. Claudius* everyone recognized a flattering picture of Sam Ward — and indeed F. Marion Crawford had every reason to write kind words about his uncle. Sam Ward had done everything he could do to further young Crawford's career — introducing him to Hurlbert of the *World*, Charles de Kay of the *New York Times*, and Jeannette Gilder of the *Critic*. And again in *Dr. Claudius*, F. Marion Crawford scored a success as he had with *Mr. Isaacs*, written at Oak Glen in Newport in his Aunt Julia's "green parlor" — as she called the ring of trees her husband had set out for her.

Louisa and her daughter Daisy spent most of the year 1881 in the United States, and it was another of Sam's delightful ideas to send for Annie Mailliard so that the three sisters could be together on Julia's birthday, May 27.

"Soon after 7 A.M. arrived Uncle Sam with my dear sister Annie Mailliard from California," Mrs. Howe wrote in her journal. "My sister is very little changed, always a most tender, sensitive woman. Sister L. . . . came in at 11 to bring me gifts, with Mr. Terry and Daisy and Uncle Sam. When Sister Annie Mailliard appeared, Sister L. almost fainted with delight and astonishment."

Sam was the one who really got the most pleasure out of his birthday surprise as he watched his three sisters, middle-aged women now, acting like girls together again. Sam gave "pearls to Daisy Terry," to Maud Howe "a new jewel which is the most beautiful I have ever seen," her mother said — and to sister Julia, for her new house, "$100 to buy curtains, $500 for carpets," a mirror and a couch.

A nervous, anxious note from Sam in November, 1881, however, indicated that once more his luck was running out. "I have been left alone to fight these demons without a helping hand," he wrote Julia, without exactly specifying what "demons" he meant. "Your presence would probably have differed me many thousands. I am working my life out for all of you and it would be more for your interest if you took life less in a happy-go-lucky style and had some thought for the poor old horse who has made himself a beast of burden to help you all in time of need."

Sam Ward always had trouble telling right from wrong. His sister, Julia Ward Howe, had no difficulty whatever in this direction. When she suspected that he wanted her eminently respectable presence in New York, in her black velvet and lace and wearing her mother's diamonds, to lend an air of solid value to a doubtful deal — she simply would not go. Sam had wanted her to escort the beautiful Maud to a gingerbread monstrosity called a Newport cottage, leased to some of his more shady clients, and Mrs. Howe went — but only once. She could forgive a good deal of vulgar display and only laughed at the Belmonts with their palace for horses — rooms for themselves on an upper floor. But there were houses she would not enter, and people she would not be seen with — once she found out what they were like.

By the middle of December, 1882, Mrs. Howe put down in her journal that she had a telegram from Sam telling her to keep all his mail. "We made up his room and expected him to arrive early next day," she said. But on the following day, "we received a letter from our dear relative, telling us of his sudden and private departure by the advice of counsel."

Sam Ward was involved in a grandiose promotion scheme centering around Long Beach, New Jersey; but, as usual, he had overextended himself. He had gone to Europe on much shorter notice than ever before. His third fortune had gone the way of the other two.

CHAPTER TWENTY-NINE
The Lamp-lighted Staircase

SAM WARD was next heard of in England, after his "sudden and private departure" from the United States "by advice of counsel." His first letter from abroad was written at the Duke of Sutherland's house, where Sam was a guest. He rose at "5:30 to catch the sunshine," he said, and to write innumerable letters "to the plash of fountains" in the garden. With obvious delight, he described the "Ducal residence" as having "sixty guest rooms and so many passages and stairways that one needs the thread of Ariadne to find one's way." If all the sixty guest rooms were occupied, then Sam was as remarkable as ever, for he described himself as "the guest of honor."

Sam commended the food, especially the Duke's cherries, which were so large that he wondered "why they were not chosen as the forbidden fruit." In his next letter it was the Earl of Dunraven with whom Sam Ward was dining, and after that he was off to Edinburgh to be the guest of Lord Aberdeen — then to "Stafford House to meet the Prince and Princess of Wales."

Then it was time for the races, and Sam was at Ascot where the "Royal enclosure was like a ball room with the top off." "The Prince was everywhere," and Sam said that he "attempted to avoid" Edward, Prince of Wales, "who was constantly running up against" him. The Prince presented Sam Ward to Lady Lonsdale, who instantly addressed him as "Uncle Sam."

"What with old acquaintances whom I did not recognize and who rushed up to me to thank me for hospitalities I had forgotten, and with new ones, male and female, I passed four exhausting hours on my feet," Sam said. But he could not deny that he had enjoyed himself hugely, whether his feet hurt him or not.

The alleged avoidance of the Prince of Wales was for home consumption — but Sam had a good reason. Prince Edward "was busy with his betting book" and even Sam realized that he was not in a position to bet with royalty right now.

But after discounting Sam's typical attitude of penitence and reform, which he always assumed after a disaster, there was for the first time a note of genuine weariness in his letters. When his friends, Lord and Lady Rosebery invited him to come to their country home for a rest, he was glad to accept. Archibald, Earl of Rosebery, was thirty years younger than Sam Ward and called him "Uncle." His lordship was an ardent follower of the turf but also a brilliant debater in the House of Lords and he eventually succeeded Gladstone as Prime Minister. Political enemies sometimes brought up the matter of his horse racing against him, but with little success; and he was genuinely fond of Sam Ward, who shared his enthusiasm for horses. Lord Rosebery's wife, Lady Hannah, was the only daughter of Baron Rothschild. Sam Ward began dictating the story of his life to Lady Hannah as they sat in Lord Rosebery's garden.

Sam had always wanted to be an author. This is not the same thing as wanting to write, as he should have learned by now. His great *History of Mathematics*, begun with ambitious fervor, had been carried on for a while by his German friend Mersch — but had been abandoned long since. In 1876, Sam privately published a volume of verse called *Lyrical Recreations*. He gave his book away to his friends with such enthusiasm that he awarded himself a second edition. Some of his poetry was almost good, capable of evoking mental pictures of strange sights and scenes. Most of it was much too long and involved. On his return voyage from Nicaragua, Sam had begun a novel, which he abandoned after writing about two hundred pages. Now he referred to his reminiscences as "my book" and felt that it was coming to an exciting climax.[1]

But Lord and Lady Rosebery decided to take a trip around the world and Sam never finished his book. He went to Sorrento. Louisa and Luther Terry and their children Daisy and Arthur were there, and so was Mimoli Crawford, now Mrs. Hugh Fraser, and her two little boys. Uncle Sam Ward loved them all, but the lodestone which really drew him to Sorrento was his favorite nephew, F. Marion Crawford.

Francis Marion Crawford had lived under a succession of names in his own family. First he was Franklino, the angel child — in appearance only. Then he was Frank, the reluctant schoolboy. Now he was Marion,

the successful novelist, and his Uncle Sam Ward was immensely proud
of him. "Marion is fagging away at his novel, which I think is likely to
prove his best," Sam wrote. And in one of his rare but excellent letters
to his uncle, F. Marion told how much better he worked with Uncle
Sam by his side. Sam Ward believed the compliment with all his genial
but egotistical heart — and as a matter of fact it was probably true.
Sam was stimulating company for titled Britishers, for American turf-
men and millionaires, for California pick and shovel men — and for a
young novelist.

One of the strongest indications that Sam Ward was weary was that
pretty girls interested him a trifle less than usual. He still sent flowers
and verses to girls he chanced to meet, but he was able to choose only
three to whom to pay court — and only in the form of letters. It was
several years since he had even jokingly offered to marry a girl of
twenty. He began to complain that girls were no longer witty, that
they only echoed back what he said to them. Underneath it all was the
faint suggestion that he himself was becoming but an echo of days
long gone.

The death of Longfellow, coming just before Sam left the United
States, was a severe blow. Sam was pleased to have his nephew F. Marion Crawford interview him about his memories of a long friendship,
and it was gratifying to have Hurlbert of the *World* take down a
dictated article and ask for another. But this did not bring back a
friend. To whom would Sam now send his poems, confident of that
word of praise for some line which Longfellow affectionately managed
to discover?

Sam was in London again in 1883, until December, when he went
to Rome to visit his sister Louisa.

Louisa Terry was now living in her third Italian palace, the Altemps.
Somehow, a little of her capital had withstood the assaults of Charlie's
efforts against it and she had a modest income. Moreover, in his tower
room at the Palazzo Altemps, F. Marion Crawford drove his pen to
good purpose and he would see that his mother never needed to worry
any more.

Sam Ward looked about him in Rome and began to collect new
friends. He found his sister's small but elegant circle of Italian nobility
delightful. Then there were Marion Crawford's friends, some of them
very strange ones. While in the Orient, Marion had dabbled in various
forms of mysticism with all a writer's instinct for dramatic experience.

Oriental mysticism was having a vogue in Boston and in Rome, following on the heels of mesmerism — which now seemed crude by comparison. Sam Ward became a Buddhist, and "aspired to the position of an Adept," he told Louisa, very much to her dismay. He was "in direct spiritual communication" with faraway Buddhist followers, he believed, and he went to tea parties given by ladies dressed in flowing garments who foretold the future by various means, including crystal balls. It was not like Sam to do anything by halves; and what he had always needed was a really reliable crystal ball.

Then there were the artists. Sam had never known many artists and he realized that he had been missing a great deal. Jack Elliott, a friend of F. Marion Crawford's, was painting in Rome, his studio being in the midst of those of other young artists who called themselves "Spanish," whether they were born in Spain or not. Their teacher was Spanish — hence their name. They delighted Sam Ward, and he in turn fascinated them. One of them modeled a bust of him and Jack Elliott asked to paint his portrait.

Jack Elliott's portrait of Sam Ward turned out to be one of the best things he ever did. There on canvas appeared a venerable old man, his great forehead and fine bald head handsomely high-lighted. Sam no longer wore the smart goatee, but a long white beard divided into two parts cascaded over his chest. A much-lengthened mustache mingled with it frostily. Sam was dressed in what might have been a bulky Prince Albert, but it gave the impression of a philosopher's dark robe. Wonderful hands, clasped right over left, the great sapphire gleaming on the ring finger, completed a picture which could have been called "Chinese Philosopher." Sam's eyes, under half-concealing lids, communed with the spirits of dead sages. Or did they? There was certainly wisdom in the glance but there was also a gleam of secret amusement which the painter's brush caught and betrayed.

When the sittings were over, Jack Elliott would walk back to the Palazzo Altemps with Uncle Sam. And now Sam seemed to throw off his weariness. They stopped at the foot of the stairs leading up out of the Piazza di Spagna to look at the flower vendors surrounded by their wares and the beautiful Italian peasant girls who gathered on the steps to offer themselves as artists' models. Uncle Sam looked the girls over and rubbed his hands — a characteristic gesture. "Jack," he said, "give me a clean shirt and a shilling and I am ready to start life all over again!" This was not Sam in his Oriental phase — Sam Ward was himself again.

Sam set out for the Island of Malta to meet Lord and Lady Rosebery, who were on their way back from their world tour. He was refreshed and rested, his mind seething with new schemes. Everyone
would help him and he would make himself a new fortune. In Naples
he ordered one of his favorite meals — steamed mussels with drawn
butter. Nothing was ever more succulently sweet unless it might be
his own native Rhode Island steamed clams. But the Bay of Naples was
not quite as clean as the waters around Newport, and Sam became
violently ill. They said he had "cholera." His friends the Roseberys
failed to arrive, and when Sam finally reached Rome again Louisa gave
one cry of dismay and ordered him to bed.

"The beloved brother was not an easy patient to nurse. He had his
own fixed ideas about medicine and was constantly insisting upon the
extraordinary remedies that he had picked up in various corners of
the world. It was difficult to persuade him that the amount of Quinine
desirable for the breaking up of a Guatemala fever could not be given
him."

Francis Marion was away and Sam occupied his room in
the tower of the Palazzo Altemps, which delighted his romantic soul
and had other advantages besides. When he was too hot with the fever,
he could get out of bed, light a cigarette and stroll up and down the
stone-paved corridor outside his room or stand in the breeze "between
door and window." When he was caught at this, they scolded him;
but when he came down with pneumonia he said it was caused by in-
sufficient quinine or lack of some strange Peruvian bark that no one
would get for him. "Not until much reduced, would he obey the doctor's orders — even then he would elude" his watchful family of
Terrys if he could, and "if he could persuade old Lucia or the handsome sailor servant to aid him in doing so."

It was a relief to Louisa when her son Francis Marion came home,
for he was the one with the most influence over Uncle Sam. The handsome sailor servant was Marion's, a crew member from his felucca
which he kept on the Mediterranean coast. But it was necessary to
send to the Convent of Bon Secours for a nursing Sister "who dominated" Sam. He came to like and trust her so that, except in the matter
of his vast correspondence, he was "tractable."

"Oh those endless letters," Louisa moaned. "The doctor expressly
forbade the labor and excitement of them but Uncle Sam was immov-
able." What a time for his sister and his doctor to propose giving up
his friends, Sam must have thought — when he needed them most!

On May 8, 1884, Louisa wrote: "I have almost lost track of the many weeks he has been ill here. They seemed to go in hopeless succession. Now we think he has reached the happy turning-point unless some new unfavorable symptom appears, and the family heart smiles anew."

As she sat by her brother's bedside, Louisa "looked back to three years ago." It had been her sister Julia's birthday and the three Ward sisters "so miraculously passed it together in Boston: Sister Annie smuggled across the plains, just to knock at" Julia's door, "that Spring morning. It was one of dear Brother's most successful coups; just one of those delicious surprises that one comes upon once in a lifetime."

The hottest days of the Roman summer were approaching and Sam, as his strength increased, began to think with longing of a little town on the Italian Riviera which he had once visited. Pegli was just six miles west of Genoa, on a high cliff overlooking the Mediterranean. A castle, in medieval style, dominated the town. In the miniature harbor clustered fishing vessels with lateen sails of blue, sienna-red or yellow; and at night the church bells called the faithful from the sea or from the terraced plots of ground where fruits and flowers grew in riotous profusion — as if to reward the patient toil with which their beds had been hollowed out of the cliffside. As Sam Ward remembered Pegli, he felt sure he could stretch out in the sun there on some flower-fragrant terrace, look out upon the sea and grow well — and young again.

If Mr. Ward could stand the trip it would do no harm to try Pegli, the doctor said. The date was set, then canceled when new symptoms appeared. But four days later, improvement was marked. Everything had been made ready for the journey, "stretcher, mattress, pillows." Francis Marion was going with his uncle and also "the beautiful Sorrento sailor whom Marion has been training as a body servant and who had been devoted to Uncle Sam throughout his illness."

At the last minute, a new difficulty arose. "The Sister of Bon Secours," a middle-aged and formidable lady, "objected seriously to going off with so many men." Margaret Terry agreed to go to Pegli to chaperone the nun.

It was about eight in the evening when Sam Ward, in dressing gown and slippers, was lifted to the stretcher. "We made the Palazzo Altemps alight with lamps and candles and flowers," Louisa said. The Terrys' faithful manservant and the Sorrento sailor carried Sam "through many rooms, down the many stairs." They wanted him to feel "as though going forth to a festival." [2]

Sam "smiled at the perfection of each arrangement." As the tower flights of stairs were succeeded by the wide ceremonial staircase, as candles gave way to lamps and, finally, in the street before the palace door the smoky torches flared, Sam Ward smiled and "waved his hand." Flowers banked the marble stairs; the palace servants gathered, bowing and curtsying. Louisa's smile and Luther Terry's cheerful handclasp did not deceive Sam Ward. He was being carried along as at a festive funeral, and he could not have devised a better one himself. Yet here he was alive and able to enjoy it. He chuckled softly to himself as they drove off — the doctor at his feet, Sister Marius at his head.

Sam lived to see his blue Mediterranean. It was amazing how well he stood the trip, they said. Ten days after he arrived in Pegli, on May 19, 1884, he was sitting up, dictating a letter to Lord Rosebery. He was accepting his Lordship's invitation to spend the summer in England, and his letter was full of future plans. But Sam Ward never quite finished this letter. His heart stopped beating.

F. Marion Crawford and Margaret Terry chose the burial spot for their uncle. It was "a lovely hilltop crowned with ilexes, overlooking the sea."

Sam would have liked that.

CHAPTER THIRTY
A Natural Saint

LOUISA TERRY was touched to find that her brother Sam had made a recent will leaving her everything. He had done a great deal for his other two sisters, and he had still hoped that there would be time to do something handsome for Louisa. As it was, his "everything" was very little. There were a few books bought abroad at different times and already in Louisa's keeping. If Sam's creditors had left any of the "bibelots" and paintings in Sam's rooms in New York, it would be difficult for Louisa to claim them. As soon as the news of Sam's death reached the family in the United States, Julia's young lawyer son-in-law, who had been instructed by Sam to burn certain letters in this event, did so — including, it was said, a most indiscreet diary. This was a real loss to later generations. To Louisa came Sam's great sapphire ring, and she gave it to her son Arthur Terry. Not surprisingly, later heirs considered it too regal to wear.

But Sam Ward left Louisa a legacy which creditors could never touch nor lawyers burn nor fashion discard. As she sat down to write to her sisters about their brother's death, she found herself remembering all the wonderful things he had done for all of them — and for her especially.

During the summer of 1881, a plan of Sam Ward's had been delightful and of far-reaching effect. Louisa and her daughter Daisy were visiting in the United States that summer — Daisy was "a debutante"; and Uncle Sam had engaged a "cliff cottage for them at Newport — one of the row of houses which had been built beyond the Cliff House." Next door was Cliff Lawn, the summer home of the Chanlers and filled with young people — Sam Ward's grandchildren. The two oldest boys, Armstrong and Winthrop, known as Archie and

Wintie, were just the right age to go sailing with their cousin Daisy Terry or take her to picnics — an informal-sounding name for most elaborate outdoor parties. "Wintie was the most entirely charming boy I had ever seen," Margaret Terry said.[1]

Wintie went to Harvard and Daisy went back to Rome. She never forgot Wintie Chanler, nor did she in any way revise her opinion of him; but during the next few years she went through a sufficiently absorbing experience. The Roman Church "had always seemed beautiful to her" but she knew that her mother and above all her father would feel unhappy if she became a Catholic. The Terrys had gone to a country village for the summer and the simple faith of the country people, the remarkable preaching of the parish priest, moved Daisy deeply. She decided to study to become a Roman Catholic, and she wrote to her half-brother Marion for advice, adding: "Do not think I am doing this behind mother's back."

It had been a sad surprise to Louisa when Mimoli, the first of her children, was drawn into the Church of Rome. Louisa had wept and called the Episcopal clergyman to come and have a talk with her daughter. Most unhappy, Mimoli gave up her project. Then Francis Marion, on his return from India, became a Catholic; and now, when Daisy who was in some ways the dearest to Louisa of all her daughters announced the same intention — Louisa had nothing to say. She felt she had made a mistake with Mimoli. Daisy must follow her heart.

It must be admitted that Julia Ward Howe, stanch Unitarian that she was, felt that here was further proof that her sister Louisa had spoiled her children. And Luther Terry, not named in vain for the great reformer Martin Luther, was unreconciled to his daughter Daisy's change of religion. There were further complications in store for Daisy when her cousin Winthrop Chanler came to Rome to visit.

It was really her son, F. Marion Crawford, around whom Louisa's life revolved, however — and that of the whole family as well. They now went most often to Sorrento for the summer — because Marion liked it there. *Dr. Claudius,* his second novel affectionately portraying his fabulous Uncle Sam, came out in 1883, the year before Sam Ward died. So often such a tribute comes too late; it must have been a great source of satisfaction to Marion to watch his uncle's proud and happy expression as he handed out to all his friends copies of the book that did him so much justice. The novel Marion was "fagging away on" just before Sam Ward died must have been *A Roman Singer.*

Title followed title in such rapid succession that there were sometimes two in one year.

Marion wrote "in a cave," for the cliffs along the Mediterranean were full of them and he had found one where he could set up a table in the cool shadows and look out upon the sea.[2] He wrote fast, "covering sheet after sheet of foolscap with his neat hand" with never a blot or a correction. The speed, the white heat at which he worked was very like his father's; and, like his father, he had great confidence in his own ability. F. Marion Crawford's good opinion was abundantly corroborated. He was a best seller and the darling of his publishers' hearts — the "first novelist to make a million dollars." [3]

Immediately after his Uncle Sam's death, Marion went to Constantinople where he was paying court to Elizabeth Berdan, a blond young lady constantly referred to in his mother's letters as "Marion's beautiful Bessie Berdan." Surrounded by various female relatives who had been beauties in their day (or so they said), Bessie had been brought up to believe that every man she met would fall at her feet. There was just enough truth in her idea to make her an accomplished flirt. Her father was General Berdan who invented the Berdan rifle used in the Civil War and spent the rest of his life trying to collect a large sum he felt the Government owed him. This unhappy legacy he bequeathed to F. Marion Crawford, for Marion married Bessie Berdan in August, 1885. For years, Crawford tried to unscramble the lawsuits and collect some money for his wife's widowed mother. But all that was far in the future, and in 1885 Louisa was writing to her sisters that there was prospect of "a Marionette."

In time, everyone but his mother knew that F. Marion Crawford's marriage fell short of success. The habit of coquetry grows less and less becoming to a married woman whose blond beauty is fading or supported by obvious art. In fairness, it should be added that F. Marion Crawford, extremely handsome, suddenly famous and with no mean opinion of himself, was perhaps not the ideal husband. In any case, Marion tried for several years to make himself believe that he was living the happy outcome of one of his own novels.

In Rome, the F. Marion Crawfords lived at the Palazzo Altemps in an apartment opposite the one occupied by Louisa and Luther Terry. The old palace was being gradually cut up into small apartments, and this one was "fitted up most charmingly." But a small apartment in a palace could not hold F. Marion Crawford for long. In summer, he had been renting the Villa Renzis in Sorrento — an enormous stone fortress rising high on a cliff far above the Mediterranean. It had a fairy-tale quality about it, and could have served as an illustration for "The Sleeping Beauty" — so Marion decided to buy it. This was easier said than done. Members of the Italian nobility were willing enough to rent a palace or two to rich Americans and live on the proceeds in still another ancient ancestral pile — or in real comfort in a Paris hotel. But to sell a palace was to relinquish a great deal of prestige, and to give an American almost the social standing of a prince. The price would have to be high.

Marion's half-brother, Arthur Terry, who worked for a Roman banking firm, arranged the loan. "I have so much work now that I think I can draw on Macmillan for almost any amount," F. Marion Crawford wrote. The sentence had a Sam Ward ring to it.

But it was F. Marion Crawford himself, warmhearted and generous, who added a confidential paragraph not once but many times to his letters to his Terry brother and sister. They were to let him know how his mother really was (she always *said* she was well) and tell him if there was anything he could do for her. They were to check into her bank account without letting her know, and write at once if she needed more money.

It was true that Louisa was not well. Rheumatism had troubled her with varying degrees of severity since the death of Thomas Crawford. It always came upon her after times of crisis when she had faced serious difficulties with courage and dignity. The tensions caused by her Cousin Charlie's failure and by her daughter Annie's heartless behavior left Louisa almost crippled with what would today be called arthritis. Yet it made no difference what the doctors called the trouble, Louisa's spirit supplied the cure. She was always certain that each attack would soon be over, and every day she tried to walk a little until she could write proudly that she had walked all the way to the church at the corner or up and down in front of the house in the sun.

At about the time of F. Marion Crawford's marriage, Erich von Rabé, Annie's husband, died. The Baroness Annie had every reason to be unhappy because her children were girls and she was no longer the wife of the heir to the estates, and would now never be the mother of the heir. She flung herself face down upon her husband's marble sarcophagus and wept for hours, having to be taken forcibly from the family tomb. At Lesnian she was less than a poor relation now, and she finally came to Rome, where she suffered neither in silence nor alone. The whole family at the Altemps put on "black bombazine" in mourning for Erich, and black bombazine exactly fitted their state of mind.

Louisa saw a notice in a paper, however. Winthrop Chanler had come to Europe for the summer and he was now in England. Louisa had never forgotten Bond Street days when she had gone each morning to her brother Sam's house to have breakfast with his motherless little girl. In spite of Astor vigilance, Margaret Astor Ward had corresponded with her Aunt Louisa. And here was Maddie's child in Europe!

Louisa Terry's family were astonished when they discovered that "Mother had mailed her letter without consulting anyone." People were always underestimating Louisa. Wintie Chanler arrived and taught Daisy to laugh again. He could even laugh at the Roman fleas that lived in the straw laid under the carpets in old palaces. "We wondered why it pleased him to stay on into the stuffy Roman summer," Daisy said — looking back. "But he was amused by everything and did not seem to mind the dullness of the dead season or the blazing heat." He was too polite to mention the fleas — till his "Aunt Loo" caught him scratching one day. Then "remedies and palliatives were administered and brought relief."

In true Ward fashion, Daisy Terry kept a journal. "Moonlight on the cypresses, nightingales in the laurels, soft summer night wind blowing the spray of the waterfalls in our faces; all pervading music of fountains. . . . Dear Villa d'Este," she wrote telling of a jaunt to nearby Tivoli. But she was not quite ready to admit that she had fallen in love with Wintie Chanler.

When Winthrop Chanler graduated from Harvard, he came straight to Rome to get himself engaged to Daisy Terry. There were difficulties. Wintie was firmly Protestant and Daisy now an ardent Catholic. Wintie did not care — except that he refused to promise that his children should be Catholic. No one had a right to bind the choice of the as yet unborn, he contended; when the children were grown they should decide for themselves. There was also the matter of their cousinship. But by now Daisy Terry admitted that she loved Winthrop Chanler and, with an iron determination of her own, she won the consent of a cardinal who waived the promise concerning children and overlooked kinship.

Julia Ward Howe now voiced what might be called the family decree — to follow the blessing of the Church. "Am glad to think of the new vista of hope and delight which Daisy's marriage will open to my sister, so sorely tried in many ways," Mrs. Howe wrote. "Daisy and Winthrop take from opposite sides of the family — she has her father's constitution with a gleam of something brighter than he has shown himself to possess. Winthrop is like his dear grandfather — a Cutler Ward."

It is only fair to add a footnote to Mrs. Howe's opinion of her brother-in-law Luther Terry. When she visited him in Rome she had called him "kind." He had since declared himself as against Woman's Suffrage.

Louisa had one of her "rampant attacks of rheumatic fever" just five days before Daisy's wedding. The bride came into her mother's room "in her white dress and long veil and crown of natural orange blossoms" to ask a "blessing most lovingly given." She wore the groom's "beautiful gift of diamonds," but Louisa, looking back upon a life of both sun and shadow, knew better than to suppose that diamonds could insure happiness to Daisy. But she loved Wintie, who must now no longer call her "Aunt" but "Mother." She was glad she had sent the letter asking him to come to visit — even without consulting any of the people who were always ready with so much advice.

In 1884, when Daisy Terry was married, Winthrop Chanler invited his cousin Maud Howe to come to Rome with him to the wedding. Maud agreed, then changed her mind. Then to Louisa's house came a very disappointed young artist, Jack Elliott — the young man who had painted the fine picture of Sam Ward. Jack had met Maud Howe when she and her mother visited Louisa in Rome in 1877 and he had been hopelessly in love with Maud ever since. Maud could not make up her mind, and Mrs. Howe disapproved of Jack Elliott because he was so masterful. She had been married to a masterful man, and she knew what it might be like for Maud. Jack Elliott now bought a sapphire ring and set out for America.

When Louisa finally heard that Maud Howe was going to marry Jack Elliott, she wrote, "I am so really attached to Jack, that despite the worldly disadvantages, I cannot help being glad that his long years of devotion to his beautiful Duchess should be thus rewarded. He is in every sense a good fellow, kind of heart, clever to the verge of genius and only needs perseverance to carry him over the line."

And speaking of genius, "I cannot expect that you should read all Marion's many books," Louisa said — doubtless hoping to be contradicted — "but I can recommend [*Sarascensca*] to you as being one of his very best. . . . The Romans are enchanted with it. The old Princess Borghese could not lay it down."

F. Marion Crawford had built over the Villa Renzis in Sorrento, by this time, adding a great sea wall and long flights of steps cut into the cliff leading down to a new pier. Within the house there was every luxury. Rarely did the natives call a historic house by anything but its original family name, but it was a tribute to F. Marion Crawford that everyone now spoke of "Villa Crawford." All of Crawford's boyish delight in the toys his money could buy was heightened by the pleasure he could give his mother. Each attack of rheumatism left Louisa weaker, but as soon as Villa Crawford was ready, her son insisted that she spend her summers there.

"We sat like royalty under a tent covered with rich Oriental stuffs, our feet resting on heavy Turkish carpets," wrote Louisa, describing one of her son's parties in Sorrento. Bengal lights were "flashing their brilliant colors on the whole scene." Professional dancers from the town of Sorrento had been hired and "the tarantella was never so well danced before." They listened to the music which they all loved so well. The "night was delicious and propitious and the long illuminated terrace lent itself to the dance and to the music."

Louisa was writing to her "dearest Eleutherio" — her name for him giving a romantic Italian turn to plain, Germanic "Luther." Everything would have been perfect if only he were with her in Sorrento. He was coming soon, but he wanted to finish a portrait of Daisy, done from sketches and from memory and intended as a surprise for his wife — now that their daughter Daisy was married and had left them. Luther Terry worked slowly and painstakingly, for his eyes troubled him and he was beginning to feel his years — which were seventy-two.

In 1892, Julia Ward Howe visited Europe once more. She found her sister Louisa at Wiesbaden, where Daisy and Wintie Chanler had brought her. The meeting between the sisters was "a little tearful but also cheerful," Julia said. Much had happened during the long eventful years since they had met, "above all many deaths of relatives and friends, dear Brother Sam, Longfellow . . . and many others." But "presently, Louisa and I were as though we had not been parted at all."

"Louisa is little changed," Julia said. "She retains all her old grace and charm of manner."

Within her own heart, Louisa knew that this might be a last meeting. If only Annie could have been with them, to return for one last time in memory to romantic girlhood days in Rome. But now there was no Brother Sam to work a miracle.

Louisa began to realize that none of the "waters" she took did her very much good, although she was willing to try them all. She had always assumed that she would live to take care of her husband, her "dear Eleutherio," all his days — but what if this was not to be? Louisa went about the difficult task of preparing her will. Both Annie and Mimoli, her two Crawford daughters, were now widowed. Hugh Fraser, Second Secretary of the British Legation, when he married Mimoli, had been "appointed to Pekin" and served, as the title of two of Mimoli's books put it, "in Many Lands." Mimoli quoted her mother as saying "People who use their brains need never break their hearts," and she began at once to write of her "many lands" — her chapters on her Roman childhood being her best. Mimoli had children to support, however, and Louisa realized that both her daughters would need all that she could leave to them. Accordingly, she left to her children her small remnant of fortune, instead of to her husband as she would have liked to do. "But my son Francis Marion Crawford and our daughter Margaret Chanler have faithfully promised to pay over to their stepfather and father during his lifetime, the entire income from their portion of my patrimony," Louisa said in her will. Luther Terry would be eighty-four when he needed the care of a devoted daughter, an affectionate son-in-law and a stepson who had long looked upon "Paterno" as his own father.

There could be only small gifts to nephews and nieces — two hundred dollars to be divided among Annie's children and the same for Julia's. But what really saddened Louisa was that she could do so little for old friends. She was not anxious about the beggars who for many years had come to her door, never to go away entirely empty-handed. They would find other doors. It was the old and the friendless — the people who had come to her "green room," who would miss her, and she would like to have had money enough for a bequest to each, instead of to only one or two.

The "green room" was a small antechamber where callers who would have felt shy or embarrassed by shabby clothes in the huge drawing room, with other guests, waited for Louisa to come to them for a private word. Aging artists could tell Louisa of past triumphs and she would listen and believe. Expatriate old ladies, too poor to go home and homesick in the city that had once seemed so glamorous, could talk to Louisa about this or that catastrophe which had brought them low. Louisa's sympathy was the bread of life to these people and the money she sometimes managed to give them no one but Louisa would have had the tact to offer without hurting their pride.

As palace succeeded palace during Louisa's long years in Rome, there was always a "green room," no matter how it was decorated. At the time of Thomas Crawford's death, "Would you have me forget my poor?" Louisa reproachfully asked her Uncle John, who wanted her to save more money. Her growing children were impatient with these friends of their mother's, whom they called her "pensioners." But one night Mimoli dreamed that she had died and gone to heaven — except that heaven itself was barred to her and she found herself in her mother's " 'green room' among the pensioners."

As Louisa's children became Catholic, one after the other, they seem to have considered trying to convert their firmly Protestant mother. "Do not disturb your mother's religion," a Roman Church official told them. "She is a natural saint." [4]

Louisa was at last so crippled with rheumatism that she could not walk. Her son brought her to Sorrento and there the sailing was what she loved. "The rougher the weather, the better she liked it," Mimoli said, watching her mother being carried down the long flights of stairs in the cliff by Marion's sailors. Louisa loved to sail in the felucca, Marion's handsome Mediterranean-built yacht with its lateen sails and crew to handle it. There was a chair for her, bolted to the deck. But if the weather were really rough enough, what she preferred was the *Margarita*, "a little open boat that Marion particularly liked," also.

Aboard the *Margarita*, an armchair for Louisa was "lashed between two thwarts." Then out they would go, just the two of them, mother and son — making "for the open sea." They would "sail for hours, neither of them saying a word." The small boat cut through the whitecaps and the hissing water was so close that the sense of speed was glorious. The wind tore at Louisa's hair and she smiled, turning her face to it, rejoicing when it rose to gale proportions. Louisa was "a natural saint," they said; she was called "gentle, pliable." Yet with her son, so strong, so like his father, she loved to leave the safe land behind and sail into the open sea. Her son Marion had found her a saint many times, but he must also have found that she was a heroine.

CHAPTER THIRTY-ONE
From Coast to Coast

THERE was now a long line of journals, a volume for each year, on the shelf in Julia Ward Howe's bedroom at 241 Beacon Street. Grandchildren looked at them with awe and knew better than to touch them. At the end of each year, it was Mrs. Howe's custom to sum up the immediate past, but most of all to look forward. On December 31, 1882, she wrote: "The last day of this year, which my young people, Maud and Marion, are preparing to celebrate by a supper and a frolic, to which I do not feel much inclination. I may confide to this page, that I feel much more worn just now than usual with cares and anxieties. My dear brother is not here to help and comfort me."

But a weary mood lasted only long enough to complete the sentence. "On the other hand, I have much to be thankful for," Mrs. Howe went on. "I pray God that the New Year may be a good one for me and mine. My truest personal desires are now and always the happy marriage of my daughter Maud, the ability to pay all my debts and a clear road for the education of my grandchildren. I shall also be glad of recognition enough to make me feel that my life has not been altogether wasted."

To see how these prayers were answered requires turning the pages of more than one year's journal, and there were unexpected episodes in store in the near future. "Marion" referred to as one of Mrs. Howe's own "young people" was her nephew, F. Marion Crawford. He spent most of the winter of 1882–1883 at his Aunt Julia's house at 241 Beacon Street, and nearby at 150 Beacon lived Mrs. Jack Gardner. She had been Isabella Stewart, her large private income coming from her father David Stewart's importing business and his ownership of the Stewart Iron Company with mines near Uniontown, Pennsylvania. Her Italian palace, Fenway Court, was yet to come.

Mrs. Jack Gardner was born in 1840, so she was now forty-two years old, a very small woman with hair exceedingly golden and eyes that burned blue fire.[1] F. Marion Crawford was born in 1854, so he was not quite twenty-eight when they met. He had disappointed hopes concerning one of the Perkins girls of Milton and he was not yet in love with Bessie Berdan. Francis Marion had seen a good deal of the world but he had never seen anything like Mrs. Jack Gardner.

Mrs. Howe knew that her nephew spent many hours with Mrs. Gardner. He spun out his plots for novels with her and she helped him greatly, for she was a witty woman. This is not to say that Marion was her only protégé, for she surrounded herself with gifted young men writers, musicians and painters — like John Singer Sargent, two years younger than F. Marion Crawford, a future favorite. But Mrs. Gardner became more and more fascinated by "Frank Marion." She always found time to see him alone and his calls were very long.

When Marion was away he wrote letters to Mrs. Gardner which she treasured all her life. Some of his phrases were so intimate and so precious to her that she cut them out of the thin sheets and burned them so that no one else might ever read the words. She left the packet of letters looking like curious lacework or a strange cryptogram which she alone remembered how to read.[2] F. Marion Crawford's Aunt Julia would not have approved of the letters any more than she did of the overlong calls which were always resumed every time Frank came to Boston.

It is not surprising that Mrs. Howe looked with disfavor upon a plan concocted by Mrs. Jack Gardner in 1883. She wanted to take Francis Marion Crawford on a trip to Japan with Mrs. Howe and Maud. Presumably, Mrs. Gardner planned to foot the bills and Maud was delighted. Mrs. Howe was not at all sure she wanted to chaperone a forty-two-year-old lady. John Singer Sargent would paint Mrs. Gardner's portrait in a low-cut black gown, the famous pearls hanging nearly to her knees — and a scandalous joke would go the rounds concerning the revealing portrait and Crawford, the novelist.

On April 7, Mrs. Howe wrote to her daughter Maud who was in New York. "You are not, darling, to say one word to anyone about Marion's departure. I will explain the reason why. The other party will wish him to go to Japan. He has his reasons for wishing to keep very quiet about his movements. I am very thankful he has decided as he has. Cannot say more on paper. Mum's the word."

Daisy Terry remembered Mrs. Jack Gardner's "much-talked-of

flirtation with Marion Crawford from which he escaped. . . . " and that "Maud was sent for by the wildly weeping Mrs. Gardner" and "had to spend many days in her house." [3]

But Mrs. Howe, released from all danger of having to chaperone Maud and Mrs. Gardner in Japan, breathed a sigh of relief. She was free to go to New Orleans, where she organized the Woman's Department for the New Orleans Exposition. Numberless letters went out beforehand as Mrs. Howe carried out an idea of hers. She wanted to "bring into notice and demand, the remote and hidden handcrafts still practiced in many parts of our country, especially in the mountain regions." This was a totally new idea in an age that was much in love with the machine. Jigsaw cutouts were stuck to the surfaces of wood to simulate hand carving; machine embroidery was admired not only because it could be produced cheaply but because it was so wonderful that a machine could do such things. It was not easy to regain acceptance of handcraft, but thanks to Mrs. Howe a new appreciation began to stir faintly. If it can be said that times of crisis produce the man for the hour, then Julia Ward Howe was the woman for the 1880's.

Mother's Day was Julia Ward Howe's original idea. She chose June 2 as the proper date, and by 1878 she was writing "a Mother's Day letter to friends . . . who help me celebrate this day." But Mrs. Howe's idea was not the sending of flowers, gifts and telegrams to mothers who could then be neglected with a clear conscience for another year. Mother's Day, as she conceived it, was the day when everyone should be dedicated anew to the task of bringing about world peace. "Mothers' Peace Day," she called it, honoring all who had lost sons in the Civil War and in other wars everywhere. She urged the newspapers to publish articles stressing the means by which lasting peace could be brought about and she wrote many such articles herself. She sent Mother's Day peace programs to women's clubs in answer to requests from all over the country.

The Peace Crusade was probably the most important in Mrs. Howe's mind, but Woman's Suffrage certainly came a close second as time went by. "Went to the Woman's Suffrage Banquet where I was to preside," she wrote. "We started speaking at 6:30 and continued till nearly 10 P.M. The speakers were mostly women and very good." She wore her "best cap" and her "long black silk — Paris made." And instead of having the "toasts given helter-skelter," Mrs. Howe "arranged a certain sequence." Pattern and plan appeared, wits grew sharp and personalities were contrasted with fine effect.

Next day it was the turn of the "Convention of Women Ministers and Preachers." And Mrs. Howe told of a reverend lady who "had undertaken to make the necessary arrangements about a place of meeting." She was "a most sweet-looking woman with dreamy eyes and a philosophizing turn of mind" — but a hall had not been reserved after all; and the lady ministers and preachers were milling around without the slightest idea of what to do. Mrs. Howe arrived just in time to set their plans in order for them.

In 1886, Mrs. Howe lost her oldest daughter, Julia Romana Anagnos. During the years when Julia Romana first went to the Institute to teach the blind, she had shown a lack of sympathy with her mother. Revelations at the time of her father's death — letters which her husband Michael Anagnos had found and burned — had been a severe shock. Julia Romana suffered a nervous breakdown — not for the first time. She had been what might now be called a "disturbed child." This was her last breakdown, however, and of late years she had been most affectionate toward her mother, whose love for her never wavered. She was childless and she died of typhoid fever from which she was thought to be recovering.

It devolved upon Laura to write to her Aunt Annie Mailliard about the death of Julia Anagnos. "Mama is very beautiful," Laura wrote. "Her hair is quite snow-white now, the black bonnet and veil showing the perfect features as if carved in ivory. The loss of her first-born has been very heavy to her, Auntie dear. For a long time, she seemed to have no power of rallying, her wonderful elasticity quite gone. But now she is better and brave and more cheerful."

The years were going by, and Mrs. Howe's earnest prayers that her daughter Maud might be happily married were still unanswered. As far back as 1878, when Maud was taken on her European grand tour, her mother had told her that she must "finally choose either a husband or a serious pursuit. Painting is what she likes best," Maud's fond mother said. So Maud took a few lessons in a so-called art suddenly become painfully popular — china painting. The rosebuds and violets which she inflicted upon innocent white procelain seemed remarkably beautiful to her mother. But Jack Elliott put in an appearance and Maud transferred her interest from art to the artist. The Howes met him on the railroad platform in Siena, and got acquainted without introductions. "Our Foundling" Maud called him; and Mrs. Howe, who did not approve of his high-handed ways, wished he had never been found.

Maud parted from her artist with little regret, apparently. Each season for the past eight years, Mrs. Howe had been her chaperone at increasingly lavish Newport functions. Her cousin, Ward McAllister, told Mrs. Howe frankly that she was a fool not to insist upon a wealthy marriage for Maud and he got roundly told off for his pains. The "little millionaire" he had trotted out was "most unattractive." The role of chaperone was not an easy one, however. Once Mrs. Howe went cruising with Maud on a yacht that could have been Maud's if she cared to bestow her lovely hand upon its owner. Mrs. Howe said that "it was ghostly to sit on deck surrounded by fog and hear the paddles of a steamer which might override us and bring us death." She was glad when the cruise was over, and glad when Maud decided against the yacht-owner.

In 1887, Jack Elliott appeared at 241 Beacon Street — a sapphire ring in his pocket. Six days later — "Much worried about Maud's precipitate intended marriage," her mother wrote. Jack might have wondered what she meant, for he had waited nine years.

Once the matter was settled, however, Mrs. Howe went about preparing for the wedding of her youngest child. She "wrote verses for a Bridal Song." Of course plans made long previously could not be broken and so, five days before the wedding, she was in Manchester, New Hampshire, delivering a lecture on Dante. The fee was most welcome. On the wedding day, February 7, 1887, Maud spent "most of the day in my room and on my bed," her mother said — but it was an evening wedding and her mother had just time to take "a carriage and go about buying rolls, etc. etc." Wedding gifts continued to arrive, some of them "very costly" from former suitors. And Mrs. Jack Gardner came to help the groom make "a bower of hibiscus and laurel" in front of the fireplace in the front parlor.

When the bride "in queenly loveliness stepped forth" her mother's heart was overflowing. "Maud's face was glorified with a new tenderness and calm of expression," Mrs. Howe said and she mentioned her son Harry's "beautiful singing of 'Integer Vitae' with words written for the occasion by J. S. Dwight." She forgot to say whether her own song, also written for the occasion, was sung or not.

Mrs. Howe's four sons-in-law differed greatly from each other. It would be unfair to say which one she cared for the most, but Jack Elliott came close to being her favorite because he gave her so much trouble. He defied her, they quarreled, they made up. Constantly she urged Maud to have patience with him. If she could save the happiness of this adored child, who could say that her own past tears had not been well shed? Jack "lost the Jay Gould order," a few months after the wedding. "With this too we must have patience," Maud's mother wrote her — and added a characteristic postscript: "Could *you* see Jay Gould about the work?"

This and further well-meant advice would not go down with the high-tempered Jack. And yet, working from old pictures and from his own impressions, Jack Elliott painted a strange, half allegorical portrait of Julia Ward Howe in her youth which was really remarkable. The water lily in her hand was a little too dramatic. But the deep-set eyes, the look of sadness and longing, must have startled Mrs. Howe when she saw it. The little book of poetry placed symbolically in her hand had the *Passion Flowers* date on it to show that the picture represented Julia Ward Howe at a time when her heart was breaking. It had mended since then. How could Jack Elliott know so much?

Julia Ward Howe's literary achievements always meant more to her than the executive gifts of which she was hardly aware. She still felt almost as hurt on reading criticism of her writing as she had in 1859 when *Passion Flowers* had been so variously received. She was youthfully elated over the recognition when she was invited to speak at the Concord School of Philosophy. It was in 1882, and she was as pleased as though she had been a young author honored for the first time. She "had great doubts" about her lecture but it went well. In 1886, she was asked again to Concord, and she said that she was glad of the work she had put into her lecture: "The Place of Women in Plato's Republic." This time the lecture not only went well, it was "warmly received."

In 1888, Mrs. Howe's comments in her journal about her first coast-to-coast lecture tour were so enthusiastic that she sounded like a young girl rather than a woman approaching her sixty-ninth birthday. In Walla Walla, she "was very kindly received . . . by Mr. and Mrs. Isaacs, people of education and refinement." She had a wonderful time in "hospitable Seattle," which she left with great regret to lecture twice in Portland, Oregon, a place where she would have liked to buy some land and settle — if only she could get at least one of her children to share as youthful a point of view as her own.

The greatest joy for Julia on this trip was her meeting with her sister Annie. For this purpose, she had corresponded and campaigned to get lecture engagements that would pay her expenses all the long distance to California. At Oakland, a young man "came in to the pullman" and Julia Ward Howe knew him at once — "from his likeness to his dear mother." He was her nephew, John Mailliard.

Annie was waiting in San Francisco, and they went to her son's house to meet his wife, then "took the train for the ranch." And now Annie could forgive all the disparaging remarks made by two of her nieces, for her sister Julia saw the same beauties in the Mailliard ranch that Annie did. It was "a cup in the hills," Julia said. And "orange-colored poppies . . . were blooming in great masses on the lawn."

Mrs. Howe lectured several times in San Francisco and Santa Barbara. In Los Angeles, Mrs. Frémont "dressed her rooms with flowers," and when Mrs. Howe returned to San Francisco she was carrying "an enormous sheaf of lilies — a sort of sceptre." [4] In Oakland, "six hundred girls sang the 'Battle Hymn!' " The Middle West now had a rival in Mrs. Howe's affections. "The middle west seems to me *no where* now that I have seen the real west," she said.

Back to Boston and Newport went Mrs. Howe, tired but triumphant — "able to pay nearly all the bills" with the proceeds of her lecture tour. Checks went out to the children as usual; to Maud a hundred dollars — to Laura only twenty because Laura had begun her own successful writing career. In July, "Flossie and her troup arrived" at Oak Glen to keep their grandmother's summer from becoming dull.

In the autumn it would be back to the Middle West again for Mrs. Howe. The "Milwaukee Club" made her an honorary member, and in Detroit she was re-elected President of the Association for the Advancement of Women "by acclamation." Mrs. Howe was thankful that "the year had carried" her to the Pacific slope and showed her "a land of promise."

Julia spent Christmas with Annie at the ranch in 1889. This time, Annie had been ill. Dr. Brown had "hoped" that "two tumors" in Annie's breast would be absorbed and advised against an operation until medicine, internal and external, had been tried. This was advice that seems shocking today but it was given by a woman doctor of a high reputation.[5] "Remember dear, that my allotted days are almost reached," Annie wrote, when an operation was at last decided upon. She survived the operation and when her sister saw her again, she "looked like herself of many years ago," Julia said. "Her hair was turned back from her little face" and she looked like the girl who had loved to roam the woods near Newport in search of wild flowers. She might almost have been once more the "maiden with the meek brown eyes," for whom Longfellow was said to have written the lines.

There were five more years of very restricted life for Annie Mailliard. She died April 7, 1895. "She was the best of us," Julia wrote in her Journal when she learned the news. Julia remembered Annie's birth — "a tiny child, left by our dear mother." They had all tried to shelter her, and Annie's marriage had been "one of pure affection." Mrs. Howe wrote that her sister Annie "had much happiness in her life although it had its tragic side." She wondered what she could say "to Adolph Mailliard who has no faith in a future life."

"At moments, I seem to see the ranch," Julia Howe finally wrote, "the lawn and the great rock, and all of you sitting in the deep shadow of a sorrow that time can hardly make less." And this proved true, at least for Adolph. His children had not realized how much their father had loved his little Annie. Now his own reason for living suddenly ceased to exist, and he died a little over a year later.

On September 22, 1897, Julia Ward Howe opened her Journal, that faithful confidante of all her thoughts and feelings. "Have just heard by cable from Rome that my dearest sister Louisa died yesterday morning. Let me rather hope that she awoke, from painful weakness and infirmity, into a new glory of spiritual life. Her life has been most blameless, as well as most beautiful. . . . She was as rare a person, in her way, as my sweet sister Annie. Alas! I, of less desert than either, am left the last of my dear mother's and father's children. God grant that my remaining years may be for good, and God help me to use faithfully my remnant of life, in setting my house in order and in giving such completeness as I can to my life work. . . ."

After her Uncle John's death in 1866, Mrs. Howe visited Bond Street no longer and when her cousin Henry died, in 1872, there were no more Wards on the street that should really have been called by their name. About twenty years later, Mrs. Howe made one last call. All the old family mansions were gone save one, and the street was now in a wholesale district for feathers and artificial flowers. The one remaining Ward house was Number 23, and it had become a sort of ghost dwelling. The front window curtains were always tightly drawn, yet the brass gleamed on the big front door and the marble steps were kept clean. No one lived there but a staff of servants.

Every afternoon at a certain time, a spare old woman dressed in black came down Bond Street, entered the house and sat in the parlor alone. At the end of the afternoon she left — to return punctually next day. She was Miss Eliza Partridge, to whom Henry Ward, a bachelor, had left a life interest in all his money, his real estate and his personal belongings — together with belongings not strictly speaking his by right. Miss Partridge was a relative of Henry's mother, Eliza Hall Ward. She had lived as a pensioner — a poor relation — in the home of Henry's aunt, Mrs. William Ward, who was also his mother's sister. Her marriage to Henry was said to have been forbidden by his mother because of the kinship. When Henry's mother died in March, 1872, all the Wards listened for the wedding bells which should have rung out for the fifty-two-year old Henry and his Elise — as she called herself. But nothing of the sort happened. Six months later, Henry died; and his will was a distinct shock to the Ward family.

Sam was especially disappointed. In the course of one of Sam's failures his Cousin Henry had acquired 32 Bond Street, the house Samuel Ward the banker had given to Sam at the time of Sam's first marriage. A good many of the Ward sisters' belongings were still in Sam's house, and he expected to get everything back — but he got nothing.

When Mrs. Howe called at 23 Bond Street she brought with her one of her daughter Laura's daughters — Rosalind Richards, a young girl resembling somewhat the beautiful Maud Howe Elliott, but with a special ethereal quality all her own. The door was opened by an aged Negro servant "in white apron and turban." Miss Partridge was seated in a great armchair in the drawing room, and in the course of the call the servant was sent to get a certain box. "You know this?" demanded Miss Partridge, taking out a miniature and thrusting it into Mrs. Howe's hands. When she looked at the young face painted on ivory, Mrs. Howe "turned pale" with the sudden shock and her eyes filled with tears. It was her brother Henry, who had died in 1840, "a glad boy of twenty-two" of whom Sam had written, "The song and dance will need his stirring voice and nimble step."

"You'd like it, wouldn't you?" said Miss Partridge — taking back the picture and locking it away. Then the old lady put into Rosalind's hand "a ring set with a magnificent carved sapphire." It had belonged to Julia Cutler Ward, the young girl's great-grandmother. "You want it, don't you?" said Miss Partridge. "*Pounce!* The claw-like fingers snatched" back the ring. It goes without saying that Mrs. Howe never called at 23 Bond Street again. She was never one to seek out the scenes of her past life very often.

The *Atlantic Monthly* asked Mrs. Howe to write her reminiscences, to appear in serial form, and this was gratifying but difficult. Maud Howe Elliott was living somewhat the life of her late Aunt Louisa in Rome and she persuaded her mother to visit her in the winter of 1897–1898 and work upon the manuscript. "My mind reverts more and more to the scenes of days long past, "Mrs. Howe wrote in her Journal. "Oh for one hour in our old square dining room at South Boston with the bright wood fire burning and dear Chev reading aloud to me and the children. Oh that I had not been so thankless for all those good things at the time. I shall never see their like again." It was sad to be in Rome now that Louisa was gone. Jack Elliott "cut armfuls of roses" from his terrace for Mrs. Howe to take to Louisa's grave in the Protestant Cemetery. "Three score years and ten — that was man's allotted span," Mrs. Howe wrote in her journal. She had lived nine years beyond this "allotted span" and suddenly she seemed to feel that she had been borrowing time.

Once she was back in Boston again, Mrs. Howe forgot all about her seventy-nine years. She must write some more chapters for Houghton Mifflin's edition of *Reminiscences*. Offers for lectures at a hundred dollars an appearance were coming in, and she must accept as many as possible. A grandson was graduating from Harvard, his education the gift of his Grandmother Howe, and there was a second boy ready for his grandmother's help. Maud's husband "painted beautifully" but it seemed to take him forever to finish a picture so Maud had written a new novel to help out and now wanted to take up lecturing. Who but her mother would correct Maud's proof and tell her how to be a successful lecturer?

Julia Ward Howe postponed indefinitely the matter of growing old. She simply had not the time for it.

CHAPTER THIRTY-TWO

"They Called Me Queen, and Kissed My Hand"

THE YEAR was 1899 and on Boston Common a Civil War Memorial was to be dedicated on May 30.[1] General Wheeler's "open carriage" called for Julia Ward Howe and she rode in the procession to the Boston Theater. The general's two daughters rode with Mrs. Howe — "*very* pleasing girls," she said, "one very pretty, the other entertaining."

This was all that Mrs. Howe wrote in her Journal about the greatest ovation she had ever received. But she pasted in a clipping headed "Philadelphia Press." "It was away over any similar celebration I ever saw," wrote the reporter and he called his piece, "Boston Warmed Up."

> There was nothing mushy or hackneyed about it. It was the real thing. I never imagined possible such genuine sweeping emotion as was awakened by the singing of "The Battle Hymn of the Republic." I always knew it was the greatest thing of its kind ever written, but it never had a fair chance before. It's the one poem — for it is a poem — that can make me cry. I'm a blatant fool every time I hear it.
>
> If Boston's cold, that song thawed it and heated it to a wild volcano on Tuesday. There was the packed, still house. Myron T. Whitney started to sing. First he bowed to the box and then we first recognized Mrs. Howe seated by the Misses Wheeler. You should have heard the yell! When Vic celebrated her eightieth birthday a few days before, she got no ovation equal to that given this octogenarian. You could see the splendid white head trembling; then her voice joined in as Whitney sang: "In the glory of the lilies, Christ was born across the sea," and by the time he reached the words, "As he died to make men holy, let us die to make men free," the whole vast audience was on its feet sobbing and singing at the top of its thousands of lungs. If volunteers were

really needed for the Philippines, McKinley could have had us all right there.

"I would be glad of recognition enough to make me feel that my life has not been altogether wasted," Julia Ward Howe had written in her Journal when she was a young woman in her seventies. Recognition had come, wave after wave of it, during the past ten years. Audiences spontaneously sprang to their feet in tribute to her when she appeared on the platform — as they did that same evening when she came to Tremont Temple to tell about her friend John Andrew, the Civil War governor. This was not merely because she had written the one great song to come out of the Civil War. A nation at war for an ideal is borne along by patriotic ardor to "die to make men free." But it is afterwards, in the dark loneliness, that a gray ebb tide sets in, leaving a nation with a sense of futility and without the strength to fight insidious evils during the time of reconstruction. Julia Ward Howe was the light of those dark times, and the leader after war-engendered enthusiasm had burned out. It takes infinitely more genius to be a leader in time of peace.

In those sacred precincts, the Chambers of the State House — which even Elizabeth Peabody had once tried in vain to enter — Mrs. Howe was a familiar figure. Well might the grafters turn pale when they saw her coming. Her weapon was wit. And what her husband, the Chevalier, had said of her was very true — she could raise a laugh in Purgatory.

Mrs. Howe never missed a "hearing" if she could help it. The august Massachusetts Representatives held a hearing on Woman Suffrage and pronounced the dictum that "women had not yet reached a sufficiently advanced mental and moral state to deserve the vote." "When did men reach this state?" Mrs. Howe wanted to know. She was told that she "might not ask a question" — but laughter drowned out the moderator's protests.

In 1900, Mrs. Howe was allowed to debate in favor of suffrage at the State House in Boston. Some antisuffrage women and the Reverend Lyman Abbott were her opponents. The Reverend Mr. Abbott said he thought that it was wrong for women to ask for suffrage when the majority of women appeared to be against it. Mrs. Howe "arose and asked the Rev. gentleman whether the twelve apostles were right in trying to bring about a better state of society when the whole Jewish nation were opposed to it."

Julia Howe was given two minutes to speak in rebuttal. This was all she needed. "This division of opinion among women reminds me of the parable of the virgins, five of whom were wise and five foolish," she said. "Time will show which will go in with the heavenly bridegroom. If the Suffragists go in, I hope the others will be given time to provide themselves with the oil necessary for admission. And I hope the Rev. Lyman Abbott will not be the one man found unprovided with a wedding garment." "This created almost an uproar of laughter," Mrs. Howe wrote in her Journal. "The women came up and kissed me."

"Abbott did not try to answer my question, saying, 'That question is a matter of rhetoric' — a most pitiful subterfuge." Mrs. Howe thanked God that she had been able to make a good speech. What the Rev. Lyman Abbott thanked God for is not a matter of record, but perhaps he was thankful just to get out of there.

Mrs. Howe was at the State House again during hearings for and against a law to control the sale of milk. Was it or was it not the duty of the state to see that wholesome milk from properly inspected dairies reached the public? Representatives of one interest and another spoke — especially those who felt that the law would reduce profits. But the day was won when Mrs. Howe got up and said simply, "I am here to represent the children — who cannot speak for themselves."

"The right word," coming like an inspiration at the right moment — that was the gift Julia Ward Howe constantly gave thanks for. But this is not to say that all her words were in behalf of some good cause of public welfare. She could still lose her temper; and sometimes her children and grandchildren — thwarting her will for her own good, as they insisted — felt the lash of her sharp tongue. There was talk of having Jack and Maud Howe Elliott live with their mother to take care of her. Mrs. Howe was by no means ready to agree. Jack had saved her life, in all probability, but it was some time before Mrs. Howe gave up her wrath against him. Against her express orders he had sent for a doctor for her. She spent a night of agony but was very angry when Jack, on his own responsibility, got a nurse next day. "The nurse made me very comfortable," the eighty-two-year-old Mrs. Howe admitted, "but I cannot have any one assume such authority in my house."

There were children, grandchildren and great-grandchildren by 1903. And even the grandchildren had to be reminded that Grandmother Howe would still do exactly as she pleased and there would be none of this nonsense about saving her strength and taking care of herself. She continued her writing schedule; and when lameness, resulting from a fall, caused her to give up a series of lectures, she consoled herself with the realization that she was able to do more work for the magazines. Articles on the great men and women she had known were most often asked for: Emerson, Longfellow, Margaret Fuller — she had known them all. But Mrs. Howe never realized that the time had come when no one would refuse one of her contributions, no matter what the subject. "A package came from McClure's Syndicate," she wrote in her journal, and she had thought it might be a rejection. "God give me strength not to cry," she admonished herself. But it was only proof for correction and a request for more material.

In 1903, the New England Women's club gave a luncheon in honor of Mrs. Howe. "I felt almost overwhelmed by the great attention shown me, and by the constant talk of speakers in reference to myself," she said. "I don't find in myself this charm, the goodness attributed to me, but I know I love the Club and the world of my own time, so far as I know it."

They had seated her in a great carved chair, after the luncheon and her friends came up to greet her. "They called me Queen, and kissed my hand," she said.

This was Julia Ward Howe of Boston. Many people thought that she had been born in Boston and had lived there all her life. But she had once been Julia Ward of New York, "a beautiful person, splendidly dressed, entering the gay theater . . . often . . . with entire delight." In 1909, she would be Julia Ward Howe of New York once more — as she stepped out on the stage of the Metropolitan Opera House to "read her poem" for the "Fulton Celebration." The stage was crowded with foreign delegates in handsome uniforms. There were "lines of sailors saluting" and four of them to carry Mrs. Howe's "rolling chair" to the platform. But she stood when introduced. And "as I came forward the whole house rose, before and behind me, and stood while I recited my verses which were very much applauded."

This standing ovation which Julia Ward Howe now invariably received delighted her. She always spoke better in response to the enthusiasm of her audience for she would always have all the instincts of a good actress. At the same time, she had not lost her perspective. In 1910, when the New England Women's Club gave her a huge birthday party and "rose in a body" as she stood up to speak — "If you don't sit down, I will," she laughed.

After all — she was only ninety-one.

In June, 1910, Mrs. Howe reached Newport late. She had sprained her knee and she shared the family tendency to suffer from rheumatism. When the rheumatic symptoms first appeared, she was put on a milk diet which caused her to gain weight — much to her dismay. The impression so many people had of her as a stout old lady, looking rather like Queen Victoria in her later years, was unflattering and also unjust. Her son-in-law, Jack Elliott, took many remarkable photographs of her, his artist's eye captivated by her beauty in old age — his camera incapable of catching it. The active, dauntless spirit which lived within her escaped both the camera and the notice of casual observers.

If proof were needed that Julia Ward Howe, at ninety-one, was both dauntless and active, her remarks on reaching Newport state her case. "I clearly announced my intention of dispensing with the services of a trained nurse," she wrote. "My good health and simple habits render one entirely superfluous." Her children were hard to handle because of their silly ideas of what a woman of ninety-one should and should not do, but their mother was still a match for them. "In spite of some opposition by Flossy," Mrs. Howe went to the Channing Church in Newport on the first Sunday after her arrival. And as a recessional, the organist played her "Battle Hymn." She "walked down the aisle . . . feeling not my feet but my wings," she said.

No matter how young her heart was, there were times when Mrs. Howe confessed to her journal that she felt the weight of her years. Since passing her "allotted span," she had said farewell to Oak Glen each autumn, confiding to her journal that she felt that each year might be last. "If I come here no more, may blessings rest upon this place, where my days have been precious." In the autumn of 1910, she had really said her last farewell to Newport.

There was one more public appearance. Early in October, Mrs. Howe went to Smith College to receive an honorary LL.D. She had already received a Doctor of Literature degree from Brown University, and these honors pleased her; but she said in her journal that she doubted if she would accept any more, "grudging the time and the expense" of the trip to Northampton. But she was glad after all that she had come when the organ rolled and a chorus of young girls began to sing, "Mine eyes have seen the glory." As so often happened, the audience could not leave it to the choir but joined in, rising to their feet at the sight of her — and singing for a great lady her stirring song.

Mrs. Howe was much touched. The girls looked so young — they sang so beautifully. But when it was all over and she was asked to sign the guest book, and add a few well-chosen lines, preferably poetry, her eyes twinkled wickedly.

> Julia Ward Howe
> Wandered to Smith College
> In pursuit of knowledge
> Leaves so much the wiser
> Nothing can surprise her.

This was what she wrote on the spur of the moment.

Faithfully, her daughters and granddaughters compiled huge scrapbooks of clippings about Julia Ward Howe's many honors. Her dream of recognition was abundantly realized. In her journal she rarely bothered to record public praise but there were actual dreams during sleeping hours that were so vivid that Mrs. Howe wrote them down. Once "dear Chev" came to see her but, not finding her, "went away leaving no message." This dream was so true to life that she awoke crying. But in recent months, peace came even to her sleeping thoughts in a still more vivid dream of a wide sea. "Dear Chev" was with her. There was no boat but he supported her and she clung to him so that safely they reached the shore.

Among the last journal entries was one dated October 11. The all too familiar query had come in, "What books have most influenced you?" And patiently Mrs. Howe set about answering the question, by no means for the first time. In childhood there had been *Pilgrim's Progress*. She paused to recall the nursery dramas enacted from this book. Sam had signed himself "Brother Faithful" at intervals all during his life, and usually when he least deserved the title. But he had tried to live up to his nursery role and take care of his sisters on their perilous journey to the Celestial City. Perhaps in seeking gold in California, he had forgotten a Pilgrim's higher aims, but he had always wanted gold to give away. Who should say he had not deserved at last to reach the golden gates?

Gibbon's *Decline and Fall of the Roman Empire* was her favorite reading when she was seventeen or eighteen years old, Mrs. Howe said. The Ward sisters had all read it and it was no wonder that they longed to go to Rome and that Rome seemed a familiar city to them when they gathered there to share Julia's honeymoon. They knew the temples, the Forum, the Baths, long before they visited the lingering ruins, guidebook in hand, and built Rome back to glory in their mind's eye. Once, Julia Howe had written that she wanted to die in Rome but now the lines in *Passion Flowers* were anything but true. They proved a prophecy for Louisa; but Julia, on her last visit to Rome, had wanted nothing so much as to get back to Boston.

"Spinoza and the Germans, studied later in life" opened the gates to a new world of philosophy. Family jokes about her study of philosophy were current — "Is it ethical, mother, for me to have a second helping?" being the way Mrs. Howe's children teased her at table. She had loved the fun even at her own expense, and laughter eased the tension of those sometimes difficult days. By way of her philosophical readings, Mrs. Howe's career as a lecturer had begun — in her own parlor. Suppose she had yielded to pressure, however, never written for publication, never spoken for a fee — what then would have become of them all after the Chevalier left them? A woman with four daughters and a son would have had a hard time without a field in which she already knew how to earn a living. It was hard enough, in any case.

The fortune left to the Ward sisters by their father had shrunk to small proportions under the efforts of Sam and Cousin Charlie; so that, if Mrs. Howe had lived on the remnants of her capital, she would long since have become dependent upon her children. As it was, she took pride in the fact that she had left her capital untouched and for the most part the income also — while she supported herself, helped her children and at times her grandchidren. The example of such courage was not wasted. Disasters came upon the Richards mills but Laura had been writing ever since the first baby had been old enough to help with the next one, and now Laura E. Richards was almost as well known as Julia Ward Howe. Florence's lawyer husband died long before his four children had grown and so Florence wrote and lectured and, with her mother's help, educated her children. Maud's writing — begun as an alternative to china painting, — turned out much better than her violets and roses, and (with her mother to correct her spelling) her list of titles increased.

Henry Marion Howe, the only living son, proved no exception to the family rule when it came to publications. It was just that his titles differed — *The Metallurgy of Steel; Copper Smelting; Iron, Steel and other Alloys* — these were but a few of the works which made him noted in his field of engineering. He too became a Chevalier — of the French Legion of Honor! This only son was able soon to help his mother, and, with gratitude, Mrs. Howe noted in her journal the arrival of regular sums of money. She was proud of his decorations but what she never ceased to marvel over was his fine singing voice. They had glorious musical evenings together still, whenever he was able to visit her.

When it came to the romantic type of writing that Julia Howe herself had once attempted, F. Marion Crawford seemed to inherit her gift more as a son than a nephew. In 1909 Francis Marion Crawford had died. A coast-to-coast lecture tour, undertaken to pay for such expensive toys as his ocean-going yacht, ended in illness. It would seem, from what was said of his last few months, that he died of cancer as his father had done. And Mrs. Howe, at ninety, had stood in the chancel of the Church of the Disciples to speak a eulogy for her nephew, dead at fifty-five. To her, he seemed a boy.

Working conscientiously on her article about books, Mrs. Howe said nothing about music. It was a pity that someone had not written in to ask her about the music in her life. In her youth, music was the barometer of her happiness. When she was happy, she sang; and when she first suffered such grief over her husband's request to leave her, it seemed as if she would never sing again. Yet, during these same years, she found her voice, because Julia Romana loved so to hear her. For her children, she had composed numerous songs which they soon learned to play on the piano and to sing with her. In 1884, a Mr. Hosmer, "teacher of the pianoforte" at the Institute, came and "took down my music beautifully," Mrs. Howe wrote in her journal with great delight. The children at Perkins Institute sang her songs for her after that, although they never could get "Flibberty-gibbet" quite gay enough in tempo.

It was amazing, people said, that Julia Ward Howe could still play the piano after she was ninety. She herself regarded it as no more than natural. Her fingers were still supple — perhaps from teaching great-grandchildren to pick out a tune. But music was now a strictly family matter, and this "screed" about the books, as she called it, was for publication. She finished it with a sigh of relief. It was time for fun — time to go to her favorite club, the "Papeterie."

The name of this club referred to the paper-backed novels which members exchanged and the meetings were devoted to nonsense of the wittiest and most intellectual variety. Humorous verses were written in Latin to be read at meetings and puns in three languages were tossed off by members in the course of events. Mrs. Howe "sparkled with merriment" that Wednesday afternoon in October.

There had been a little trouble in getting to the meeting. Both Flossy and Maud were determined to take care of their mother and had objected, but Mrs. Howe had won the victory and it went to her head a trifle. On the way home in the carriage, she had insisted on having the top down. It was a lovely warm day.

And it was just like the girls to say that this had given their mother the cold in her chest — pouncing upon the very thing that had been the most fun. Mrs. Howe said her cold was of no consequence. She had no time for illness because a most exciting event was in the offing. Her Greek play in verse, *Hippolytus*, written in 1857, was to be produced at last. Margaret Anglin, after a series of New York successes co-starring with E. H. Sothern, had sparked a Greek revival by producing the *Antigone* of Sophocles in California in 1909. Now she wanted another Greek play and she had chosen *Hippolytus* by Julia Ward Howe to produce in Boston in 1910. After the bitter disappointment when Charlotte Cushman and Edwin Booth had been forced to break their promise to appear in *Hippolytus,* this fulfillment of a long-lost hope was almost too wonderful to contemplate.

But the cold which Mrs. Howe had said was of no consequence proved to be pneumonia. Maud and Florence called not one but two doctors, and this time their spirited mother was too weak to protest. Amazed at her vitality, however, the younger doctor thought she would pull through. But the older man shook his head. "Perhaps," he said — if improvement continued for another twenty-four hours. It was then Sunday night.

In the early hours of Monday morning, October 17, 1910, Maud Howe Elliott was alone with her mother. "I am so tired," Maud heard her mother say.

There had always been a family language spoken by Julia Ward Howe and her children — each child adding a word or two. They all loved to play with words the way their mother taught them to do and now, as Maud sat by her mother's bedside, she heard the word which had been coined just for her. It meant "Good-by."

Julia Ward Howe had lived during a time when great men of letters and great reformers walked the earth. That generation was gone now and as they left her, one by one, she told of their passing in her journal. There was Longfellow and James Russell Lowell and James T. Fields —

she paid tribute to each memory and she described vividly the funeral of John Andrew and of her own Chevalier. She would have been glad to know that the children from Perkins Institute for the Blind came to sing at the Church of the Disciples in her memory, as they had done in memory of Dr. Howe. The crowded church was her friends' final tribute and it would have pleased her. But Julia Ward Howe was not a woman to look back — even from Heaven's gate. She belonged to the new century and it would have pleased her most of all to know that, on her last earthly journey, eight grandsons formed her guard of honor.

"I stand between the old and the new," Mrs. Howe once said and this was true. All that the nineteenth century gave her she brought as a gift to the twentieth, which was really her time. After her death, her daughters gathered together some of her prayers found in her journals. But when friends thought of Julia Howe they remembered her delighted laughter. "Autos" were "fun" and the telephone was "wonderful." *At Sunset* was the title of her last book of poems — but for Julia Ward Howe the word was sunrise. She looked not west but east, into the morning.

Acknowledgments

Julia Ward Howe, by Laura E. Richards and Maud Howe Elliott, assisted by Florence Howe Hall, the two-volume biography published in 1916 — receiving the Pulitzer Prize — is the most lasting and perfect memorial that two devoted daughters could create in their mother's memory. Florence Howe Hall, eldest surviving daughter, in her books, *Memories Grave and Gay*, and *Julia Ward Howe and the Woman's Suffrage Movement*, throws light on Mrs. Howe's later life. There was not one of the Howe children, attaining maturity, who failed to appear in print on many subjects, with their children and their children's children often following in their footsteps. Without the active assistance of living Ward descendants this book could never have been written.

I wish first of all to express my heartfelt thanks to Mr. Henry Marion Hall for his help and guidance at the beginning of my project and for his belief that, with the aid of many unpublished manuscripts, still another inspirational story might be told. While I was the guest of the Halls at Newport, Mr. Hall's sister, Mrs. Caroline Hall Birkhead, described for me the "Doctor's Wing" as she remembered it at Perkins Institute for the Blind in South Boston. She showed me a remarkable portrait which she herself painted of Mrs. Howe. I owe an equal debt of gratitude to Mr. Hall's daughters, Mrs. Julia Ward Howe Stickley, Mrs. Francis Minturn Howard and Miss Rosalys Haskell Hall. Mrs. Stickley placed at my disposal the results of her own family research, especially in the field of genealogy. From Mrs. Howard's collection of family pictures I not only chose those I wished for reproduction but used others as a basis for description.

During the preparation of this book, I was privileged to visit the Yellow House, home of the Richards family in Gardiner, Maine. The great treasure-trove of Ward letters, bestowed by Julia Ward Howe upon Laura E. Richards and by her on her second daughter, are now at the Houghton Library, the gift of Miss Rosalind Richards and her brother, Mr. John Richards, who are literary executors of these Howe papers; and hitherto no one outside the family has seen the Julia Ward Howe Journals. There is increased interest in the part played in history by this remarkable family, and because misunderstandings on the part of the researchers arise and misinterpretations of episodes in the life of Julia Ward Howe occur, Miss Richards has permitted me to read and quote passages from the journals which, more than a generation ago, were omitted. In this way, Julia Ward Howe speaks for herself in her own words, and emerges as one of the truly great women of her time, not only in her public life but in her private life as well. Her example of steadfast love and courage, particularly in her private life, is one we need today.

Coming now to the second of the Ward sisters, Louisa Ward Crawford and after Thomas Crawford's death Louisa Ward Terry, I wish to thank MR. LAWRENCE TERRY, her grandson, for his cordial assistance. Mr. Terry turned over to me all the papers in his possession concerning his grandmother and told me of the great sapphire ring, once the property of Sam Ward and now his by inheritance. In Mr. Terry's home hangs the fine portrait which is a tribute both to the beauty of his grandmother and to his grandfather's skill as an artist.

The California Mailliards have made it possible for me to bring to life Annie Ward Mailliard, youngest of the Ward sisters. Family papers also provided color and variety for the portrait of Sam Ward — the fourth subject of this biography. I wish especially to thank MRS. KATE PETERSON MAILLIARD, wife of the late JOHN WARD MAILLIARD, JR.; MR. ERNEST CHASE MAILLIARD, grandson of Annie Ward Mailliard, and his cousins, MRS. MARION-LEIGH MOORE and MRS. ANITA BRIDGMAN, granddaughters of Annie Mailliard. It is with deep regret that I learn of the death of Mrs. Bridgman, whose kindness to me I do not forget. At the invitation of Mrs. John Ward Mailliard Jr., I went to San Francisco — where I found not only papers awaiting me but a schedule of calls arranged whereby I met other members of the family, saw portraits and heirlooms, and visited the San Geronimo Ranch, where Annie and Adolph Mailliard's house still stands. Such firsthand impressions are of inestimable value.

MRS. MARGARET LIVINGSTON CHANLER ALDRICH most helpfully answered my many questions concerning her grandfather Samuel Ward, fourth of the name. Mrs. Aldrich, being both a Ward and an Astor, understands as no one else the New York background of this book. The late MR. WILLIAM WARD, long a resident of the Columbia Club in New York City, was more than kind to me at the beginning of my research. He went with me to the New-York Historical Society, where we examined family papers and diaries which he had deposited there and where he talked of the New York of other days which he knew so well. He remembered the rose gardens at Hamilton Grange, at one time his grandmother's home. I deeply regret that I may not again thank him personally for all his help to me.

The Ward family descendants form an impressive group and I am sorry that I have not met and talked to them all. The gracious reception accorded me by the many with whom I have become acquainted constitutes one of the richest rewards of my research.

Among the institutions of greatest importance to me, I must first mention the HOUGHTON LIBRARY OF HARVARD UNIVERSITY and speak with gratitude of PROFESSOR WILLIAM A. JACKSON, Director, who permits me to quote from Harvard-owned manuscripts — the Howe papers being quoted of course with the kind permission of MISS ROSALIND RICHARDS and her brother MR. JOHN RICHARDS, donors. I greatly appreciate Professor Jackson's sound advice in connection with my research and his interest in my problems. MISS CAROLYN E. JAKEMAN and her staff were of the utmost assistance, their patience unfailing.

I doubt if such a book as this, with its Boston as well as New York background, could be completed without the help of the BOSTON ATHENAEUM — and my thanks are due first of all to DR. HAROLD BOWDITCH for his gift of a reader's card. MR. WALTER MUIR WHITEHILL, Director and Librarian of the Athenæum, was most helpful in discussing with me American nineteenth-century sculpture and Crawford's "Orpheus" in particular, which was first shown at the Athenæum. MISS MARGARET HACKETT, Reference Librarian, has given me many constructive suggestions as to lines of inquiry.

At Craigie House I was welcomed as a guest by MR. THOMAS DE VALCOURT, whose intimate knowledge of Longfellow and his circle was of the greatest use to me. It is an inspiration to be allowed to work in Longfellow's own home surrounded by his books and belongings, and it was my good fortune to find Professor Wagenknecht also at work there upon his book, *Longfellow, a Full-length Portrait*. I benefited greatly by his advice and generous sharing of discoveries among the manuscripts.

I wish to thank MR. M. A. DEWOLFE HOWE for calling to my attention the diaries of Mrs. James T. Fields, which are at the MASSACHUSETTS HISTORICAL SOCIETY. MR. STEPHEN T. RILEY was helpful as always, at the Society's library. The manuscript room of the Boston Public Library with its antislavery collections also proved useful, MR. ZOLTAN HARASTI most kind.

At the BOSTON MUSEUM OF FINE ARTS, I learned much from a discussion with MR. RICHARD McLANATHAN concerning the types of marble used by American sculptors in Rome. Crawford's "Orpheus" is now at the museum.

As might be expected, New York proved a fertile field of research where the Ward family was concerned. Archives of New York City yielded family wills and inventories, the property settlements of the Ward heiresses, their real estate holdings. In the manuscript room of the NEW YORK PUBLIC LIBRARY I found a small but rich vein of letters of Samuel Ward the banker and others. The NEW YORK GENEALOGICAL AND BIOGRAPHICAL SOCIETY's library was of greatest value, and I wish to thank MRS. LOUISE H. ZIMM for her assistance upon many occasions.

The NEW-YORK HISTORICAL SOCIETY provided the most valuable material on my subject and I wish to thank MR. WAYNE ANDREWS, in charge of manuscripts, and Mr. DAVID H. WALLACE, for calling to my attention the Evangeles diaries — a most valuable find for me. The John Ward diaries shed a great deal of light on my entire subject. Miss GERALDINE BEARD, Chief Librarian, and all her staff were most kind. At the New-York Historical Society are Crawford's "Indian" and a miniature by Miss Anne Hall. The portrait bust of Louisa Ward by her sculptor husband Thomas Crawford is at the MUSEUM OF THE CITY OF NEW YORK.

Sources

ONLY THOSE TITLES which have been of the most use to me are here listed, books by Ward descendants coming first. Other sources are listed in notes.

JULIA WARD HOWE, 1819–1910.
Laura E. Richards and Maud Howe Elliott assisted by Florence Howe Hall. Houghton, 1916. (2 vols.)

REMINISCENCES.
Julia Ward Howe. Houghton, 1899.

THE WORLD'S OWN.
Julia Ward Howe. Ticknor & Fields, 1853.

PASSION FLOWERS.
Julia Ward Howe. Ticknor & Fields, 1853.

MEMORIES GRAVE AND GAY.
Florence Howe Hall. Harper, 1918.

JULIA WARD HOWE AND THE WOMAN'S SUFFRAGE MOVEMENT.
Florence Marion Howe Hall. Estes, 1913.

THE STORY OF THE BATTLE HYMN OF THE REPUBLIC.
Florence Marion Howe Hall. Harper, 1916.

STEPPING WESTWARD.
Laura E. Richards. Appleton, 1931.

SAMUEL GRIDLEY HOWE.
Laura E. Richards. Appleton, 1935.

NINETY YEARS ON.
Henry Richards. Kennebec Journal Press, 1940.

THREE GENERATIONS.
Maud Howe Elliott. Little, Brown, 1923.

UNCLE SAM WARD AND HIS CIRCLE.
Maud Howe Elliott. The Macmillan Co., 1938.

THIS WAS MY NEWPORT.
Maud Howe Elliott. The Mythology Co., 1944.

My Cousin F. Marion Crawford.
Maud Howe Elliott. The Macmillan Co., 1934.

The Eleventh Hour in the Life of Julia Ward Howe.
Maud Howe Elliott. Little, Brown, 1911.

Roman Spring — Memoirs.
Mrs. Winthrop Chanler. Little, Brown, 1934.

A Diplomatist's Wife in Many Lands.
Mrs. Hugh Fraser. Dodd, Mead, 1910. (2 vols.)

Reminiscences of a Diplomatist's Wife.
Mrs. Hugh Fraser. Dodd, Mead, 1912. (2 vols.)

The Diary of Philip Hone.
Ed. by Allan Nevins. Dodd, Mead, 1927.

The Diary of George Templeton Strong.
Ed. by Allan Nevins and Milton Halsey Thomas. The Macmillan Co., 1952.

Memories of a Hostess.
M. A. DeWolfe Howe. Atlantic Monthly Press, 1922.

A Venture in Remembrance.
M. A. DeWolfe Howe. Little, Brown, 1941.

Longfellow: A Full-Length Portrait.
Edward Wagenknecht. Longmans, 1955.

Sam Ward in the Gold Rush.
Ed. by Carvel Collins. Stanford University Press, 1949.

"Samuel Gridley Howe as Phrenologist."
Harold Schwartz. *American Hist. Review*, Vol. LVII, No. 3, April, 1952.

Doctoral Theses of John Pilkington, Jr., and Harold Schwartz. Houghton Library, Harvard University.

Chapter Notes

CHAPTER ONE: *This Was New York*

1. Principal sources for this chapter are *American Notes*, by Charles Dickens; *The Diary of Philip Hone*, edited by Allan Nevins; letters at Craigie House, Cambridge, Mass., from Felton and other members of the Five of Clubs — together with family letters at Houghton Library, Harvard University.

A pencil sketch of Annie as a child is in the home of Mrs. John Ward Mailliard, Jr. It is by an unknown artist, and shows Annie with flowers braided in her hair.

2. According to Mary Crawford, who described her Aunt Julia as a young woman, Mrs. Howe's eyes were blue. French passport authorities put down hazel and great-granddaughters remember that in later life Mrs. Howe's eyes were gray.

3. Hone diary.

4. *Reminiscences*, by Julia Ward Howe.

5. *Uncle Sam Ward and His Circle*, by Maud Howe Elliott (The Macmillan Co., 1938).

CHAPTER TWO: *Three Graces of Bond Street*

1. For the addresses of members of the Ward family, I have used New York directories, made available at the New York Genealogical and Biographical Society. These directories were published once a year, for the most part, so changes of address were sometimes slow in appearing. Family letters contributed information in this respect.

2. According to the *Dictionary of American Biography*, it was James Gore King who was the partner of Samuel Ward and not Charles King, as sometimes stated.

3. Names of other Bond Street residents are from "Bond Street," by Sturges S. Dunham, in *Valentine's Manual*, Vol. II.

4. Deeds, New York County Court House.

5. The Wanton-Lyman-Hazard House now belongs to the Newport Historical Society and is open daily to visitors during the summer months.

It is on Broadway, just north of the Colony House, and is listed in *The Fifty Best Historic American Houses,* by Ralph E. Carpenter Jr. (Dutton, 1955).

6. Ward letters are from *The Correspondence of Governor Samuel Ward, May 1775–March 1776,* edited by Bernhard Knollenberg and published by the Rhode Island Historical Society. All of the correspondence is well worth reading. Much of the genealogical material is from *The Genealogy of the Ward Family,* compiled by Clifford Monahan and included in the above volume, but I am indebted to Mrs. Julia Ward Stickley for corrections and for further information.

7. President Eisenhower chose this Biblical selection to read at his inauguration.

8. *Samuel Ward of Rhode Island, A Memoir,* by John Ward, 1875. For an interesting and readable treatment of Arnold, see *The Traitor and the Spy,* by James Thomas Flexner.

9. *The Old Merchants of New York City,* by Walter Barrett, Clerk (1872).

10. It has been said that Samuel Ward the banker "at fourteen . . . entered as a clerk the banking house of Prime and King." I think it may be true that he went to work at fourteen — but with some other firm, if Walter Barrett is right about Prime's arrival in New York.

CHAPTER THREE: *Cinderella Story*

1. At the Museum of the City of New York, there is a scale model called "Bowling Green, 1831," which may be seen in the Altman Foundation Gallery on the main floor. Here is the corner of Nathaniel Prime's house, with No. 5 Bowling Green in the background. *The Museum of the City of New York, Its Collections and Activities* contains a description of this house.

2. The letters of Julia Cutler to her mother were sent to me for my use by Miss Rosalind Richards and her brother, Mr. John Richards, and are now at the Houghton Library, Harvard University. Other family letters of this period are at the Rhode Island Historical Society in Providence.

3. According to *The Life of Marion,* by Horry and Weems, Benjamin Marion, the first American ancestor, received a letter beginning: "Your damnable heresy well deserves, even in this life, that purgation by fire which awfully awaits it in the next. But in consideration of your youth and worthy connection, our Mercy has condescended to commute your punishment to perpetual exile." Benjamin Marion's eldest son Gabriel had six children, of whom Esther was the eldest and Francis Marion the youngest. Esther Marion was twice married, first to John Allston of Charleston and the Waccamaw River, and second to Thomas Mitchell of Georgetown. She had fifteen children, one of whom was Sarah Mitchell, grandmother of the Ward sisters and Sam.

4. It is possible that Mrs. Graham had left the big house when little Julia Cutler was her pupil; but in that case, she would still have been told about so important a mansion.

5. The McAllisters, grandfather, father and son Ward, are all to be found in the *Dictionary of American Biography*, and I have quoted *Society as I Have Found It*, by Ward McAllister (1890).

6. *A Century of Banking in New York*, by Henry Wysham Lanier, quotes *The Rich Men of 1822*, a pamphlet produced by Moses Y. Beach, editor of the *Sun*. In this list the value of Samuel Ward's house, Number 5 Bowling Green, is given as $18,000. His personal property amounted to $30,000.

CHAPTER FOUR: *The Young New Yorkers*

1. Sam Ward's schoolboy correspondence is in the Manuscript Room of the New York Public Library.

2. *Uncle Sam Ward and His Circle*, by Maud Howe Elliott.

3. *Ibid.*

4. Poe wrote of Dr. Francis in an article entitled "The Literati," for *Godey's Lady's Book*, 1846.

5. "From the album of one of his kindred," according to material in the Manuscript Room of the New York Public Library, comes the following, very much in the style of Julia Ward:

> Who on the sofa loves to sit
> And see his wife beside him knit
> Which scintillates her ready wit?
> > The Doctor.
> And when the cruel bell doth ring
> Who frowning from the couch doth spring
> Doff his gray jacket and take wing?
> > The Doctor.
> Who thinks that Pleasure comprehends
> Books where great Truth with Reason blends
> Green tea, cigars and genial friends?
> > The Doctor.

There were still more verses about Dr. Francis.

6. *The Memorial History of the City of New York*, and *America and the Americans*, by Achille Murat.

7. Oyster cellars are described in *New York in Slices*, a tract signed "Foster" and selling in 1849 for 3½ cents.

CHAPTER FIVE: *"Julietta"*

1. See *The Columbia Historical Portrait of New York*, by John A. Kouwenhoven, page 170, for a picture of Samuel Ward's house. In this same

volume, on page 220, is an interior of No. 38 Bond Street, with carved fireplace like that described in Ward family letters.

2. Ward letters in the Manuscript Room of the New York Public Library contain this, and most of the other material for this chapter. There is only one Sam Ward diary in this collection, and it is from this that I quote. Maud Howe Elliott referred to the diary, but for my more liberal interpretation I am indebted to Ward descendants.

3. *Uncle Sam Ward and His Circle*, by Maud Howe Elliott.

4. *Ibid.*

5. *Ibid.*

6. This letter from Francis Marion Ward is at Houghton Library, Harvard University.

7. These letters were preserved in the family of Major David Bates Douglass, and were made available to me through the kindness of the late Moses Hale Douglass, a grandson of the Major, and his family.

8. The manuscript of the Evangeles diary is in the New York Historical Society. In 1834, Christy said his name was Christopher Lysemochus Matthews Evangeles, but he broke with Dr. Matthews, who had been his first patron — and changed his two middle names.

9. Mrs. Mary Douglass Rackliffe writes me that Sarah Douglass married Samuel G. Cornell, went to live in Buffalo and became in due course the great-grandmother of Katharine Cornell.

10. This letter is at the Houghton Library in Harvard, and is especially interesting because it is sometimes stated that Sam Ward was the one who suggested "The Skeleton in Armor" idea.

CHAPTER SIX: *The Astor Wedding*

1. This portrait of Sam Ward now belongs to Annie Ward's direct descendant, the Honorable William S. Mailliard, member of the United States House of Representatives from California, and it hangs in Mr. Mailliard's Washington home. Sam had his favorite dog painted in later.

2. This panic, its cause and effect, is discussed in various volumes including James Blaine Walker's *Epic of American Industry* and Hickernell's *Financial and Business Forecasting*.

3. *Reminiscences*, by Julia Ward Howe.

4. *The Diary of George Templeton Strong*, edited by Allan Nevins and Milton Halsey Thomas, furnished the basis for these identifications.

5. *Uncle Sam Ward and His Circle*, by Maud Howe Elliott.

CHAPTER SEVEN: *End of an Era*

1. Howe papers, Houghton Library, Harvard University.

2. Longfellow papers, read at Craigie House.

3. *Reminiscences*, by Julia Ward Howe.

4. Longfellow papers. Some of these letters are also quoted by Maud Howe Elliott in *Uncle Sam Ward and His Circle*, but after seeing the original manuscripts, I departed from the printed version to a certain extent. The reading — one might almost say the decoding — of Sam Ward's handwriting presents problems.

5. This is shown by entries in the Journals of Julia Ward Howe.

6. Mrs. Margaret Aldrich tells me that in all probability Emily Astor, like Julia Cutler Ward, died of puerperal fever.

7. Items mentioned are from the inventory of the estate of Samuel Ward the banker, New York County Courthouse, New York City.

8. Howe papers, Houghton Library, Harvard University.

9. For more about John Louis O'Sullivan, see F. L. Mott: *A History of American Magazines*. Also see J. W. Pratt: *John L. O'Sullivan and Manifest Destiny* (*N. Y. Hist.*, July, 1933).

10. O'Sullivan's poetry is in the Sterling Library, Yale University, the gift of the late John Ward Mailliard Jr.

CHAPTER EIGHT: *Stormy Courtship*

1. Manuscripts at Craigie House, Cambridge, Mass.

2. Howe papers, Houghton Library, Harvard University.

3. *Reminiscences*, by Julia Ward Howe.

4. At the Sterling Library, Yale University, there is a passport made out in French to Julia Ward Howe and dated June 19, 1851. Her height is given as "1 metre, 53 centimetres." Mrs. Howe's hair was considered by the French to be brown; her eyes, hazel; her face, oval; and her complexion, white.

5. Dr. Howe had come to New York to ask the American Bible Society for money to put the Bible into Braille and had received a grant.

CHAPTER NINE: *Crowded Honeymoon*

1. This letter and the correspondence between Dr. Howe and the Wards, and the comments within the Ward family, are all to be found in the Howe papers at the Houghton Library, Harvard University.

2. Julia Ward Howe's wedding dress is in the Smithsonian Museum in Washington, the gift in 1911 of her daughter, Maud Howe Elliott. A photograph of it appeared in *Woman's Day*, January, 1954. The wedding slippers were presented to the Smithsonian by Mrs. Eleanor Hall Saunders of Washington, great-granddaughter of Julia Ward Howe.

3. Information on the Howe family was supplied by Major George McRory to Mrs. Julia Ward Howe Stickley for my use. Mrs. Stickley also supplied the name of the frigate.

4. New York County Courthouse, New York City.

5. The inscription within the ring is told by Maud Howe Elliott in a

letter to the *New York Herald Tribune* written from Newport, R. I., May 1, 1943.

6. Longfellow to Mrs. Cleveland, read at Craigie House.

7. Sterling Library, Yale University, presented by the late John Ward Mailliard, Jr., of San Francisco. Quoted with permission.

8. Howe to Sumner, Howe papers, Houghton Library.

CHAPTER TEN: *Sam's Medora*

1. Howe papers, Houghton Library, Harvard University.

2. Deeds, New York County Courthouse, New York City.

3. *Reminiscences of a Diplomatist's Wife*, by Mrs. Hugh Fraser (Dodd, Mead & Company, 1912). Mrs. Hugh Fraser was Mary, daughter of Thomas Crawford and Louisa Ward Crawford.

4. Louisa had a cousin John Ward, son of her father's brother William, whose diaries are in the New-York Historical Society. But he was fifteen years younger than Louisa. It was not until I read the letter of Julia Ward Howe to her sister Annie (quoted in a subsequent chapter) that I realized that the Boston Wards not only had a son named Samuel, but one named John, and that this John was briefly Louisa's fiancé. The *Dictionary of American Biography* mentions Samuel G. and John G. Ward as continuing the business of their father, Thomas Wren Ward, after he died in 1856.

5. This letter from Howe to Sumner was returned, with others, to the Howe family. They were considered unsuitable for publication in a contemplated life of Sumner, to be written soon after his death in 1874. Since the letters show both Howe and Sumner as human beings, they would never do for the sort of eulogistic work then the fashion.

6. Part of the information concerning Crawford's life comes from *A Diplomatist's Wife in Many Lands* by Mrs. Hugh Fraser. *Thomas Crawford: A Eulogy* by Thomas Hicks, N.A. is more of interest because Hicks knew Crawford personally. In the Terry papers at the Houghton Library is a letter to Julia Ward Howe signed Thalia Peters and dated May 7, 1887. Thalia Peters was a daughter of John Frazee, Crawford's early employer. According to Mrs. Fraser, Crawford was born "21 March 1811," while according to Thomas Hicks, it was "22 March, 1813."

7. The Boston Athenæum kindly supplied material on their acquisition of the "Orpheus." See also Acknowledgments.

CHAPTER ELEVEN: *A Tempest on Bond Street*

1. Howe papers, Houghton Library, Harvard University. All the quotations are taken from Dr. Howe's letters to Charles Sumner unless otherwise stated in text.

2. Louisa's letters to Uncle John Ward are from the Chanler papers at the Houghton Library.

3. Longfellow papers.

4. I describe here Louisa's appearance as shown in the Crawford marble. I do not positively know that this was her wedding costume, but it could be. The letter written by Annie might tell but so far I have not been able to locate it. Quotation here is from the Mailliard papers in San Francisco.

5. Deeds, New York County Courthouse, New York City.

6. For an excellent presentation of American artists in Rome, see *Travellers in Arcadia* published by the Detroit Institute of Arts and the Toledo Museum of Art, in 1951. I talked with Mr. Edgar P. Richardson, Director of the Detroit Institute of Arts, who was most helpful concerning this phase of American art.

CHAPTER TWELVE: *Royal Bordentown*

1. This skit, written by Julia Ward Howe and sent to her sister Annie, is among the Mailliard papers in San Francisco.

2. Howe papers, Houghton Library, Harvard University.

3. An unidentified newspaper clipping among the papers of David Prescott Hall told of the jewels, the story in turn being related to me by Mr. Hall's son, Henry Marion Hall.

4. A miniature of Adolph Mailliard belongs to Mrs. John Ward Mailliard, Jr., and this, together with the almost life-size portrait in Mrs. Mailliard's home in San Francisco, forms the basis for descriptions. The name Adolph is spelled without a final e by Annie herself. Mrs. Fraser adds the e, as did Julia Ward Howe.

5. In preparation for this chapter, I visited Bordentown, New Jersey, with my husband during the summer of 1954. We saw the site of the Princess Zenaïde's house, also Spring Villa on Park Street — now the Bordentown Military Institute — and what remains of the artificial lake.

A large mansion stands on the site of Joseph Bonaparte's home, Point Breeze, the second house built by King Joseph having also been destroyed, although it was still standing in Annie Ward's time. Bonaparte Park is now owned by the Divine Word Missionaries and is used as a seminary for young priests studying to enter the foreign mission field.

Remains of a pier on Cross Creek may be traced and the brick archway and part of the passage under the bluff are clearly to be seen. Formal gardens are still cultivated, but in the wilderness that was once the lake and pleasure park, the ghosts of the Bonapartes would be most at home.

Adolph and Annie's extensive gardens can still be traced, and although their house has been altered the old parts of it can be identified. Adolph's stables — themselves impressive buildings — are still standing.

6. With the Honorable William S. Mailliard of California, I had the privilege of examining the Bonaparte documents given by his father to the Sterling

Library, Yale University. These papers were most kindly placed at my disposal and from these come the figures.

7. A list of Annie's assets is in the New York County Courthouse — Index of Grantors. No nuptial agreement was on file. Sales by Annie and Adolph Mailliard are also recorded.

CHAPTER THIRTEEN: *Annie and Adolph*

1. Descriptions of Point Breeze may be found in several sources but the best, in my opinion, is in *Joseph Bonaparte en Amerique*, by Georges Bertin, and from it I drew the material for Annie's imaginary tour of Point Breeze with Monsieur Mailliard. It is a matter of fact, not fancy, that Annie knew the place well and that the Mailliard family still owns Bonaparte furnishings and paintings and the silver-gilt camp kit of Napoleon.

2. *Emigrés in the Wilderness*, by T. Wood Clarke (The Macmillan Co., 1941), contains by far the best account of this transaction.

3. Howe papers, Houghton Library, Harvard University.

4. *History of Burlington and Mercer Counties, N. J.*, with biographical sketches by Major E. M. Woodward and John F. Hageman (1883).

5. F. Marion Crawford, "Joseph Bonaparte in Bordentown," in *Century Illustrated Monthly Magazine*, May–Oct. 1893, Vol. XLVI. This article is illustrated by an etching of a portrait of Joseph Bonaparte by J. Goubaud, the portrait now being in the home of Mrs. John Ward Mailliard, Jr., in San Francisco.

Annie Mailliard's own account as told to her by Louis Mailliard is among the Bonaparte papers at Sterling Library, Yale. It is this version I have followed for the most part.

6. Bonaparte papers, Sterling Library, Yale University.

CHAPTER FOURTEEN: *Sam Ward, Forty-niner*

1. Papers on the Ward failure are among those deposited at the New York Historical Society by the late Mr. William Ward.

2. This letter is from Sam Ward to his sister Annie and is among the Mailliard papers in San Francisco.

3. Joseph Mailliard, son of Adolph, states as follows in a letter to Salvator published in the *Thoroughbred Record:*

"My father and my uncle, Samuel Ward, visited California in 1850 when they bought the brig *Niantic*, then lying deserted in San Francisco Bay, had it hauled up on the beach at what is now N. E. corner of Sansome and Clay Streets and fitted it up as a warehouse with deck housing for offices, but it was burnt in the great fire of April, 1851."

The trouble with this recollection of Joseph Mailliard's is that Adolph and Annie were in Europe in 1850, and that Adolph's first trip to California was on March 30, 1852, according to Mailliard papers in San Francisco. Doubtless young Joseph was told that the *Niantic* was just as proper as he states. And of course perhaps it was!

4. See *Sam Ward in the Gold Rush*, edited by Carvel Collins (Stanford University Press, 1949).

CHAPTER FIFTEEN: *Flood Tide*

The *Calendar of State Papers, Richmond, Virginia*, provides details of specifications for the Richmond monument, money involved, arrangements for delivery etc., in this chapter.

1. *A Diplomatist's Wife in Many Lands*, Vol. I, by Mrs. Hugh Fraser.
2. *Yankee Stonecutters*, by Albert Teneyck Gardner (published for the Metropolitan Museum of Art by Columbia University Press, 1945).
3. Correspondence between Thomas Crawford and the Honorable John H. Rice, Chairman of the Committee on Public Buildings, as found in *Thomas Crawford, a Eulogy*, by Thomas Hicks, N.A.
4. Howe to Sumner, Howe papers, Houghton Library, Harvard University.
5. Longfellow's diary, Longfellow papers.
6. *Reminiscences*, Julia Ward Howe.

CHAPTER SIXTEEN: *Passion Flowers*

1. Howe papers, Houghton Library, Harvard University.
2. Bonaparte papers, gift of John Ward Mailliard, Jr., to Sterling Library, Yale University.
3. *Reminiscences*, by Julia Ward Howe.
4. Houghton Library.
5. Longfellow papers.
6. According to Ernest Longfellow in *Random Memories*, a young German poet by the name of Emmanuel Scherb, probably a political refugee, was a constant visitor at Craigie House. He had dark hair worn like Liszt's, was poor but "cultivated," and Longfellow seemed fond of him. When asked why Scherb came around so much, Longfellow replied, "Who would be so kind to him if I were not?"

It is to be feared that Scherb was pretty much a hanger-on, for he had been visiting the hospitable Mailliards in Bordentown for quite a while. His end was sad. In 1862 or '63 he "was detected in bounty-jumping" — or enlisting to get the bounty paid recruits and then deserting. Longfellow bailed him out.

CHAPTER SEVENTEEN: *Back to the Gold Mines*

1. *Sam Ward in the Gold Rush*, edited by Carvel Collins (Stanford University Press, Stanford University, 1949).

Sam Ward wrote the story of his adventures in the gold fields for *Porter's Spirit of the Times,* a magazine devoted to racing and the theater, which he must have enjoyed. These articles, published in 1861, were unsigned, but the scholarly detective work of Carvel Collins uncovered the author and, in *Sam Ward in the Gold Rush,* Mr. Collins has done a splendid job of abridging Sam's verbiage, where necessary, adding notes from contemporary sources, and making this a most readable volume, which I highly recommend.

2. *Uncle Sam Ward and His Circle,* by Maud Howe Elliott, and *Sam Ward in the Gold Rush.*

3. I am indebted to descendants of the Ward sisters and Sam Ward for the tall tales. They are to be taken with a grain of salt — how much salt, exactly, I leave to the reader to decide.

4. Howe papers, Houghton Library, Harvard University.

5. See *The Wolf Cub: The Great Adventure of Count Gaston de Raousett-Boulbon in California and Sonora,* 1850–1854, translated from the French of Maurice Soulié by Farrel Symons.

My San Francisco, by Joseph Henry Jackson, is useful. And of still more value were the personal recollections of Mrs. Amelita Page. *San Francisco Street Names,* by Henry C. Carlisle, gives sketches of pioneers.

6. Letter of Joseph Mailliard, Adolph's son, for *Thoroughbred Record.*

7. I take the liberty of recording personal impressions during a recent visit to Mexico, when my husband and I traveled over Sam's route and saw here and there a remnant of the ancient road he followed. The Franklin Library in Mexico City contains historical volumes of interest concerning this period.

8. Howe papers. Later, the blind children at the Institute enjoyed the pony cart.

CHAPTER EIGHTEEN: *End of an Eagle's Flight*

1. All direct quotations attributed to "Mimoli" are reprinted by permission from *A Diplomatist's Wife in Many Lands,* by Mrs. Hugh Fraser (Dodd, Mead & Company). Mary Crawford Fraser, "Mimoli" of these pages, "died in the 72nd year of her life with 18 novels and books of travel and memoirs to her credit, all written since her husband's death in 1894," according to the *New York Times,* May 6, 1923.

2. Louisa to Annie; Terry papers, Houghton Library, Harvard University.

3. *The Calendar of State Papers, Richmond, Virginia.*

4. In *Reminiscences,* Mrs. Howe tells of discovering the "family portraits" in bronze while on a visit to Washington.

5. Eulogy by Thomas Hicks.

6. See *Memories of a Hostess,* edited by M. A. DeWolfe Howe (Atlantic Monthly Press, 1922).

7. Among the Ward papers at the New-York Historical Society is a letter

from David Hall, son-in-law of Julia Ward Howe, to John Ward, Louisa Crawford's first cousin. It is dated 1890 and tells of Crawford works displayed at Tymper's [?] for some years past. "Owing to the change of taste, they do not sell," Mr. Hall said, suggesting that John Ward might like to buy them. John Ward refused, proposing the New-York Historical Society, but the statuettes are not listed there. The list follows, and if these pieces should come to light in some forgotten attic, it is safe to say that various museums would be interested.

1. Boy Hunter with Dog (about 2½ ft. high).
2. Peri (copy of large one) (about 3 ft. high).
3. Girl with Tambourine (about 2½ ft. high).
4. Raphael (like Charlie's. About 18 in. high). [Refers to Charlie Ward.]
5. Bust of Flora.
6. Bas relief (Psyche and Bacchante).

CHAPTER NINETEEN: *Sam Ward, King of the Lobby*

1. Sources for Sam's Paraguayan adventures are *La Plata and the Argentine Confederation and Paraguay*, by Thomas Jefferson Page, USA. (Harper and Bros. 1859). Also, *Paraguay: an Informal History*, by Harris Gaylord Warren (Univ. of Oklahoma, 1949).
2. *Uncle Sam Ward and His Circle*, by Maud Howe Elliott.
3. *Society as I Have Found It*, by Ward McAllister.
4. My attention was called to this investigation through reading *All-Time Champ of the Lobbyists*, by Beverly Smith, in the *Saturday Evening Post* for Dec. 23, 1950. The Congressional Record is the source.
5. Mailliard papers, San Francisco.
6. William Russell friendship is drawn from *My Diary North and South*, edited by Fletcher Pratt (Harper, 1954). Also, *The First War Correspondent, William Howard Russell of the Times*, by Rupert Furneaux (Cassell and Co., Ltd., 1944); also *The Diary of George Templeton Strong*, edited by Allan Nevins and Milton Halsey Thomas.

CHAPTER TWENTY: *Lords of the Lash and Lords of the Loom*

1. Correspondence: Julia Cutler to her children, the gift of John Richards and Rosalind Richards, Howe papers, Houghton Library, Harvard University.
2. Knowing he had no chance of election, Mann had already accepted the Presidency of Antioch College.
3. Longfellow's diary; see also *Longfellow — A Full-length Portrait*, by Edward Wagenknecht.
4. Howe papers, Houghton Library, Harvard University.
5. *Reminiscences*, by Julia Ward Howe.

6. The *Liberator* quotes articles from other papers giving the proslavery side a considerable amount of space. I have indicated in text the sources of the *Liberator* quotations.

7. Sometime after these events occurred, the idea that Dr. Samuel Gridley Howe's departure for Canada was a cowardly flight appeared in print. This was thoughtlessly accepted and copied. I have tried here to show the situation by means of newspaper accounts, and I hope I have been able to prove that physical cowardice was never a characteristic of Dr. Howe.

8. Quoted here are letters and journal entries never before published. The reason is understandable; but times have changed, and after conferences with Miss Richards, she and I together concluded that, for a complete understanding of Mrs. Howe's character, the truth ought to be told. As will be seen, Mrs. Howe's own words are used as much as possible.

CHAPTER TWENTY-ONE: *Battle Hymn*

1. For the background of this chapter, see *Campaigns of the Army of the Potomac*, by William Swinton (1882). Wartime files of *The New York Herald* were made available with the kind co-operation of Miss Grace Walmsley, Research Librarian at the Ferguson Library, Stamford, Conn.

2. See *The Heroic Story of the U. S. Sanitary Commission 1861–'65*, by William Howell Reed, reprinted from the *Christian Register*; also *What They Have to Do Who Stay at Home*, by Fred Law Olmstead, General Secretary, U. S. Sanitary Commission; *Annual Report of the New England Women's Auxiliary Association, Branch of the U. S. Sanitary Commission*, Boston, 1863 — and final report, 1865; and *What Women Did for the War and What the War Did for Women*, a Memorial Day address by Joseph H. Banton, Jr., 1894.

3. *Reminiscences*, by Julia Ward Howe.

4. In *Julia Ward Howe, 1819–1910*, there is a photograph of the original Battle Hymn manuscript.

5. Lines from final verse of the Battle Hymn, as published.

CHAPTER TWENTY-TWO: *War Years*

1. *A Diplomatist's Wife in Many Lands*, by Mrs. Hugh Fraser.

2. The *Thoroughbred Record*. Photostats were supplied by the Mailliard family.

3. The Misses Parsons lived at 54 Garden Street. Miss Carrie and Miss Kitty lived to a ripe old age. They were daughters of Theophilus Parsons, professor at the Harvard Law School and the author of *The Law of Contracts*.

CHAPTER TWENTY-THREE: *Editorial Mrs. Howe*

1. Abby Williams May's "Appeal," Boston.

2. *Commonwealth*, January 8, 1864.

3. Mrs. Howe's account of writing her poem is from her journal, and her description of the railroad journey with Holmes is from *Reminiscences*.

4. A bound volume of the *Boatswain's Whistle* is in the New York Public Library, inscribed "To Mr. Bancroft from the Editor."

5. This first mention of Sam's sapphire is from the John Ward Diary in the New-York Historical Society.

6. This meeting between Mrs. Howe and her brother is retold from various sources. The incident is not in Mrs. Howe's Journal and I do not know that it happened at this time but this is the most probable date, because of references in the John Ward Diary.

CHAPTER TWENTY-FOUR: *Louisa's Second Romance*

1. Terry Papers, Houghton Library, Harvard University. Material concerning this period of Louisa Ward's life comes from this source. Letters from Luther Terry are there, and letters from Louisa to her children.

2. *Roman Spring*, by Mrs. Winthrop Chanler, says that the Palazzo Odescalchi was designed by Bernini (1598–1680). In Baedeker's *Italy*, the Palazzo Odescalchi is described as "in the Florentine style," erected in 1887–1888; but this is the modern wing facing the Corso, as Mrs. Chanler explains.

3. Howe papers, Houghton Library.

4. *My Cousin F. Marion Crawford*, by Maud Howe Elliott (The Macmillan Co., 1934).

CHAPTER TWENTY-FIVE: *Annie the Pioneer*

1. Bonaparte Papers, gift of Mr. John Ward Mailliard, Jr., to the Sterling Library, Yale University.

2. Artist's name is given in *Uncle Sam Ward and His Circle* as Von Vogelstein, but as C. Vogel by the Frick Art Library.

3. Acreage and house in San Rafael, distance from San Rafael, and date are according to the letter by Joseph Mailliard, son of Adolph, published in the *Thoroughbred Record*.

4. Built in 1872, according to the Joseph Mailliard letter.

5. Mr. Ernest Mailliard wrote these recollections for Mrs. John Mailliard at my request.

6. Mr. Ernest Mailliard explained this curious transaction.

7. Mailliard papers, California.

8. Personal recollections of Mrs. Amelita Page of San Francisco.

CHAPTER TWENTY-SIX: *The Chevalier*

1. Journal, Julia Ward Howe.

2. The John Ward papers, New-York Historical Society.

3. *From Oak to Olive*, by Julia Ward Howe, also journal and letters.

4. In *Ninety Years On*, by Henry Richards.

5. This family anecdote, much enjoyed when the teen-agers grew up, is not dated.

CHAPTER TWENTY-SEVEN: *My Dear New Found*

1. *Reminiscences*, and *Julia Ward Howe, 1819–1910*. General sources such as the *Dictionary of American Biography* under Charles Sumner and others supply further information.

2. For "Charlie's failure," I have used Ward papers, New-York Historical Society, and also letters in the Howe, Terry and Chanler papers, Houghton Library, Harvard University. The remainder of this chapter is from journals for the most part, as indicated in text.

3. Mrs. Howe's personal financial report that she made to herself at the end of the year's journal — a custom of hers.

CHAPTER TWENTY-EIGHT: *Gamblers' Luck*

1. Quotations attributed to "Daisy" are from *Roman Spring*, by Mrs. Winthrop Chanler, the former Margaret Terry.

2. Chanler and Terry papers, Houghton Library, Harvard University.

3. In *Uncle Sam Ward and His Circle*, Maud Howe Elliott lists Sam's descendants through Margaret Astor Ward, who married John Winthrop Chanler. Her children were John Armstrong Chanler, b. 1862; Winthrop Ames Chanler, b. 1863 — the one who married Louisa Ward Terry's daughter Margaret in 1886; Elizabeth Winthrop Chanler, b. 1866; William Astor Chanler, b. 1867; Lewis Stuyvesant Chanler, b. 1869; Margaret Livingston Chanler, b. 1870; Robert Winthrop Chanler, b. 1872; Alida Beekman Chanler, b. 1873; Egerton White Chanler, b. 1874; Marion Ward Chanler; Emily Chanler, died in infancy.

4. *The Horse and Buggy Age*, by E. V. Mitchell (Coward-McCann, 1937).

CHAPTER TWENTY-NINE: *The Lamp-lighted Staircase*

1. In *Uncle Sam Ward and His Circle*, Mrs. Maud Howe Elliott quotes most of Sam's unfinished autobiography.

2. Terry papers. His new friends never came by to see Sam after he was taken ill.

CHAPTER THIRTY: *A Natural Saint*

1. *Roman Spring — Memoirs*, by Mrs. Winthrop Chanler.

2. *My Cousin F. Marion Crawford*, by Maud Howe Elliott (Macmillan, 1934).

3. Doctor's Thesis of John Pilkington, Jr., at Widener Library, Harvard University; read and referred to by kind permission.

4. *Roman Spring*.

CHAPTER THIRTY-ONE: *From Coast to Coast*

1. This is how Mrs. Jack Gardner looked to me in 1917. At that time, she was required to open her Italian palace, Fenway Court, to the public once a year. Tickets were printed and distributed to art students but Mrs. Gardner was not happy about her guests. She stationed herself in one of the rooms, saying at brief intervals, "Don't touch! don't touch!"

2. I am indebted to Mr. John Pilkington, Jr., for information concerning the present condition of letters from Crawford to Mrs. Gardner.

3. *Roman Spring*, by Mrs. Winthrop Chanler.

4. In September, 1888, the Century Club of San Francisco was formed with 111 charter members. This was the first exclusively women's club in Northern California and had "as mentor and guide . . . the inspiration of Julia Ward Howe who was present at their first meeting."

5. Dr. Charlotte Brown was a good doctor for her time. She was the mother of Doctors Adelaide and Philip King Brown, according to Mr. Ernest Mailliard.

CHAPTER THIRTY-TWO: *"They Called Me Queen, and Kissed My Hand"*

1. Material for this final chapter comes from Mrs. Howe's journals and from *The Eleventh Hour in the Life of Julia Ward Howe*, by Maud Howe Elliott. See also *Julia Ward Howe, 1819–1910*.

Index